W9-BTE-486

Principles of Software Engineering and Design

PRENTICE-HALL SOFTWARE SERIES
Brian W. Kernighan, Advisor

Principles of Software Engineering and Design

MARVIN V. ZELKOWITZ

Department of Computer Science
University of Maryland

ALAN C. SHAW

Department of Computer Science
University of Washington

JOHN D. GANNON

Department of Computer Science
University of Maryland

Prentice-Hall, Inc., Englewood Cliffs, New Jersey 07632

Library of Congress Cataloging in Publication Data

ZELKOWITZ, MARVIN V (date)
Principles of software engineering and design.

Bibliography: p.
Includes index.
1. Electronic digital computers—Programming.
I. Shaw, Alan C., (date) joint author.
II. Gannon, John D., (date) joint author.
III. Title. IV. Title: Software engineering and design.
QA76.6.Z438 001.6'42 78–27315
ISBN 0–13–710202–X

Editorial/production supervision and interior design by Marianne Thomma Baltzell
Cover design by Edsal Enterprises
Manufacturing buyer: Gordon Osbourne

Printed in the United States of America

10 9 8 7 6 5 4 3

PRENTICE-HALL INTERNATIONAL, INC., *London*
PRENTICE-HALL OF AUSTRALIA PTY. LIMITED, *Sydney*
PRENTICE-HALL OF CANADA, LTD., *Toronto*
PRENTICE-HALL OF INDIA PRIVATE LIMITED, *New Delhi*
PRENTICE-HALL OF JAPAN, INC., *Tokyo*
PRENTICE-HALL OF SOUTHEAST ASIA PTE. LTD., *Singapore*
WHITEHALL BOOKS LIMITED, *Wellington, New Zealand*

Contents

PREFACE *xi*

1 LARGE-SCALE SOFTWARE DEVELOPMENT *1*

Marvin V. Zelkowitz

1.1 Stages of Software Development *2*
- 1.1.1 Requirements analysis *3*
- 1.1.2 Specification *4*
- 1.1.3 Design *5*
- 1.1.4 Coding *7*
- 1.1.5 Testing *7*
- 1.1.6 Operation and maintenance *9*
- 1.1.7 Themes of software engineering *11*

1.2 Management Issues *12*
- 1.2.1 Project personnel *13*
- 1.2.2 Estimation techniques *17*
- 1.2.3 Milestones *23*
- 1.2.4 Development tools *24*
- 1.2.5 Reliability *24*

1.3 Programmer Issues *26*
1.3.1 Verification and validation *27*
1.3.2 Programming techniques *30*
1.3.3 Performance issues *32*
1.3.4 Theory of specifications *35*
1.4 Other Design Strategies *37*
1.4.1 PSL/PSA *37*
1.4.2 SADT *39*
1.4.3 Other techniques *41*
1.5 Summary *42*

2 PROGRAMMING METHODOLOGY *45*

Marvin V. Zelkowitz

2.1 Program Design Languages *45*
2.2 Design Strategies *50*
2.2.1 Top-down design and development *50*
2.2.2 Structured programming *55*
2.3 Data *60*
2.3.1 Survey of data structures *60*
2.3.2 Abstractions *65*
2.4 Program Certification *81*
2.4.1 Axioms *82*
2.4.2 Certification of a program *85*
2.5 Testing *88*
2.5.1 Stub development *91*
2.5.2 Test data *93*
2.5.3 Compiler aids *93*
2.5.4 Formal Testing *97*
2.6 Design Techniques *99*
2.6.1 Divide and conquer and balancing *99*
2.6.2 Recursion and dynamic programming *100*
2.6.3 Simulation *101*
2.6.4 Searching *102*
2.6.5 Sorting *107*
2.6.6 Backtracking *108*
2.6.7 Finite state and table-driven algorithms *109*
2.6.8 Storage allocation *111*
2.6.9 Coroutines *112*

3 EXAMPLES OF PROGRAM DESIGN *116*

John D. Gannon and Marvin V. Zelkowitz

3.1 Fibonacci Sequence *117*
  3.1.1 Recursive solution *117*
  3.1.2 Dynamic programming solution *118*
3.2 Sort a List *119*
  3.2.1 Exchange sort *119*
  3.2.2 Merge sort *122*
3.3 Parking Cars Problem *126*
  3.3.1 Simulation solution *127*
  3.3.2 Corrected simulation solution *133*
  3.3.3 Efficient simulation solution *135*
  3.3.4 Recursive solution *136*
3.4 Coin-changing Problem *138*
  3.4.1 Recursive solution *138*
  3.4.2 Dynamic programming solution *141*
3.5 Path through a Maze *144*
  3.5.1 Breadth-first search solution *144*
  3.5.2 Depth-first search solution *153*
3.6 Airline Reservation System *157*
  3.6.1 Abstraction solution *158*
  3.6.2 More efficient solution *174*

4 DESIGN OF A SINGLE-LANGUAGE MULTIPROGRAMMING SYSTEM *179*

Alan C. Shaw

4.1 Introduction *179*
  4.1.1 Purpose and type of system *179*
  4.1.2 Design methodology *179*
4.2 System Overview *180*
  4.2.1 Hardware components *180*
  4.2.2 User job flow *182*
  4.2.3 Single-language interpreter and user workspaces *184*
  4.2.4 The operating system *184*
4.3 The User Interface *187*
  4.3.1 Job input *187*
  4.3.2 Job output *188*

4.4 The Nucleus *189*
4.4.1 Process management kernel *189*
4.4.2 Resource management kernel *191*
4.4.3 Resource definitions *192*
4.4.4 Process scheduling *195*
4.5 Interrupts and Input-Output *196*
4.5.1 Interrupt and trap handling *196*
4.5.2 Input-output device driver processes *197*
4.6 File Structures *198*
4.6.1 Job tables and files *198*
4.6.2 Directory structure *200*
4.6.3 File descriptors *200*
4.7 Scheduling and Allocation Policies *202*
4.7.1 Job and process scheduling *202*
4.7.2 IO buffering methods *204*
4.7.3 Storage policies *205*
4.8 Process Elaboration *206*
4.8.1 Job supervisor *207*
4.8.2 Loader *209*
4.8.3 User processes *210*
4.8.4 Spoolin *211*
4.8.5 Spoolout *214*
4.8.6 Operator communication *214*
4.8.7 The root process *216*
4.9 File System Routines *217*
4.9.1 Directory manipulation *217*
4.9.2 Initialization and termination *218*
4.9.3 Read and write routines *221*
4.10 Performance Measurements *223*
4.11 Conclusions *224*
4.12 Acknowledgments *225*

5 DESIGN OF A COMPILER *226*

Marvin V. Zelkowitz

5.1 Compiler Design *226*
5.2 Background *233*
5.2.1 Grammars and languages *233*
5.2.2 Finite state automata *240*
5.2.3 Postfix *246*

5.3 Project Methodology *247*
5.3.1 Source programming language *248*
5.3.2 Target machine language *248*
5.3.3 Iterative enhancement *249*
5.4 Compiler Organization *250*
5.4.1 Requirements analysis *250*
5.4.2 Top-level design *252*
5.4.3 Diagnostic features *255*
5.5 Symbol Table Organization *256*
5.5.1 Keywords and constants *259*
5.5.2 Detailed design *260*
5.6 Scanner *264*
5.7 Parser *268*
5.7.1 Interface specifications *268*
5.7.2 Recursive descent parsing *270*
5.7.3 Parser design *271*
5.7.4 Parser summary *281*
5.8 Code Generation *281*
5.8.1 Internal forms *283*
5.8.2 Code generation techniques *284*
5.8.3 Machine organization *285*
5.8.4 Code generator organization *287*
5.8.5 Execution environment *291*
5.8.6 Machine dependencies *295*
5.8.7 Symbolic code generation *295*
5.8.8 Code generator summary *311*
5.9 Enhancements *311*
5.9.1 Compiler improvements *311*
5.9.2 Code improvements 312
5.9.3 Language extensions *315*
5.10 Interpreters *317*
5.11 Summary *317*

BIBLIOGRAPHY *319*

INDEX *325*

Preface

Software engineering is rapidly emerging as a discipline for managing the development of computer systems. As such it incorporates many ideas from engineering, management, and computer science. This book was written to bring together many of the topics into one location.

It is not possible to totally describe in one book all the facets of software development so that the complexity of the problem can be fully understood and appreciated. Instead, this book concentrates on the design aspects of programming, although sections are presented that cover the entire realm of the software development life cycle.

This book is not designed as an introduction to programming. Knowledge that programming is hard is a necessary prerequisite for adequately understanding the issues presented. It is assumed that the reader has had at least one course in programming, preferably with a block-structured language like ALGOL, PL/1, or PASCAL. In addition, the reader should have knowledge of data structures and probably should have previously taken an introductory course in operating systems or compiler writing (for Chapters 4 and 5), although that is not absolutely necessary.

The book's five chapters may be thought of as being divided into two sections. The first two chapters discuss the general principles of good software design and development. The last three chapters present several small and large examples of program design. These examples also include discussions of why certain design decisions were made.

Chapter 1, "Large-scale Software Development," presents a summary of the software engineering field and describes the major issues and some of the proposed solutions. Several of these solutions are described in greater detail in later chapters. The major goal is to give an account of the professional software environment—its problems and proposed solutions.

Chapter 2, "Programming Methodology," describes several programming techniques. The program design language used to describe the examples presented in this book is defined. In addition, concepts like top-down development, structured programming, data abstractions, certification, and testing are explained. A short list of common programming algorithms is also given.

Chapter 3, "Examples of Program Design," coauthored with John Gannon, presents six different short designs. Unlike other treatments of this topic, each problem is solved by at least two different algorithms to demonstrate that there is not always only one correct way to solve a problem. Various advantages of each solution are described.

Chapter 4, "Design of a Single-Language Multiprogramming System," by Alan Shaw, and Chapter 5, "Design of a Compiler," present two larger, complete designs. Both of these designs are given in complete detail and can be implemented in several hundred PL/1 statements. They present most of the issues encountered in developing systems and compilers.

I would like to acknowledge the contributions of John Gannon, who coauthored Chapter 3 with me, and Alan Shaw, who contributed Chapter 4, on operating systems. Except for these two chapters, I must take full responsibility for the contents of this book. Chapter 1, "Large-scale Software Development," is an extension of an earlier paper, "Perspectives on Software Engineering," which appeared in the June 1978 issue of *ACM Computing Surveys*. I am indebted to Peter Denning of Purdue University for his detailed comments on this earlier paper.

MARVIN V. ZELKOWITZ

Principles of Software Engineering and Design

1 Large-scale Software Development

It is natural at first to dismiss mistakes in programming as an inevitable but temporary evil due to lack of experience, and to assume that if reasonable care is taken to prevent such mistakes occurring, no other remedy is necessary. [Gill, 51]

In the late 1940s and early 1950s programming errors were no great problem. Mistakes happened only because we were inexperienced in using these new machines. Once we had practice in writing programs, the process would be as easy as riding a bicycle or driving an automobile.

The 1950s became the 1960s, and the 1960s became the 1970s, and still the maturation process has not occurred. After 30 years we are still making mistakes and are writing incorrect programs. Why? Is the overall process itself incorrect? Do we need new techniques to use in developing computer software?

In order to answer these questions, the discipline of *software engineering* has been developing for the last 10 years. In this book we shall define software engineering as the specification, design, implementation, testing, and operation of computer programs. Later chapters will expand on this, but will concentrate mostly on the design phase of development. Thus individuals who generally are good at coding programs from detailed designs, such as flowcharts, will be given experience in more stages of the software development life cycle. However, why study this field at all?

When the Verrazano Narrows Bridge in New York City was started in

1959, it was estimated to cost $325 million and was to be completed by 1965. It was the largest suspension bridge ever built, yet it was completed in November 1964, on target and within budget [ENR, 61] [ENR, 64]. Would anyone care to base his reputation on such predictions for a large-scale software development?

Software is often delivered late. It is unreliable. It is expensive to maintain. The IBM OS project, which involved over 5000 man-years of effort, was years late [Brooks, 75]. Why can engineering be so exact while software development flounders?

Part of the answer is that it is easier for an engineer to see the added complexity of a larger bridge than for a software engineer to see the complexity of a larger program. Part of today's "software problem" is our attempt to extrapolate from personal experiences with smaller programs to large-systems programming projects.

We begin this chapter by outlining the general approach used in developing program products, emphasizing aspects which are still poorly understood. Later, we will enumerate the techniques which have been used to solve these problems. We have not attempted to cover all the topics in depth, but we have given many references for further reading.

Currently, software engineers are studying the causes of these problems and the mechanisms of software development; they seek constraints on programming which will render software less expensive and more reliable; they seek the theoretical foundations upon which programs are built. Software engineering is not programming, although programming is certainly an important component. It is not the study of compilers and operating systems common to many academic computer science programs, although compiler writers and operating system implementors (should) use the techniques. It is not electrical engineering, although electronics does implement the computer [Jeffery and Linden, 77].

Software engineering is interdisciplinary. It uses mathematics for analyzing and certifying algorithms; engineering to estimate costs and define trade-offs; management to define requirements, assess risks, oversee personnel, and monitor progress.

1.1 STAGES OF SOFTWARE DEVELOPMENT

A large software system surpasses the ability of any one individual to understand and build. To better control the development of the project, software managers have identified six separate stages through which software projects pass; these stages are collectively called the *software development life cycle*.

1. Requirements analysis
2. Specification

3. Design
4. Coding
5. Testing
6. Operation and maintenance

The pie chart of Figure 1.1(a) shows roughly the amount of time each stage takes. The stages are summarized in the following subsections.

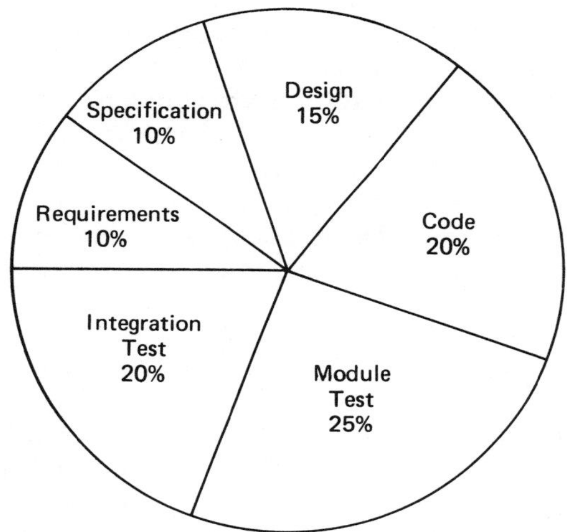

Figure 1.1(a) Effort required on various development activities (except maintenance).

1.1.1 Requirements Analysis

This first stage, curiously absent from many projects, defines the requirements for an acceptable solution to the problem. The statement "Code a program in COBOL of not more than 50,000 words to produce payroll checks" is not a requirement. It is the partial specification of a computer solution to the problem. The computer is merely a tool in a complex man/machine system for solving a problem. Requirements analysis focuses on the interface between the tool and the people who need to use it. For example, to pay its employees, a company may consider several alternatives:

1. Pay employees in cash.
2. Use a computer to print payroll checks.
3. Produce payroll checks manually.
4. Deposit payroll directly into employees' bank accounts.

Other aspects—such as processing time, costs, error probability, chance of fraud or theft—must be considered among the basic reqiurements before an appropriate solution may be chosen. Requirements analysis can help understand both the problem and the tradeoffs among conflicting constraints, contributing thereby to the best solution.

The hard requirements must be distinguished from the optional. Are there time or space limitations? What facilities of the system are likely to change in the future? What facilities will be needed to maintain different versions of the system at different locations?

The resources to implement the system must be determined. How much money is available for the project? How much is actually needed? How many computers or computer services are affordable? What personnel are available? Can existing software be used? After these questions are answered, project schedules must be planned. How will progress be controlled and monitored? What has been learned from prior efforts? What checkpoints will be inserted to measure this progress? Once all of these have been answered, the specifications for a computer solution of the problem may begin.

1.1.2 Specification

Whereas requirements analysis seeks to determine whether to use a computer, *specification* (also called *definition* [Fife, 77]) seeks to define precisely what the computer is to do. What are the inputs and the outputs? In the payroll example: Are employee records in a disk file? on tape? What is the format for each record in the file? What is the format of the output? Are checks to be printed? Is another tape to be written containing information for printing the checks off-line? Are there printed reports along with the checks? What algorithms will be needed for computing deductions such as taxes, unemployment and health insurance, or pension payments?

Since commercial systems process considerable amounts of data, the data base is a central issue. What files are needed? How will they be formatted? accessed? updated? deleted?

When the new system takes over an older process (e.g., an automatic payroll system replacing a manual system), the conversion of the existing data base to the new format must be part of the design. Conversion may require a special program which is discarded after the first and only use. Since the company may be using the older system in its day-to-day operation, how is the new system brought on-line? Are the old system and the new system run side by side for awhile?

The answers to these questions are set forth in the *functional specification*, a document describing the proposed computer solution. This document is important throughout the project. By defining the project, the specification gives both the purchaser and the developer a concrete description. The more precise the specifications, the less likely are errors, confusion, or recriminations later. The specifications enable test data to be developed early; this means that the performance of the system can be tested objectively since the test data will not be influenced by the implementation. Because it describes the scope of the solution, this document can be used for initial estimates of time, personnel, and other resources needed for the project.

These specifications define only what the system is to do, but not how. Detailed algorithms for implementation are premature and may constrain the designers unduly.

1.1.3 Design

In the design stage, the algorithms called for in the specifications are developed, and the overall structure of the computer system takes shape. The system must be divided into small parts, each the responsibility of an individual or a small team. Each such module thus defined must have its constraints: its function, its size, its speed.

In describing the software life cycle, the terms "requirements," "specification," and "design" are often given different interpretations. Our definitions can be represented by Figure 1.1(b).

The user first perceives a need in the real world. When explicitly stated,

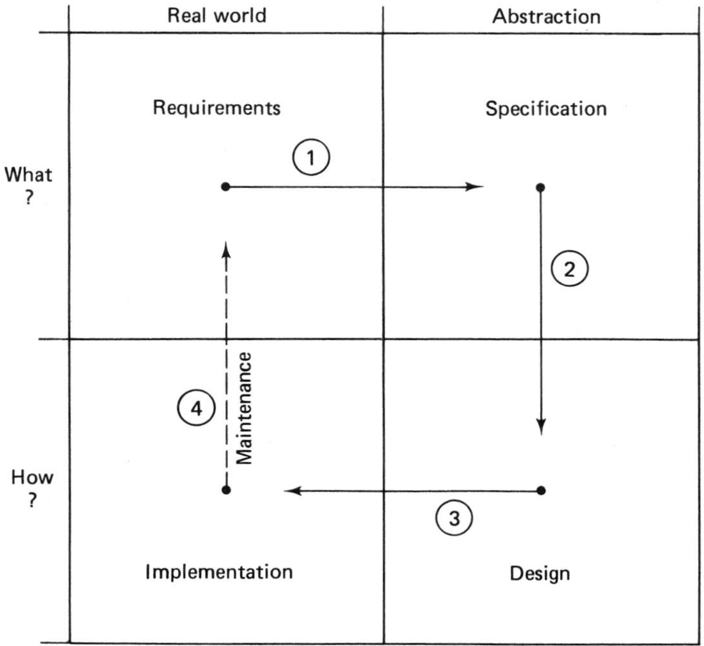

Figure 1.1(b) Software life cycle progression.

these needs represent the requirements. However, the computer cannot solve the problem directly. Real-world data must somehow be encoded and entered into the computer via sensors, cards, or keyboard. This model of the problem is an abstraction of the real-world need and represents the specification.

Given the specification of what the program is to do, the next step is to describe how the process is to occur. This represents the design phase. Since the program must be used to solve the real-world problem, the conversion of this abstract design into an executing program represents the implementation stages (coding and testing).

Finally, the user can compare what the program is to do in the real world with how it is doing it. These seldom agree exactly. Thus the maintenance stage closes the loop to altered requirements, altered specification, altered design, etc.

During design, as submodules are being specified, they are represented in a tree diagram showing the nesting of the system's components. Figure 1.2 illustrates this for a typical compiler. This picture, sometimes called a *baseline diagram*, is not by itself an adequate specification of the system.

Because the solution may not be known when the design stage starts, decomposition into small modules may be quite difficult. For older applications (e.g., compiler writing) this process may become standardized, but new ones (e.g., defense systems, spacecraft control) may be quite difficult.

A common problem is that the buyer of a system often does not know exactly what he wants, especially in state-of-the-art areas such as defense systems. As he sees the project evolve, the buyer often changes the specifica-

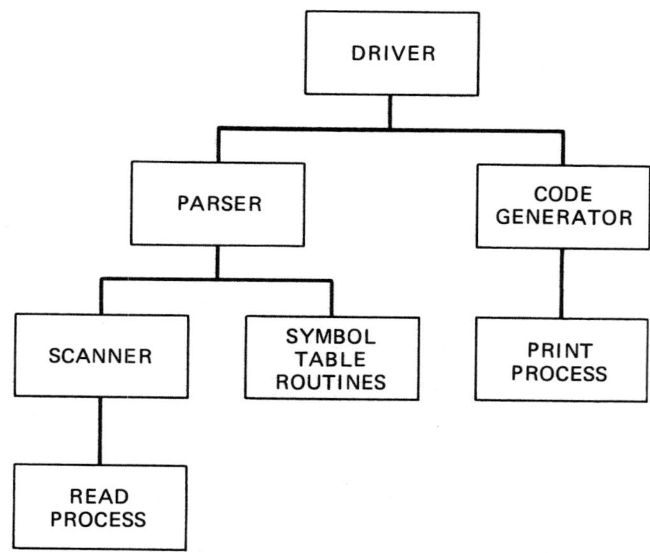

Figure 1.2 Sample baseline diagram for a compiler.

tions. If this occurs too often, the project may flounder. We will return to this problem later.

1.1.4 Coding

This stage is usually the easiest. High-level languages and structured programming simplify the task. Coding is the least troublesome stage. In one study, Boehm [75] found that 64% of all errors occurred in design, but only 36% in coding. Hamilton and Zeldin [76] report that in the NASA Apollo project about 73% of all errors were interface (design) errors. We have mastered coding better than any other stage of software development.

1.1.5 Testing

The testing stage may take up to half of the total effort. Inadequately planned testing often results in woefully late deliveries as schedules slip due to insufficient test time.

During testing, the system is presented with data representative of that for the finished system; thus test data cannot be chosen at random. In fact the test plan should be designed early, and most of the test data should be specified during the design stage of the project.

Testing is divided into three distinct operations: module testing, integration testing, and systems testing. In *module testing* each module is subjected to the test data supplied by the programmer. A test driver simulates the software environment of the module by containing dummy routines to take the place of the actual subroutines that the tested module calls. This is sometimes called *unit testing*, with the unit being tested called the *unit under test* (or UUT). A module that passes these tests is released for integration testing.

During *integration testing* groups of components are tested together. Eventually, this produces a completely tested system. Integration testing frequently reveals errors missed in module tests. Correcting them may use about a quarter of the total effort.

The final test is the *systems* or *evaluation test*, a test of the completed system by an independent group. The independence of this group is important. The buyer may also insist on his own systems test, the *acceptance test*, before accepting the product formally. If the performance of several systems is being compared (such as when a given software product is already available from several sources), this is called a *benchmark test*.

During testing, many criteria are used to determine correct program execution. Four important ones are:

1. The program is considered correct if every statement has been executed at least once by the test data and the program produces the correct answer.

2. The program is considered correct if every branch in the program has been executed and the program produces the correct answer.

3. The program is considered correct if every path through the program has been executed at least once by the test data and the program produces the correct answer.

4. The program is considered correct if for each specification of the program there is test data that demonstrates that the program performs that specification correctly.

Although (1) and (2) appear to be similar, they are actually quite different. For example, for the FORTRAN arithmetic IF statement:

IF (expression) n_1, n_2, n_3

rule (1) only implies that the IF has been executed, while rule (2) implies that different test data causes control to jump to n_1, n_2 and n_3.

These three different conditions show that there is no single acceptable criterion defining a "well-tested" program. Goodenough and Gerhart [76] proposed a set of consistent terms for "testing," and they showed that some of the above definitions of testing are, in theory, insufficient. We shall return to this subject later. For a survey of good testing techniques, see Huang [75].

Closely related to testing are verification and validation (V/V). A system is *validated* by testing to show that it performs according to its specifications. A system is *verified* if it can be proven that the program meets its specifications. Current technology is inadequate for achieving both of these concepts. A validated system may misbehave for cases not among the test data. A verified system is correct relative only to the initial specifications and assumptions about the operating environment; formal proofs tend to be long, making them subject to error or incredulity. *Certification* refers to the overall process of creating a correct program by validation and verification techniques.

In certifying a program, three terms are sometimes used interchangeably, but are different. A *failure* in a system is a noticeable event where the system violates its specifications. An *error* is an item of information which, when processed by the normal algorithms of the system, produces a failure. Since error recovery may be built into the program (e.g., ON units in PL/1), not every error will produce a failure. A *fault* is a mechanical or algorithmic defect which will generate an error (e.g., a programming "bug") [Denning, 76].

Reliability is a concept which must not be confused with correctness. A *correct* program is one that has been proven to meet its specifications. In contrast, a *reliable* program need not be correct but gives acceptable answers even if the data or environment do not meet the assumptions about them. We would like a system to be highly robust, i.e., accept a large class of input data and process it correctly under adverse conditions. Parnas [75] defines a system as being correct if it is free of faults and its internal data does not contain errors; it is reliable if failures do not seriously impair satisfactory operation.

Operating systems with "fail-soft" procedures illustrate the difference between reliability and correctness. A detected error causes the system to shut down without losing information, possibly restarting after error recovery. Such a system may not be correct because it is subject to errors; but it is reliable by its consistent operation. A real-time program may be correct as long as a sensor reports correctly; but it may be unreliable if bad sensor readings have not been considered in the specifications (and hence in the implementation).

Exercise 1.1: Are all failures the result of faults? Explain.

Exercise 1.2: Give examples of programs that are:

1. Reliable but not correct.
2. Correct but not reliable.

1.1.6 Operation and Maintenance

Figure 1.1(a) shows the disposition of software costs in developing a new project. Although correct, it is simply the wrong chart to look at. The activities of Figure 1.1(a) are only one-fourth to one-third of the effort required during the entire life of the system. Figure 1.3 better illustrates the true situation.

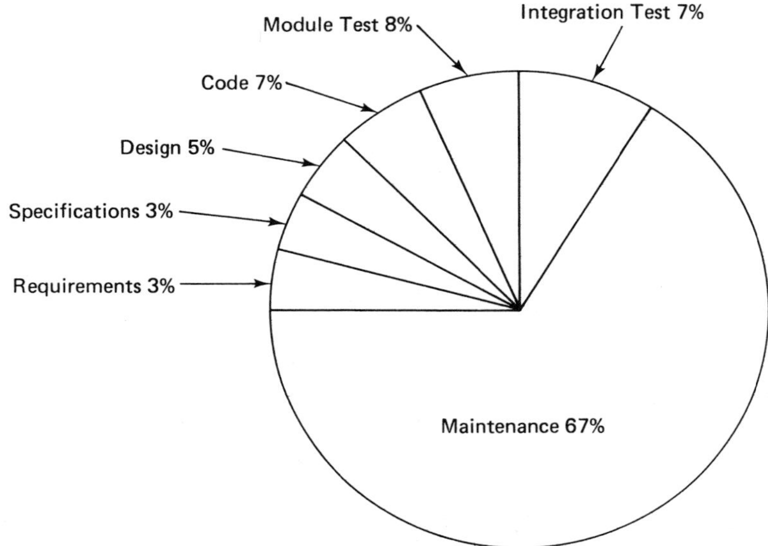

Figure 1.3 True effort required for many large-scale systems.

No computer system is fixed. Since a buyer seldom knows what he wants, he seldom is satisfied; he will request changes in the delivered system. Errors missed in testing will be discovered. Different installations will need special modifications for local conditions. The managing of multiple copies of a system is again a difficult problem that must be handled—and at an early stage in the development. Once the first line of code is ever written, the structure of the resulting maintenance operation may already be fixed; so it is best to plan for it at that time.

The division of effort indicated by Figure 1.3 greatly affects system development. Due to the "hidden" maintenance costs, techniques that rush development and provide for very early initial implementation may be trading early execution with a much more extensive maintenance operation. Basing development on the earlier figure 1.1(a), clearly suffers from this. Therefore good techniques should not be geared to produce "lines of code" early in the development cycle. While this code production may be quite pleasing to a manager, early code production with an equivalent lack of design may lead to many testing and maintenance problems later.

The maintenance problem is sometimes referred to as the *parts number explosion*. For example, a certain system contains components A, B, and C and is installed at 3 installations (I, II, and III) (Figure 1.4). Installation I finds and reports an error. The developer fixes the error and sends a corrected module A′ to all installations using the system.

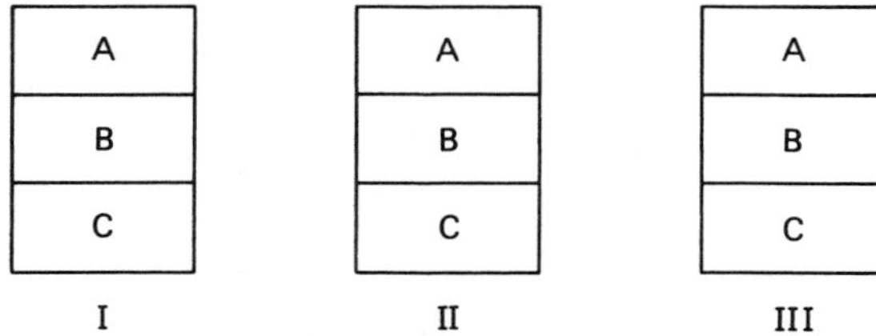

Figure 1.4 Initial systems: all the same.

Due to the history of unreliable software, most installations are very wary of changes to a system. Therefore, installations II and III did not experience the problems encountered at I and choose to use the original system, using the "principle" of "if it works, leave it alone" (Figure 1.5). Now installations I and II discover another error in module A. The developer must now determine whether both of these errors are the same since different versions of module A are involved. The correction to this error involves a correction to both A′ (for I) and A (for II), yielding A″ and A‴. There are now three versions of the system (Figure 1.6). In many cases most of the

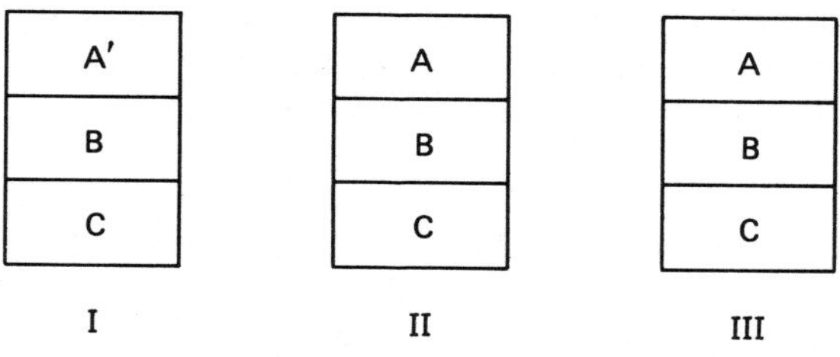

Figure 1.5 After one error: two different versions.

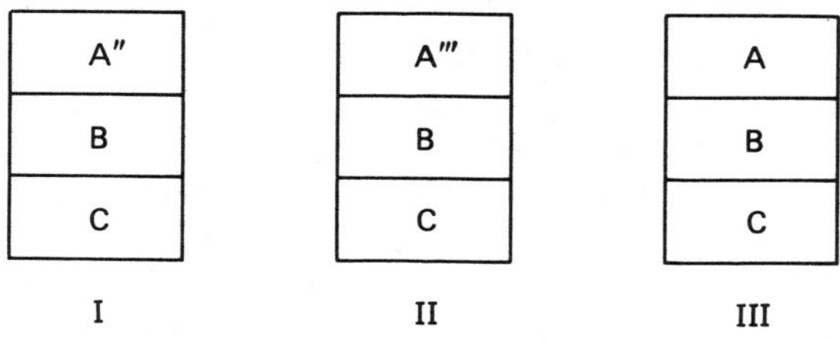

Figure 1.6 After two errors: three different versions.

developer's efforts are spent at rediscovering previous errors already found in other versions of the system.

To avoid this growth, systems are often updated at fixed intervals called *releases.* A useful tool for dealing with myriad maintenance problems is a "systems data base" started during the specifications stage. This data base records the characteristics of the different installations. It includes the procedures for reporting, testing, and repairing errors before distributing the corrections.

1.1.7 Themes of Software Engineering

It should be clear that each software development stage may influence earlier stages. The writing of specifications gives feedback to evaluate resource requirements; the design often reveals flaws in these specifications; coding, testing, and operation reveal problems in design. The goals of software engineering can be stated as:

1. Use techniques that manage system complexity.
2. Increase system reliability and correctness.
3. Develop techniques to predict software costs more accurately.

In the following sections, we discuss approaches towards some of these problems. The list of techniques is divided into management and programmer issues. Management issues concern the effective organization of personnel on a project. Programmer issues concern the techniques used by individual programmers to improve their performance.

1.2 MANAGEMENT ISSUES

A manager controls two major resources: personnel and computer equipment. This section surveys techniques for optimizing the use of these resources.

A project may fail when management is not aware of developing problems. A year's delay comes "one day at a time" [Brooks, 75]. Faced with a catastrophic failure (e.g., needed hardware is delayed six months), a resourceful manager can usually find alternatives. However, it is easy to ignore day-to-day problems (e.g., sick employees, many errors during testing).

Most problems occur in the interfaces between modules written by different programmers. Since the number of such interfaces connecting N individuals is $N(N - 1)/2$, and thus is on the order of the square of the number of individuals, this is unwieldy when the development group grows to four or more.

As an example of the communications problem, assume that a single programmer is capable of writing a 5000-line program in a year and a programming system requires about 50,000 lines of code and is to be completed in two years. Five programmers seem to be sufficient (Figure 1.7).

5000 lines/year = 50,000 lines in two years
No communication between programmers

Figure 1.7 Single projects.

However, the five programmers must communicate among one another. Such communication takes time, and also causes some loss in productivity since misunderstood aspects will require additional testing to be found. For this simple analysis, assume that each communication path "costs" a programmer 250 lines of code per year. Therefore each of the five programmers can produce only 4000 lines per year, and only 40,000 lines are completed within two years (Figure 1.8).

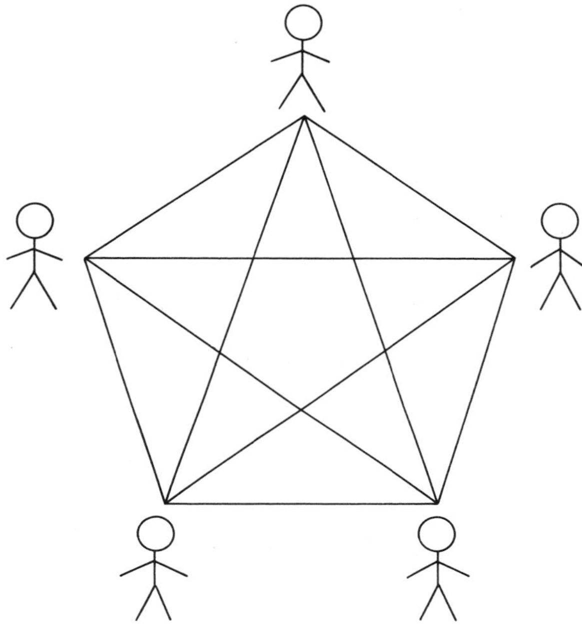

4000 lines/year = 40,000 in two years
Ten communication pairs

Figure 1.8 Five-member team.

This means that eight programmers producing 3250 lines per year are actually needed in order to produce the required 50,000. With this large effort, a manager is required for direction. Therefore, in summary, eight programmers and a manager producing an average of 3000 lines per year are actually needed (Figure 1.9).

As we shall see, simply counting lines of code is not a good estimate of productivity. Also, the figures in this example are only given to illustrate a point, but they are representative of the problems. There are techniques for limiting this communication "explosion" and increasing programmer productivity.

1.2.1 Project Personnel

Software can usually be divided into three categories: control programs (e.g., operating systems), systems programs (e.g., compilers), and applications programs (e.g., a file management system). From previous experience,

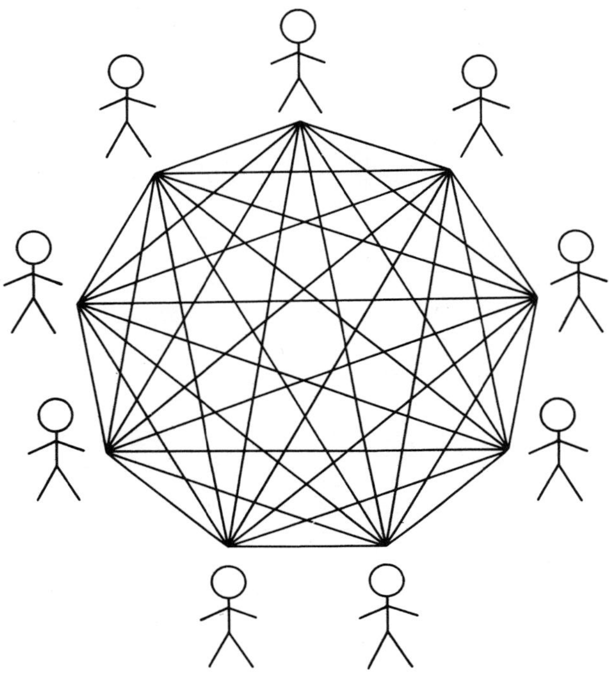

3000 lines/year = 50,000 in two years
Thirty six communication pairs

Figure 1.9 Nine-member team.

a single programmer working on a control program can produce about 600 lines of code per year, and he can produce about 2000 lines if working on a systems program and about 6000 lines if working on an applications program [Wolverton, 74].

These figures must be used very carefully. For example, what is a "line of code"? Does it include comments? data declarations? lines of generated machine instructions? library subroutines? source lines or source statements? The underlying assumptions can easily vary this figure by a factor of 2 or more.

The type of task certainly affects the productivity one can expect from a given programmer. However, as the previous example demonstrates, the organization of personnel also affects performance. For example, with approaching deadlines, documentation is often given low priority. However, since 70% of the total system cost may occur during the maintenance stage, this may be a false savings of effort.

Use of a librarian is one way to avoid this problem. A *librarian* is the interface between the programmer and the computer. Programs are coded and given to the librarian for insertion into the on-line project library. The actual debugging of the module is carried out by the programmer, but changes to the official copy in the library are performed by the librarian. The use of a library is further enhanced if an on-line data management system is used.

The use of a librarian has a beneficial side effect. All changes to modules in the project library are handled by one individual and are easy to monitor; they are often reviewed by the project manager before insertion. This prevents "midnight patches" from being quickly incorporated into a system and forces the programmer to think carefully about each change. It also gives the manager disciplined product control and helps with audit trails.

On still larger projects, a technical writer is added to write much of the documentation. This frees programmers for the tasks for which they are most skilled.

The culmination of this idea is the *chief programmer team* as developed by IBM [Baker, 72]. The concept recognizes that programmers have different levels of competence; therefore, the most competent should do the major work, with others in support roles. As the earlier example shows, interfacing problems greatly reduce programmer productivity. The chief programmer team is one way of limiting this complexity.

The *chief programmer*, an excellent, creative, and well-disciplined individual, is the head of the team. He may be five or more times more productive than the lowest member of the team [Boehm, 76]. He is the technical manager of the project who designs the system and writes the top-level interfaces for all major modules.

If a project is large, a team may also have an *administrative manager* to handle such responsibilities as scheduling time, vacations, office space, and budgets and reporting to upper management. The administrative manager often administers several programming teams.

The *backup programmer* works with the chief programmer and fills in details assigned by the chief programmer. Should the chief programmer leave the project, the backup programmer takes over. This means that he also must be an excellent programmer. The backup programmer also fulfills an important role in providing the chief programmer with a peer he can use in discussing the design.

There are two or three more *junior programmers* assigned to the team to write the low-level modules as defined by the chief programmer. The term "junior" in this context means "less experienced" and not "less capable." As Boehm states, the best results occur with fewer and better people.

Using the example illustrated in Figure 1.5, a chief programmer team of five individuals has only seven communication paths, and the chief programmer, being that rare good individual, can produce more than his "quota" of 5000 lines (Figure 1.10). Thus productivity per programmer can be over 5000 lines per year instead of the previous figure of only 4000.

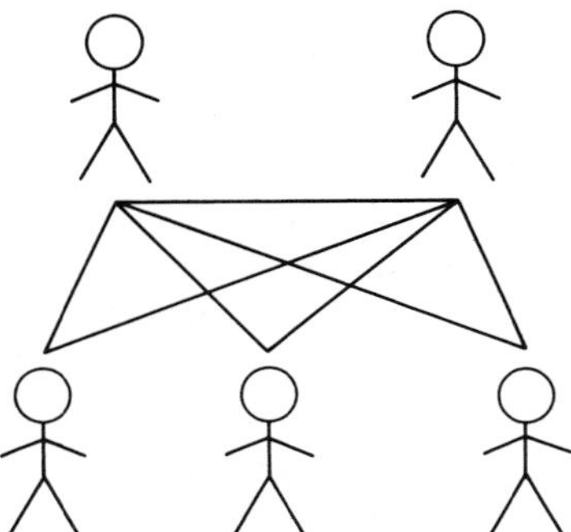

Figure 1.10 Fewer communication pairs using a chief programmer team.

The team has a librarian to manage the project library—both the on-line module library and the off-line project documentation (also called the *project notebook*). The project notebook contains, among other things, records of compilations and test runs of all modules. The project notebook is an important part of the team structure. All development is now accountable and open for inspection; code is no longer the "private property" of any individual programmer.

Programmers have traditionally been reluctant to exhibit their products until finished—the discovery of errors has traditionally been viewed as a personal failure. The absurdity of this approach is clear enough. If the "ego" is removed from programming, programmers are open to ask others for advice when needed, instead of trying to solve all problems themselves [Weinberg, 71].

The team may include other supporting personnel such as secretaries and technical writers. Experience shows that 10 is an upper bound to the size of any team.

This structure, however, will not cure all ailments in development. With the small number of individuals involved, competence is crucial. It is not possible to "work around" a nonproductive individual, as is possible in a large project. The success or failure of the team is totally dependent upon the chief programmer. If that rare creative individual is not employed by the organization, then a chief programmer team should not be used to avoid catastrophic failure. There are also extremely large projects where a group of 10 is simply insufficient to tackle development. Larger teams are not efficient. Also, this organization provides nothing towards the actual design process. That is still the creative undertaking of one individual—the chief programmer in this case. In Section 1.5 other approaches towards development will be described.

A *man-month,* or the amount of work performed by one individual in one month, is a common, but deceptive, measure for estimating project productivity. A project requiring four programmers for a year cannot be completed by 48 programmers in one month. The example of the 50,000-line system needed in two years shows some of the problems in trying to exchange programmers for time. As Brooks [75] states, "Adding manpower to a late software project makes it later." New personnel divert existing personnel to train them; they require more supervision; they complicate communication and interfere with the design since they are unfamiliar with the project structure.

However, man-months do serve a purpose as a useful measure of the size of a completed project. Stating that a project required 100 man-months does give some indication of the effort involved. However, this figure by itself is insufficient. As shown in the next section, additional data can be combined with this figure, such as the *rate* of using man-months, to produce an accurate cost estimation technique.

1.2.2 Estimation Techniques

One of the most important aspects of engineering is estimating the resources needed to complete a project. As previously mentioned, the Verrazano Narrows Bridge in New York City was completed at the projected time and within the estimated budget. How was such accuracy achieved?

Engineering estimation techniques

Most engineering disciplines have highly developed methods of estimating resource needs. One technique is the following [Gallagher, 65]:

1. Develop an outline of the requirements from the request for quotation (RFQ). The RFQ is produced by the organization needing the new system and is used to notify potential developers that a new system is being contemplated. Often this document is a "wish list" of desirable features, and a requirements analysis must be performed to accurately identify the needed resources to build the system. Ideally, the purchaser of a system has performed an adequate requirements analysis, but this unfortunately is not always the case.
2. Gather similar information, such as data from similar projects.
3. Select the basic relevant data.
4. Develop estimates.
5. Do final evaluation.

Although this approach has been advocated for software development, software projects have difficulty passing step (1) [Wolverton, 74]. Engineers have been building bridges for 6000 years, but software systems for only 30. The experience to understand the true requirements may not be available. Moreover, with very little background to build on, the developer has little knowledge of similar systems to use in evaluation (step (2)).

In developing the estimates (step (4) above), the following tasks must be undertaken:

4a. Compare the project to previous similar projects.

4b. Divide the project into units, and compare each unit with similar units.

4c. Schedule work by month, and estimate resources per month.

4d. Develop standards that can be applied to work.

Note that step (4a), the lack of previous experience, is a continuing problem. In (4b), what do we mean by a "unit" of a software system? We do not have any definition of a module or component of a system that is agreeable to all. Also, in (4d), an adequate set of standards does not yet exist. In the construction industry, for example, various handbooks list precise formulas for utilizing glass, steel, and other components in buildings; however, nothing comparable exists for software.

Several independent techniques should be used for developing these estimates. If they generate inconsistent results, the inconsistencies should be resolved before continuing. Estimation techniques should also be conservative to minimize cost overruns later. Several of the approaches (both good and bad) to cost estimation include the following:

1. *Expert judgment.* The estimate is based upon the personal experiences of the (chief) designers. For many applications designers may have a feeling about the complexity of the system that can be translated into an accurate cost estimate even though no apparent algorithms can be specified for this computation. This estimate is usually based upon the designers' previous experiences on similar projects. Unfortunately, subjective biases are unavoidable and the technique is no better than the skill of the individual designers. However, with no explicit theory or body of empirical data to go on, this technique is generally the crux of any cost estimation strategy on most projects.

2. *Algorithmic analysis.* Some algorithm is used to explicitly specify the cost estimate; it is objective and repeatable. Much of the current research in software engineering is in the development of such algorithms that can be applied to many projects. Unfortunately, few algorithms currently exist that are applicable. In addition, the algorithm is only as good as the data used

in the algorithm (e.g., the system's specifications), and these are rarely precise enough.

3. *Top-down and bottom-up*. The system is specified in a top-down or bottom-up manner (Section 2.2), and each such identified task is separately estimated. This is a semi-algorithmic process that can be used effectively with other techniques, like expert judgment, to develop accurate estimates for each subtask and for the project as a whole.

4. *Parkinson's Law*. For many tasks, people will spend whatever time is allocated to that task, whether absolutely necessary or not. Or specified another way, work fills the time available. Regardless of how individuals are used on a project, all will somehow contribute in some way and charge their time to the project. This "technique" is usually the result of applying other techniques. That is, once an estimate is made (such as via expert judgment), all people allocated to the project will be busy performing some function, whether necessary or not.

One result of this is that the design of any system often reflects the organization of the committee that designed it. Thus if three designers work on a system, the finished project will probably consist of three major segments; if the design group consisted of four designers, then four major segments will probably result.

While this technique is not especially fruitful, it is probably an unavoidable consequence of human nature.

5. *Cost-to-win*. Sometimes a contract is intentionally underbid with the expectation by the developer that contract modifications and system specification changes can be used to greatly increase the cost. Once a contract is given for a particular piece of software, changes in specifications are usually negotiated between the developer and purchaser without any new bidding by other developers. At this point the developer is in a more powerful position since significant resources may have already been spent on the project, and it may be too expensive to restart the project with another developer.

A buyer of such a system should be very wary of any bids that seem too out of line from the others. In addition, the buyer should protect himself from such tactics by first performing a good requirements analysis and avoid the necessity of changing specifications. (Since any change of specifications results in increased system costs and decreased reliability, a good requirements analysis is a must in any case.) While not a recommended technique, it is often used.

6. *Psyche bidding*. On some proposals, bidders will often submit cost estimates that are remarkably similar. Their algorithmic analysis of the problem seems truly outstanding until the actual technique is revealed. In these cases, the bidders simply know how much money is available for the project and then bid that amount, after "psyching out" the competition by trying to minimally underbid all other potential developers.

Experience is the key to accurate estimation. Even civil engineering projects may fail badly when established techniques are not adhered to. Although the Verrazano Narrows Bridge was the world's largest, its engineers had much experience with other large suspension bridges. The architectural firm that designed the bridge had also designed the George Washington Bridge in New York, which was also the world's largest when it was built 25 years previously.

On the other hand, the Alaskan oil pipeline was estimated to cost $900 million, yet upon opening in 1977 the cost had risen past $9 billion [ENR, 77]. In this case, the design kept changing as the United States government imposed new environmental safeguards (i.e., changed specifications) and new technologies were needed for moving large quantities of oil in a cold weather environment. Previous experience was only marginally helpful.

Rayleigh curve estimation

Results from computer hardware reliability theory are now starting to play a role in software estimation [Putnam and Wolverton, 77] [Putnam, 78]. The cumulative expenditures over time for large-scale projects (over 50 man-years) has been found to agree closely with the following equation:

$$E(t) = K(1 - e^{-at^2})$$

where $E(t)$ is the total amount spent on the project up to time t, K is the total cost of the project, and a is a measure of the maximum expenditures for any one time period. This relationship is usually expressed in its differential form, called a Rayleigh curve:

$$E'(t) = 2Kate^{-at^2}$$

where $E'(t)$ is the rate of expenditures, or the amount spent on the project during year number t. Since 60% of the cost of a project occurs during the maintenance stage, it is not surprising that the maximum expenditures will occur just before the product is released, a time when it has traditionally been assumed that the effort is winding down towards termination (Figure 1.11).

The applicability of the Rayleigh curve developed from the following argument:

1. The number of problems to solve in building a software product is a finite but unknown number.

2. The process of information gathering, thinking about possible solutions, and identifying alternatives all consume time. All design decisions convert one of the unsolved problems into a solved problem.

3. The assumption is made that the occurrence of these events (of converting unsolved problems into solved problems) is independent and random.

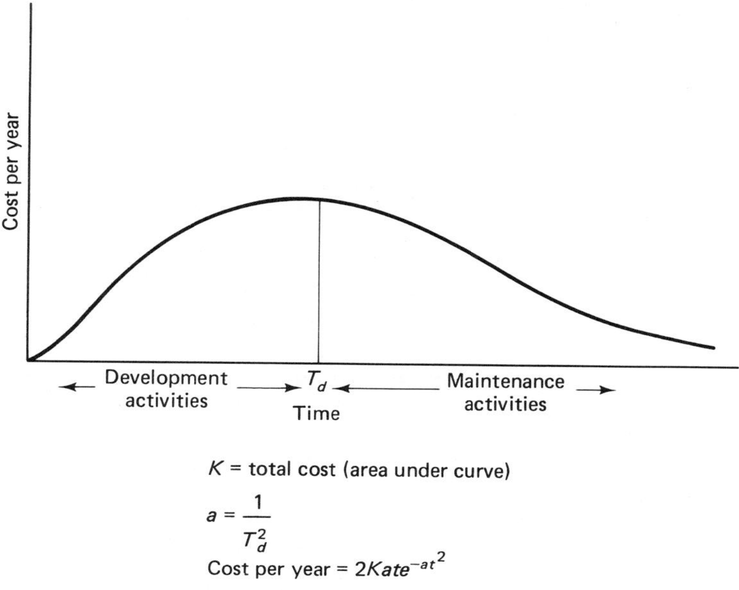

Figure 1.11 Yearly rate of expenditures approximates the Rayleigh curve.

This leads to a solution that is Poisson with an exponential interevent arrival time satisfying the equation:

$$y = e^{-\lambda t}$$

where y is the probability of the problem remaining unsolved by time t.

4. The number of people working in a group at any time is proportional to the number of problems "ripe" for a solution. This also assumes that each individual is working independently on unsolved problems to solve.

If we let

$$\Pr(T > t) = \text{probability that no event occurs in the interval } [0, t]$$

then from the Poisson assumption

$$\Pr(T > t) = e^{-\lambda t}$$

Since $\Pr(T \leq t) + \Pr(T > t) = 1$, we know that the probability of the event occurring in the interval $[0, t]$ is just

$$\begin{aligned}\Pr(T \leq t) &= 1 - \Pr(T > t) \\ &= 1 - e^{-\lambda t}\end{aligned}$$

The frequency distribution, or the rate of solving problems, is the derivative of the probability function, or

$$f(t) = -\lambda e^{-\lambda t}$$

Let us now refine our previous assumption (3).

3′. Assume that after an event occurs, p is the probability that the event is actually solved (e.g., the correct decision was made). This leads to the solution:

$$\Pr(T \leq t) = 1 - e^{-p\lambda t}$$
$$f(t) = -p\lambda e^{-p\lambda t}$$

If we further assume that the probability of success (p) is a function of time ($p(t)$), then the solution becomes

$$\Pr(T > t) = e^{-\lambda \int_0^t p(\tau)\, d\tau}$$

or

$$\Pr(T \leq t) = 1 - e^{-\lambda \int_0^t p(\tau)\, d\tau}$$
$$f(t) = \lambda p(t) e^{-\lambda \int_0^t p(\tau)\, d\tau}$$

According to empirical data for large-scale software systems [Norden, 64], the best fit for p is an equation of the form

$$p(t) = \alpha t$$

This gives the following solution:

$$\Pr(T \leq t) = 1 - e^{-(\lambda \alpha t^2)/2}$$

Letting $a = (\lambda\alpha)/2$ and multiplying by the total project cost (K) to convert the probability into an approximate cost per unit of time results in the standard equations

$$\Pr(T \leq t) = K(1 - e^{-at^2})$$
$$f(t) = 2Kate^{-at^2}$$

If we let $y(t)$ represent the total expenditures on the project, then the rate of spending (or the rate of solving problems) can be written as

$$y'(t) = 2at(K - y)$$

This equation contains two variable terms: t and $(K - y)$. As a project moves towards completion, t increases so the rate of progress (y') increases. This is due to the effect of the "learning curve" as the personnel become more familiar with the problem and hence become more productive.

Working against this trend, however, is the term $(K - y)$, which represents the work still to be done. As a system nears completion, it grows more complex, which has a tendency to diminish worker productivity.

The Rayleigh curve has two parameters, K and a; however, a system can be described by three general characteristics:

1. Its total cost
2. Its rate of development
3. Its completion date

Two of these characteristics are enough to determine the constants K and a. When a project is initiated, the proposed budget is an estimate of K and the available personnel permits a to be calculated. Assuming that requirements analysis determines that these figures represent an accurate assessment of the complexity of the problem, the estimated completion date (the date when the expenditures reach a maximum) can be *computed* and cannot be set arbitrarily during the requirements or specification stage. This is the basis for a cost estimation strategy that has been applied to smaller projects in the 100 man-months range [Basili and Zelkowitz, 78]. We may be close to a mathematical theory of cost estimation which will greatly reduce our need to "guess" at project costs.

Exercise 1.3: Show that $y'(t) = 2at(K - y)$.

Exercise 1.4: Given the development costs K_d and the time needed to develop, t_d, compute for the Rayleigh curve the total costs K and the maximum height of the curve a.

1.2.3 Milestones

A *milestone* is the specification of a demonstrable event in the development of a project. Milestones are scheduled by management to measure progress. "Coding is 90% complete" is not a milestone since the manager cannot know when 90% of the code is complete until the project itself is complete.

There are many candidates for milestones: publication of the functional specifications, writing of individual module designs, modules compiling without errors, units testing successfully, and so on. Milestones are scheduled fairly often to detect early slippage.

Reporting forms can give information which is useful for estimating when a future milestone will be reached. A general project summary, describing such overall characteristics as system size, cost, completion dates, or complexity, can be resubmitted with each milestone. Change reports can be submitted each time a module is altered. The use of a librarian probably means that such a form already exists. Weekly personnel and computer reports monitor expenditures. Although they add a minor overhead to the project, the information helps management keep abreast [Walston and Felix, 77].

In one study several projects were monitored via a set of reporting forms [Basili and Zelkowitz, 78]. Some of the projects were on schedule and had little trouble with the data collection procedures. On the other hand, some projects were late and had little time for the reporting requirements. While the overhead on filling out the forms was blamed for part of the delay, investigations revealed that those projects were actually delayed before data collection even began.

This may possibly lead to one simple algorithm for measuring probable success on a project:

1. Have all projects fill out reporting forms for several months.
2. All projects having trouble with the forms should be investigated for possible organizational problems which may surface later.

1.2.4 Development Tools

Compilers and certain debugging facilities have been available for some time. In contrast, other programming aids are new, and experience with them less extensive. Aids can be of considerable help. Auditors or data base systems can help to control the organization of the developing system. Cross references, attribute listings, and symbolic storage maps are such examples. The problem statement language/problem statement analyzer (PSL/PSA) of the ISDOS project of the University of Michigan is one of the first data base systems geared towards providing a module library for storing source code, and it includes a language for specifying interfaces in system design which can be checked automatically [Teichroew and Hershey, 77]. RSL (requirements statement language) is a similar system designed to specify requirements and design interfaces via a data management system [Davis and Vick, 77]. Both of these will be described in greater detail in Section 1.4.

An alternate approach is the programmer's workbench developed by Bell Telephone Laboratories [Dolotta and Mashey, 76]. A PDP 11–based system provides a set of support routines for module development, library maintenance, documentation, and testing. Proper use of these facilities allows accessing information in a more easily controlled environment.

1.2.5 Reliability

Conceptual integrity—the uniformity of style and simplicity of structure—is usually achieved by minimizing the number of individuals in the project. A chief programmer team greatly enhances conceptual integrity since the chief programmer does most of the design.

From the user's perspective, this idea is often called *human engineering*. Features should follow from a logical structure and should not be the result of arbitrary decisions.

Many examples of poor design exist:

1. In the PL/1 language, for example, the PICTURE attribute declaration may be abbreviated as either "PIC" or "P", but in format specifications it may only be "P" [ANSI, 76].

2. In the old 1966 FORTRAN standard, the right side of an assignment statement can be an arbitrary arithmetic expression, but DO loop indices must be integer constants or variables, and subscripts to arrays are limited to seven basic forms [ANSI, 66]. These are difficult idiosyncracies to remember, and while applicable to efficient compiler design when FORTRAN was first developed in the late 1950s, they no longer apply.

3. The tradeoff between logical simplicity and functional requirements is not an easy one to agree upon. The example of an operating system's command language is a case in point. In IBM's 360/370 OS job control language (JCL) the command to assign a file named X residing on a disk to a program takes the format:

```
//X DD DSN=X,UNIT=DISK,DISP=(MOD,PASS),SPACE=(TRACK,(100,10,1))
```

This is quite unwieldy for the casual user who may simply need temporary disk space for a single job step and is unconcerned as to its location or format. On the other hand, in the Univac 1100-series operating system, the same operation could be achieved with the command:

```
@ASG X
```

However, for complicated user applications the situation may differ from the previous example. Under 360/370 OS, if the user needs a disk file of 256 tracks, then the only change needed to the previous DD statement is a change to the SPACE parameter, as in:

```
SPACE=(TRACK,(256,10,1))
```

since knowledge of the logical structure of the DD statement leads to easy adaptation of alternative operations. On the other hand, the equivalent Univac command would be:

```
@ASG X,F///256
```

and no amount of understanding of the short form of ASG leads to knowing how to extend the command for specific applications.

Requirements analysis must consider the alternatives. Since operating system command languages are used by all classes of users, they should have the flexibility of IBM JCL and the simplicity of Univac's commands for the novice—not an easy task.

Certification of a system, unlike buying an air conditioner or an FM radio for a new car, is not an "add-on" option purchased after a system is completed. A system must be designed to be correct at all stages of development. At each level of design, coding, or testing, it is necessary to show that correctness is preserved by any new additions to the system. Several techniques aid in this effort.

A *walkthrough* is a management review to discover errors in a system. In one study, TRW discovered that the cost of fixing an error at the coding stage is about twice that of fixing it at the design stage, and catching it in testing costs about 10 times that in design [Boehm, 77].

A walkthrough is scheduled periodically for all personnel. In attendance are the project manager (chief programmer), the person reviewed, and several others knowledgeable about the project. One section of the system is selected for review, and each individual is given information about that section (e.g., design document for a design walkthrough, code for a coding walkthrough) before the review. The person being reviewed then describes the module under study.

The walkthrough is for detection of errors and not for their correction. Also, the walkthrough is brief—not more than two hours. By explaining the design to others, the person reviewed is likely to discover vague specifications or missing conditions.

An important point for management is that the walkthrough is *not* for personnel evaluation. If the person reviewed perceives that he is being evaluated, he may attempt to cover up problems or present a rosy picture.

Another technique, often used by good programmers, is quite effective in insuring system validity. When stumped by a hidden error, they will often discuss the code with a colleague. Even if the colleague says nothing, the technique is quite often successful at revealing problems. This technique has been more standardized as the concept of *code reading*. In order to perform code reading, a second programmer reviews the code for each module. This technique frequently turns up errors when the second reader, failing to understand some aspects of the code, asks the author for an explanation. Code reading has been found to be one of the most cost effective techniques for finding problems in a system.

1.3 PROGRAMMER ISSUES

Each stage of the software development life cycle has its own set of problems and solutions. The most advanced techniques apply to the last stages, and the first stages are the least developed. For example, testing and debugging problems are apparent to every programmer; these tools are the oldest and most advanced. Techniques for improving coding were developed next. The most recent developments have related to requirements and specifications. While all technical problems have not been solved, an effective methodology is emerging. Some of these techniques are presented next.

1.3.1 Verification and Validation

Verification and validation (module and integration testing) of a system occupies about half of the development time of a project. Many debugging aids were developed to lessen this effort; most are implemented as programs to test some feature of a system.

The earliest and most primitive tools were the dump and the trace. A *dump* is a listing of the contents of the machine's memory. From this collection of gibberish, errors may sometimes be found. Unfortunately, a dump may not be taken until long "after the fact," and the cause of the error may not be apparent. A *trace* is a printout showing the values of selected variables after each statement is executed. It may help a programmer discover errors. These techniques are not usually very effective because they supply much data with little or no interpretation. More advanced methods are needed to reduce this data to an intelligible form.

Flowgraph analyzers are capable of detecting references to variables which are never initialized or never reused after receiving a value; these usually indicate errors. There are test data generators to generate test data for a program. Assertion checkers validate that given conditions are true at indicated points of a program. Automatic verification systems have been implemented for small languages, and symbolic execution has been proposed as a practical means for validating programs in a more complex language. The PSL/PSA system is an example of a tool for assisting with design and specification. Symbolic dumps and traces are generated with compilers like PL/C [Conway and Wilcox, 73] or PLUM [Zelkowitz, 75]. Ramamoorthy and Ho [75] survey many of these tools.

When discussing correct program development, the term "correct" can have many interpretations. Conway [78] lists eight different meanings for a correct program:

1. A program contains no syntactic errors.
2. A program contains no compilation errors or failures during program execution.
3. There exists test data for which the program gives correct answers.
4. For typical sets of test data, the program gives correct answers.
5. For difficult sets of test data, the program gives correct answers.
6. For all possible sets of data which are valid with respect to the problem specification, the program gives correct answers.

7. For all possible sets of valid test data and all likely conditions of erroneous input, the program gives correct answers.
8. For all possible input, the program gives correct answers.

A student running his very first computer program will generally be satisfied to simply get a clean compilation (level (1) above). However, as most programmers already realize—and as the novice is quickly going to discover—that level of correctness is far from acceptable. On the other hand, level (8) correctness is not always attainable or even needed. If the data is known to be correct, then level (6) might be sufficient. Also, if failures are rare enough, the reliability of level (5) might be acceptable.

The achievement of each of these levels requires a cost in developing and testing the system. The appropriate level of correctness needed for any application should be determined by the requirements stage.

Some people are optimistic that one day complete automatic program verification will be possible. Today's tools operate a posteriori, demonstrating that a *given* program works. Tomorrow's tools will also operate a priori, helping to develop programs which are correct before they are ever run. Such tools can reduce the amount of testing required for a completed project [Dijkstra, 76].

Verification techniques have the following general structure: A program is represented by a flowchart. Associated with each arc in the flowchart is a predicate called an *assertion.* If *Ai* is the assertion associated with an arc entering statement *S*, and *Aj* is the assertion on the arc following the statement, then the statement "If *Ai* is true, and if statement *S* is executed, then assertion *Aj* will be true" must be proven (Figure 1.12).

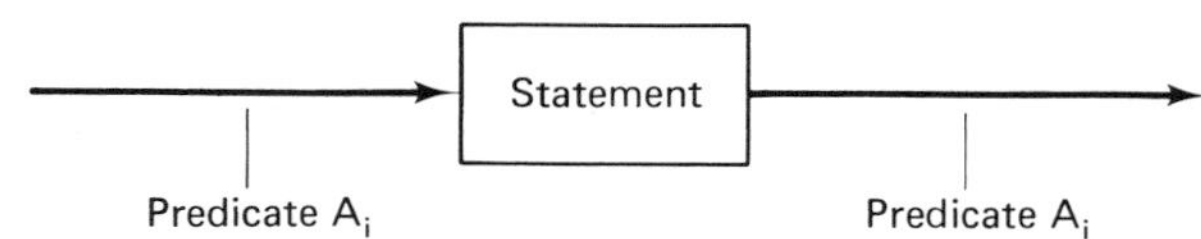

Figure 1.12 Assertions A_i and A_j surround each statement of a program.

This process can be repeated for each statement in a program. If *A*1 is the assertion immediately prior to the input node to the flowchart (i.e., the *initial* assertion), and if *An* is the assertion at the exit node (e.g., the *final* assertion), then the statement "If *A*1 is true, and the program is executed, then *An* is true" will be the theorem that states that the program meets its specifications (*A*1 and *An*) (Figure 1.13). This approach was formalized by Hoare [69], who defined a set of axioms for determining the effects upon the assertions (*pre-* and *postconditions*) by each statement type in a language. Thus program correctness reduces to proving a theorem of the predicate

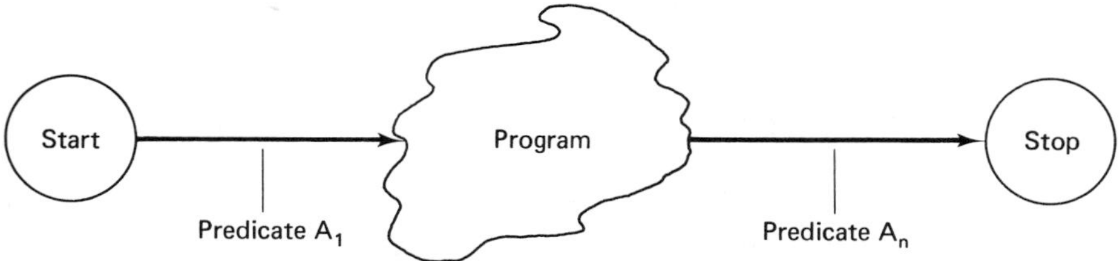

Figure 1.13 Predicates A_1 and A_n specify input-output behavior of program.

calculus. In Chapter 2 this axiomatic approach to program certification will be outlined in greater detail.

Note one important point that must not be overlooked. In both Conway's eight levels of program correctness and in Hoare's axiomatic approach, the effects of a program must be compared with its specification. *Every* program is correct with respect to *some* set of specifications: However, are these specifications equivalent to the program requirements? Also, are the stated specifications the same ones the program is correct with respect to? This issue is the main one behind the desire to create languages and systems for automating the requirements and specification phases of a project.

Exercise 1.5: Prove the above statement that every program is correct with respect to some set of specifications. What about programs that do not terminate for all input? What can you say about the following fairly common statement: "Here is a program written in some programming language. Is it correct?"

Certification will not solve all our software problems, although it is an important tool. Gerhart and Yelowitz [76] have shown that there are many published "certified" programs that contain errors. Even experts err.

Although useful for focusing our attention, analogies with other engineering fields must be used with care. Reliability is one area of incomplete analogies. The concept of *mean time between failure* (MTBF) does not apply directly to software, although it sometimes is used as if it does.

Systems built of physical components wear out, transistors fail, motors burn out, soldered joints break. This is certainly true of the hardware of the computer. However, the logical components of software are durable. A given program will always produce the same answer for the same input (as long as the hardware does not fail). When a software module "fails," it has been presented with an input that finally revealed a fault present from the start.

The concept of mean time between failures measures the time between revelations of errors. This will depend on the kinds of inputs presented. A compiler used only for short jobs from students may have a long MTBF; but if it is suddenly used for other applications, its MTBF may decrease sharply as unsuspected errors surface. Thus a large MTBF can be interpreted only as an indication of possible reliability, not a proof of it.

Since formal certification of large classes of programs is still unattainable, techniques for estimating the validity of programs are being considered. Most of these techniques measure the number of found errors, which are assumed to be representative of the total number of errors present in the system and hence a measure of the reliability of the system.

Mills [76] defines an *error-day* as a measure stating that one error remains undetected in a system for one day. The total number of error-days in a system is computed by summing, for each error, the length of time that error was in the system. A high error-day count may reveal many errors (due to poor design) or long-lived errors (due to poor development).

The assumption is made that if a program is delivered with a low error-day count, then there is a good chance that it will remain low during future use. However, two major problems remain before this measure can be widely used. For one, it is difficult to discover when a particular error first entered a system. Secondly, for a delivered product, it may be difficult to obtain such information from the developer.

1.3.2 Programming Techniques

Several authors have mentioned that the number of lines of code produced by a programmer in a given time tends to be independent of the language used; thus higher level languages enhance productivity [Brooks, 75] [Halstead, 77]. This is true even though assembly language programs are potentially more efficient (the potential is seldom realized in practice).

In developing early higher level languages, the goals were to be able to clearly express an algorithm and to be able to translate the algorithm into efficient machine language programs. Efficiency of the resulting code was all important. This led to some anomalies in FORTRAN due to the structure of the IBM 704 for which it was developed (e.g., the three-way branch of the arithmetic IF). Even ALGOL, which was developed independent of any particular machine and had some inefficient features such as call-by-name parameters, still defined data types (real and integer) which translate closely to actual computer hardware.

By the late 1960s the concepts that the language should facilitate writing the program, and that the machine should be designed to create an efficient run-time environment, was more widely accepted. Today there is a definite shift toward using the language to make programming and documentation easier and to produce reliable and correct software.

This does not mean, however, that efficiency is ignored. For example, whereas PL/1 permits writing simple programs whose execution time is quite long, PASCAL was carefully designed to exclude constructs whose machine code is inefficient. Hardware being less expensive than programmers, reliability is now a major factor: let the task be made easier for the programmer; let the computer do more work.

A major development in easing the programming task is *structured programming*, which has been erroneously called "gotoless" programming. Fortunately, the "debate" about "to goto or not to goto" has mostly disappeared, and some clear ideas have emerged. The premise of structured programming is to use a small set of simple control and data structures whose proof rules are well understood. A program is built by nesting these statements inside each other. This discipline restricts the number of connections between program parts and improves the comprehensibility and reliability of the program thereby. In Chapter 2 the issues of structured programming will be explored in greater detail.

A related technique to structured programming is *top-down design.* A programmer first writes a subroutine as a single statement. This statement is then expanded into greater detail. At each level the function is expanded into more and more detail until the resulting description is the actual source language program in some programming language.

Other design techniques have also been proposed for software development. The goal is to simplify the design process by outlining a concrete sequence of steps that can be applied in arriving at a design. In Chapter 2, top-down design, as well as several other strategies, will be explained further.

The concept of a *program design language* (PDL) to aid in this development has been defined [Caine and Gordon, 75]. This type of language contains two structures. There is a concrete *outer syntax* of basic statement types, such as **if-then-else, while**, and **sequence**, for connecting components. There is also an *inner syntax* that corresponds to the application being designed. The inner syntax is English-statement oriented, and is expanded, step by step, until it expresses the algorithm in some programming language. Figure 1.14

```
max: procedure (list);
    /* Find maximum element in a list */
    declare (maximum, next) integer;
    declare list list of integers;
    maximum = first element of list;
    do while (more elements in list);
        next = next element of list;
        maximum = largest of next and maximum;
        end;
    return(maximum);
    end max;
```

Figure 1.14 PDL of program to find the largest element in a list.

is an example of a PDL design. Chapter 2 gives the PDL which is used throughout this book.

It should be noted here that PSL/PSA and PDL complement each other. PSL/PSA is a specifications tool that validates correct data usage (interfaces) between two modules. A system like PDL is useful for describing a given module at any level of detail. Both tools can contribute to success in a large project.

1.3.3 Performance Issues

The chosen algorithms and data structures have a much greater influence over program performance than code optimization or the programming language. Before choosing an algorithm, the programmer faces the questions:

1. Can previously written software be used?
2. If a new module must be written, what algorithms and data structures will give an efficient solution?

Programming languages usually include standard mathematical functions such as sine, logarithm, and square root. They give the programmer ready access to libraries of standard software packages. This helps the programmer by allowing him to use results of previous work. However, on preparing programs for standard libraries, analysts have included many options into a single package, thereby permitting the user to select the special case of interest. The effect can be a large cumbersome package which is inefficient because only a small part of it is applicable at any one time. This can be avoided by installing multiple versions of the module for each special case.

There remains considerable room for more packaging and use of existing software. Some of the difficulties in achieving this are:

1. Identifying the standard algorithm to package. This is easier in mathematical areas such as statistical testing, integration, differentiation, and matrix computations than in many nonnumerical areas such as business applications.
2. Transporting and interfacing with packaged software. Some progress has been made with programs stored in read-only memories which plug into microprocessors, or with interface processors on computer networks. A major problem area is interfacing software directly to other software—there are no conventions. Some help is afforded by such concepts as the "pipeline" in UNIX, which provides a general communications channel between programs [Ritchie and Thompson, 74].

Sometimes the program specification is not changeable; the analyst must find the best possible algorithm. However, sometimes the specifications can be altered to permit a more efficient solution. Sometimes we can show that there are no algorithms guaranteed to be efficient in all cases, whereupon approximate algorithms that are efficient in most cases but need not give exact solutions must be used.

The fast Fourier transform illustrates the most efficient form for computing the Fourier transform, a technique useful in waveform analysis [Cooley and Tukey, 65]. This transform is based on a finite set of points rather than a complex integral that is harder to compute. Although computed for only a finite set of points, the desirable properties of the transform are preserved. Language analysis (parsing) in a compiler illustrates how changing the specification can permit a more efficient solution. Any string of N symbols in an arbitrary context-free language can be parsed in time of order $O(N^3)$ [Younger, 67]; however, a programming language need not include all features of an arbitrary context-free language. PASCAL is an example of a language which can be parsed by a deterministic top-down parser in average time of order $O(N)$ [Aho and Ullman, 72]. Thus if we are free to set language specifications, we can choose the language and be rewarded with efficient compilers.

Many practical problems involve enumerating a combinatorially large number of alternatives and selecting a best solution. Examples include job scheduling or network commodity flow problems. In these cases it may be better to restrict the search for a suboptimal but good answer. We recommend the paper by Weide [77] for a discussion of the issues and a state-of-the-art survey of analyzing algorithms. Chapter 2 will present a short catalog of some of the major algorithms in use today.

In many cases the results of algorithmic analysis do not go far enough to help a programmer. Thus we need to offer techniques which can help locate and remove sources of inefficiency. One tool is an optimizing compiler which, for some languages, can yield significant improvements [Lowry and Medlock, 69]; but the value of such tools is limited [Knuth, 71] and may be realized only for programs which are used often enough to justify the investment in optimization.

One of the most powerful aids is the *frequency histogram* that reveals how often each statement of a program is executed. It is not unusual to find that 10% of the statements account for 80% of the execution time. A programmer who concentrates on those "bottlenecks" in his algorithms can realize significant performance improvements at a minimum investment. This technique has been used in some interactive operating systems; UNIX and MULTICS, for example, started out as high-level language operating systems. Bottlenecks have been replaced by assembly language routines in less than 20% of the system.

For example, the frequency histogram of Figure 1.15(a) shows that in one case only six statements accounted for 1440 of the 2873 statements executed

```
EXECUTION HISTOGRAMS      EACH * =  19 EXECUTIONS
    1        1                       52        50     **
    2        0                       53        50     **
    3        1                       54        50     **
    4        1                       55        50     **
    5        1                       56        50     **
    6        1                       57        50     **
    7        1                       58        50     **
    8        1                       59        50     **
    9        0                       60        50     **
   10        1                       61        50     **
   11        1                       62        50     **
   12        1                       63         1
   13        1                       64         0
   14        1                       65         1
   15        1                       66         1
   16        1                       67         1
   17        1                       68         1
   18        0                       69         1
   19        0                       70         1
   20        0                       71         1
   21        1                       72         0
   22        1                       73         0
   23        1                       74         0
   24        0                       75         1
   25        1                       76         1
   26        1                       77         1
   27        0                       78         1
   28        1                       79         1
   29        1                       80         1
   30        0                       81         1
   31        1                       82         1
   32       41    **                 83        50     **
   33      240    ************       84         0
   34      200    **********         85        50     **
   35      200    **********         86        50     **
   36       40    **                 87        50     **
   37        1                       88        50     **
   38        1                       89        50     **
   39        1                       90        50     **
   40        1                       91        50     **
   41        1                       92         1
   42       51    **                 93         0
   43       50    **                 94         1
   44      300    ***************    95         1
   45      250    *************      96         1
   46      250    *************      97         1
   47       50    **                 98         1
   48       50    **                 99         0
   49       50    **                100         1
   50       50    **                101         0
   51       50    **                102         0
STATIC/DYNAMIC STATEMENT COUNTS
  COMMENTS = 5     STATEMENTS = 100    EXECUTED STATEMENTS =  2873
```

Figure 1.15(**a**) Frequency histogram of unmodified program.

by a 100-statement PL/1 program. Looking at the code revealed the following characteristics:

1. Statements 32 to 37 were the sequence:

```
SUM = 0;
DO I1=1 TO WEEKSCNT;
      DO I2=1 TO 5;
            SUM=SUM+A(I1,I2)*WEIGHTS(I2);
      END;
END;
```

2. The statements beginning at statement 42 were:

```
DO I=1 TO NRECORDS;
      J=0;
      DO K=1 TO 5;
            J=A(I,K)*WEIGHTS(K)+J;
            END;
      . . . code not involving SUM . . .
      END;
```

According to the specifications of this program, *NRECORDS* will always be greater than *WEEKSCNT*. Therefore statements 33 to 37 could be deleted with the following addition to the code beginning at statement 42:

```
DO I=1 TO NRECORDS;
      J=0;
      DO K=1 TO 5;
            J=A(I,K)*WEIGHTS(K)+J;
            END;
      IF I<=WEEKSCNT THEN SUM=SUM+J;
      . . . code not involving SUM . . .
      END;
```

With this addition of the IF statement which was executed 50 times in the test run displayed in Figure 1.15(b), the total number of executed statements dropped from 2873 to only 2242—a drop of over 20%. Total elapsed time to study the program and design the change: *under* five minutes!

1.3.4 Theory of Specifications

An area of software engineering that is now under study is in "system specifications." The objective is to state the specifications early using a metalanguage. This places restrictions on the design, and may help establish whether the specifications are met.

```
EXECUTION HISTOGRAMS      EACH * =  19 EXECUTIONS
   1       1                        50      50     **
   2       0                        51      50     **
   3       1                        52      50     **
   4       1                        53      50     **
   5       1                        54      50     **
   6       1                        55      50     **
   7       1                        56      50     **
   8       1                        57      50     **
   9       0                        58      50     **
  10       1                        59      50     **
  11       1                        60       1
  12       1                        61       0
  13       1                        62       1
  14       1                        63       1
  15       1                        64       1
  16       1                        65       1
  17       1                        66       1
  18       0                        67       1
  19       0                        68       1
  20       0                        69       0
  21       1                        70       0
  22       1                        71       0
  23       1                        72       1
  24       0                        73       1
  25       1                        74       1
  26       1                        75       1
  27       0                        76       1
  28       1                        77       1
  29       1                        78       1
  30       0                        79       1
  31       1                        80      50     **
  32       1                        81       0
  33       1                        82      50     **
  34       1                        83      50     **
  35       1                        84      50     **
  36       1                        85      50     **
  37      51     **                 86      50     **
  38      50     **                 87      50     **
  39     300     ***************    88      50     **
  40     250     *************      89       1
  41     250     *************      90       0
  42      50     **                 91       1
  43      40     **                 92       1
  44      50     **                 93       1
  45      50     **                 94       1
  46      50     **                 95       1
  47      50     **                 96       0
  48      50     **                 97       1
  49      50     **                 98       0
 STATIC/DYNAMIC STATEMENT COUNTS
   COMMENTS = 5     STATEMENTS =  97   EXECUTED STATEMENTS =  2242
```

Figure 1.15(b) Frequency histogram of modified program.

An early example of such a specification was once called "the goto controversy" [Dijkstra, 68a] [Knuth, 74]. It is properly called *structured programming*. It does restrict the form of statements a programmer may use, and this restriction contributes to comprehensibility and enhances a correctness proof.

A second set of such rules employs the concepts of levels of abstraction, information hiding, and module interfacing to restrict access to the internal structure of data. Parnas [72] formalized these ideas which were standard practices of expert programmers. The basic idea is to define data as a collection of logical objects, each with a set of allowable states. Procedures are written to hide the representation of these objects inside separate modules. The user manipulates the objects by calling the special procedures.

Several languages that facilitate the use of these features have been developed. Among these are Alphard, Clu, and Euclid [Popek et al., 77], [Liskov et al., 77], [Wulf et al., 77]. These languages permit programmers to define *abstract data types* having the property to *encapsulate* the representation of the logical objects (abstract data types) within separate modules [Liskov and Zilles, 75]. When concurrency is an issue, the abstract types also need synchronization primitives (e.g., locks, signals), and such modules are called *monitors*. In Section 2.3 the abstraction issue will be described in greater detail.

Another addition to this area are the higher order software axioms (HOS) [Hamilton and Zeldin, 76], which are a set of six axioms that specify allowable interactions among processes in a real-time system. For example, one axiom prohibits a process from controlling its own execution. This eliminates recursion as a possible design. Another axiom states that no module controls its own input data space and therefore no module is able to alter its input variables. While these axioms are not complete, they are a first step at formalizing the specification aspects of system design.

1.4 OTHER DESIGN STRATEGIES

While the chief programmer team using top-down development, structured programming, and walkthroughs has been the major technique emphasized so far, other approaches have been proposed. These strategies vary between manual and automated systems, with most being a blend of the two. Some of the techniques will be described in the following subsections.

1.4.1 PSL/PSA

PSL (problem statement language) is a language designed to express functional and performance requirements. It was developed by the ISDOS project at the University of Michigan [Teichroew and Hershey, 77]. It contains a set of declarations that allow the user to define *objects* in the proposed system, to define *properties* that each object possesses, and to connect the objects via *relationships*.

PSA (problem statement analyzer) is the implemented processor that validates PSL statements. It generates a data base that describes the system's requirements and performs consistency checks and completeness analyses on the data. Many different reports can be generated by the PSA processor. These include: data base accesses and changes, errors, lists of objects, and relationships among the data in the data base.

PSL is mostly keyword-oriented, with a relatively simple syntax. Some of the statements are the following:

PROCESS ⟨name⟩. Define ⟨name⟩ as a new process.
DESCRIPTION ⟨text⟩. ⟨text⟩ is an English description of the function performed by the process.
SUBPARTS ARE ⟨name⟩. The process ⟨name⟩ is related to the current process and is lower in the hierarchy tree than is the current process.
PART OF ⟨name⟩. Process ⟨name⟩ invokes the current process.
DERIVES ⟨file⟩. File ⟨file⟩ is output from the current process.
USING ⟨file⟩. File ⟨file⟩ is input to the current process.
PROCEDURE ⟨text⟩. ⟨text⟩ is a PDL-like description of the algorithm executed by the process.

As an example of the error-checking capabilities of PSL, if process Y has the statement

```
PART OF X;
```

then process X must include the statement

```
SUBPARTS ARE Y;
```

From user experience with PSL/PSA [Basili, 78], the system has the following characteristics:

1. It forces the user to understand the problem in a disciplined manner.
2. It documents requirements in a uniform manner.
3. It assists in the identification of certain error conditions—noticeably incompleteness and inconsistency.

As with any general purpose tool, PSL/PSA is not universally applicable:

1. The system is too general for many specific applications. Ad hoc conventions (e.g., naming conventions, limited attributes, etc.) not checked by PSA must be used to keep the design manageable.
2. PSA uses large amounts of computer time.

3. The system is oriented towards a transactions-based business environment.

In summary, for the definition of large business-oriented applications, PSL/PSA is an effective processor for formalizing system requirements. However, for smaller applications (e.g., less than five or six programmers), the overhead of using such a system may be excessive.

1.4.2 SADT

Structured analysis and design technique (SADT—a trademark of SofTech, Inc., Waltham, Mass.) is a manual graphical system for systems analysis and design [Ross and Schoman, 77]. The SADT graphics language is based upon a hierarchically structured set of diagrams, each box in the diagram being defined in greater detail by another diagram (Figure 1.16). A model is structured to show more and more detail as the design develops.

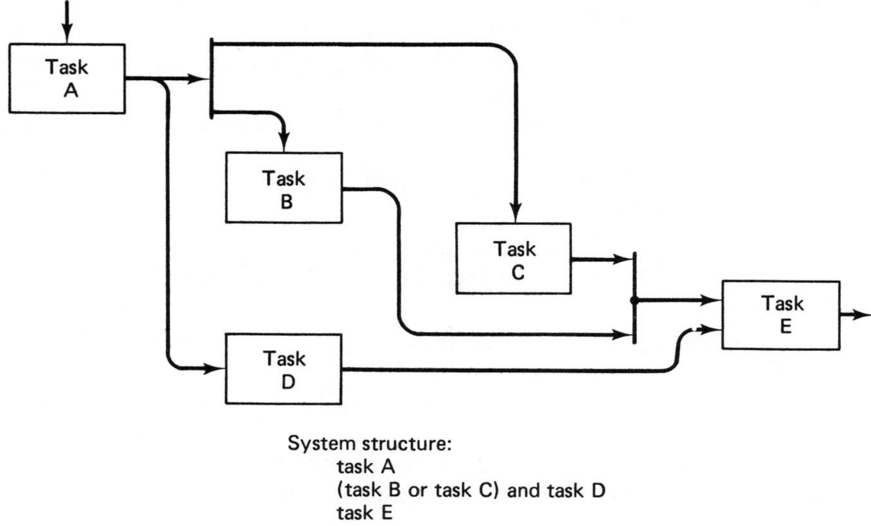

System structure:
task A
(task B or task C) and task D
task E

Figure 1.16 SADT structure. SA is a formal language for specifying relationships among design components.

Similar to the chief programmer team, SADT assumes that the personnel on a project have clearly defined roles. The following set of positions are used in SADT. Their description gives a flavor of the SADT design process.

Authors. Personnel who study requirements and constraints and represent them by SADT models.

Commentators. Usually, authors who review the work of other authors and comment on them.

Readers. Reviewers who may read other designs but may not be obligated to comment on the work of others.

Technical Committee. A group of senior technical personnel assigned to review the design at major levels of decomposition.

Project Librarian. The person assigned the responsibility of maintaining the process file.

Project Manager. The person with the ultimate technical responsibility for the project.

Chief Analyst. A "language lawyer" in the use of SADT. This person understands the use of SADT and advises others on its use.

Instructor. A person who trains others to use SADT.

One basic assumption made in using SADT is that requirements definition ultimately requires user input to choose among conflicting goals and constraints. This is difficult (or impossible) to automate. While SADT is a design technique, it assumes the existence of other automated tools to provide for the on-line data bases that may be needed. For example, PSL/PSA provides the relationships that can be used to represent the hierarchical structure of SADT objects.

Some of the positive aspects of SADT include the following [Basili, 78]:

1. SADT promotes teamwork. It also promotes agreement on specifications before continuing on the design.
2. Written comments by the committees result in a continual walk-through of the system, one of the desired characteristics for continual systems validation.
3. Interviews of experts provide an efficient means of obtaining specified information.
4. High-level decisions must be made early, thus it provides a sound basis for other decisions.
5. SADT permits nonsoftware people to understand the process.
6. SADT provides an easy way to measure progress.

As with any system, there are a few problems:

1. It is not automated.
2. It is sometimes hard to think only in functional terms.
3. The lack of a specific design methodology hurts this technique (and others, as well).

Similar to the use of PSL/PSA, SADT requires a disciplined individual to maintain certain conventions that are not automatically checked by any automated processor. However, in general, the use of SADT with an automated data base like PSL/PSA results in an effective technique for specifying large-scale systems.

1.4.3 Other Techniques

Several other methodologies have been devised to help in system specifications and design. A brief description of some of these follows:

SREM

The software requirements engineering methodology (SREM) is a system like the previously mentioned PSL/PSA-SADT system for automating the requirements stage of development [Davis and Vick, 77]. It consists of a requirements statement language (RSL) to specify the relationships among the objects of a system. The requirements engineering and validation system (REVS) is a processor which checks the consistency of RSL statements.

The steps involved in an SREM definition are the following:

1. *Translation.* The requirements structure consisting of data descriptors and processing steps are developed.
2. *Decomposition.* Detailed designs are developed.
3. *Allocation.* Aspects of the design are simulated by REVS for appropriate tradeoff considerations. The output of this step is a set of computational requirements of the data processing subsystem which are generated by REVS.
4. *Analytic feasibility demonstration.* The user checks all requirements for feasible development.

This system has many of the same characteristics of PSL/PSA. Its main difference is that it was developed to be used in an *embedded system* environment, where the computer is only one small aspect in solving a larger complex problem. Defense systems and spacecraft control are two such examples of embedded systems where the computer plays an important but secondary role.

Structured design

Structured design is a manual system for creating a detailed design [Constantine and Yourdon, 79]. A system is assumed to consist of the following levels of components:

Subsystem. A major functional area.

Process. An identifiable user function that is part of a subsystem. The process is the lowest level of system visible to the user.

Activity. One of the individual components that helps to make up a process. Activities are executable programs or job steps. While the process is oriented towards the user's requirements, the activity is oriented towards the structure of the computer (and its operating system) that will execute the system. In many cases a process and its activity will be essentially the same.

Module. A single subroutine that is part of an activity. Modules are denoted by six-character names. For example ABC123 would be module 123 in process BC of subsystem A.

Structured design is applied at the process or activity level. Design documentation includes a hand-drawn baseline diagram and a completed *module description form* for each module. This form defines the function of a module in sufficient detail to allow its implementation independent of any other supporting documentation. One drawback to this is that the design often requires pseudocode or PDL for an accurate description, thus violating the goal of telling what a program is to do but not how.

Jackson methodology

As developed by Michael Jackson, the methodology incorporates the technologies of top-down development, structured programming, and structured walkthroughs [Jackson, 75]. Programs are hierarchically structured with four basic components, which are similar to the usual control structures used in structured programming:

Elementary. Functions that are not dissected further.
Sequence. The parts are executed once, in order.
Selection. One of a series of parts is executed.
Iteration. One part is executed zero or more times.

An explicit assumption in this methodology is that the system structure must parallel the data structures used. Thus a tree chart of the system organization should reflect the data structure records; if not, then the design is incorrect. This methodology uses many of the techniques already described, although in a slightly different notation.

1.5 SUMMARY

In reviewing all the techniques presented in this chapter—chief programmer team, structured programming, PSL/PSA, SADT, etc.—a common characteristic can be found. While the techniques provide for a good structure for developing a software system, they do not give any real indication of how to proceed with a design. A creative mind is still needed to begin the basic requirements-specification-design process. Anyone who has carefully studied these techniques will clearly see that there is no justification to the sometimes stated argument that forcing programmers to use these techniques will destroy their creativity. Just the opposite is actually true. A creative mind is needed to develop such systems; these techniques simply provide a mechanical means for handling necessary but uninteresting organizational details. This leaves more time available for the truly interesting parts of software design.

Several strategies exist for combining the different techniques mentioned in this chapter into a complete methodology. We close this chapter by mentioning one. Boehm [77] has identified seven basic principles common to good software development:

1. *Manage using a sequential life cycle plan.* This means to follow the software development life cycle outlined earlier. This allows for feedback which updates previous stages as the consequences of previous decisions become known. It encourages milestones to measure progress.
2. *Perform continuous validation.* Certify each new refinement of a module. Use walkthroughs and code reading to aid in this process. Display the hierarchical structure of the system clearly in all documentation throughout the project.
3. *Maintain disciplined product control.* All output of a project—design documents, source code, user documentation, and so forth—should be formally approved. Changes to documents and program libraries must be strictly monitored and audited. Code reading, project reporting forms, librarians, a development library, and a project notebook all contribute towards this goal.
4. *Use enhanced top-down structured programming.* If available, PL/1 and PASCAL have good control and data structures. There are preprocessors to augment FORTRAN with these structures. Description techniques such as stepwise refinement, nested data abstractions, and data flow networks should be used.
5. *Maintain clear accountability.* Use milestones to measure progress. Use the project notebook to watch each individual's efforts.
6. *Use better and fewer people.* The chief programmer team aids in this effort. Each individual is skilled and accountable for his actions. Good results are rewarded.
7. *Maintain commitment to improve process.* Settle only for the best. Strive for improvement. Be open to new developments in software engineering, but do not sacrifice reliability or modifiability while pursuing them.

Progress has been made in understanding how large-scale software systems are built, yet more needs to be done. Management aids need to be improved, and project control techniques need to be developed. Software management is becoming more like engineering management in other disciplines. We can no longer afford costly mistakes; systems are too large and integrated into our daily lives for this to happen. Finally, we must also be patient—we need the experience on which future theories will be based.

2 Programming Methodology

In the previous chapter, a considerable number of techniques were presented outlining facets of the software development life cycle. It is not possible to study all of them in detail. Software engineering is currently a major research area, and many different ideas are under study. However, several topics are emerging as central to good program design, and these will be discussed in this chapter.

2.1 PROGRAM DESIGN LANGUAGES

In "designing" programs, a student typically uses two approaches. Either a flowchart of the program is constructed or the actual code is written directly (typically on the back of an old listing). The second approach obviously suffers from a lack of thought about program structure. However, even the good old flowchart leads to poor program structure, as we shall see later in this chapter. We do need some notation in which to specify the design of the resulting system. This is especially true in larger projects where 10 to 20 designers, who may spend several months just on the design phase, must communicate with each other.

In order to provide such a notation, the concept of a *program design language*, or PDL, has been developing. PDL's are patterned after the common programming languages like ALGOL or PL/1. As stated in the previous chapter, the coding phase of a project is generally well understood. Coding estimates are relatively accurate, and the number of coding errors is small when compared to design errors. The idea then is to use a form of programming language in other phases of the project.

Problems occur when the role of a design language is compared with that of a programming language. While programming languages manipulate explicit data structures created by programs, a design language would have to contain general primitives like "solve problem" or "invert matrix" and in general cannot be explicit. If the exact language statements were known, a design phase would be unnecessary.

In order to avoid this problem, design languages generally consist of two components: an explicit set of primitives patterned after programming languages and a general, mostly undefined syntax from the application area to be solved. With all the current research on structured programming, the better aspects of existing languages can be incorporated into the design language.

One aspect of a program design language is a concrete *outer syntax* which describes the control flow through a design. This control flow is patterned after the control structure present in most programming languages and includes statements like the **while**, **if-then-else**, and **call** statements. In this book, we assume that the reader has programmed in PL/1, so our PDL will be similar to it.

The other aspect of a PDL is an undefined *inner syntax*, including all the data structures and operations on the data. Essentially any English statement could be used to describe manipulations on the data. This inner syntax is intentionally kept undefined in order not to restrict the designer's choice. For example, to take the square root of a number *X*, the following PDL could be written:

```
if  X is not negative
    then
          return (square root of X
                     as a real number);
    else
          return (square root of -X
                     as an imaginary number);
```

In this case, the explicit **if-then-else** control flow is fixed by the PDL but the internal operations (e.g., "square root of *X*") is undefined. A PDL is called a design language since the next step in the process would be to design, in PDL, the code for "square root of *X*." Since the language consists of a mixture of programming language statements and English text, the term *pseudo code* is often applied to it.

In this book, the PDL that will be used consists of six groups of statements. In the following description, terms like "*X*list" will mean "an arbitrary list of *X*'s."

1. Selection

(a)

```
if expression
    then statement₁ ;
    else statement₂ ;
```

Statement$_1$ is executed if the expression is true, and statement$_2$ if the expression is false. Either statement$_1$ or statement$_2$ may be a sequence of statements by using a **do-end** group. "**else** statement$_2$" is optional as it is in PL/1.

(b)

```
do case(expression);
    \prefix₁\ statement₁ ;
          .
          .
          .
    \prefixₙ\ statementₙ;
  else  statementₙ₊₁ ;
end;
```

Since the **if** statement only provides a two-way decision procedure, the **case** statement is included to extend this to a multi-way branch. The **case** statement evaluates the expression and then executes the statement whose constant prefix matches the value of the expression. If no prefixes match the expression, then the **else** statement (if present) is executed. As with the **if** statement, each of the statements in each alternative may actually be a **do-end** group.[1]

In expanding the **do case** into a programming language that does not have a **case**, repeated **if**s can be used, as in:

```
if expression=prefix₁
    then statement₁ ;
else if expression=prefix₂
    then statement₂ ;
    .
    .
    .
else if expression=prefixₙ
    then statementₙ;
else statementₙ₊₁ ;
```

[1]The **case** statement was implemented by the author in the PLUM PL/1 compiler. The syntax used in that implementation is used in this PDL. Some IBM compilers call this the SELECT statement.

2. Iteration

(a)

```
do while(expression);
       Statementlist;
       end;
```

Statementlist is executed as long as the expression remains true. This may be zero or more times.

(b)

```
do variable = expr1 to expr2 by expr3;
       Statementlist;
       end;
```

This has a definition similar to the PL/1 iterative DO group. $Expr_1$, $expr_2$, and $expr_3$ are evaluated upon entering the loop for the first time. The increment portion ($expr_3$) may be positive, negative, or omitted (with a value of +1 assumed). The loop may be executed zero or more times.

3. Data declaration

```
declare name attributes;
```

Name is declared to be a variable with the listed attributes. The attributes may be standard programming language data types (e.g., real, fixed, float, character) or may be high-level data structures (e.g., symbol_table, parser_stack, etc.) Section 2.3 of this chapter will expand this "data abstraction" concept for defining and implementing data structures.

For defining more complex records, PL/1 structures may be used. For example, the declaration:

```
declare 1 A,
          2 B,
             3 C,
             3 D,
          2 E,
          2 F;
```

results in the tree structure pictured in Figure 2.1. Dot notation is used to reference items in these structures. Thus node *C* is the reference *A.B.C*, although *C* can be used by itself if it is unambiguous.

4. Other statements

(a) Variable = expression;
(b) **call** procedurename (argumentlist);
(c) **return** (value);

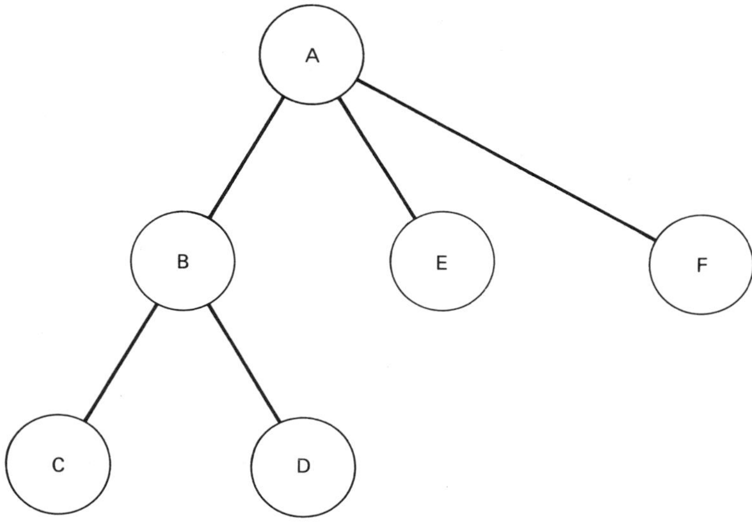

Figure 2.1 PDL data structures.

(d) name: **procedure** (parameterlist);
Statementlist;
end;
(e) **get** (inputvariablelist);
(f) **put** (outputexpressionlist);

These have the usual PL/1 interpretations. **get** is the input statement and **put** is the output statement. All parameters to a procedure are *call by reference* (i.e., the address of the argument is passed to the procedure). The scope rules for variables are the same as in PL/1. That is, if a variable is used without being locally declared, then the declaration used is the one in the smallest block containing the reference.

5. Leave

The **leave** statement causes control to immediately exit from the currently executing iterative **do** statement. This is a controlled form of transfer that avoids the problems with the general **goto** described in Section 2.2.2 on structured programming.

6. Text

Besides the above five categories, any English sentence may be used as a valid PDL statement. It is this type of statement that takes a PDL out of the realm of programming languages and makes it a design language. Any statement may be coded here. Examples include the following:

(a) Find the maximum element in array *B*.

(b) **do** for all *X* in $\{a, b, c\}$.

(c) A = first member of *B* that is greater than *C*.

In addition, any other statement from PL/1 may be used and will have its usual PL/1 interpretation.

The use of a PDL is still in its infancy. Unfortunately there are few implemented processors for them, and these do not provide very many features. They are useful for formatting listings; they provide an easy way to read code in the design phase; and they could be used to keep track of data references between different procedures. They also provide a source of documentation which is greatly needed in understanding and maintaining any system.

Even with all these problems, PDLs have been of great help to organizations that use them. The necessity of writing the design in an almost explicit programming language style greatly reduces the number of errors. The designs that are presented in this book depend very heavily on the use of a PDL.

2.2 DESIGN STRATEGIES

2.2.1 Top-down Design and Development

In both the design and coding phases of a project, there are two approaches to development that are generally used: top-down and bottom-up. While top-down and bottom-up design techniques are used often, top-down and bottom-up coding practices are not as well known.

In order to explain these four terms, the system pictured in Figure 2.2 will be used. This is an example of a *baseline diagram* since each box represents a module in the system and each module below another module is called by that module (e.g., module AC calls both modules ACA and ACB).

In *top-down design*, the functions of the driver are designed first. For example, the driver of Figure 2.2 might be representable by the following PDL:

```
DRIVER:  procedure;
    Perform task A;
    do while (condition is true);
        Perform task B;
        end;
    Perform task C;
    end DRIVER;
```

Each of the pseudocode statements would then be expanded, and other modules would be created. For example, if tasks A, B, and C are sufficiently

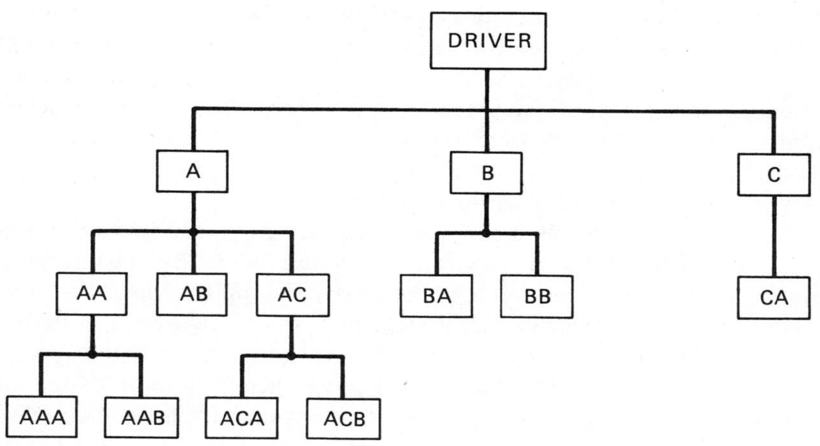

Figure 2.2 Sample baseline diagram.

complex, they could be separate procedures. Thus, a complete design for the driver could look something like:

```
DRIVER;  procedure
    Set up task A;
    call A;
    do while (condition is true);
        Set up task B;
        call B;
        end;
    Set up task C;
    call C;
    end DRIVER;
```

Procedures A, B, and C could then be defined in a similar manner. It should be apparent that a PDL is quite suited for top-down design.

In top-down design, also called *stepwise refinement* [Wirth, 71] [Wirth, 74], the program is hierarchically structured and is described by successive refinements. Each refinement describes its actions by referring to other refinements in a top-down manner.

In *bottom-up design*, the low-level routines are generally designed first. For example, if certain capabilities are needed, modules AAA and AAB might be designed. Then module AA could be added, which uses the capabilities of AAA and AAB in order to provide a new capability. This could be continued until all capabilities needed for the system are created.

Operating systems are often modeled as hierarchies of *abstract* or *virtual* machines [Brinch Hansen, 77]. At the lowest level is the physical hardware.

Each new level of system provides additional *capabilities*, or allowable functions on data, and hides some of the details of a lower level. For example, one level accesses the paging hardware of the computer and provides a large virtual memory for all other processes. Therefore, other abstract machines at higher levels can be implemented as if they had unlimited memory with this detail controlled by a lower level. Because of this, most real-time programs are designed in a bottom-up manner.

In many non-real-time cases, bottom-up design is inferior to top-down design, and will not be used extensively in this book. By starting at the bottom, and randomly putting together pieces, the top level may not fit and a clumsy (or nonimplementable) system may result. However, bottom-up design is practical in some cases. If a system is similar to a previously developed system and its general structure is known, then bottom-up design may work. For example, parts of the operating system of Chapter 4 use this technique. A top-down approach is used early in the design until the design progresses to several small, well-understood components. At this point, a bottom-up design is used to finish the product.

The situation is almost exactly the opposite when it comes to implementation. While many systems are designed in a top-down manner, a bottom-up implementation is the most common technique used. That is, modules AAA and AAB (of Figure 2.2) are coded and tested since they do not call any other components of the system. Module AA is then added since it uses only previously checked out pieces. AB is next, etc. (Figure 2.3). The bottom-up implementation is seemingly attractive since the amount of *scaffolding*, the

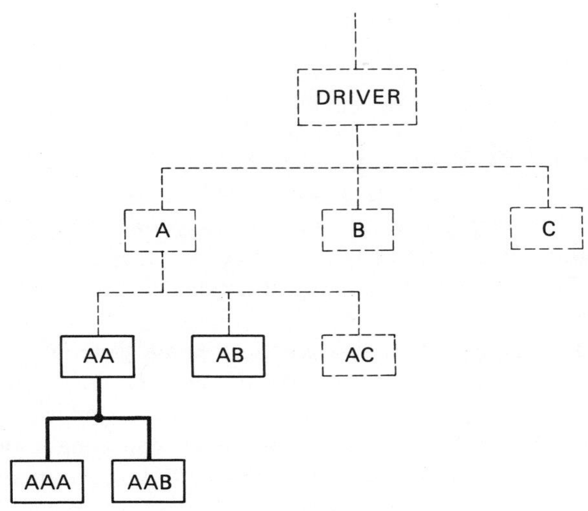

Figure 2.3 Bottom-up testing.

additional code needed to test the developing system, is small since few auxiliary routines are needed for testing.

This approach is quite satisfactory when the problem to be solved is well understood, such as in writing a compiler. In this case, even though languages differ, compilation techniques are relatively standard and there is not much chance that the product will differ radically from expectations.

However, if the problem to be solved is not well understood or well defined, serious problems may arise with the bottom-up coding approach. The purchaser of a system, for example, would not get to see it operate according to specifications until the top-level driver is tested. However, this will not happen until the entire hierarchical structure is tested (e.g., at the end of the project). At this time, changes will be hard to design and expensive to install.

In order to avoid these problems, a top-down coding technique can be used. In this case, the driver and modules A, B, and C are tested first. Now the purchaser of a system sees the top-level operation early in the development lifetime so that any necessary changes to the specifications will be easier to make.

The only problem with this approach is that in order to test modules A, B, and C, modules AA, AB, AC, BA, BB and CA will also be needed. This is handled via *stubs*, i.e., short routines that are specially written to simulate the unwritten modules and to return known test values (Figure 2.4). Section 2.4 will expand upon the development of stubs as a testing strategy.

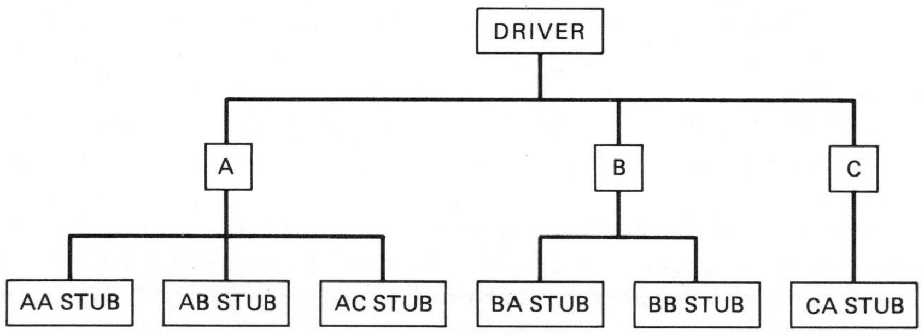

Figure 2.4 Top-down testing.

If used carefully, this technique can be useful; however, the system's correctness is assumed, *not* proven, until the last stub has been replaced. The documentation specifies the assumptions on each stub. For example, if

$$f(x) = \textbf{if } p(x) \textbf{ then } g(x) \textbf{ else } h(x)$$

is a program fragment calling stubs g and h, then f will be correct only if the eventual modules replacing the stubs g and h are correct.

Top-down development is not quite as easy as it looks since there are three possible "tops" to a system:

1. The start of execution
2. The focus of control
3. The user interface

To demonstrate the differences between the three, a compiler built by the author will be used as an example.

To the computer hardware, the top of the system is the module where execution begins. This module, called PLEX, is the main interface with the operating system. It loads from disk storage the various compilation phases and then branches to this code. All other code can be considered to be subroutines to this one module.

To the systems programmer, the top of the system is where execution centers. In a compiler this point is the main language analysis loop that is looking for the next statement to analyze. Thus the logical top of the system is a loop inside the module SYNTAX that has the code:

```
do while(more to compile);
        Read until start of next statement;
        Analyze this statement;
        end;
```

From the user's point of view, a compiler reads a statement and then compiles it. Thus his "top" is the card reading routine that waits for the next input to be inserted—either into a card reader or typed into an interactive terminal.

We will consider the second definition as the preferred meaning of *top*. The control logic is what drives the program, and it should drive the design as well.

Via top-down development, a user sees very early the top-level interfaces in the system. Changes can then be made relatively easily and early in the development cycle. Another approach with this same goal of early exhibition of the specifications is *iterative enhancement* [Basili and Turner, 75]. Using this technique, a subset of the problem is designed and implemented. This gives the user a running system early in the life cycle, when changes are easier to make. The process is repeated with successively larger subsets until the final product is delivered.

Brooks [75] believes that the first version of a system is always "thrown away" since the concrete specifications to a system are often not defined until the system is completed—a time when the initial product meets those specifications rather poorly. It is often cheaper and faster to rebuild a system from scratch than to try to modify the existing product to meet these specifications. However, a developer will often deliver such a system as a "prerelease" if the schedule is slipping and the purchaser is demanding results. This version, replete with errors, is used by the buyer who then suffers with it until he throws it away or has the product rebuilt. Iterative enhancement is a useful method in this practice since there is a running system, although it does not meet all of the requirements, available early in the development cycle. Various design decisions can be tested early. And from a practical point of view, the buyer has something that he can use without putting undue pressure on the developer.

Thus, while top-down implementation seemingly involves the additional overhead of writing stubs for unfinished components, the payoffs are worth the expense.

2.2.2 Structured Programming

Stepwise refinement was described as a technique for program development. The use of a PDL in a top-down design is a natural outgrowth of this technique. A programmer thinks of a design in greater and greater detail, each step being an "intellectually manageable" component of the entire problem.

Initially a programmer thinks of a solution as a set of tasks:

```
do task A;
do task B;
do task C;
```

Each of these tasks is then explicitly defined via a set of specifications and expanded. Each task, if small enough, will simply be a few PDL statements in the same procedure. If complex, then it will become a separate procedure.

In expanding each task, only the PDL statements can be used. These statements have not been chosen randomly; they all provide a means to keep the design manageable. For example, the **goto** statement is replaced by the more restrictive **leave**. However, why such restrictions? The following discussion, based upon the work of Mills of IBM, should make this clearer.

Consider a program to be a function. For any statement we can write $y = f(x)$ to describe the effects of that statement. (The variables x and y can be vectors to take into account multiple variables.) Thus the effects of the assignment statement

$$A = B+C*D$$

can be represented by the function

$$F(X,Y,Z) = X+Y*Z$$

and the assignment statement can be replaced by the statement

$$A = \mathrm{F}(B,C,D)$$

This approach can be expanded to include multiple statements. An entire program is then simply a function from its input variables to its output variables.

Let us define a *proper program* as a program represented by a flowchart of function and decision nodes which has the following properties:

1. There is one input arc and one output arc.
2. For each node, there is a path from the input arc to that node to the output arc.

The flowcharts in Figure 2.5 are all proper, while none of the flowcharts in Figure 2.6 is proper.

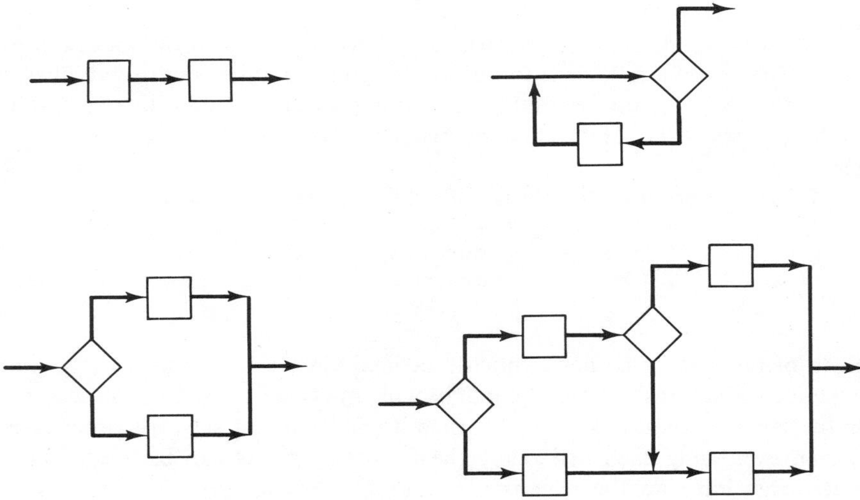

Figure 2.5 Proper programs.

Exercise 2.1: Why are the flowcharts in Figure 2.5 proper, and the ones in 2.6 not proper?

Stated in this notation, top-down development consists of the following algorithm:

```
Let a program be represented by a single function node;
do while(design not finished);
        Replace some node by a proper program;
        end;
```

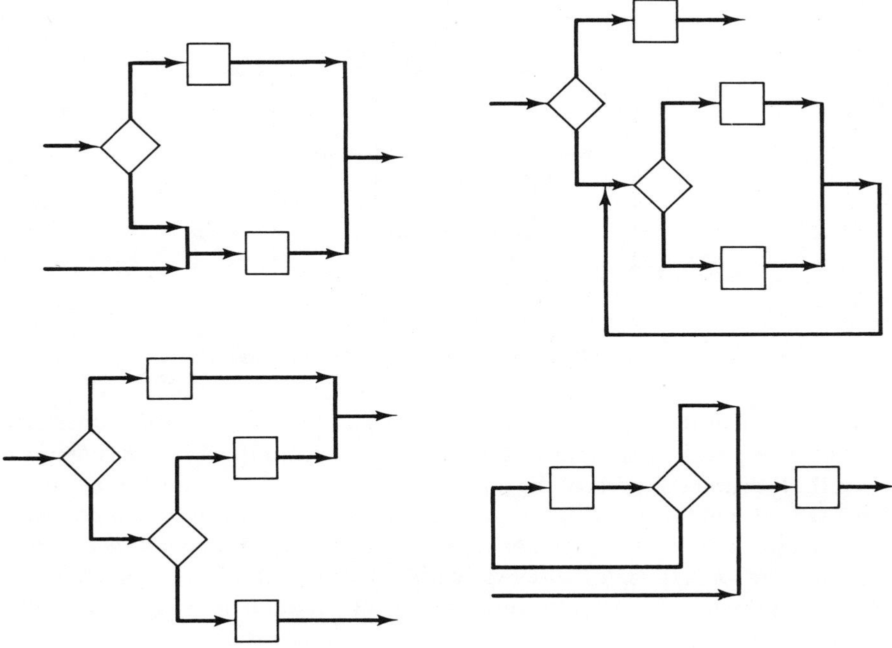

Figure 2.6 Nonproper programs.

This algorithm, by its very nature, makes the use of arbitrary **goto** statements difficult and requires that the programmer think more about the problem than is usually the case. However, there are more mathematical reasons for this stepwise refinement approach.

Define a *prime program* to be a proper program that has no proper subprogram in it of greater than one node that is prime. All of the flowcharts in Figure 2.5 are prime. Figure 2.7 represents a program which is not prime since the three-node **if-then-else** is embedded within the entire program.

Exercise 2.2: Show that there are an infinite number of prime programs.

Consider the process of reading and understanding a program. In general a programmer starts with single statements and then combines groups of them together when he understands that group of statements. This process of understanding is almost the exact opposite from the stepwise refinement process used in program development. A single function node will ultimately be an assignment statement, and its function will be relatively easy to determine. As small numbers of nodes merge into prime subprograms, their functions will also be relatively understandable. Thus an **if-then-else** consists

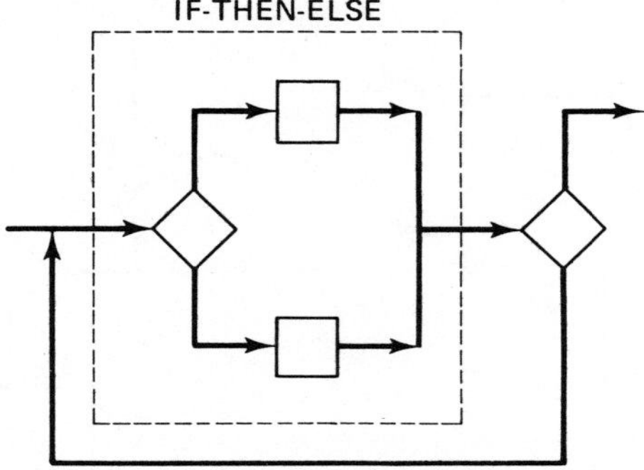

Figure 2.7 Prime decomposition of a program.

of three nodes (one predicate, two function) and will be a function that can be relatively easily determined (even informally) from the functions composing the **then** and **else** parts of the statement. Understanding a complex program consists of building up understanding of the smaller constituent components.

However, consider a program that has an arbitrary number of **goto** statements (Figure 2.8). In this case, the entire program (or a large segment of it) may be prime. Thus understanding may require initially looking at all of the nodes since no proper subprogram may exist. Thus it is not possible to build up understanding by studying smaller pieces of the program. "Intellectual manageability" is destroyed.

The **if-then-else**, the **while-do**, and the **sequence** statements are a commonly suggested set of control structures for programming in this discipline. However, there is nothing sacred about them. That the **goto** statement is irrelevant to the true goals of structured programming has been argued by Knuth [74].

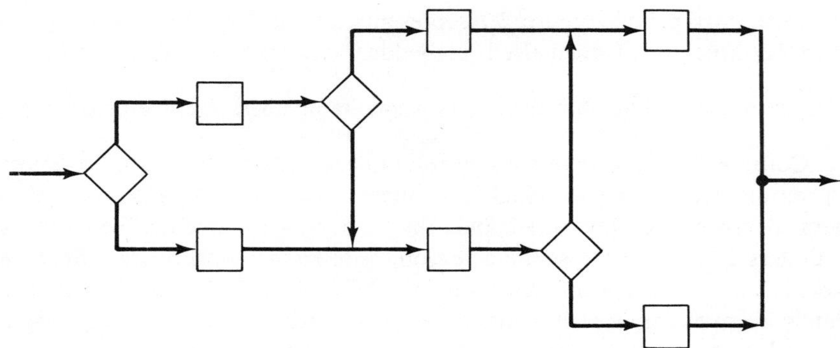

Figure 2.8 Complex prime program.

These simple control structures help programmers certify programs, even at an informal level. For example, using a functional approach, a program can be represented as a function from its input data to its output data. Suppose f(x) represents a segment of a program given by the following **if-then-else** statement:

```
if p(x) then g(x) else h(x)
```

Functions g and h are simpler than the total fragment f, thus their specifications should be simpler. If their specifications are known, the overall function f is defined by

$$f(x) = (p(x) \Longrightarrow g(x)) \cup (\neg p(x) \Longrightarrow h(x))$$

The programmer can come close to the formal definition of f by knowing the simpler functions g and h.

Such languages as ALGOL, PASCAL, and certain subsets of PL/1 contribute good programming practices by providing a set of good control structures. In order to repair FORTRAN's lack of structure, well over 50 preprocessors for translating well-structured pseudo-FORTRAN programs into true FORTRAN have been developed [Reifer, 76]. An IF-THEN-ELSE has been added to the ANSI FORTRAN-77 standard, although a general WHILE is still missing from the language.

For this reason the PDL uses prime subprograms with small numbers of nodes. The **if** and **do while** are a minimal sufficient set since it has been proven that any program function can be simulated by a program using only these two control structures; however, others are possible. For example, a **repeat-until** is often used.

```
repeat
        Statementlist;
until(expression);
```

can be defined as:

```
Statementlist;
do while(expression);
        Statementlist;
        end;
```

In this book, a **do case** is also included even though it may have an arbitrarily large number of nodes. However, it is a proper program that does have a rigid, easily understood structure. A **leave** is also added even though it is a transfer of control. However, it is a transfer that essentially says "stop this function" and does not add much to the complexity of the program function.

Note that "intellectual manageability" and not "no **goto**s" is the driving force in the design process. **goto**s are not explicitly eliminated in all cases simply because they are **goto**s. As noted by Mills [72], "Programs should be characterized not by the absence of **goto**s, but by the presence of structure." For example, the operating system in Chapter 4 uses **goto**s to perform one operation in only one procedure. The **goto** is to terminate processing and restart the process. In this case, the value of the program function is irrelevant since the program is restarting. To reprogram this procedure, simply to remove the **goto** may unnecessarily complicate an otherwise quite understandable design.

Exercise 2.3: Prove that any program function is equivalent to one using only **if-then-else** and **do while** control structures. One approach is the following:

1. Number each statement.
2. Include the statement LC = next_statement_number after each statement.
3. Use a **do case**(LC) to control execution.

How do you handle **if**s and loops using this technique? How do you convert the resulting **do case** into **if**s and **do while**s? (Note: Nobody said that the resulting program was good, well structured, or understandable, only that it was the same program function! This is why programs which automatically "structure" a program by deleting all **goto** statements are doomed to fail in most cases.)

Exercise 2.4: Assume that the **repeat—until** is a primitive control structure. Define the **while—do** in terms of **repeat**, **if**, and **sequence**.

2.3 DATA

2.3.1 Survey of Data Structures

As described in Section 1.1.3, a computer program is an abstraction of some real-world problem which needs to be solved. As part of this solution, real-world data must also be abstracted so that the program may compute some value. In order to facilitate this process, computer languages include a set of primitive data types. Since no language designer can anticipate all possible applications for which the language will be used, the set of data types is necessarily not complete.

For each variable in a program, its basic attribute is its *type*, or the set of values the variable may contain and the set of operators permitted to access the variable. The *integer* data type takes on the values 0, +1, −1,

+2, −2, +3, −3, . . . , and most languages permit the operators of addition (+), subtraction (−), multiplication (*), and division (/).

Every programming language has some set of primitive types. FORTRAN implements *real*, *integer*, and *complex*. PL/1 also includes *character* and *bit*. Other languages have additional types. Even assembly languages have types, i.e., only one type called *word* consisting of some hardware defined number-of-bits, with all possible operators defined on these words.

As programs become more complex, additional data types will be needed to accurately model the real-world problem. These must be created by the programmer using collections of existing data types. Variables declared to be of a primitive data type will be called *scalar* variables while variables consisting of collections of existing data types will be called *aggregate* variables. From these aggregate variables, new types can be constructed by implementing special operators to manipulate their contents. In this section a short list of aggregate data will be outlined; in the next section the concept of data abstraction will be explained as a way of using these aggregates to create new user-defined data types. See [Knuth, 68] for a more complete discussion of data structuring.

Arrays

Arrays are the simplest aggregate data built into a programming language. An array is an ordered set of variables, all of the same type. Thus

```
declare A(10) FIXED BINARY;
```

declares *A* to be an array of ten FIXED BINARY variables with the names *A*(1), *A*(2), *A*(3), . . . , *A*(9), *A*(10). Similarly,

```
declare B(5:10) FIXED BINARY;
```

declares *B* to be a six element array with the names *B*(5), *B*(6), . . . , *B*(10). It is assumed that the reader is well acquainted with single and multiple dimensioned arrays.

Structures

Structures are generally the most complex data available in a programming language. A structure is a named set of types. For example,

```
declare 1 X,
          2 Y FIXED BINARY,
          2 Z BIT(12);
```

declares *X* to be a structure consisting of a FIXED BINARY variable named *X.Y*, and a BIT string of length 12 named *X.Z*.

Structures can generally be used to create variables of a new type. In the next section, the current data abstraction approach to data structures will be discussed and it will be shown how the basic COBOL, PL/1, or PASCAL structure (**record** in the case of PASCAL) can be used to form a correct data typing mechanism. In most programming languages, arrays and structures are the only aggregate data provided. In the remainder of this section, these two features will be combined to form other aggregate structures.

Lists

A list is an ordered set of variables of the same type. It differs from an array in that the size of the list is generally variable, and entries can be added and deleted from the list. A list can be declared by the following structure:

```
declare 1 LIST (N),
            2 DATA_ENTRIES TYPE(some data type),
            2 SIZE;      /* current size of list */
```

The entries in the list are *DATA_ENTRIES*(1), *DATA_ENTRIES*(2), . . . , *DATA_ENTRIES*(*SIZE*).

Note that this is not the only implementation of a list. If a list can grow arbitrarily long then this approach will fail when *SIZE* gets to be larger than *N*. An alternate strategy is to implement a list as a set of BASED variables:

```
declare 1 LIST BASED,
            2 DATA_ENTRIES TYPE(some data type),
            2 FPTR POINTER, /* pointer to next item in list */
        LIST_HEAD POINTER; /* pointer to first element in list */
```

In the first case, the items in the list are:

LIST.DATA_ENTRIES(1),
LIST.DATA_ENTRIES(2),
LIST.DATA_ENTRIES(3),
. . .
LIST.DATA_ENTRIES(*SIZE*)

while in the second they are:

LIST_HEAD ⟶ *DATA_ENTRIES*
(*LIST_HEAD* ⟶ *FPTR*) ⟶ *DATA_ENTRIES*
((*LIST_HEAD* ⟶ *FPTR*) ⟶ *FPTR*) ⟶ *DATA_ENTRIES*
. . .

The operators which are usually permitted on LIST data include:

1. ADD, place a new entry into a list (Figure 2.9(a)).
2. DELETE, remove an entry from a list.
3. SEARCH, check whether an entry is in the list.

In Section 2.6.4 various list searching strategies are discussed.

Queues

A queue is an ordered list whose entries are added at one end and accessed at the other (Figure 2.9(b)). Thus a queue is like a pipe where information is entered and then processed in the same order as received, much like waiting in line at a supermarket checkout counter. A queue is also called a FIFO (First In, First Out) list since the first entry into the queue will be the first entry processed from the queue.

A queue can be implemented using either of the two approaches mentioned for lists above; however the second BASED approach is more efficient. (Why?) In general, a queue needs two operators:

1. INSERT, which adds an entry to a queue
2. DELETE, which takes an entry from a queue

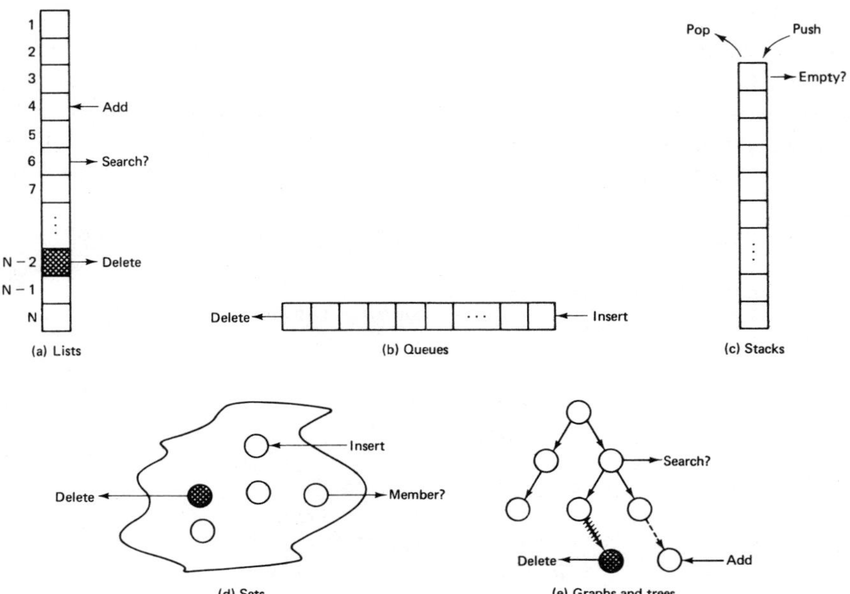

Figure 2.9 Aggregate structures and their operators

Stacks

A stack is an ordered list whose entries are added and accessed in reverse order, i.e. a LIFO (Last In, First Out) list. As with queues, a stack can be implemented using either of the two approaches for lists; however, the list array implementation is most efficient. (Why?)

Stacks generally need three operators (Figure 2.9(c)):

1. PUSH, places an entry on the top of the stack.
2. POP, takes an entry off the top of the stack.
3. EMPTY, a function which returns true if the stack is empty.

Sets

A set is an unordered collection of variables of the same data type. A set is similar to a list, except that the name of the variable (its location in the list) is unimportant. Sets are usually implemented as lists, using either of the previously mentioned implementation techniques.

Operators usually defined on sets are (Figure 2.9(d)):

1. INSERT, add a new member to a set.
2. DELETE, remove a member from a set.
3. MEMBER, a function that is true if a given variable is in the set.

Directed graphs

A directed graph is a structure consisting of *nodes* and *edges* with the property that each edge connects one node to another. Graphs are generally implemented as BASED structures where the edges are pointer variables. For example, the second implementation of a LIST using a BASED structure is actually a graph where each node in the graph is connected via an edge to only one other node, its successor node in the list.

For multiple edges from each node, the implementation could be:

```
declare 1 GRAPH BASED,
              2 DATA_ENTRIES TYPE(some data type),
              2 EDGES(N) POINTER;
```

For *undirected graphs*, where edges point in both directions, both forward and backward pointers are needed:

```
declare 1 GRAPH BASED,
              2 DATA_ENTRIES TYPE(some data type),
              2 FORWARD_EDGES(N) POINTER,
              2 BACKWARD_EDGES(N) POINTER;
```

Various graph operators are explained in Section 2.6.4 (Figure 2.9(e)).

Trees

A tree is a directed graph with the properties:

1. Only one node has no edge pointing to it (the *root* node).
2. All nodes have 0 or 1 edges pointing to them.
3. Every node can be reached via a series of edges from the root node.

(Note that conditions 2 and 3 insure that trees contain no loops, i.e., paths from a given node back to itself.)

2.3.2 Abstractions

In programming language design, perhaps the greatest change that has occurred is in the role that data plays in program development. Control structures have not materially changed since the early days of ALGOL. Except for the addition of a **case** statement and the deletion of the **goto**, little has been added to ALGOL **if**, **for**, or procedure invocation statements.

However, data structures have undergone considerable evolutionary change since those early days. Then the purpose of data was to describe, in a convenient notation, aspects of the machine's hardware structure. Hence, the early languages were almost exclusively restricted to real and integer data which were designed to mimic a machine's floating-point and fixed-point hardware.

COBOL and PL/1 expanded this definition by adding strings. In addition, hierarchically composed structures of items could be grouped under a single name. The programmer could compose data structures of arbitrary complexity.

The problem with this approach is that as data structures became more complex, so did the problems of testing and maintaining those systems using such data structures. Small changes to one data structure could cause ripples throughout an entire system and make maintenance a complex and expensive item. In addition, the aggregate structures were still collections of machine-defined objects. The programmer still had to think in terms of programming language ideas (e.g., integer, real, character) rather than in terms of the application area itself (e.g., symbol table, scheduling queue, input transaction).

In order to avoid such problems, the current approach is to use the concept of *information hiding* in the design of a system. The basic idea is to restrict knowledge of the structure of data to only one module (e.g., hide the information). All access to this data is controlled by this module. Thus, changes to the data structure would be easy since only one module would need to be altered.

In languages like PL/1, PASCAL, and FORTRAN, the names of an object and their representation are closely coupled. If a user codes:

```
DECLARE 1 STACK,
          2 TOP FIXED,
          2 ENTRIES(100) FIXED;
```

as a structure to define a stack, then any module that accesses the stack must also know its internal structure as a FIXED number and a FIXED array. The purpose of information hiding is to uncouple this binding of name to representation. The user of a stack would simply know that a certain variable is of type STACK, while only the module implementing the stack operations would know the representation.

The concept of a *data abstraction* is a means of implementing information hiding. Programs are assumed to provide transformations on data. Each module in a system has the following general structure:

```
modulename: module
      Representation of data structure
fcn1 : function
      Code for function
      end
fcn2: function
      Code for function
      end
      end modulename
```

Other modules in the system access this module via its function names (fcn1, fcn2), and only this module knows the detailed structure of the data itself.

In order to explain data abstraction further, two forms of program design will be discussed: control-oriented programming and object-oriented programming. We will define a data abstraction as data created in object-oriented programming.

In *control-oriented* programming, the basic goal is to decide "what to do next." Programs developed via flowcharts are almost always control-oriented. The programmer typically writes a decision box on a flowchart and then decides what to do if either branch is taken (Figure 2.10(a)). In this case, the flow of control is quite apparent, but the effects on data are not clear (Figure 2.10(b)).

In *object-oriented* programming, a programmer creates objects and uses them only on a restricted set of operations. To the declarer of an object, only the name of the object and the functions that can manipulate the object are known. For example, Figure 2.11 models an object called a stack. In order to

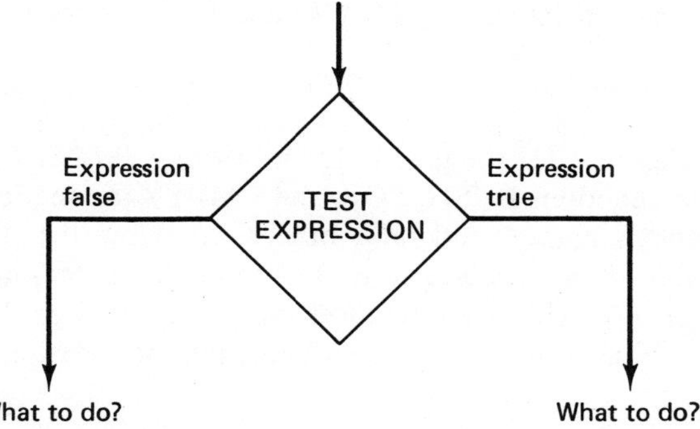

Figure 2.10(a) Control-oriented programming : developing control-oriented programs.

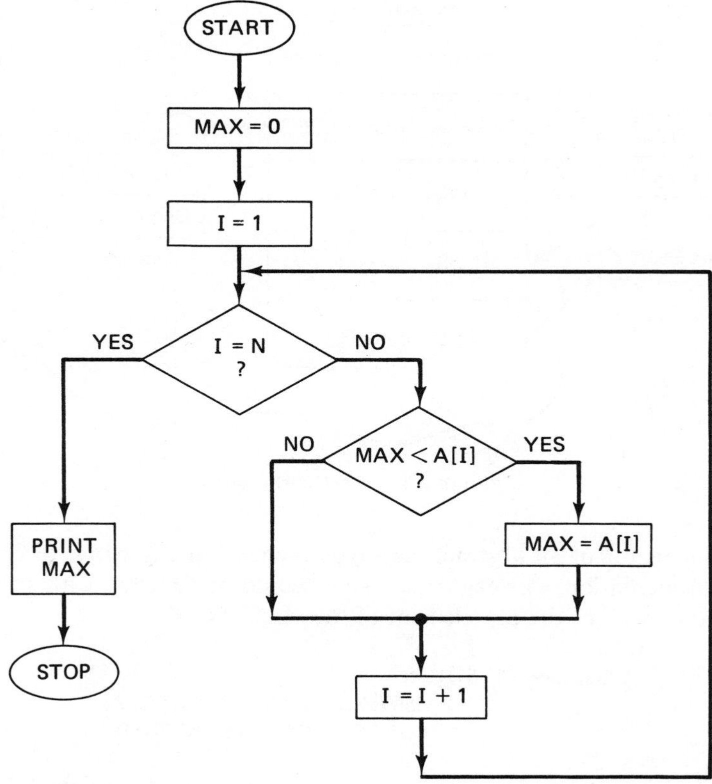

Figure 2.10(b) Control-oriented programming : control-oriented flowchart.

declare a stack named *PARSER_STACK*, a user would code:

```
declare PARSER_STACK TYPE (STACK);
```

According to Figure 2.11, the user only knows that *PARSER_STACK* may be passed to the functions PUSH, POP, and EMPTY (a function that returns true if the stack is empty, and false otherwise). How the three functions operate and what data structures are used to create a stack are immaterial to the user of a stack. All stack references must filter through the abstraction, and changes are relatively easy. This enforces the information-hiding aspect of the design.

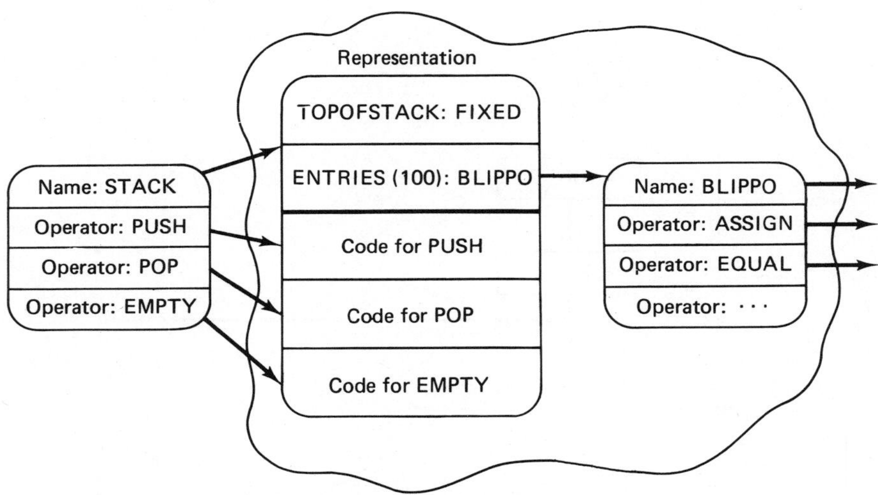

Figure 2.11 Stack abstraction.

The creator of an abstract data type then has the freedom of choosing the implementation. For example, a stack could be an array with an integer giving the index of the top element of the stack, as in:

```
declare 1 STACK,
            2 ENTRIES(100) TYPE(INTEGER),
            2 TOPOFSTACK TYPE(INTEGER);
```

This process can be repeated iteratively. For example, the stack abstraction may be a stack of BLIPPOs which are created in some other abstraction.

The definition of such a stack might be:

```
declare  1 STACK,
              2 ENTRIES(100)   TYPE(BLIPPO),
              2 TOPOFSTACK TYPE(INTEGER);
```

Each time PUSH, POP, or EMPTY is invoked to perform an operation on the stack, the stack abstraction would have to call a function within the BLIPPO abstraction to perform more primitive operations on the elements of the stack.

For example, consider the following code to push a BLIPPO on a stack:

```
PUSH: function(STACK,ITEM);
      declare 1 STACK,
                  2 ENTRIES(100) TYPE(BLIPPO),
                  2 TOP TYPE(INTEGER);
      declare ITEM TYPE(BLIPPO);
      if TOP<100 then TOP=TOP+1;
                 else call ERROR ('stack overflow');
      call BLIPPO_ASSIGN(ENTRIES(TOP),ITEM);
                 /* ENTRIES(TOP) := ITEM */
      return;
      end PUSH;
```

In this case, the call to BLIPPO_ASSIGN is needed as the operation to access the variable *ITEM* of type BLIPPO and to move it to the array which is simulating the stack. The PUSH function is unable to perform this operation directly since only the BLIPPO abstraction knows the actual structure.

In creating concrete programming languages from these ideas, the actual syntax need not be "cluttered" by all these **call** statements. For example, in Clu [Liskov et al., 77], "syntactic sugar" is added to simplify the structure. Thus the statement:

```
call BLIPPO_ASSIGN(ENTRIES(TOP),ITEM);
```

could have been coded in Clu as:

```
ENTRIES(TOP) := ITEM;
```

with the compiler subsituting for := the code:

```
call BLIPPO$ASSIGN
```

Procedures in Clu are denoted as "abstracttype $function", and the information is available during compilation to make sure that both arguments to := are of the correct data type. The creator of the module for "abstract-type" must include a function named ASSIGN in order for the code to be complete.

The major problem with this approach towards program design is that programming language design has not kept up with these developments. No widely used programming language fully implements the abstraction mechanism described here. For example, in PL/1, the declaration of a stack as a structure consisting of an array and an integer must be used each time such a stack is declared. There is no way to uncouple the name of an object from its description. This uncoupling is crucial in order to provide an appropriate enforcement and protection mechanism against errors.

Even so, programs can be designed in terms of abstractions. Data can be created, and then functions for this data can be defined. All accesses to this data could be restricted to procedures in the module implementing the abstraction. While the enforcement mechanism will be lost in the translation from a design into code in some language that doesn't include data abstraction features, a good design will result in good code being written.

In order to implement abstractions, two features of a programming language are needed: the ability to create data structures to represent an abstract data type, and the ability to write procedures to access that data. Using PL/1 as a model, three different implementations are presented.

Static abstractions

In this model, the burden of correct program design rests mostly with the programmer. Unfortunately, the compiler will not be able to check for errors in data usage since the programmer simply defines the abstract type as a structure and writes each operation as a separate procedure, passing the structure as a parameter.

For example, in order to create a stack, a programmer would add the following declaration to each procedure that needed a stack:

```
DECLARE 1 STACK,
               2 ENTRIES(100) FIXED,
               2 TOPOFSTACK FIXED;
```

The programmer would then code separate procedures for PUSH, POP, and any other stack functions. If the program was well designed with this organization in mind, then the translation into executable code will preserve these data abstraction structures.

This solution has the obvious advantage that it can be implemented in any programming language, although in languages like FORTRAN without any data structuring facility, the implementation can get somewhat awkward. Unfortunately this implementation does have a significant drawback since the components of any data structure are known in all procedures that use the structure (Figure 2.12). The programmer must be on guard to alter the structure only via its defined operations, and not insert "innocent" statements that access a component directly. This type of statement may cause disaster if each component of the data structure is not altered in a consistent manner.

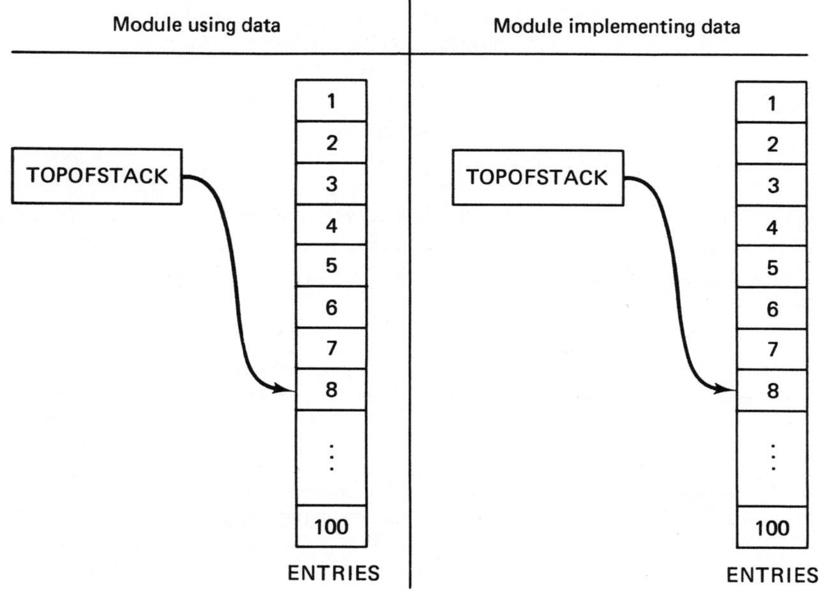

Figure 2.12 Static abstractions.

In spite of this disadvantage, this solution may be the only one possible since most current languages do not support abstractions.

Pointer allocation

Using pointer variables, a PL/1 solution can come close to true abstractions—although we will see that it too has an element of danger associated with it. In PL/1 a pointer variable refers to an area of storage, but the format of that storage is defined by a template called a BASED variable. In order to use abstractions, the user of an abstract data type simply defines the data as a pointer variable and calls an operation (PROCEDURE) to allocate and access the structure.

Using the previous stack example, the user of a stack would encode:

```
DECLARE STACK POINTER;
CALL STACK INITIALIZATION(STACK);
```

In this case, the procedure STACK_INITIALIZATION must be explicitly called in order to allocate space for the stack.

The procedure STACK_INITIALIZATION would then have the structure:

```
STACK_INITIALIZATION: PROCEDURE(X);
        DECLARE X POINTER;
        DECLARE 1 STACK BASED(X), /* X points to stack */
                  2 ENTRIES(100) FIXED,
                  2 TOPOFSTACK FIXED;
        ALLOCATE STACK SET(X);
        TOPOFSTACK = 0;   /* Set stack empty */
        END;
```

This procedure is the only one which knows the fine structure of the data referenced by the pointer *STACK*, so there is less temptation to alter this structure outside of the abstraction procedures (Figure 2.13).

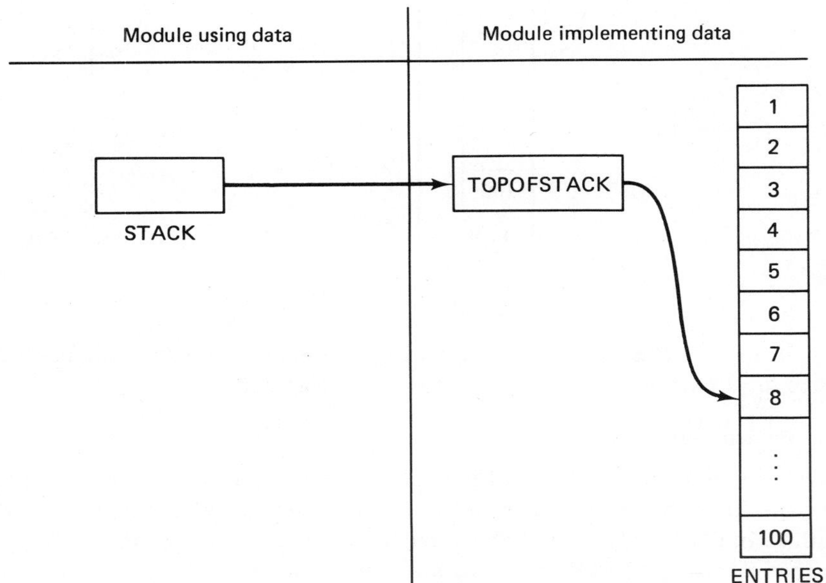

Figure 2.13 Pointer allocation.

In order to provide multiple functions on stacks, ENTRY statements could be used. Thus the complete STACK abstraction would have the format:

```
STACK: PROCEDURE;
       DECLARE X POINTER;
       DECLARE 1 STACK BASED(X),
                    2 ENTRIES(100) FIXED,
                    2 TOPOFSTACK FIXED;
STACK_INITIALIZATION: ENTRY(X);
        /* allocate stack */
        . . .
PUSH: ENTRY(X,element);
        /* put element on stack X */
        . . .
        RETURN;
POP: ENTRY(X,element);
        . . .
        RETURN;
        . . .
        END;
```

This solution has all the characteristics we want: the names of the structure and its representation are uncoupled, and the operations for a stack are encapsulated within a single procedure with only this procedure having access to the representation. However, this solution shares a serious defect with the first solution. While this implementation does permit abstractions, there is no enforcement mechanism to ensure that the encapsulation is not subverted. For example, in the above stack procedure, there is nothing to ensure that STACK_INITIALIZATION was indeed called for each such pointer variable, and there is nothing to prevent the programmer from defining his own template for a stack in order to access directly the data referenced by the pointer. As with the first solution, PL/1 does not provide an efficient enforcement mechanism; however, it does go part way towards a solution.

Exercise 2.5: This solution can be simulated in FORTRAN using arrays in a named COMMON area to provide storage and coded integers to signify individual abstractions for the "allocated" storage. Design this solution in FORTRAN.

Protected allocation

PLUM allocation. A final solution that will be described has been designed by the author for the PLUM PL/1 compiler, and a preliminary version has been implemented [Zelkowitz and Larsen, 78]. This solution is based upon the previous solution, but provides the enforcement mechanism missing from standard PL/1 in order to catch violations in its usage.

In order to declare an abstract type (i.e., pointer), the ENVIRONMENT attribute was added, as in:

```
DECLARE X ENVIRONMENT(STACK);
```

In the user's environment, *X* is allocated as a stack and can only be passed to entry points within a procedure named STACK (e.g., PUSH, POP, EMPTY), much like if *X* were real and had the operations + and * defined. The user has no idea, however, of what a stack is composed, and does not know and cannot get its internal structure, just as most programmers do not know or care how floating-point values are stored in the machine's hardware.

Unknown to the user, the stack *X* is actually declared by the compiler to be a pointer variable (as in the previous solution), but has the additional restrictions that:

1. *X* can only be passed to a FUNCTION in an ABSTRACTION named STACK.
2. *X* can only be assigned to point to a REP (representation) variable with the name *STACK*.
3. Only this representation can be used in accessing *X*.

From the user's point of view, data of an abstract type should be no different from any other variable in a program. However, there is one crucial difference so far between a variable of type FIXED and one of type BLIPPO. The variable of type FIXED is allocated when the procedure containing the declaration is entered, and freed when that procedure is terminated. However, for the variable of type BLIPPO, the storage must be explicitly allocated. This could lead to confusion. Since one of the goals of abstraction is to extend data types into the application area, this difference between compiler-generated data and user-generated data could lead to confusion. Therefore, one of the design goals in an abstraction mechanism should be to automatically allocate abstract types every time that they are used, so that there would be no difference between storage allocation strategies of any two program variables.

In order to provide this automatic storage allocation, the variable *X* is initialized via a call to STACK. In essence the above ENVIRONMENT declaration is compiled as if the following were coded:

```
DECLARE X POINTER INITIAL(STACK);
```

The initial call to STACK will allocate storage for *X* and return its address as a pointer variable.

The stack abstraction has the following general format:

```
STACK: ABSTRACTION;
REP 1 STACK [X], /* X is name of stack parameter */
              2 ENTRIES(100) FIXED,
              2 TOPOFSTACK FIXED;
         /* Allocate a stack */
         /* Initialization code for new stacks */
         TOPOFSTACK = 0;
PUSH: FUNCTION(X,element);
         ...
         END;
POP: FUNCTION(X,element);
         ...
         END;
         ...
END;
```

The incorporation of these ideas into PL/1 is quite straightforward, and can generally be handled by a preprocessor on any PL/1 compiler. For each of the added concepts, existing PL/1 features can be used. The following substitutions are made:

1. The initial code for an ABSTRACTION procedure is for allocation and initialization of the abstract type; however, the actual storage allocation is handled automatically by the compiler. This is to preserve compatibility with primitive types like FIXED and REAL. After declaring an object with an abstract type, the user should assume that storage for it exists and not be concerned with its allocation.

As stated above, the abstraction procedure for a STACK begins with the code:

```
STACK: ABSTRACTION;
REP 1 STACK [X], /* X is name of stack parameter */
              2 ENTRIES(100) FIXED,
              2 TOPOFSTACK FIXED;
         /* Allocate a stack */
         /* Initialization code for new stacks */
         TOPOFSTACK = 0;
```

For ABSTRACTION, the token PROCEDURE is substituted and the RETURNS (POINTER) attribute is added. In addition the following statements are added:

```
DECLARE DUMMY POINTER;
ALLOCATE datatype SET(DUMMY);
```

These statements permit storage for the abstract type to be automatically allocated.

Before the first FUNCTION, the following statement is added to ensure that the allocation routine returns to the appropriate DECLARE statement allocating this instance of an abstract type:

```
RETURN(DUMMY);
```

For the REP declaration, a declaration of a BASED structure is substituted. So when the abstraction function is called via the ENVIRONMENT declaration, storage will be allocated for the abstract data and the following code is actually compiled by the compiler:

```
STACK: PROCEDURE RETURNS(POINTER);
       DECLARE 1 STACK BASED(X),
                   2 ENTRIES(100) FIXED,
                   2 TOPOFSTACK FIXED;
       DECLARE DUMMY POINTER;
       ALLOCATE STACK SET(DUMMY);
       TOPOFSTACK=0;
       RETURN(DUMMY);
```

2. For FUNCTION, the sequence ENTRY BEGIN is substituted. In addition, the compiler checks that this entry point is only into an ABSTRACTION procedure. For the corresponding END, a RETURN is included. This makes each FUNCTION-END pair a separate block within the global ABSTRACTION procedure.

With all of these changes, the compiler is actually compiling the following program:

```
STACK: PROCEDURE RETURNS(POINTER);
       DECLARE 1 STACK BASED(X),
                   2 ENTRIES(100) FIXED,
                   2 TOPOFSTACK FIXED;
       DECLARE DUMMY POINTER;
       ALLOCATE STACK SET(DUMMY);
       TOPOFSTACK=0;
       RETURN(DUMMY);
PUSH: ENTRY(X, element);
       BEGIN;
       ...
       RETURN;
       END;
```

```
POP: ENTRY(X, element);
     BEGIN;
     . . .
     RETURN;
     END;
     . . .
     END STACK;
```

Note that parameters can be added to the abstraction very easily. To create a stack that can hold up to *N* elements, the declaration would be:

```
DECLARE X ENVIRONMENT(STACK(N));
```

while the abstraction module would contain the code:

```
STACK: ABSTRACTION(SIZE);
       DECLARE SIZE FIXED BINARY;
       REP 1 STACK(SIZE) [X],
       . . .
```

This solution has the advantage of providing the abstraction mechanism based upon PL/1 pointer variables, yet the ENVIRONMENT attribute prevents misuse of the feature and avoids all the problems in using pointers.

Exercise 2.6: Since a declaration of STACK(*N*) is easy to handle, comment on the problems of allowing the data type to be a parameter. That is, the same abstraction module should be able to handle the code for STACK(FIXED), STACK(CHARACTER), STACK(FLOAT), etc.

Access rights. With the abstraction mechanism so far, only part of the necessary protection that is needed has been achieved: a module cannot obtain the representation of any variable of an abstract type defined in some other module. However, should a given module have access to a given abstract type at all?

A finished program has the general structure:

$$\begin{array}{l}\text{Module}_1\\ \text{Module}_2\\ \text{Module}_3\\ \dots\\ \text{Module}_n\end{array}$$

With this structure, one module can access any function in any other module. However, this may not be desirable. Assume that module *X* uses abstract type *Y*, which in turn accesses abstract type *Z* (Figure 2.14). During mainte-

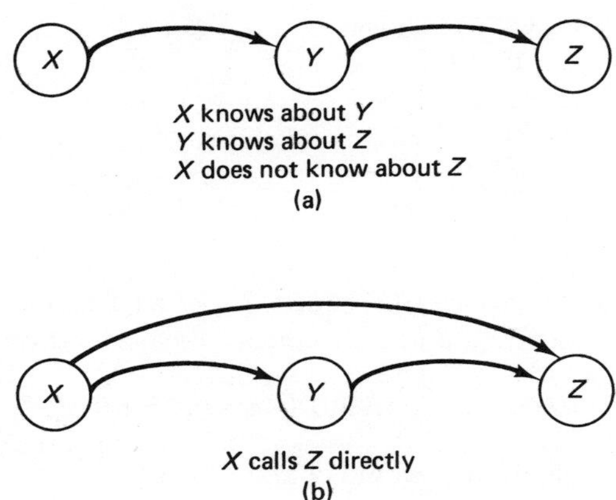

Figure 2.14 Violation of information-hiding attribute.

nance, the programmer codes a call from *X* to *Z* for efficiency, thus inadvertently violating the specification that *Z* is known only to module *Y*. However, the compiler is unable to check for this violation, and the error may only appear at some later date—e.g., if *Y* ever gets altered.

Using a concept from operating system design, this form of protection can be added to programming languages. In an operating system, associated with each independently executing process is a vector, the *capability vector*. This vector describes the functions (*capabilities*) that a given process is allowed to call (e.g., certain file operations, memory accessing, special operating system functions). Since processes start and stop as new user jobs enter and exit the system, the maintenance of this capability vector is dynamic and checking the legality of operations must occur during system execution.

In a programming language such a vector is called an *access right* [Jones and Liskov, 77]. In this case the concept is similar, but has one significant advantage: the checking can be performed at compile time, thus avoiding the necessity of generating any execution time code. A program is static (although the data that it manipulates may not be): all of the procedures are known before execution begins. All abstract types are known, and such legality checking can be performed by the compiler.

Note that the purpose of an access right is to enforce the abstraction mechanism, and not to provide system security, as is the case with operating system capabilities. Since it is assumed that the programmer has access to all of the code, the access rights to any module can be altered. The purpose of the access rights, however, is to ensure that the translation of the specifications to design to code does not introduce any errors in the abstraction structure.

In the PLUM implementation, access rights are denoted as additional parameters in the ENVIRONMENT attribute. For example, to declare a variable *X* of type STACK, and to permit *X* to be passed to the procedure SPECIAL_OP, as well as to the stack operators (PUSH, POP, EMPTY), the user codes:

```
DECLARE X ENVIRONMENT(STACK:SPECIAL_OP);
```

The user can also restrict access to certain functions within an abstraction. For example, if variable *X* above is permitted to PUSH new elements on the stack or test for EMPTY, but not POP elements, then access to the STACK abstraction can be restricted, as in:

```
DECLARE X ENVIRONMENT(STACK[PUSH,EMPTY]:SPECIAL_OP);
```

The compiler will allow *X* to be passed to the functions PUSH, EMPTY, and to SPECIAL_OP, but any attempt to pass it to POP will result in a compile time message.

Variables may not be *widened* when passed to another routine. For example, in the previous declaration, since *X* is restricted in its access to the stack function POP, the parameter in SPECIAL_OP that represents *X* may also not be passed to the POP function. In order to widen a variable, a special function within the STACK abstraction must be created, and widening can only occur within this module, since it is assumed that since the STACK abstraction creates stacks, it has the power to decide which variables get widened.

With this addition the programmer can carefully control the total environment for each variable of an abstract type. The ABSTRACTION mechanism provides information hiding while the addition of access rights enforces module boundaries and prevents accidental usage of one abstract type by another.

Other abstraction languages. PLUM is by no means the only solution to the abstraction problem. Several other languages have been developed to provide similar enforcement mechanisms. All of them provide the essential attributes of:

Abstraction of data type
Representation of data structure
Implementation of functions on data type

SIMULA67. SIMULA67 [Dahl and Hoare, 72] is perhaps the original language to include a form of abstraction mechanism. SIMULA67 is essentially ALGOL 60 with some extensions. One of these extensions is the declaration of a *class* object to represent what we now call an abstract type.

A SIMULA67 class has the format:

```
class abstracttype
    begin
        Declaration of objects of this class;
        procedure function1 ;
            <statement>;
        procedure function2;
            <statement>;
        . . .
        Initialization code for the representation;
    end;
```

The representation of objects is a set of ALGOL 60 declarations (e.g., **real** *X*, **integer array** *Y*[1 : 10], etc.). When a new object is allocated, then the initialization code is executed. Each function for a class object is an ALGOL 60 procedure.

New instances of class objects are allocated via the expression NEW(abstracttype). This generates a call to the **class**, which generates storage for the object and executes the initialization code.

Clu. In Clu [Liskov et al., 77] abstractions are modeled via *clusters.* The format of a cluster is:

```
abstracttype = CLUSTER IS
      List of function names known
          outside of cluster
   REP = structure representing abstract type
function1 = PROC;
      Code for function1 ;
      END function1 ;
function2 = PROC;
      Code for function2;
      END;
   . . .
 END abstracttype;
```

As stated previously, functions in Clu are denoted by abstracttype function. The language has many of the same features as the previously described PLUM and SIMULA67 implementations. In this case, although pointer variables are needed to implement the abstract types, the pointers are hidden from the user and are generated by the compiler to handle the abstract type storage allocation.

Alphard. Alphard [Wulf et al., 77] encompasses more than just an abstraction mechanism. As stated in Chapter 1, every program is correct with respect to *some* set of specifications. The problem is to determine if those specifications are the desired ones. Thus Alphard also includes a formal specifications part to help the system determine whether the source program indeed meets those specifications.

The basic abstraction mechanism in Alphard is the **form**. Every **form** has the format:

```
form abstracttype =
        SPECIFICATIONS . . .
        REPRESENTATION . . .
        IMPLEMENTATION . . .
        endform
```

The REPRESENTATION and IMPLEMENTATION sections are similar to the corresponding concepts in PLUM and Clu. The SPECIFICATIONS part provides a formal way to characterize the functions of an abstract type.

The SPECIFICATIONS part includes several components. Some of these are:

REQUIRES expression. Expression must be true in order to allocate storage for the representation.

INVARIANT expression. Expression must always be true.

INITIALLY expression. Expression must be true when the representation is initially allocated.

FUNCTION functionname PRE expression POST expression. Pre- and postconditions that must be true when functionname is entered and exited.

One of the goals of Alphard is to merge the specifications stage of development with the design and coding stage. This permits an extension to the methodologies proposed by such systems like PSL/PSA, SADT, and SREM (see Section 1.4). Although still a research project, some of the goals of Alphard should be applicable to commercially available languages in the future.

2.4 PROGRAM CERTIFICATION

One of the more recent developments to have an effect upon program design is the concept of program *verification*, or a mathematical proof that the program executes according to its specifications. One approach, an axiomatic one, attempts to extend the predicate calculus to include programs [Hoare, 69]. While not yet applicable to all programming, the techniques developed for the formal theory are applicable to real programs. We will briefly describe the formal system and show its applicability to program design.

Assume that each statement in a program has a predefined action depending only upon its syntax. Thus given two predicates, P and Q, and a statement S, the object is to determine whether the following statement is true:

If P is true and if S is executed, then Q will be true.

P will be the specifications for the correct execution of statement S; afterwards, Q will be true and will be the specification for the statement following S. As we stated in Chapter 1, if we extend this to include all program statements and if P is now the specification on the initial statement of the program and Q is true after the program terminates, then we have proven the correctness of the entire program with respect to P and Q.

We will write the above statement as:

$$\{P\}\ S\ \{Q\}$$

and we call P the *precondition* for Q to be true after S executes. The goal of our logic system will be to determine whether $\{P\}S\{Q\}$ is true with respect to its input specifications represented by P, its output specifications represented by Q, and program statements represented by S. If $\{P\}S\{Q\}$ is true, then S is *verified* with respect to P and Q.

2.4.1 Axioms

Even if we assume all the rules of the predicate calculus, we must still add rules that account for the dynamic execution of program statements. We call these the *rules of consequence* and are stated as follows:

1. If $\{P\}S\{Q\}$ and $Q \Rightarrow R$ then $\{P\}S\{R\}$.
2. If $\{Q\}S\{R\}$ and $P \Rightarrow Q$ then $\{P\}S\{R\}$.

The first states that if P is a precondition for Q and if $Q \Rightarrow R$ is a theorem of the predicate calculus, then we may state that P is a precondition for R (to be true). Thus if P is true and S is executed, then we know that R (as well as Q) will be true. The second rule of consequence is similar.

These rules can also be written in a more formal notation. The "numerator" of the expression will be the antecedent, and the "denominator" will be the consequent. Therefore we can restate the rules of consequence as follows:

1. $$\frac{\{P\}S\{Q\},\ Q \Longrightarrow R}{\{P\}S\{R\}}$$

2. $$\frac{\{Q\}S\{R\},\ P \Longrightarrow Q}{\{P\}S\{R\}}$$

The rules of consequence give this theory the operational structure defined in Chapter 1. Assume that a program is represented by the flowchart of Figure 2.15. The S_i's are statements and the P_i's are the predicates attached to every arc. According to the axioms, the following are true: $\{P_1\}S_1\{P'_1\}$ and $\{P_2\}S_2\{P'_2\}$ for some predicates P'_1 and P'_2. If we can prove that $P'_1 \Rightarrow P_2$ and $P'_2 \Rightarrow P_3$, then by the transitive nature of these rules, we can derive a rule to show that $\{P_1\}S_1;S_2\{P_3\}$ is true.

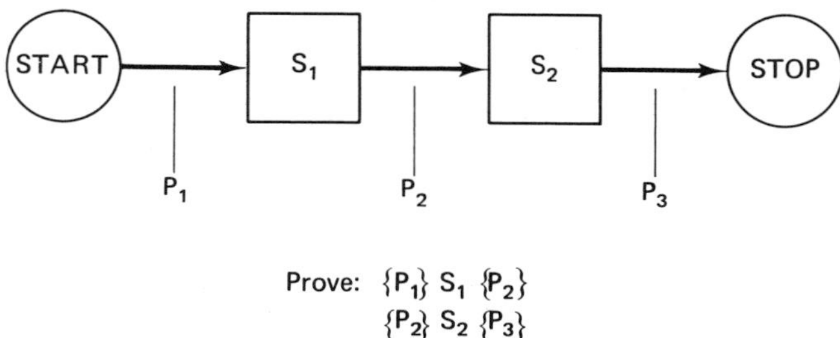

Prove: $\{P_1\}\ S_1\ \{P_2\}$
$\{P_2\}\ S_2\ \{P_3\}$

Figure 2.15 Basic approach towards axiomatic certification.

We must now determine the effects that a single statement has on a program. Assume that programs only consist of sequences of assignment, **if**, and **do while** statements. We know from Section 2.2.2 that these are sufficient.

Since only the assignment statement can change the value of a variable, a single axiom can account for changes in the data. We call this the *axiom of assignment*, and it is stated as follows:

$$\frac{x = \text{expr},\ P(x)}{\{P(\text{expr})\}x = \text{expr}\{P(x)\}}$$

This states that if P is to be a true statement involving variable x after the execution of the assignment statement, then P, where each occurrence of x is replaced by expr, must be true before the assignment statement is executed.

For example, if $P(x)$ is the predicate $x > 0$, and $x = x + 1$ is the assignment statement, then the precondition $P(x + 1)$ is the predicate $(x + 1) > 0$ or $x > -1$. Thus x must be greater than -1 if x is to be positive after the execution of $x = x + 1$.

By the rules of consequence, if we can prove that $Q \Rightarrow P(x + 1)$ for some predicate Q, then we can also state $\{Q\}x = x + 1\{x > 0\}$ as a theorem, and Q is also a precondition for P.

In order to complete this development, we need to determine the effects of the various control structures on a program. These are given by the following axioms:

1. *Sequencing axiom*

$$\frac{\{P\}S1\{Q\},\ \{Q\}S_2\{R\}}{\{P\}S_1;S_2\{R\}}$$

Two statements can be combined in the "obvious" way. If execution of S_1 results in Q being true, and S_2 requires Q as a precondition, then P is a precondition for $S_1;S_2$.

2. *Axiom of iteration*

$$\frac{\{P\&B\}S\{P\}}{\{P\}\textbf{do while}(B);S;\textbf{end};\{\neg B\&P\}}$$

This states that if the truth of P is unaltered by statement S (i.e., is *invariant*), then P is invariant in the loop containing S. In addition, upon exit from the loop, the control expression B will be false.

3. *Axioms of selection*

(a) $$\frac{\{P\&B\}S_1\{Q\},\ \{P\&\neg B\}S_2\{Q\}}{\{P\}\textbf{if } B \textbf{ then } S_1;\ \textbf{else } S_2\{Q\}}$$

(b) $$\frac{\{P\&B\}S_1\{Q\},\ P\&\neg B \Longrightarrow Q}{\{P\}\textbf{if } B \textbf{ then } S_1\{Q\}}$$

These give a straightforward representation for the **if** statement.

In addition to these rules, we need to add various axioms to account for the valid transformations performed on the data. For example, in the case of integer arithmetic, the following axioms cover most operations:

1. *Commutative rules*
   (a) $x + y = y + x$
   (b) $x * y = y * x$
2. *Associative rules*
   (a) $(x + y) + z = x + (y + z)$
   (b) $(x * y) * z = x * (y * z)$
3. *Distributive rule*
   $x * (y + z) = (x * y) + (x * z)$
4. *Subtraction*
   $x - y + y = x$
5. *Constants*
   (a) $x + 0 = x$
   (b) $x * 0 = 0$
   (c) $x * 1 = x$

2.4.2 Certification of a Program

Using these rules, programs can be proven correct. For example, consider the following program to multiply two numbers by repeated addition:

```
1   MULTIPLY(R,A,B);
2       declare X;
3       declare R; /* R=A*B */
4       declare A,B; /* B≥0 */
5       R=0;
6       X=B;
7       do while(X≠0);
8          R=R+A;
9          X=X-1;
10         end;
11      end MULTIPLY;
```

The input assertion is simply the predicate $B \geq 0$. The output assertion is $R = A * B$. An outline of the proof of this program is as follows:

Line 5

$\{0=0 \ \& \ B \geq 0\}\ R=0\ \{R=0 \ \& \ B \geq 0\}$ by the axiom of assignment.

$\{B \geq 0\}\ R=0\ \{R=0 \ \& \ B \geq 0\}$ by the rules of consequence since the following are theorems of the predicate calculus:

$$\text{true} \Longrightarrow 0=0$$
$$B \geq 0 \Longrightarrow (B \geq 0 \ \& \ \text{true})$$

Line 6

$\{B=B \ \& \ R=0 \ \& \ B \geq 0\}\ X=B\ \{X=B \ \& \ R=0 \ \& \ B \geq 0\}$ by axiom of assignment,

$\{R=0 \ \& \ B \geq 0\}\ X=B\ \{X=B \ \& \ R=0 \ \& \ B \geq 0\}$ by rules of consequence,

$\{B \geq 0\}\ R=0; X=B\ \{X=B \ \& \ R=0 \ \& \ B \geq 0\}$ by sequencing axiom.

We have so far shown that if $B \geq 0$ (precondition on the function), then after line 6 $(X=B \ \& \ R=0 \ \& \ B \geq 0)$ will be true.

Lines 7 to 10

We need an invariant for predicate P of the **do while** loop. This invariant should describe the action performed by the loop. In this case, the loop is computing the partial product; thus let the invariant be: $R=A*(B-X)$. By the axiom of iteration if we can show that this is invariant through the loop, and that it is true when the loop terminates, then we will have the following situation:

$$R=A*(B-X) \quad \text{(loop invariant)}$$
$$X=0 \quad \text{(loop expression now false)}$$

Thus $R=A*(B-X)$ & $(X=0)$ will be true, resulting in $R=A*(B-0)$ & $(X=0)$ being true, which results in $R=A*B$ being true—our desired result.

Therefore to complete this proof, we have to show that $R=A*(B-X)$ is true at line 7, and that it is invariant through the loop.

The proof that it is invariant through the loop is just:

Line 8

$\{R+A=A*B-A*X+A\}$ $R=R+A$ $\{R=A*B-A*X+A\}$ by axiom of assignment;

$\{R=A*B-A*X\}$ $R=R+A$ $\{R=A*B-A*X+A\}$ by axioms of arithmetic;

$\{R=A*(B-X)\}$ $R=R+A$ $\{R=A*B-A*X+A\}$ by distributive law.

Line 9

$\{R=A*(B-(X-1))\}$ $X=X-1$ $\{R=A*(B-X)\}$ by axiom of assignment;

$\{R=A*B-A*(X-1)\}$ $X=X-1$ $\{R=A*(B-X)\}$ by arithmetic axioms;

$\{R=A*B-A*X+A\}$ $X=X-1$ $\{R=A*(B-X)\}$ by arithmetic axioms.

Combining lines 8 and 9 by the sequencing axiom results in:

$$\{R=A*(B-X)\}\ R=R+A;X=X-1\ \{R=A*(B-X)\}$$

which is our desired invariant relation.

In order to complete this proof, we must show that the invariant is true at line 7, which is equivalent to showing by the rules of consequence that the following is a theorem:

$$X=B \ \&\ R=0 \ \&\ B\geq 0 \text{ (true at line 6)}$$
$$\Longrightarrow R=A*(B-X)$$

This is left as an exercise.

Although we were able to prove this simple program, several important points about certification should be apparent:

1. Proofs are long and complex, even for such simple programs as the example shown here.

2. Once you extend data to types other than integers, the writing of axioms are difficult. String operations, floating-point calculations, and data base accessing are all difficult to axiomatize.

3. Even with relatively "tame" integers, problems exist. For example, all common computers use fixed length words in which to store integral values. This means that integer overflow is a real problem, and the axioms must include this condition. In our example, we totally ignored overflow and assumed (implicitly) that all possible integer values were valid.

4. Real programming languages have built-in structures that do not lend themselves easily to certification techniques. No widely used language uses only the **do while**, assignment, and **if** statements. Even the simple language defined in Chapter 5 of this book is more complex than that. **goto** statements may be included, and global variables may have their values changed by a procedure. All of these complicate an already difficult problem. (Note: There is some work on defining languages that only contain structures that can be certified. GYPSY [Ambler et al., 77] and the PL/CS dialect of PL/C [Conway, 78] are two such examples.)

In addition, the axiomatic certification presented here is a weak form of certification. The statement $\{P\}S\{Q\}$ actually states that *if S terminates*, then P is a precondition for Q to be true. Thus the termination problem is a separate issue, and may actually be an unsolvable problem.

Since axiomatic methods are incapable of proving such termination, other techniques must be used. One such technique which can be used, even informally, to show termination is to show that the following two attributes are true for each loop in a program:

1. Find some number P that is always nonnegative within the loop.
2. Show that for each execution of the loop, P is decremented by at least a fixed amount.

By condition (1), P is never negative within the loop. By condition (2) if m is the fixed amount that P is decremented by and if k is the initial value of P, then in at most k/m iterations of the loop, P will become negative. Therefore the loop must terminate before this point. A programmer who uses such rules, even informally, will seldom write nonterminating loops.

Consider this program fragment:

```
do while (x<y)
    . . .
    x = x+1
    . . .
    end
```

Let quantity P be the expression $y - x$, and let $P(i)$ refer to the value of P during the ith execution of the loop. Because $x < y$ must be true for each next iteration, $y - x$ is always nonnegative and condition (1) is satisfied for each execution of the loop.

Since the loop contains the statement $x = x + 1$,

$$\begin{aligned} P(i) &= y - x \\ &= (y - x) - 1 + 1 \\ &= (y - (x + 1)) + 1 \\ &= P(i + 1) + 1 \end{aligned}$$

so $P(i + 1) = P(i) - 1$, satisfying condition (2). Therefore the loop must terminate.

Even with these restrictions, certification does have a place in program development. The techniques developed to certify programs in the formal system can be used formally or informally on real programs as they develop. As a program is developed, the necessary preconditions should be determined. Even if not formally proven, simply stated they can greatly aid in understanding the structure of a given program. The adding of preconditions follows very closely the discussion of understanding prime programs in Section 2.2.2. In addition, as will be discussed in the next section on testing, these preconditions can form the basis for testing the program. They can be coded as IF statements and then executed as part of the test.

Several important issues have been uncovered via a study of program certification. The development of loop invariants has gone a long way towards understanding the complexity of the general loop structure in a program. The extension of these ideas to include other control structures and to add multiple data structures is a current area of research in computer science.

2.5 TESTING

As stated in Chapter 1, the testing stage of project development can use up to half of the total development time. It is therefore important to adequately design test procedures early. Unfortunately, this is not usually the case. A program is typically written with every expectation of working. When it fails, special debugging statements are scattered through the code in an attempt to find problems. If it is realized that programs must be tested, then these tests can more easily be developed early and testing problems can be minimized.

Testing cannot be accomplished in a vacuum. The strategy used greatly depends upon the methodology used in developing the program. As such, the following briefly summarizes the ideas that have been recommended by the preceding sections of this book:

1. Develop programs using top-down development and stepwise refinement. This implies that higher levels of a system (drivers) will be written before the routines that they call can be coded. Results of this technique mean that the systems are built as collections of small pieces. Each piece should be tested as it is built.

2. Use structured programming control structures. As in stepwise refinement, this limits the complexity of a given procedure. As a corollary to this, programs should be coded in a straightforward manner. Clever code that does not work is of no use to anyone, and testing such routines often involves more resources than are saved by the clever coding. Similarly, routine sizes should be limited to about a printed page in order to be able to grasp the entire function easily.

3. Design modules around the data abstraction concept. By defining programs as transformations on data, it is easier to understand the operation of these functions on that data, and therefore easier to design test routines for those functions. In addition, the use of data abstractions limits the occurrence of *side effects*, the changing of the value of a global variable within a procedure. Side effects are to be avoided since there is no documentation in the code at the point of the procedure call that the value of a variable before a procedure call may be different from the value of the same variable after the call.

4. Use (formal or informal) certification techniques to verify each level of a system as it develops. Programs are certified as they are built; certification is not an "add-on" feature performed at the completion of the coding stage.

Many reasons exist for the occurrence of errors. Inadequate or incomplete specifications are probably the greatest cause. A routine will pass to a called routine a value that the called routine does not know how to process. One way to avoid this is to encode all specifications as IF statements within the called procedure. This special debugging code will be explained shortly.

Another cause of errors is incorrect algorithm design. Stepwise refinement is an attempt to minimize these problems.

Accidents and clerical errors are a third minor, yet not insignificant, cause of errors. For example, mistyped variable names are not detected as errors by either FORTRAN or PL/1 compilers, yet are obviously wrong. Always declare every variable name and print a cross-reference listing to discover such errors.

Since the occurrence of some errors in a large program is unavoidable, a program should be written with the knowledge that it probably contains an error, and some person, probably not the author, will have to find that error. As such, the following guidelines are presented:

1. *Variable names.* Explicitly declare all variables. Similarly, use symbolic names that mean something. COBOL allows for 30 character names, and ANSI PL/1 allows for 63. Use these wisely. Make sure that all variables are initialized to some value. The use of a good set of names goes a long way to eliminating much (but not all) extra documentation.

2. *Constants.* "Magic numbers" have no place in a program. There is nothing special or meaningful about numbers like 7, 26, or 63. Use symbolic names to specify such quantities. Some languages permit constants to be given symbolic names (*manifest constants*). Use these if available.

Consider the following two identical algorithms as part of a scanner:

```
if PTR ≤ 63 then PTR = PTR+1;
             else PTR = PTR-64;
```

and

```
declare LINELENGTH INITIAL(64);
if PTR ≤(LINELENGTH-1) then PTR=PTR+1;
             else PTR = PTR-LINELENGTH;
```

The second case describes the code much more clearly than the first without the need for any comments. In addition, the second is independent of the actual length of the line. If that should change, then only the INITIAL attribute need be changed. In the first, all occurrences of 63, 64, and possibly a 65 or two would have to be searched for and altered.

3. *Input data.* All input data should be printed upon reading in order to check that the correct value was read at the correct point of the program.

4. *Parameter lists.* Check that there is agreement between number and types of arguments and parameters. Are all specifications to the procedure fulfilled? Are appropriate data abstraction concepts being applied?

5. *Assertions.* Add assertions in the form of **if** statements to the program. This allows the executing program to check its own status. In addition, make sure that all loops terminate.

The specifications to a procedure can be used to develop predicates to be tested. Each such specification translate into the code:

```
if specification is true then do;
    algorithm
    end;
```

In addition, the invariant in a loop can be tested as in:

```
do while(condition is true);
    if invariant false then call ERROR ('invariant error');
    Code for loop;
    end;
```

In addition, predicates can be added to ensure that there is some property *P* that is decreasing for each execution of the loop.

2.5.1 Stub Development

From these guidelines, the major impact on testing will be the first, top-down development, and the need for stubs to test a given module. When a module is written, the functions that it calls are named, and some specifications written for those functions. These specifications should immediately be encoded into a simple testing procedure so that the higher level modules can be tested.

The simplest type of stub is merely a routine that prints a message indicating that control reached that point, as in:

```
INPUTREADER: procedure;
    put SKIP LIST('INPUTREADER CALLED');
    end;
```

For most routines this is insufficient since the calling routine expects some action by the stub. This can easily be simulated, as in:

```
INPUTREADER: procedure(VALUE);
    declare VALUE;
    put SKIP LIST('INPUTREADER CALLED');
    VALUE = 7;
    end;
```

Returning the same value each time may not adequately test the routine, so a stub can use a set of "canned" responses, as in:

```
INPUTREADER: procedure(VALUE);
    declare VALUE;
    declare SWITCH STATIC INITIAL(0),
            DATA(10) STATIC INITIAL(3,6,1,4,12,43,10,12,7,0),
            NUM_TEST_ITEMS INITIAL(10);
    put SKIP LIST('INPUTREADER CALLED');
    if SWITCH<NUM_TEST_ITEMS then SWITCH = SWITCH + 1;
    VALUE = DATA(SWITCH);
    end;
```

The routine now returns a set of predefined values to the calling routine.

Certification techniques can be used to help in developing stubs. If a specification in a procedure indicates that a certain condition is to hold, then this can be checked for. For example, if a certain input value must be positive, the following stub can be used:

```
INPUTREADER: procedure (OLDVALUE, VALUE);
    declare (OLDVALUE, VALUE);
    put SKIP LIST('INPUTREADER CALLED');
    if OLDVALUE ≤0 then do; /* specification error */
        /* ERROR CONDITION */
        put LIST('INPUTREADER ERROR', OLDVALUE);
        call ERRORROUTINE;
        end;
    /* DO STUB CODE */
    . . .
    end;
```

In addition, loop invariants can be tested as **if** statements before and after a loop. The additional code that must be executed can be minimized by the use of conditional execution techniques, explained below.

As the program develops, the stub may either be replaced or expanded into the complete function. As such, many of the initial tests on the data may be deleted for efficiency considerations. However, should a later problem arise, these tests will again be needed, but will now be unavailable.

A method for incorporating this debugging code without undue overhead in the finished product is to leave the code in the program, but control it by a "debugging" switch which is normally turned "off," as in:

```
INPUTREADER: procedure(OLDVALUE,VALUE);
    declare(OLDVALUE,VALUE);
    declare DEBUGSWITCH BIT INITIAL('0'B); /* 0=off, 1=on */
    . . .
    if DEBUGSWITCH then do; /* debug code on */
        put SKIP LIST('INPUTREADER CALLED');
        . . .
        end;
    /* rest of procedure */
    . . .
    end;
```

In this case execution time is increased insignificantly to test the **if** expression, although the size of the program will grow to include the added code. However, if space is not at a premium, then this technique should be used.

2.5.2 Test Data

Although stubs may be written, it takes data to execute the program. The development of test data is aided by the following general guidelines:

1. Use simple test cases first and then work towards more complex ones. One or two successful test runs are insufficient for testing a reasonably complex program.
2. Use extreme values for some of the test data. For example, if *VALUE* should be in the range *A* to *B*, then values of $A - 1$, A, $A + 1$, $B - 1$, B, and $B + 1$ should be tested.
3. Use special values. This includes the constants 0 and 1 and the null string for string variables.
4. Use control flow to determine test data. Every statement must be executed by some test run (although a single test run cannot in general test every statement). For each **if** statement, choose values that cause the expression to be both true and false. Similarly for **do** loops choose values to make the loop execute 0, 1, or a maximum number of times. For example, in the code:

```
do while(X<Y);
   . . .
end;
```

choose a value of *X* less than *Y*, choose *X* equal to *Y*, and choose an *X* greater than *Y*.

5. The desired test results should be known before the test is run. It is of little use to pick a few random tests, try them on the program, and then spend hours with a paper and pencil simulation of the program to see if they are correct. This technique takes too much time, and there is little guarantee that major parts of the program will even be tested.

Stating these rules is certainly easier than generating the data in many cases. It is hard to know what values to pick for input data in order to cause an IF statement three procedures deep to be true. However, that is the purpose of top-down development. One is always testing at a level reasonably close to the level where the program is known to be correct.

2.5.3 Compiler Aids

Several compilers exist for aiding in program development. Examples include the PL/C compiler for the IBM 360/370 [Conway and Wilcox, 73] and the PLUM compiler for the Univac 1100-series computer [Zelkowitz, 75].

These include many features mentioned in this section to help in testing the program. Besides syntactic checking of the source language, these compilers provide many of the necessary semantic checks, e.g., checking on parameter list agreement between called and calling procedures.

As an example of the features provided, some of PLUM's features will be described.

1. The writing of stubs is aided by a FLOW PROC statement. Use of this statement causes all procedure calls and returns to be automatically printed, as in:

```
⟨CALL INPUTREADER AT 47 FROM 14⟩
⟨....RETURN TO SCANNER AT 14 FROM 67⟩
```

The two numbers represent the two statement numbers involved. This can be controlled by the following code in the main procedure of the program:

```
DECLARE FLOWSWITCH BIT INIT('0'B); /* 0=off 1=on */
IF FLOWSWITCH THEN FLOW PROC;
```

Normally the code will be ignored; however, if an error occurs, the program can be rerun with *FLOWSWITCH* initialized to '1' B. (PL/C also includes a FLOW statement for tracing a program's execution.)

2. Since PLUM is an interactive system, the user controls execution of a program at a terminal. Any error causes control to return to the terminal, where the programmer can inspect variables and then resume execution. Thus a programmer can more easily simulate a program stub. For example, INPUTREADER can be coded as:

```
INPUTREADER: PROCEDURE(OLDVALUE, VALUE);
      DECLARE OLDVALUE, VALUE;
      SIGNAL ERROR;
      END;
```

When the SIGNAL statement is executed, the programmer at a terminal will gain control. PLUM will print out:

```
**** IN STMT 73 SIGNAL
*
```

Now the programmer can:

```
Display OLDVALUE       (Print value of OLDVALUE)
Alter VALUE=newvalue   (Set new value of VALUE)
Resume                 (Resume execution)
```

3. The use of debugging code is aided by conditional code generation. *Pseudo comments* are included and are interpreted by the compiler as regular code if a certain compiler option is set. Thus the FLOW PROC example above can be coded as:

```
/*D DECLARE FLOWSWITCH BIT INITIAL('0'B); */
/*D IF FLOWSWITCH THEN FLOW PROC; */
```

Normally these are interpreted as comments and no code is generated. However, if an error occurs, the programmer can set an option in order to have the /*D deleted and the remaining part of the comment compiled as regular code. This allows for such debugging "documentation" to remain within the finished program with no additional execution or space overhead.

Any other code can be "hidden" by such conditional comments, as in:

```
/*D PUT DATA(variables to test); */
/*D Any other testing code        */
```

In addition, this program can be run without any changes on a production PL/1 compiler, where minimal execution time, rather than diagnostics, is the major goal. In this case the pseudo comments will be ignored by the compiler since they are valid PL/1 comments.

PL/C extends this concept further. Pseudo comments have the syntax

```
/*n TEXT */
```

where *n* takes on the value 1 to 9. In this case the programmer can specify up to nine different classes of special code and only have those desired classes compiled during any one test.

4. Variables in PLUM are also initialized with a special value which usually results in an error if misused. Other systems such as PL/C detect all usages of uninitialized variables. PLUM and PL/CS also have an option to force all variables to be explicitly declared and to prohibit implicit declarations.

5. The CHECK option in PL/1 allows for easy echoing of all input data. This option can easily be included as part of a conditional code generation statement as follows:

```
GET LIST(A,B,C) /*D CHECK */ ;
```

As with the previous example, this code can be enabled or disabled by a simple compiler switch.

6. PLUM will automatically indent all listings depending upon the prime

program decomposition of the source. The input might look like the following:

```
MAX: PROCEDURE(B,N);
DECLARE B(N);
A=0;
DO I=1 TO N;
IF B(I)>A THEN A=B(I);
END;
PUT LIST('MAXIMUM VALUE',A);
END MAX;
```

This will be printed out as:

```
MAX:PROCEDURE(B,N);
    DECLARE B(N);
    A=0;
    DO I=1 TO N;
        IF B(I)>A THEN A=B(I);
        END;
    PUT LIST('MAXIMUM VALUE',A);
    END MAX;
```

This enhances "intellectual manageability" of the program and enables certain errors (e.g., missing END statements) to be determined more easily.

7. PL/CS provides an assertion mechanism.

```
ASSERT(expression)
```

will be checked during program execution and generate an error message if false. The expression can be any logical expression, and PL/CS also has the capability of checking assertions for all variables within a certain range.

The ASSERT statement comes in three forms:

(a) ASSERT (expression);
(b) ASSERT (expression)
FOR ALL variable=expr1 TO expr2 BY expr3;
(c) ASSERT (expression)
FOR SOME variable=expr1 TO expr2 BY expr3;

These assertions can be used to test pre- and postconditions according to a procedure's specifications. (In the language GYPSY [Ambler et al., 77], assertions are also provided. The GYPSY system first tries to verify the correctness of those assertions via an automated verifier. If that fails, then the programmer is able to tell the system to generate code to test the assertion during program execution.)

8. The execution histogram, mentioned in Chapter 1, can be automatically generated. In addition a count of statement types compiled and exe-

cuted and a symbolic dump of a program's memory can be provided (Figure 2.16). In PL/1, the statement:

```
PUT DATA;
```

can be used to "snapshot" the state of all the program's variables at any time during program execution.

These few examples only represent a small set of the features that a debugging compiler can provide for effective program development. The important points are that such facilities are provided in a semiautomatic manner by the compiler and such debugging code can remain as part of the permanent documentation for the program. This documentation makes it easier to understand the rest of the program, and if necessary, it can be reactivated with a simple compile-time option. It is unfortunate that many programmers do not have access to such a compiler and must use a production compiler for all their runs. Debugging compilers are more than just tools to teach students how to write "toy" programs. Perhaps their usage will spread.

2.5.4 Formal Testing

There are generally two approaches which are used to show that a program is correct. In one approach programs are verified by formal proofs in order to show correctness. The more common technique is to use testing to validate a program's usefulness. Goodenough and Gerhart [75] have made an important contribution to this area by defining a theory that merges the two concepts.

A *test* is a subset of the permissible inputs to a program. A *testing criteria* specifies what is to be tested (e.g., specifications, all statements, all paths).

A test is *complete* if the test performs all the requirements of the testing criterion. For example, if the criterion specifies that every statement is to be executed, then a test is complete if this is true. A complete test is *successful* if the program gives correct results for each input in the test.

With these definitions, we can define reliability and validity. A testing criterion is *reliable* if every found error is revealed by any complete test. Thus any one complete test is sufficient for finding all errors that the testing criteria are capable of finding. Note that some errors may still be present since reliability allows for errors not discoverable by any test according to the criterion to remain.

A testing criterion is *valid* if every error is revealed by some complete test. This means that a finite set of complete tests can be used to find all errors in the program.

TYPE	COMPILATION COUNT	%	EXECUTION COUNT	%
BEGIN	0	.0	0	.0
CALL	3	3.0	52	1.8
CLOSE	0	.0	0	.0
DECLARE	14	14.0	0	.0
END	6	6.0	541	18.8
ENTRY	3	3.0	0	.0
FORMAT	0	.0	0	.0
GET	2	2.0	2	.0
GOTO	0	.0	0	.0
IF	0	.0	0	.0
OPEN	1	1.0	1	.0
PROC	2	2.0	54	1.8
PUT	18	18.0	67	2.3
RETURN	3	3.0	52	1.8
STOP	0	.0	0	.0
NULL	0	.0	0	.0
DO	0	.0	0	.0
DO WHILE	0	.0	0	.0
DO ITER	4	4.0	632	21.9
DO CASE	0	.0	0	.0
ASG GEN	16	16.0	856	29.7
ASG 0 OP	21	21.0	266	9.2
ASG 1 OP	7	7.0	350	12.1
–	0	.0	0	.0
FLOW	0	.0	0	.0
EXIT	0	.0	0	.0
ON	0	.0	0	.0
REVERT	0	.0	0	.0
SIGNAL	0	.0	0	.0
DELETED	0	.0	0	.0
ALLOCATE	0	.0	0	.0
FREE	0	.0	0	.0
LEAVE	0	.0	0	.0
READ	0	.0	0	.0
WRITE	0	.0	0	.0
–	0	.0	0	.0
SYSTEM	0	.0	0	.0

```
At line 100 in procedure P
RR= 7.26438066E-001        LB=          81          LA=           4
NEW=             0         L=           0           K=            6
OLD=             0         I2=           6          I1=          41
SUM= 1.06000000E+003       WEEKSCNT=          40    COUNT=       1115
J=            0            NRECORDS=          50    PROJTITLE='PAS HNDLS'
STR='
'                          I=          51           TEMP= 2.64091002E+001
T= 5.00000000E+001         KKE= 1.68270000E+004     KB= 8.87669999E-004
KA= 9.02419999E-004        KE= 1.02489999E+003      V= 1.62361397E+002
ROLD= 4.00000000E+000
Program statistics (words) : Program : 1009 Symbol table : 1518 Source :
        803 Runtime stack : 909 Unused : 3822
EXECUTION TIME    3266  MSEC.
```

Figure 2.16 Symbolic dump following program termination.

With these definitions, several important results can be proven. Among these are:

1. If a criterion is both reliable and valid, then it is correct if and only if any complete test is also successful. This is easy to show. If the criteria are valid, then each error is found by some complete tests. If the criteria are reliable, then any error found by one complete test is found by all. Thus if the criteria are reliable and valid, all errors are found by all complete tests. If one such complete test is successful, then no errors exist in that or any other test.

2. The criterion "execute every statement" is not a valid criterion; there exist programs all of whose test sets succeed, but which produce the wrong results for some input.

Exercise 2.7: Give a program such that if all the statements in the program are executed, the program may give either correct or incorrect answers.

While reliability and validity can be used to prove program correctness, the difficult problem still remains to show that a given testing criterion *is* reliable and valid for a given program. Therefore, this formalism is currently more useful in describing the overall certification process than in applying it to real programs. It is, however, an important step in formalizing this area. We now have a basis for talking about such concepts as reliability and correctness.

2.6 DESIGN TECHNIQUES

Although the development of a program is mostly a creative activity, there are many standard algorithms that can be used to simplify the process. Having some knowledge of how the algorithm operates often makes it easier to state a problem in terms applicable to that algorithm.

In this section, many of the standard techniques used in programming are presented. The list is by no means exhaustive, and each technique is only given a brief introduction. However, the information should be sufficient for knowledge of how to choose the appropriate algorithm. For more detailed information on many of these techniques, see Aho et al. [74] or Knuth [68].

2.6.1 Divide and Conquer and Balancing

Divide and conquer

Divide and conquer is the basic algorithm behind any problem solving activity. In order to solve task A, it is first necessary to break down the task into independent subtasks B, C, D (etc.). For example, if a task A consists of the three components B, C, and D, task A can be represented by the following procedure:

```
A: procedure;  /* DO TASK A */
        Task B;
        Task C;
        Task D;
        end A;
```

How these subtasks are created is the major role of the remaining algorithms.

Balancing

While divide and conquer is inherent in all programming activities, the concept of balancing should also be used. This means to divide the problem into subtasks which are as equally complex as possible in order to make each subtask significantly easier to solve than the original problem.

Searching a list for a desired element is a good example of balancing (Section 2.6.4). In a linear search, the algorithm is:

```
Check first element;
if not found then search remaining elements;
```

In this case, the problem is divided into two pieces: the first element and the remainder. This does not divide the problem equally.

However, a binary search has the structure:

```
Check middle element;
if not found then search either top or
                 bottom half;
```

In this case the problem has been divided into two pieces: each about the same complexity. (Note: This is also an example of a recursive solution (Section 2.6.2).)

2.6.2 Recursion and Dynamic Programming

Recursion

Although an exact solution to a problem may not be known, it may be possible to state such a solution as a known transformation of another (simpler) variant of the same problem. If this process is repeated until a known value is obtained, the solution is called a recursive solution.

The factorial function is often cited as a recursive solution. FACTORIAL(N) is $1*2*3...*N$. For example, if one wants FACTORIAL(460), although its value may be unknown, it can be computed easily (although tediously) by multiplying the 1001 digits of FACTORIAL(459) by the integer 460. This simplifies the problem somewhat since 459 is less than 460. If this is repeated 458 more times to get FACTORIAL(2) = 2*FACTORIAL(1), the solution is known since FACTORIAL(1) is just 1.

If F is a function, then we will state that F is a recursive function if:

1. $F(N) = G(N, F(N - 1))$, for some known function G, and
2. $F(1) =$ some known value.

The function F can be a function of several parameters, with the N in the equations above being a derived quantity (similar to property P for loop termination). This N can be the elements in a set, size of an interval, or some other property of the problem. See for example the definition of binary search and, in Chapter 3, the fourth solution to the parking problem for recursive solutions. Recursive solutions are often shorter than their nonrecursive counterparts. In terms of execution speed, they may be shorter or longer than their nonrecursive solutions.

Dynamic programming

Dynamic programming is a tabular method related to recursion for computing all subproblems of a given problem. In dynamic programming, a solution, once found, is stored in a table for later use. In this way, it need not be recomputed later.

Solution 2 to the Fibonacci series, and the breadth-first search solution of the maze problem of Chapter 3 are examples of dynamic programming problems. In these cases all possible solutions are computed at one time and kept in a table (a set for the search problem and two temporary variables for the Fibonacci series).

2.6.3 Simulation

Often it is not possible to construct an exact solution to a problem—due to cost, complexity, or size. This will often occur in trying to solve physical problems about the real world such as in traffic control, economic predictions, or military situations, etc. In these cases a representation of certain features of the problem, called a *model*, is constructed with all other features ignored. This model is then analyzed for its behavior on the desired features. This is called *simulation*.

Simulations occur in many fields. Models of boats and planes are often tested in miniature in model basins and wind tunnels, respectively, before full-scale production is undertaken. Cardboard models of buildings are often constructed to determine functional and aesthetic aspects before development begins. Most engineering fields use models to simulate operation before construction.

One of the problems with software engineering is the insufficient use of simulation. While a computer simulation is often used to model a physical process, especially when the mathematical behavior of the process is known via a set of mathematical equations, it is rarely used to model a computer program, e.g., model an operating system before investing 100 man-years to build one. Simulation is an effective tool that deserves more exposure to the computer science community. Solution 1 to the parking problem in Chapter 3 is an example of simulation.

2.6.4 Searching

Searching is the process of finding a desired value among a set of possibilities. We will restrict our discussion here to those situations which have a finite number of alternatives.

In general, a collection of entries may be either structured or unstructured. If unstructured, then searching usually means the finding of a desired entry in a list. If structured, such as in a tree or graph, then searching means the finding of the correct path through the structure.

Each entry will have three components: a key, an argument, and a structure. The *key* is the item used to access the data. This key may be an alphabetized name in a directory, a word in an index, or a chapter name in a table of contents. The *argument* is the associated value of the entry. This can be an address and telephone number in a directory or a page number in an index or table of contents. The *structure* is additional information used by the implementation for describing the data, such as the address of the following or related entries in the collection. The structure information is usually not made available to the one who accesses the data.

We separate searching algorithms into two sections: searching lists (unstructured items) and searching trees (structured items). For a more complete description of searching see Knuth [68, vol. 3].

Searching lists

In order to search a list, four different techniques will be presented: direct, linear, binary, and hash. Each has distinct advantages and disadvantages.

(a) Direct search. In a direct search, the location of an entry is computed directly from the key. For example, room numbers in an office building are often direct searches. The first digit is often the floor number, and the last two digits are generally the location of the room on that floor, sequentially numbered from one end of the building.

In a more computer-oriented application, the symbol table for the BASIC language is often organized around a direct search. Since BASIC limits variable names to a single letter and digit, 260 entries are sufficient for all possible combinations. Since this is a relatively small number for most large computers, BASIC interpreters frequently preallocate all possibilities.

A direct search is often used when the number of entries is fixed and relatively small. In addition, the number of entries must be close to the total number of possible entries. It is very efficient since the location of the argument can be obtained directly from the search key.

(b) Linear search. A linear search is the easiest to program although it has the highest average search time. In this case, entries are checked sequentially, one at a time, until the desired key is found. Unlike the direct search, there is no order assumed for the keys. If a list has N entries, then $N/2$ of them will be checked on the average each time. Thus a linear search is not particularly fast.

However, a linear search does have the advantage that it is extremely easy to add to the list (at the end). It is also very easy to program and is reasonably efficient for small lists that change repeatedly. If there is no structure to the data, it may be hard to use an alternative search strategy.

One should not overlook the usefulness of a linear search in many applications. A well developed program usually has a straightforward, simple design. In searching applications, there is no need to show off your creativity by programming the most elegant, abstract, convoluted searching algorithm you know. In many cases a straightforward linear search can be programmed in five minutes and has the advantage of avoiding the hours of debugging time that more complex algorithms may require. If the search list is short, consider this possibility.

(c) Binary search. A binary search assumes that the keys can be ordered numerically or lexigraphically (alphabetically). In this case, the ordering can be used to make the search time of a list of length N to be on the average $\log_2(N)$.

In a binary search, the middle element of the list is compared with the key. If the key is larger, then the same algorithm is repeated with the second part of the list; if smaller, then the algorithm is repeated with the first part. Thus half of the remaining list is eliminated at each step of the process.

The major problem with a binary search is how to insert new entries. Since the list is ordered, an insertion may require all the entries to be moved in order to create a slot for a new entry in the correct location.

Exercise 2.8: A tree structure can be used to store an ordered list. The left son pointer can point to entries less than a given entry, and the right son pointer can point to entries greater than a given entry. This has the advantage that new entries can always be physically located at the end of the storage area; movement of the list is not necessary. Design a search routine to search, add, and delete entries from this structure.

(d) Hash search. The hash search is an attempt to use the direct search strategy since it is the fastest on larger collections of data. In this case a pseudo key called the *hash code* is computed from the real key, and this hash code is used to index into the table of entries. As long as all keys hash to unique codes, a single direct search will locate any entry.

For example, a FORTRAN compiler may allocate 1000 slots for variable names in its symbol table. However, FORTRAN permits names consisting of letters and digits of up to six characters. This allows for over 26^6 names, which is much greater than the symbol table size of 1000. But if each name is now reduced to a number between 0 and 999, they can be stored (up to 1000 of them) in the table.

Algorithms for computing hash codes are varied. For example, the name (key) can be considered to be a number using the internal binary representation of the character string. This number can be divided by the table size, and the remainder used as the hash code. Since this algorithm will result in the names A1, A2, A3, and A4 being in successive slots in the table, and since names like these are common in programming, this is not a very good hashing algorithm. Other algorithms include adding together bits within the number or some other function on the key.

As the FORTRAN example shows, with only 1000 symbol table entries and much more than 1000 possible names, many names must hash to the same value. Therefore, the major aspect in writing a hashing algorithm is to decide how to handle *collisions*, i.e., two keys hashing to the same value.

Obviously, the first time a certain hash value is encountered, the entry is simply placed in that slot of the table since it is not yet known that a collision will occur. However, if a collision occurs, some other slot is used for the entry. The insert algorithm for such a hash code is given by:

```
INSERT: procedure(key, argument);
        declare 1 TABLE(size),
                    2 KEY,
                    2 ARGUMENT;
        declare hashcode;
        Compute hashcode from key;
        if TABLE(hashcode).KEY=key then return;
                                        /* entry already in table */
        /* Resolve collision. */
        do while(TABLE(hashcode).KEY≠0 &
                 TABLE(hashcode).KEY≠key);
            hashcode = new value depending upon (hashcode,key);
            end;
```

```
/* found slot */
TABLE(hashcode).KEY = key;
TABLE(hashcode).ARGUMENT = argument;
end INSERT;
```

In order to complete this algorithm, the **do while** loop must know when to terminate, such as when the table is full.

Exercise 2.9: Write the routines to look up an entry in a hash table and to delete an entry from such a table. Due to multiple collisions, deleted entries cannot be simply set to 0.

Algorithms for resolving collisions include: go the entry following the entry causing the collision, go a constant number of entries past a collision, or compute a new hashcode from the current key and current hashcode. This latter method is preferable. For example, in a dense table (over half full), clumps of collisions resulting in long search times may result due to sequentially resolved collisions.

For large tables which are sparse, hashing provides the most effective retrieval. A hash table under 50% full will require under two searches to find any entry. When 80% to 90% full, hash tables start to become inefficient due to the number of collisions found.

Searching trees

Since the data is organized as a tree structure, the searching algorithm reduces to an algorithm to visit every node of the tree. Two basic algorithms exist for this operation: a depth-first search and a breadth-first search.

(a) Depth-first search. The depth-first search visits each path in a tree from "left to right" (Figure 2.17). For binary trees, it has a simple recursive structure:

```
DEPTHFIRST: procedure(TREE);
      declare 1 TREE,
                      2 KEY,
                      2 ARGUMENT,  /* data */
                      2 RIGHTSON,  /* null, if no son */
                      2 LEFTSON;   /* null, if no son */
      if TREE=null then return;
      if current node not KEY then do;
                call DEPTHFIRST(LEFTSON);
                call DEPTHFIRST(RIGHTSON);
                end;
      end DEPTHFIRST;
```

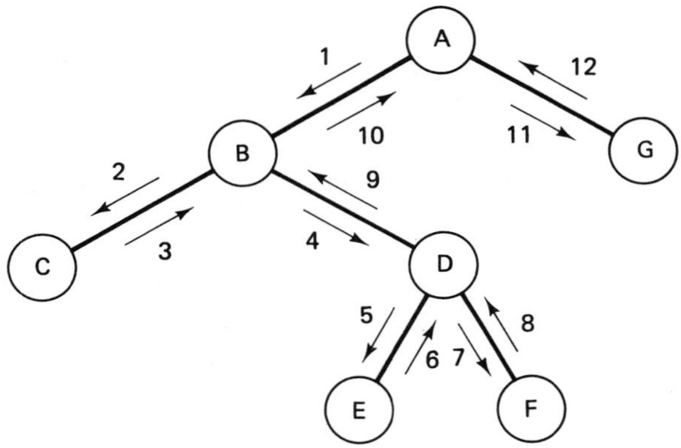

Figure 2.17 Depth-first search.

Note that if the tree is ordered so that *LEFTSON* has a key less than the value of the root node, and if *RIGHTSON* has a key greater than the root node, then this algorithm is similar to a binary search (see Exercise 2.8). Solution 2 of the maze problem in Chapter 3 is another example of a depth-first search.

Exercise 2.10: Give the algorithm for a depth-first search which stores a tree via the items: father, left son, right brother.

(b) Breadth-first search. The breadth-first search is a parallel search algorithm that progresses one level at a time down a tree (Figure 2.18). This is

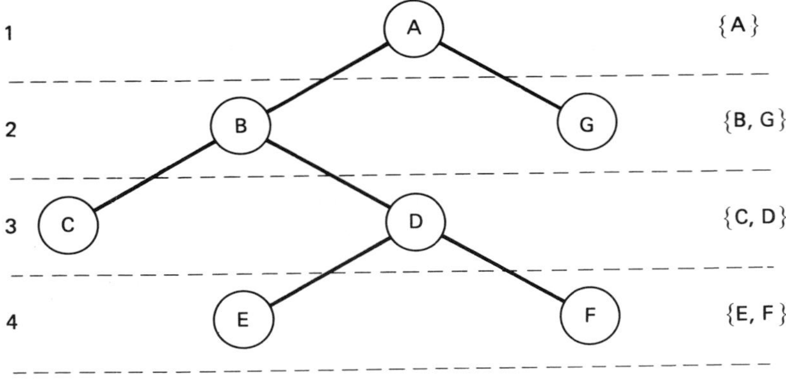

Figure 2.18 Breadth-first search.

a parallel solution which has the side effect of finding the shortest solution to the problem. The general algorithm is:

```
BREADTHFIRST: procedure(SOLUTION);
        declare 1 TREE,
                        2 ARGUMENT, /* data */
                        2 SONS(N);   /* arbitrary trees */
        declare(SOLUTION, NEXTSTEP) SET OF TREES;
        do while(SOLUTION≠null); /* go down each level */
               NEXTSTEP = {TREE.SONS(I) for all TREE
                                 and I in SOLUTION};
               call BREADTHFIRST(NEXTSTEP);
               end;
        end BREADTHFIRST;
```

Solution 1 to the maze problem of Chapter 3 is a breadth-first solution.

2.6.5 Sorting

Sorting is the process of placing a list of items into some numerical or lexigraphical ordering. Of all algorithms in computer science, sorting problems have been studied the most. Several simple sorting algorithms are as follows:

(a) Exchange sort. In this algorithm, the smallest entry moves to the top, the next smallest to position 2, etc. For a list of N elements, it takes $N*(N-1)/2$ steps (or $O(N^2)$), so is not practical for very large N. The basic algorithm is:

```
EXCHANGESORT: procedure(LIST,N);
        declare LIST(N); /* array to sort */
        do I = 1 to N-1;
            do J = I+1 to N;
                if LIST(J)<LIST(I) then
                    Reverse(LIST(J),LIST(I));
            end;
        end;
end;
```

(b) Merge sort. The merge sort is an example of the divide-and-conquer and recursive techniques. First the unsorted list is divided into two parts, and each part is then sorted independently. The lists are then merged. The PDL for this algorithm is:

```
MERGESORT: procedure(LIST,N);
        declare LIST(N);
        if N>1 then do; /* divide by 2 */
              call MERGESORT(LIST(1:N/2),N/2);
                              /* sort items 1. .N/2     */
              call MERGESORT(LIST(N/2+1:N),N/2);
                              /* sort items N/2+1. .N */
              end;
        call MERGE(LIST(1:N/2),LIST(N/2+1:N),N);
                              /* merge two sorted sublists */
        end;
```

The merge procedure merges two lists of size K in $2*K$ operations by looking at the first element in each list and moving the smaller of the two into a new list. These two tests are repeated for each of the $2*K$ elements of the merged list, giving $4*K$ operations. Since each sublist is already sorted, only the first element need be checked.

While this does require more storage than the exchange sort (an auxiliary array the size of the sorted list as opposed to space for a single element), the time to sort is reduced to $N \log_2 N$. In order to compute this time complexity, consider the following: For each sublist of length 1, there are $N/2$ calls to merge, each requiring 4 compares, or $2*N$ steps. For each list of length 2 there are $N/8$ calls to merge with 4 compares, etc. This results in a total of $2*(N/2*2 + N/4*4 + \ldots + N/2*2)$ compares. This is just $2*(N + N + N + \ldots + N)$ compares, with $\log_2 N$ terms in the sum, or a total of $2*(N \log_2 N)$ compares, which is $O(N \log_2 N)$.

(c) Other sorting procedures Many other sorting algorithms have been developed—enough to easily fill this chapter. For further infomation see Knuth [68, vol. 3].

2.6.6 Backtracking

Frequently it is necessary to try alternative strategies for a solution. One such technique is called backtracking and has the following general solution:

```
Generate first partial solution;
do while(not finished);
      Get next part of solution;
      do while(not possible to continue);
            Backup to previous level;
            Try alternative at this level;
            end;
    end;
```

The depth-first search algorithm is an example of a backtracking solution. It uses the following substitutions to the general algorithm.

1. Generate first part of solution;

becomes

Start at root node;

2. Get next part of solution;

becomes:

Go to left son node, if any;
else go to right brother;

3. **do while** (not possible to continue);

becomes:

do while (no left son and right brother);

4. Backup to previous level;

becomes

Go to father node;

5. Try alternative at this level;

becomes

Go to right brother node, if any;

The complete algorithm then becomes:

```
Start at root node;
do while (current node exists);
        Go to left son node, if any;
                else go to right brother;
        do while (no left son or right brother);
                Go to father node;
                Go to right brother node, if any;
                end;
        end;
```

Backtracking is quite common in searching trees and in recursive solutions.

2.6.7 Finite State and Table-driven Algorithms

Often a problem can be reduced to a set of operations depending only upon the current state of the program. Such a solution is called a finite state solution, and usually involves a table describing the action to be performed.

The rows of the table define the states of the program and the columns define the possible alternatives. The intersections define the possible actions to be performed—often the name of a subroutine to call to perform the action (Figure 2.19).

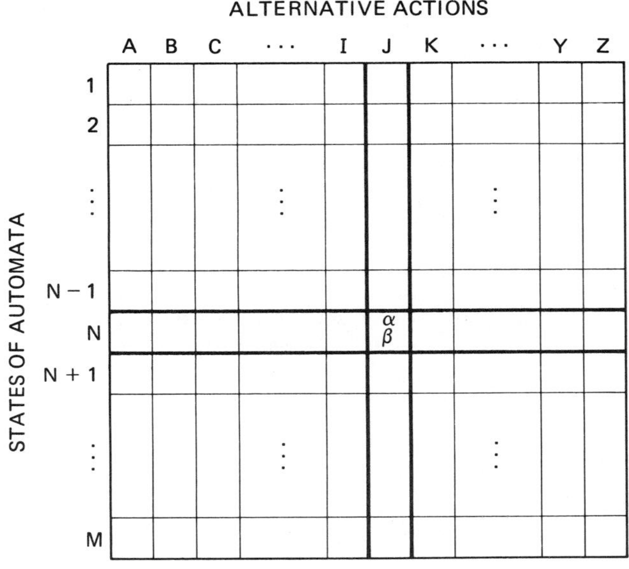

α = Next state if current state is N and alternative J occurs.
β = Subroutine name to process alternative J.

Figure 2.19 Finite state action table.

In order to execute such an algorithm, a variable is set to a certain state and the proper alternative determined from the external environment (e.g., read in data). The intersection of these entries in the decision matrix will define an action to be performed and a new state to enter.

There are many examples of finite state processes. A lexical scanner in a compiler is based upon this technique, where the current state is the type of token being read (e.g., name, number, operator) and the alternatives are the next characters to be read (e.g., letter or digit). The intersection defines the possible actions (e.g., add symbol to current token, terminate token, raise error condition). The arrays *INEXT*, *JNEXT*, and *NEWDIRECTION* in solution 2 of the maze problem of Chapter 3 is a variant of a finite state solution.

Finite state solutions are patterned after the mathematical model of a finite state automata. Chapter 5 contains a formal presentation of this model.

2.6.8 Storage Allocation

One class of searching strategy is the storage allocation problem, which is usually encountered in operating systems implementation, but may be applicable in many data dependent problems. If the amount of data to be processed by a program is unknown before execution begins, then a common approach is to allocate units of memory as they are needed.

Given a fixed area of storage, the problem is to allocate and free smaller areas within this larger area without running out of space. As storage gets allocated, small unused areas tend to appear. These areas are too small to be allocated, and hence the memory becomes *fragmented.* Techniques to reduce this fragmentation include the following:

1. *First fit.* Sequentially look through the area until the first area large enough to contain the allocation is found. All areas are kept on a linked list in address order (Figure 2.20). Search this list sequentially until an area large enough to contain the storage is found. The area is removed from the list, with any leftover area returned as a smaller available area at that point in the list.

This technique makes it very easy to free unneeded areas. The list is searched. Since it is in address order, the correct place to place the freed area is easily found. Since adjacent machine addresses are adjacent in the list, it is also possible to easily combine two smaller freed areas into one larger area.

This technique is probably the easiest to program; however, since it looks for only the first area to use, regardless of size, it may quickly lead to a fragmented memory.

2. *Best fit.* Sequentially look through all areas, choosing the smallest one greater than or equal to the desired allocation. In this case, the areas are linked together in size order rather than in order of machine addresses. The basic allocation-free algorithms are similar to the first-fit algorithms. However, in this case the allocation strategy leads to less fragmentation since the minimal size area to contain the new allocation is used. Unfortunately, since freed areas are not in order, the algorithm to combine two freed areas into a single larger area is more complex.

3. *Buddy system.* Areas are on N chains of size 2^N each. If no area of size 2^K is available, a free area of size 2^{K+1} is obtained and broken down into two areas of size 2^K. After being freed at a later times these two "buddies" will form two areas of size, 2^K, which can be collapsed into one area of size, 2^{K+1}.

Exercise 2.11: Implement these allocation strategies. Note that an important point in all of them is to be able to combine contiguous free areas into one larger free area.

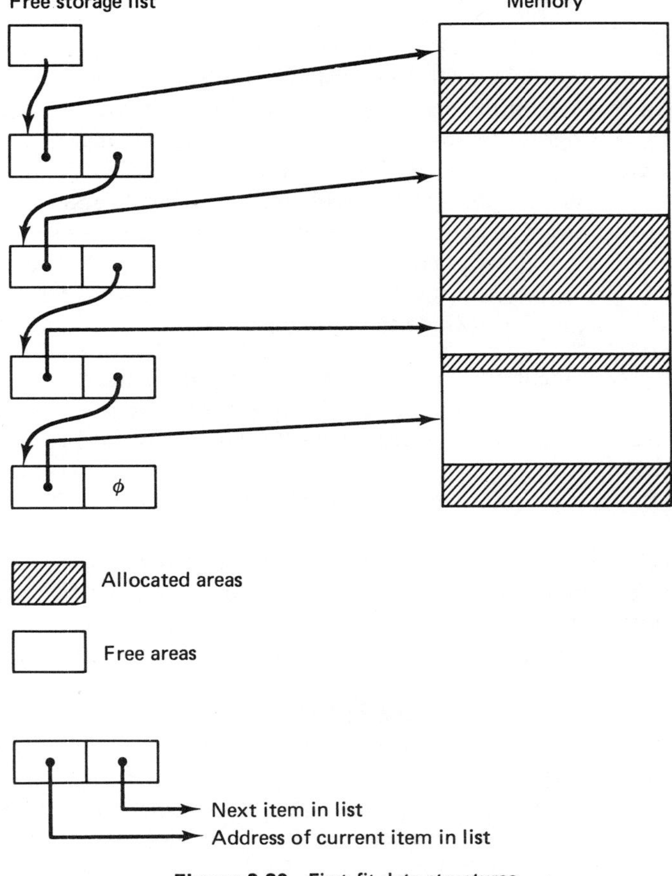

Figure 2.20 First-fit data structures.

Exercise 2.12: What is the advantage of the buddy system for storage allocation? If the area to contain all allocations begins at binary address 101000000, and there are 64 words available for allocation, what are the buddies for: 101000100, 101100000, 101101010? Give a simple algorithm for finding the address of a given area's "buddy."

2.6.9 Coroutines

In some applications, two or more tasks must be processed in segments, each progressing at different rates (Figure 2.21). In these cases, a simple subroutine structure is often insufficient. The use of a coroutine may sometimes be a more useful control structure.

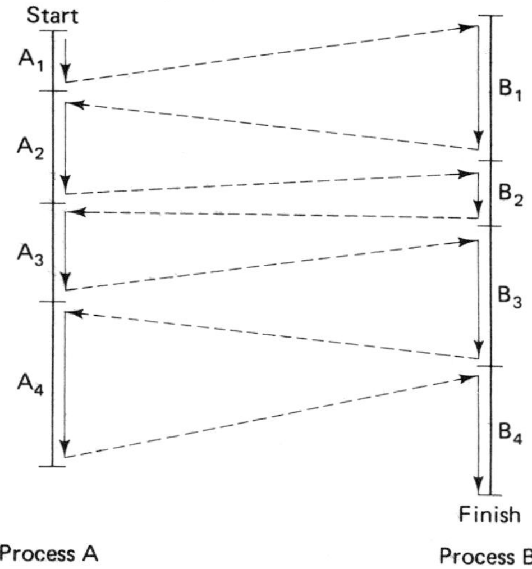

Figure 2.21 Coroutine execution.

A *coroutine* is a form of subroutine return that preserves the current location counter. When this subroutine is called again, execution resumes at this location rather than at the beginning of the subroutine. As an example, FORMAT specifications in PL/1 or FORTRAN are usually implemented as coroutines. In these cases, the language specifies for the execution of such an I/O statement:

```
do while (data items in I/O list);
        Let DV = next data value;
        Let FS = next format specification;
        call I/O_process (DV,FS);
        end;
```

The problem occurs since data values and format specifications are in separate lists and the number of items in each list can differ, as in:

```
PUT EDIT (A,B,C) (F(5), F(3));
```

In this case, the language specifies:

1. Terminate the I/O statement after the last data item is processed (and ignore any remaining format specifications).
2. If there are any remaining data items after processing the last format specification, repeat processing the entire list of format specifications.

Let us define a coroutine return to procedure X as:

resume X;

With this addition to our PDL, the PUT EDIT statement can then be described by the following code:

```
call DATA;
goto next_statement;
/* For data items */
DATA: procedure;
        declare FS, DV;
        DV = data value1;
        resume FORMAT(FS);
        call I/O_process (DV, FS);
        DV = data value2;
        resume FORMAT(FS);
        call I/O_process(DV, FS);
        . . .
        DV = data valuen;
        resume FORMAT(FS);
        call I/O_process(DV, FS);
        end DATA;

/* For FORMAT specifications */
FORMAT: procedure(FS);
        LOOP: FS = format specification1;
              resume DATA(FS);
              FS = format specification2;
              resume DATA(FS);
              . . .
              FS = format specificationk;
              resume DATA(FS);
              goto LOOP;
              end FORMAT;
next_statement: . . .
```

Note that one added benefit to this structure is that each coroutine can be considered to be the caller of the other. Thus the data routine calls the format processor for the next format item, while the format routine calls the data routine to process the next data item. This often increases understanding of some processes.

Unfortunately, coroutines do not exist in any commonly used programming language. The FORMAT procedure above can be simulated in PL/1 as a **case** statement (or a set of nested **if** statements):

```
FORMAT: procedure (FS);
        declare RESUME STATIC INITIAL(1);
        do case (RESUME);
           \1\ do; FS = format specification1;
                   RESUME = 2;
                   end;
           \2\     do;
                   FS = format specification2;
                   RESUME = 3;
                   end;
           . . .
           \k\     do;
                   FS = format specificationk;
                   RESUME = 1;
                   end;
           end    /* case */
           return;
           end FORMAT;
```

3 Examples of Program Design

In Chapters 1 and 2 literally dozens of techniques, methods, and ideas were presented describing ways of producing better software systems. By this time, some may get the impression that software design has been reduced to a trivial mechanical process. This motion has even been found in industry, where some programmers have resisted such notions as structured programming, claiming that such formal rules restrict creativity and lead to "assembly-line" programming.

Nothing could be further from the truth. The notion that good software development techniques restrict creativity is like saying an artist can paint without learning the details of form and a musician does not need knowledge of music theory. While it is true that a few geniuses do survive without such training, the vast majority need and appreciate the formal training that they receive.

The development of software proceeds along similar lines. While structured programming and top-down design do lead to better systems, the basic ideas of how to begin and what the eventual system will look like are still the products of a creative mind. Thus, even if everyone were taught good design techniques, some would develop into expert designers while others would struggle along, much like anyone can learn to play (somewhat) a musical instrument, but only a few can create new musical pieces.

In order to develop a design, it has been observed that most programming can be broken down into a few basic techniques. Such concepts as recursive programming, backtracking, divide and conquer, and simulation are some of the basic design strategies behind most programs. If a given problem can be restated in terms of one of these techniques, then the initial creative guess of how to begin the design is much easier.

This, in short, is the purpose of this chapter. Several problems will be posed and solved several ways. Each solution will point out one or more aspects of a design technique. After reviewing all the designs, the reader should have an idea of how various design strategies proceed. In the final two chapters of this book, two larger projects—an operating system and a compiler—will be developed using many of the same techniques.

3.1 FIBONACCI SEQUENCE

Problem statement: The Nth Fibonacci number is defined recursively as:

$$F(N) = \begin{cases} 0 \text{ if } N = 0 \\ 1 \text{ if } N = 1 \\ F(N-1) + F(N-2) \text{ if } N > 1 \end{cases}$$

Compute the Nth Fibonacci number.

This problem has an obvious recursive solution. Here, we present two solutions, one recursive and one using dynamic programming, in order to contrast these two techniques. Several of the later designs will also make use of these techniques, although the recursive nature of the solution will not be as obvious.

3.1.1 Recursive Solution

Often we wish to calculate a quantity that is defined recursively. While this type of definition makes a recursive implementation particularly attractive because of its ease, the resulting implementation is not necessarily the most efficient one. The obvious recursive implementation of a program to compute the Nth Fibonacci number first computes the $(N-1)$st and $(N-2)$nd Fibonacci numbers and then sums the two.

```
FIBONACCI:procedure(N) returns(FIXED BINARY) recursive;
  declare N FIXED BINARY;
  if N = 0
    then
       return(0);
```

```
        else
            if N = 1
                then
                    return(1);
                else
                    return(FIBONACCI(N-1)+FIBONACCI(N-2));
    end;
```

Note that this program is not totally correct! The input specifications are never checked, and there is the possibility of obtaining improper results using this function.

Exercise 3.1: What are the specifications for this program, and what will happen if input that does not meet these specifications is used?

3.1.2 Dynamic Programming Solution

Even though the recursive solution is often an obvious one, it is not always the best. The problem with it is that the smaller Fibonacci numbers are repeatedly computed each time we compute a larger Fibonacci number. In Figure 3.1, the procedure invocation FIBONACCI(N) causes FIBONACCI($N-1$) to be computed once, FIBONACCI($N-2$) twice, FIBONACCI($N-3$) three times, FIBONACCI($N-4$) four times, etc.

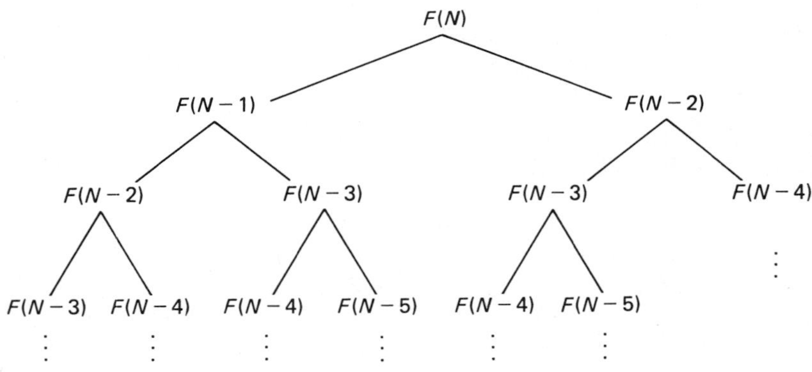

Figure 3.1 Procedure invocations to compute the Nth Fibonacci number.

Instead of recomputing the smaller Fibonacci numbers each time one is needed in the computation of a larger number, we can employ a solution based on dynamic programming. We compute the smaller Fibonacci numbers first and save the last two in a table (i.e., two temporary variables). In computing a larger Fibonacci number, we merely sum the values saved in our table and update the contents of the table.

```
FIBONACCI:procedure(N) returns(FIXED BINARY);
  declare (N,I,NEXT,OLD,NEW) FIXED BINARY;
  if N = 0
    then
       return(0);
    else do;
       /* Initialize FIB(0) and FIB(1) */
       OLD = 0;
       NEW = 1;
       NEXT = 1;
       do I = 1 to N;
          /* FIB(I) = FIB(I-1)+FIB(I-2) */
          NEXT = OLD + NEW;
          /* Save previous two values */
          OLD = NEW;
          NEW = NEXT;
          end;
       return(NEXT);
       end;
  end FIBONACCI;
```

Even though this solution is faster than the first solution, recursion is a powerful technique for solving problems. Many of the examples in this chapter use it.

3.2 SORT A LIST

Problem statement: Sort a sequence of $N (N > 0)$ integer values into ascending order.

As with the previous example, this is a straightforward example to show several design algorithms from Chapter 2. The two sort algorithms from Chapter 2 form the basis for the two solutions.

3.2.1 Exchange Sort

In using a divide-and-conquer strategy on a problem, we try to segment a problem until we find small enough parts to solve. We then combine our partial solutions into a single solution for the entire problem. Consider sorting. We could break our problem of size N into two pieces of sizes $N - 1$ and 1 respectively.

1. Find the smallest value in *First. .N*.
2. Swap the First and smallest values.

At this point, those values in the range 1. .*FIRST* are sorted and those in FIRST + 1. .N remain unsorted. If we now increment FIRST, we can again use the two pieces of our solution to solve the remaining problem of size *N* — 1. Repeating this process *N* times, we reach solutions to successively smaller problems until a solution for the entire problem is achieved. Thus, our solution has the form:

```
Obtain N and the N values;
do for each value in the range FIRST. .N;
   Find the smallest value in FIRST. .N;
   Swap FIRST and smallest values;
   Increment FIRST;
   end;
Print the sorted values;
```

We can refine all but the innermost abstractions to obtain:

```
/* Obtain N and the N values */
 get LIST(N);
 begin;
 declare A(N)  FIXED  BINARY;
 get LIST  (A);
     /* For each value in the range FIRST. .N */
     do FIRST  =  1 to N;
        Find the smallest value in FIRST. .N;
        Swap FIRST and smallest values;
        end;
     /* Print the sorted values */
     put SKIP  LIST(A);
     end;
```

One of the recommended procedures in Chapter 2 is to check all specifications as a stub is developed in order to find all errors. The major specification here is that *N* must be positive. We can check this condition by inserting an **if** statement before the **begin** block, as in:

```
if N>0            /* Check specification */
      then begin;
             /* Obtain N values */
             /* Sort list of values */
             end;
```

In order to find the smallest number in *FIRST. .N* and place it first, we can:

```
Assume that the first value is the smallest;
If any other value is smaller, make that the smallest;
```

Finding the smallest expands to:

```
/* Find the smallest value in FIRST. .N */
MIN = FIRST
do I = FIRST to N;
  if A(MIN) > A(I)
    then
      MIN = I;
  end;
```

and swapping it with the FIRST value is:

```
/* Swap the first and smallest values */
T = A(FIRST)
A(FIRST) = A(MIN);
A(MIN) = T;
```

We can now put the pieces together and insert the appropriate declarations to obtain:

```
SORT:PROCEDURE OPTIONS(MAIN);
DECLARE N FIXED BINARY;
GET LIST(N);
IF N > 0 /* Check specification */
  THEN BEGIN;
      DECLARE A(N) FIXED BINARY;
      DECLARE (MIN,T,I,FIRST) FIXED BINARY;
      GET LIST (A);
      /* For each value in the range FIRST. .N */
      DO FIRST = 1 TO N;
         /* Find the smallest value in FIRST. .N */
         MIN = FIRST;
         DO I = FIRST + 1 TO N;
            IF A(MIN) > A(I)
                THEN
                   MIN = I;
            END;
         /* Swap the first and smallest values */
         Y = A(FIRST);
         A(FIRST) = A(MIN);
         A(MIN) = T;
         END;
```

```
            /* Print the sorted values */
            PUT SKIP LIST(A);
            END;
      END;
```

Exercise 3.2: Why is a BEGIN block used in this solution instead of a DO group?

3.2.2 Merge Sort

Consider the cost of the first solution in terms of the number of comparisons made. In order to sort, we find the smallest value N times and put it in an appropriate place. The first time we do this we must consider all N values, which requires $N - 1$ comparisons. However on the next attempt, we can consider the first value to be sorted and restrict our attention to the remaining $N - 1$ values. We need to make $N - 2$ comparisons among our $N - 1$ items. On any pass through the remaining values, the values in the interval 1. .*FIRST*-1 are sorted and we seek the smallest value from among those values in *FIRST*. . *N*. Finally, $FIRST = N$ and we swap the last value with itself without any comparisons. Thus, the total number of comparisons is given by:

$$
\begin{aligned}
N-1 + N-2 + \ldots + N-N &= (N*N)-1-2- \ldots -N \\
&= N*N - N*(N+1)/2 \\
&= N*(N-1)/2
\end{aligned}
$$

The trouble with out first division of the problem is that the parts of our solution do not significantly reduce the number of values to be considered on each application of the solution. (That is, the problem is not well balanced. First we find the smallest value among N values, then the smallest among $N - 1$, etc.) Thus at each stage in reaching a solution, we work with almost all the values of the previous stage. We prefer to find a solution that reduces the size of the problem more quickly so that we need apply the solution less frequently and deal with fewer values. The quickest way to balance a problem is to divide it into two equal parts. In our second solution, we perform the following steps:

1. Sort the first $N/2$ values.
2. Sort the second $N/2$ values.
3. Merge two sorted sequences into one sorted sequence.

Steps (1) and (2) are just recursive solutions of the same problem. While the merge is the same size as our original problem, we shall see that merging is a simpler operation than sorting. Also we apply it to much smaller lists, handling all N values only once. If we restrict N to be a power of 2, we can divide a list of N values in half only $\log_2(N)$ times. After this many divisions, we have sequences of values of length 1 that are obviously sorted (i.e., the known trivial case required for a recursive solution). Thus, we must apply our solution at most $\log_2(N)$ times. Our solution has the form:

```
Obtain N and place the N values in A;
SORT:procedure(A,FIRST,SIZE) recursive;
   if SIZE > 1 /* Check for non-trivial case */
     then
        call SORT(A,FIRST,SIZE/2);
                     /* Sort first half */
        call SORT(A,FIRST+SIZE/2,SIZE/2)
                     /* Sort second half */
        call MERGE(A,FIRST,SIZE);
                     /* Merge two halves */
        end;
   end;
MERGE:procedure(A.FIRST,SIZE);
   MIDDLE = FIRST + SIZE/2;
               /* MIDDLE is start of second sorted list */
   LAST = FIRST + SIZE - 1;
   Combine A(FIRST..MIDDLE-1), A(MIDDLE..LAST) in A;
   end;
call SORT(A,1,N);
Print the sorted values in A;
```

Next we complete the design of merge. We must merge two sorted lists in adjacent locations of an array into a single sorted list in the same positions within the array. Merging is much easier than sorting because we need only consider two values, those at the head of each of our lists. We pick the smaller of these two values, remove it from its list and install it in some temporary storage, which we call B. Eventually one of the two lists becomes empty and we simply append the other list to the values we have already accumulated in B. Finally, we copy the sorted list in B back to our original array.

```
/* Combine A(FIRST..MIDDLE-1), A(MIDDLE..LAST) in A */
do while(FIRST ≤ MIDDLE -1 AND MIDDLE ≤ LAST);
   Pick the smaller of FIRST and MIDDLE and put in B;
   Reduce the appropriate interval;
   end;
Copy remaining values from A(FIRST..MIDDLE-1) to B;
Copy remaining values from A(MIDDLE..LAST) to B;
Copy B to A(FIRST..LAST);
```

The finished program, including the code to read in the values and check the specifications appears below:

```
SORTMERGE:PROCEDURE OPTIONS(MAIN);
 DECLARE N FIXED BINARY;
 GET LIST (N);
 IF N > 0         /* Check specification */
   THEN BEGIN;
        DECLARE A(N) FIXED BINARY;
        SORT:PROCEDURE(A,FIRST,SIZE) RECURSIVE;
            DECLARE A(*) FIXED BINARY;
            DECLARE (FIRST.SIZE) FIXED BINARY;
            IF SIZE > 1        /* Check for trivial case */
              THEN DO;
                  CALL SORT(A,FIRST,SIZE/2);
                                 /* Sort first half of A */
                  CALL SORT(A,FIRST+SIZE/2,SIZE/2);
                                 /* Sort second half of A */
                  CALL MERGE(A,FIRST,SIZE);
                                 /* Merge two halves of A */
                  END;
            END SORT;
        MERGE:PROCEDURE(A,FIRST,SIZE);
            DECLARE A(SIZE) FIXED BINARY;
            DECLARE (FIRST,SIZE) FIXED BINARY;
            DECLARE (FIRSTSTART,FIRSTEND) FIXED BINARY;
            DECLARE (MIDDLE,LAST,I) FIXED BINARY;
            DECLARE B(SIZE) FIXED BINARY;
            FIRSTSTART = FIRST;
            MIDDLE = FIRST + SIZE / 2;
                          /* MIDDLE is start of sorted list */
            FIRSTEND = MIDDLE - 1;
            LAST = FIRST + SIZE - 1;
            /* Combine A(FIRST..MIDDLE-1), */
                 /* A(MIDDLE..LAST) in A */
            /* DO WHILE(FIRST ≤ MIDDLE -1 & MIDDLE ≤ LAST) */
            /*    Pick the smaller of FIRST and MIDDLE and */
            /*          put in B; */
            /*    Reduce the appropriate interval */
            I = 1;
            DO WHILE (FIRSTSTART≤FIRSTEND & MIDDLE≤LAST);
               IF A(FIRSTSTART) < A(MIDDLE)
                  THEN DO;
                       B(I) = A(FIRSTSTART);
                       FIRSTSTART = FIRSTSTART + 1;
                       END;
```

```
                    ELSE DO;
                        B(I) = A(MIDDLE);
                        MIDDLE = MIDDLE + 1;
                        END;
                I = I + 1;
                END;
                /* Copy remaining value from A(FIRST..MIDDLE-1) */
                        /* to B */
            /* If interval is zero, loop executed 0 times */
            DO FIRSTSTART = FIRSTSTART TO FIRSTEND;
                B(I) = A(FIRSTSTART);
                I = I + 1;
                END;
            /* Copy remaining values from A(MIDDLE..LAST) */
                        /* to B */
            DO MIDDLE = MIDDLE TO LAST;
                B(I) = A(MIDDLE);
                I = I + 1;
                END;
            /* Copy B to A(FIRST..LAST) */
                FIRSTSTART = FIRST;
            DO I = 1 TO SIZE;
                A(FIRSTSTART) = B(I);
                FIRSTSTART = FIRSTSTART + 1;
                END;
            END MERGE;
        /* Driver program to read data and sort */
        GET LIST (A);
        CALL SORT(A,1,N);
        PUT SKIP LIST(A);
        END;
    END;
```

As explained in Chapter 2, the merge sort requires $N*\log_2(N)$ comparisons, which is significantly better than the approximately $N*N$ comparisons needed for solution 1. However, there is the cost of additional storage for the array B in procedure MERGE.

Exercise 3.3: These sorting techniques are based upon arbitrary data. Knowledge of the range of the data can be used to improve sorting times. Reprogram this sorting problem using the following algorithms:

1. Assume that the numbers to be sorted are in the range 1 to m. Create m *buckets*; each bucket can contain one number. In one pass through the data place the unsorted elements into their correct buckets. Concatenate the buckets.
2. In (1), if m is too large to create m independent buckets, then create k

buckets of size m/k. In one pass through the data create k smaller sorting problems.

3. In (2), assume each bucket holds only one item. Sort the data in one pass by placing each item in its probable final bucket, and adjust the list as items are added.

3.3 PARKING CARS PROBLEM

Problem statement: Assume that a certain city block is 20 car lengths long and the block is not marked with parking spaces. Cars can park randomly along the curb (see Figure 3.2). How many cars can be expected to fit on this block?

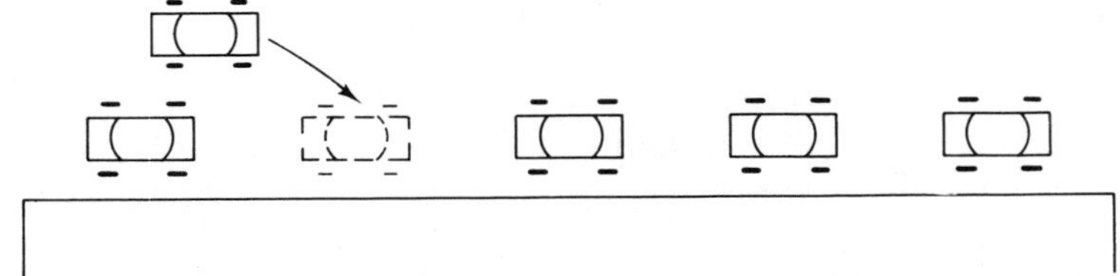

Figure 3.2 Parking problem.

On first inspection this problem seemingly has nothing to do with computer programming. Here is a case where an analysis of the requirements of the problem shows that the use of a computer will lead to a useful solution.

After studying the problem statement, we can see that the answer can range between a low of 10 and a maximum value of 20. The maximum will occur if each car is parked immediately behind the car in front (Figure 3.3). Similarly, the minimum number is 10 (Figure 3.4). The maximum space between any two cars is $1 - x$ for some $x > 0$. Thus each car uses up to $2 - x$ spaces. The actual answer will lie somewhere between these extremes.

While we can solve this problem analytically, let us not do so since this problem is representative of a large class of problems that do not have analytic solutions. Instead we will use simulation. In this case, the problem will be "executed" and the number of cars that are parked will be counted, giving us the answer.

One possible solution is to experiment with real cars and a city block.

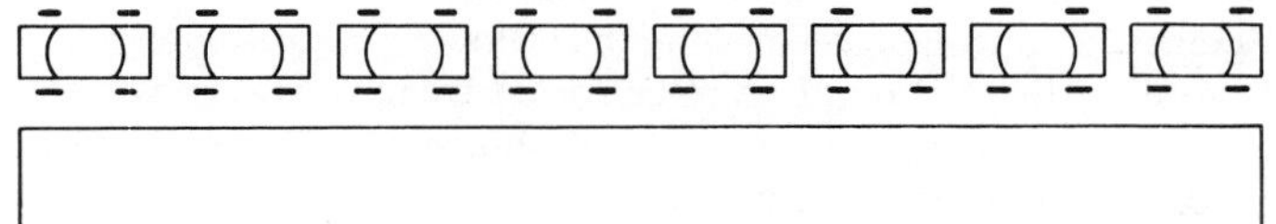

Figure 3.3 Maximal solution.

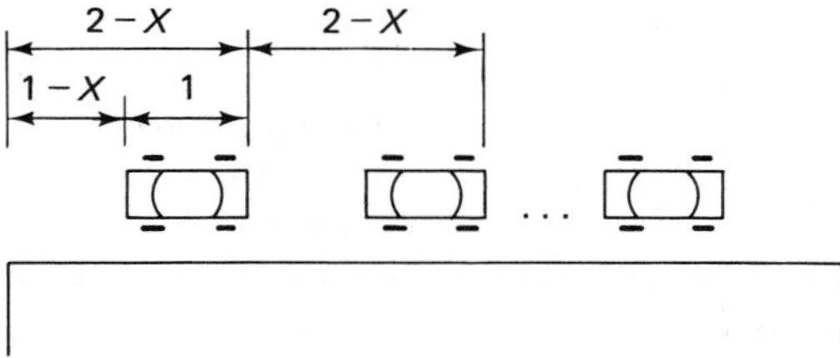

Figure 3.4 Minimal solution.

Find a block that matches the problem specifications and count the cars. Since the number may vary, it will be necessary repeat the experiment on different days and average the number of cars present over a period of time.

Unfortunately, this solution has two principal defects:

1. Only one data point is acquired each day, thus it will take many days to get an accurate solution.
2. In real life, cars are of varying lengths. If a full-sized station wagon does not fit into a space, a small compact might. Thus, there is no real-world situation that exactly matches the problem specifications.

Another possibility is to build a model of a city block and fixed-length cars and run the experiment. Since we have access to a computer, we will build a computer model of the problem and solve it.

By a *model*, we mean a representation of the problem such that some of the relationships between attributes in the real world are also true in the representation. In this case, the only aspects of the real world that we care about is where the cars are parked along the length of the block. Other aspects like color of car, weather conditions, width or height of car, etc., are irrelevant.

The length of the car is not important, only its relationship to the length of the block. Let us assume a length of 1 for each car and a length of 20 for the block. If we know where the front of a car is along a block, then we know the entire space occupied by the car. Thus, if a car begins at location A, then the following car must start at or after location $A + 1$.

3.3.1 Simulation Solution

At this point, several different computer solutions may come to mind. Let us first investigate an obvious one. Generate a point randomly between 0 and 20, and check if that is a valid place to park a car. If so, place the car at that point. Repeat the process as long as there remains a space of at least length 1 to contain a car.

In order to obtain random numbers, we will use what is called a *pseudorandom number generator*. It is a function that returns a sequence of numbers that have most of the properties of random numbers. While the sequence is actually well determined, it is sufficiently long as not to duplicate itself in any realistic computer run. Since the sequence is well determined, if two runs begin with the same number, then they will generate the same "random" sequence.

Most computer systems have random number generators as standard system subroutines, and most operate as follows. A single number is chosen as the starting point, called the *seed*. This is usually a real number in the range of 0 to 1. A statement of the form:

```
X = RANDOM (X)
```

is then executed. *X* will be reassigned as the next number in the sequence. Since the sequence is reproducible, the program can be rerun. In order to test the program with a different sequence, it is only necessary to start with a new seed.

In order to solve this problem, two different tasks must be solved. One is to keep track of where cars are parked and whether a new car will fit. The other task is to generate random numbers, try to park cars at these locations, and terminate the program at the appropriate time. This leads us to our first major design decision. We will separate the program into two sections, a main program to control the execution and an abstraction called PARKEDCARS to manage the cars.

In reading the problem statement, it appears as if the main procedure needs access to four functions about cars.

CANPARK(*X*). A function that determines whether a car can park at location *X*. The function returns true if the car can park, and false otherwise.

PARK(*X*). A procedure that parks a car at location *X*.

FINDMAX. A function that returns the maximum space available. Obviously, if the maximum space available is less than the length of a car, no more cars can be parked.

INITIALIZE. A procedure that initializes the block to no parked cars. This will be needed since we already know that the program will have to be rerun several times in order to get an average value.

With these procedures, the function SIMULATE, which returns the number of cars parked, can be written as the following top-level design:

```
SIMULATE: procedure returns (FIXED BINARY);
        Initialize block to no cars;
        do while (space for more cars);
                Find next car to park;
                Park it;
                end;
        Return count of cars parked;
        end SIMULATE;
```

This, in turn, can be expanded with the following code:

```
SIMULATE: PROCEDURE RETURNS (FIXED BINARY);
        DECLARE COUNT FIXED BINARY,
                LOCATION FLOAT; /* Random number */
        LOCATION = .5;  /* Initial seed */
        COUNT    = 0;
        /* Initialize block to no cars */
        CALL INITIALIZE;
        /* DO WHILE (space for more cars) */
        DO WHILE (FINDMAX ≥ 1);
                LOCATION = RANDOM (LOCATION);
                /* Find next car to park */
                DO WHILE (CANPARK (LOCATION) = FALSE);
                        LOCATION = RANDOM (LOCATION);
                        END;
                /* Park car */
                CALL PARK (LOCATION);
                COUNT = COUNT+1;
                END;
        /* Return count of cars parked */
        RETURN (COUNT);
        END;
```

In order to implement the PARKEDCARS abstraction, we need a mechanism to keep track of the cars of our model. Since the front of a car is a single point along the curb, an element of an array seems like a possible implementation. Therefore, we will keep, in increasing order, the set of all fronts of cars that are parked. An implementation of this model of cars is then the declarations:

```
declare BLOCKLENGTH INITIAL(20);
declare CARS(BLOCKLENGTH) FLOAT, /* Location of cars */
        NUMBERPARKED FIXED BINARY;
```

The four procedures that implement this abstraction can be developed as follows:

Initialize

This procedure eliminates all cars from the block, i.e., *NUMBERPARKED* is zero.

```
INITIALIZE: procedure;
    NUMBERPARKED = 0;
    end;
```

Canpark

CANPARK checks whether the current location is a valid parking space. Since the input parameter is a random number between 0 and 1 signifying the location, and since the array CARS is ordered by location, it is necessary to:

1. Scale the input parameter by *BLOCKLENGTH* so it is in the range *START* (i.e., 0) to *BLOCKLENGTH* and signifies the desired location.
2. Find the car before this location in *CARS* and the car after this location.
3. See if the new car fits between the two cars found.

There is one problem with this solution. What if the new location is not between any two cars such as when the new car is (1) before the first car on the block, (2) after the last car on the block, or (3) the first car to be parked. In these cases there may not be a preceding or a following car. While we can write code to incorporate all of these special cases, there is a technique that will make all of these cases seem regular so that no special checking need be done.

We know that the input parameter represents the front of a car located between *START* and *BLOCKLENGTH*. What if "phantom" cars were placed at each end point? Since *START* is the start of the block, a car at location *START*-1 will end at *START*, and since a car cannot go past the end of the block, let us "park" one at location *BLOCKLENGTH*. Thus, if cars are at *START*-1 and *BLOCKLENGTH*, and all new cars are in the range *START* to *BLOCKLENGTH*, the new car will always be between two cars. This eliminates the need for special cases in the code.

The easiest way to implement is to rewrite INITIALIZE. Note the use of the constants START and BLOCKLENGTH. These identifiers allow for more readable code, and allows us to change lengths simply by redefining these identifiers.

```
DECLARE CARS(START:BLOCKLENGTH+1) FLOAT,
            /* Leave room for two phantom cars */
        NUMBERPARKED  FIXED BINARY;
INITIALIZE:  PROCEDURE;
        CARS(START) = START-1;   /* Phantoms */
        CARS(START+1) = BLOCKLENGTH;
        NUMBERPARKED = 2;
        END;
```

With this change, CANPARK will have the following design:

```
CANPARK: procedure (X)  returns (BIT);
        declare X FLOAT, /* Random number input */
            LOCATION FLOAT, /* Car location */
            (PRECEDE, FOLLOW) FLOAT; /* Found cars */
        /* Scale input */
```

```
LOCATION = BLOCKLENGTH * X;
Find Preceding and following car;
     PRECEDE = preceding car;
     FOLLOW = following car;
if X fits between PRECEDE and FOLLOW
     then
        return(TRUE);
     else
        return(FALSE);
end;
```

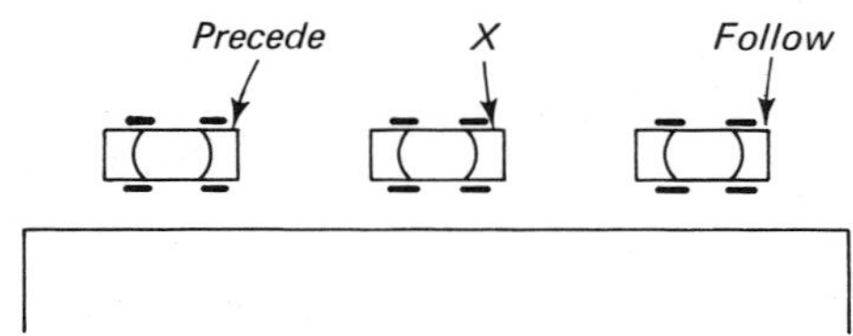

Figure 3.5 INSERT function.

The Find statement is simply a loop looking for the first location greater than LOCATION. By the previous discussion and our rewritten INITIALIZE, there must be one. The code is then:

```
I = START+1; /* No need to check first car */
do while (LOCATION > CARS(I) );
     I = I+1;
     end;
/* CARS(I) is now FOLLOW */
FOLLOW = CARS(I);
PRECEDE = CARS(I-1);
```

Exercise 3.4: Why is I initially $START + 1$ above?

The car at *LOCATION* will fit if it begins at least one unit after *PRECEDE* (to account for the length of the car at *PRECEDE*) and *FOLLOW* is at least one unit past *LOCATION* (to account for the new car's length). Thus, the **if** statement of CANPARK is simply:

```
if ((LOCATION-PRECEDE)≥1) &
   ((FOLLOW-LOCATION)≥1)
        then
           return(TRUE);
        else
           return(FALSE);
```

Park

Since CANPARK checks for the validity of a location, PARK simply inserts a car at the specified location. Thus, the code is:

```
PARK: procedure (X);
      declare (X, LOCATION) FLOAT;
      LOCATION = BLOCKLENGTH * X;   /* Scale input */
      Find preceding and following car;
      Insert car at LOCATION;
      end;
```

The Find statement is identical to the code in CANPARK and can be duplicated here. Alternatively, this common code could be made an internal subroutine for both CANPARK and PARK.

Assume that the variable *I* is the index of *FOLLOW* (as in CANPARK). The Insert statement is then:

```
MOVE CARS(I) through CARS(NUMBERPARKED)
      to CARS(I+1) through CARS(NUMBERPARKED+1);
CARS(I) = LOCATION;   /* New car */
NUMBERPARKED = NUMBERPARKED+1;
```

Findmax

FINDMAX finds the largest gap remaining between two consecutive cars. The code for this is just:

```
FINDMAX: PROCEDURE RETURNS (FLOAT);
      DECLARE (MAX,TEMP) FLOAT,
            I FIXED BINARY;
      MAX = 0;
      DO I = START+1 TO NUMBERPARKED;
            TEMP = CARS(I)-CARS(I-1)-1;
            IF TEMP > MAX
               THEN
                  MAX = TEMP;
            END;
      RETURN (MAX);
      END;
```

Exercise 3.5: Why was 1 subtracted from assignment to *TEMP*?

At this point, the design is almost complete. However, at the beginning of this section it was mentioned that the program would have to be run several times to get an average value. In order to do this, the following must be done:

1. A routine DRIVER must be written to repeatedly call SIMULATE and keep track of the returned values.

2. The initial random number in SIMULATE must be a parameter to the routine, and not coded as:

```
LOCATION = .5; /* Initial seed */
```

These changes will be left as exercises.

Exercise 3.6: Why must the random number be a parameter to SIMULATE?

After we make these changes, the program is almost ready to go, except for one thing: it will not work! The glaring defect is cleared up in the following solution; however, before reading it try to discover the problem yourself.

3.3.2 Corrected Simulation Solution

In order to solve the parking problem, we would like a solution that is both correct and efficient. Unfortunately, while the previous solution is correct, it is not efficient. If you have not discovered the problem yet, we will give a hint by stating that the problem is in the following loop in SIMULATE:

```
do while ( CANPARK (LOCATION) = FALSE );
    LOCATION = RANDOM (LOCATION);
    end;
```

The problem is that this loop may never terminate. As discussed in Section 2. 4. 2, all loops should be proven to terminate. This can be done by showing the following two facts:

1. Show that there is some property P that remains positive within the loop.

2. Show that this property P decreases by at least 1 for each iteration of the loop.

While the other two loops in solution 1 meet these conditions and hence must terminate, the above loop does not satisfy the criteria. The only other loop in SIMULATE begins with the statement:

```
do while (FINDMAX ≥ 1);
```

In this case, let property P be $FINDMAX$-1. If $FINDMAX \geq 1$, then $FINDMAX$-1 will be greater than or equal to 0. (The case where FINDMAX equals 0 does not alter this condition as long as condition 2 remains true.)

FINDMAX is the maximum space available between two adjacent cars. It is initially bounded by the length of the block. However, each iteration of the loop parks one more car, so this total available space drops by at least 1. In at most *BLOCKLENGTH* interations, *FINDMAX* is bounded by 0.

The only other loop is in the PARKEDCARS abstraction. This code is:

```
do while ( LOCATION > CARS(I) );
    I = I+1;
    end;
```

In this case. case, *LOCATION* is constant and bounded above by *BLOCKLENGTH*. The following properties are also true:

1. *LOCATION-CARS(I)* ≥ 0 for $I \geq$ *START* (which is property *P*).
2. *CARS(I)* increases by at least 1 as *I* increases. Thus, *LOCATION-CARS(I)* decreases by at least 1.

Exercise 3.7: Show that the above two statements are true, and prove that the loop must terminate.

However, now consider the initial **do while** in the procedure SIMULATE. In this case, the body of the loop is simply:

```
LOCATION = RANDOM (LOCATION);
```

and no property is necessarily decreasing. The physical phenomenon causing nontermination to which this corresponds is the case where only one more car remains to be parked between cars at locations X and $X + Y$. At this point, FINDMAX will return the value $1 + Y$ that is between 1 and 2. Only a car whose front is within the interval X and $X + Y$ can be parked. If Y is small, then the probability of generating a random number within that interval is also small.

For example, if FINDMAX is 1.1 (which gives a Y of .1), then the probability of generating a random number between X and $X + .1$ is $.1/20 = .005$, which translates into one random number in this interval every 200 executions of the loop. This case will occur about every 10 programs. Similarly, about once every 20 programs, Y will have a value of .05 and about 400 executions will be needed. Thus, while the loop will eventually terminate, if RANDOM really is a random number generator, the expected execution time gets quite large.

One simple way to correct this problem is to observe the following: if a distance between 1 and 2 remains between two parked cars, exactly one car can be parked there, irrespective of where the front of the car is placed.

One way to fix this is to add a function SMALLSPACE. After each car is parked, SMALLSPACE checks for the above condition and deletes those spaces, returning the number of spaces deleted. In SIMULATE, the update to the variable COUNT should be changed to:

```
COUNT = COUNT+1+SMALLSPACE;
```

SMALLSPACE would have the following design:

```
SMALLSPACE: procedure returns (FIXED BINARY);
    For all I such that
        2≤(CARS(I+1)-CARS(I)) &
        (CARS(I+1)-CARS(I))<3 do
        Park car at location CARS(I)+1;
    return (Number found);
    end;
```

With this change, FINDMAX will return a value of at least 2 if any space is available, so the minimum probability of generating a valid random number between X and $X+1$ is 1/20 or .05 (or approximately 20 executions of the loop). The detailed design of SMALLSPACE will be left as an exercise.

3.3.3 Efficient Simulation Solution

Solution 2, while better than solution 1, still has the property that the troublesome **do while** loop can execute an arbitrary number of times. The following changes to solution 1 eliminate this problem.

Rather than generating a random number signifying some arbitrary place on the block to park a car, generate the random number signifying some arbitrary place along all space available for parking. It turns out that this requires no change to SIMULATE and can be entirely implemented in the abstraction PARKEDCARS.

Since the random number signifies a location among the available spaces, there is never a car already at that location. This means that CANPARK should never fail and should always return true. (Alternatively, CANPARK can be deleted and the corresponding **do while** in SIMULATE eliminated.)

In PARK, compute the total length available for the front of a car, as in:

```
LENGTH = 0;
For all I in the interval such that
    2≤ (CARS(I+1)-CARS(I)) &
    (CARS(I+1)-CARS(I))<3 do
        LENGTH=LENGTH+(CARS(I+1)-CARS(I)-2);
```

LENGTH contains the total length available for fronts of cars. Park the car at the place represented by $X*LENGTH$, where X is the input random number. Figure 3.6 represents this solution. Note that when the first car is to be parked,

$$\begin{aligned} LENGTH &= CARS\,(START + 1) - CARS\,(START) - 2 \\ &= 20 - (-1) - 2 \\ &= 19 \end{aligned}$$

which says that the front of the first car must start somewhere between location 0 and location 19. The details of this design are left as exercises.

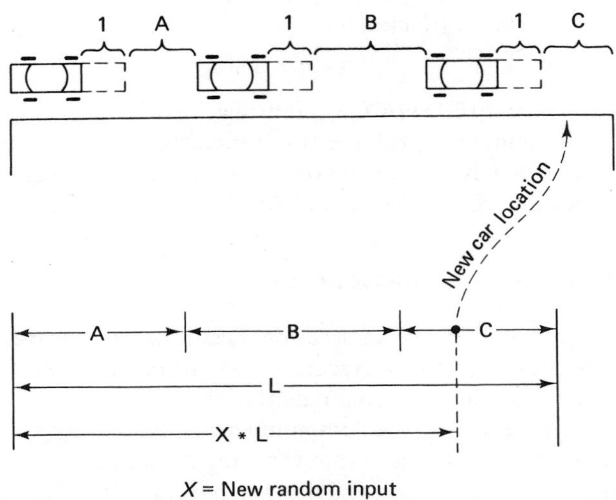

Figure 3.6 Efficient simulation solution.

Exercise 3.8: Redesign this solution using a linked list structure to represent the parked cars. For example, cars can be represented by the following structure:

```
declare 1 CARS,
          2 LOCATION FLOAT, /* Start of car */
          2 NEXTCAR; /* Pointer to following car */
```

3.3.4 Recursive Solution

For this final solution to the parking problem, let us try a totally different approach. It may be apparent that the problem has the following property: if any car is parked, that car divides the remaining space into two pieces. From then on, each piece is independent of the other. We can consider each interval as a separate problem. In this way a general algorithm could be:

```
Park first car;
Solve parking problem for space left of car;
Solve parking problem for space right of car;
return (left solution+right solution+1);
```

This is an example of a divide-and-conquer strategy resulting in a recursive solution. The more complex problem is solved by solving two simpler problems. If the length should be less than 1, then the solution is trivial, namely 0.

In order to give this solution, assume that X is a random variable and global to the procedure to park cars. In addition, the procedure needs two parameters, a left location and a right location, delineating the length of the block. With these specifications, the program can be written down almost directly:

```
PARKING:  PROCEDURE (LEFT,RIGHT)
                  RECURSIVE RETURNS (FIXED BINARY);
          DECLARE (Y,LEFT,RIGHT) FLOAT;
          /* Park cars in interval LEFT..RIGHT */
          IF RIGHT-LEFT<1
                  THEN RETURN (0);  /* Trivial case */
          X = RANDOM (X);  /* New location */
          Y = LEFT+(RIGHT-1-LEFT)*X;
                  /* Y to Y+1 is car location */
          RETURN(PARKING(LEFT,Y)+
                      PARKING(Y+1,RIGHT)+1);
          END;
```

Exercise 3.9: Explain assignment to Y in above solution.

This recursive solution can be called via a driver as in:

```
DRIVER:  PROCEDURE;
       DECLARE X FLOAT;
       X = .2;  /* Initial seed */
       NUMBERPARKED = PARKING (START,BLOCKLENGTH);
       ...
       END;
```

As in solutions 1, 2, and 3, the design must be modified for computing an average value.

These solutions were all coded and tested in PL/1; solution 4 had a much lower execution time than solution 3. As the following exercise demonstrates, unlike the Fibonacci example, here is a case where a recursive solution actually results in a much more efficient solution.

Exercise 3.10: If a given test run of solution 3 and solution 4 both result in 14 cars being parked, how many procedure calls are executed by the two programs? Does this explain why solution 4 is the fastest? What about for solutions 1 and 2?

3.4 COIN-CHANGING PROBLEM

Problem statement: Find the minimum number of coins whose values sum to a desired amount of change. There is an unlimited number of coins in each of N different denominations. The input to the program will be a list of numbers, the first of which is the amount of change desired, the second is the number of different denominations of coins, and the remainder are the values of each denomination.

Since the program requires the values of the coins to be read in as data, we can use an array V to store this information with $V(1)$ containing the smallest demonination, and $V(N)$ the largest.

3.4.1 Recursive Solution

Before solving the general problem, let us solve a simpler one. Assume that the denominations for the coins are the standard United States denominations of 1, 5, 10, 25, and 50. In this case an obvious algorithm is:

```
Choose as many of the coins of denomination 50 as possible;
From the remainder, choose as many coins of denomination 25;
. . .
From the remainder, choose as many coins of denomination 1;
```

This easily generalizes to:

```
declare V(5) INIT(1, 5, 10, 25, 50);
do I = 5 to 1 by -1;
    Choose as many coins of denomination V(I) as possible;
    end;
```

Unfortunately, intuition fails us if we try to generalize this solution to coins of arbitrary values. For example, if our coins have denominations 1, 5, 10, 25, 50, the minimum number of coins totalling 40 is three (one 25, one 10, and one 5). However, using the same algorithm and adding coins of value 20, we would still get the same answer although two 20s also total 40.

In designing an algorithm to solve this problem, we consider how many coins of the *J*th denomination should be included in the change. The possibilities include 0, 1, . . . , *CHANGE*/*V*(*J*), where *V*(*J*) is the value of the *J*th denomination and "/" represents integer division. If we decide to use *I* coins of value *V*(*J*), then we must still find coins for the remainder of the change:

$$CHANGE - I * V(J)$$

from among the coins of the remaining values. Thus we would like to minimize the following quantity:

$$(I + \text{coins for } (CHANGE - I * V(J))) \text{ for all } I,\ 0 \leq I \leq CHANGE/V(J)$$

Since *CHANGE-I∗V*(*J*) is less than *CHANGE*, we have another example of a recursive solution. If we again start with the coins of the largest (*N*th) denomination, we can state our problem recursively:

$$\text{Coins}(N,CHANGE) = \begin{cases} \min(I + \text{Coins}(N-1,CHANGE-I*V(N)) & \text{if } N > 1 \\ CHANGE/V(1) & \text{if } N = 1 \end{cases}$$

This solution is easily written in the form of a recursive function.

```
COINS:procedure(N,CHANGE) recursive returns(FIXED BINARY);
  if N = 1
    then
      return(CHANGE/V(1));
    else do;
      do I = 0 to CHANGE/V(N); /* I=0 is possible */
        MIN_NUMBER = min(I + COINS(N-1,CHANGE-I*V(N)))
                        for all I;
        end;
      return(MIN_NUMBER);
      end;
    end COINS;
```

As with the earlier sort program, we will construct this minimum value by first setting the minimum value to the first element; and if any other element is smaller, we will replace it as the minimum. Therefore the inner abstract instruction is expanded to:

```
MIN_NUMBER = COINS(N-1,CHANGE); /* I=0 case */
do I = 1 to CHANGE/V(N);
  MIN_NUMBER = MIN(MIN_NUMBER,I+COINS(N-1,CHANGE-I*V(N)));
  end;
```

If we define the function MIN and add some initialization code to obtain the values of *CHANGE* and the *V*(*i*)'s, we obtain the following program.

```
MAKECHANGE:PROCEDURE OPTIONS(MAIN);
DECLARE (N,CHANGE) FIXED BINARY;
GET LIST(CHANGE,N);
BEGIN;
   DECLARE V(N) FIXED BINARY;
   DECLARE I FIXED BINARY;
   COINS:PROCEDURE(N,CHANGE) RECURSIVE RETURNS(FIXED BINARY);
      DECLARE (N,CHANGE,MIN_NUMBER,I) FIXED BINARY;
      MIN:PROCEDURE(A,B) RETURNS(FIXED BINARY);
          DECLARE (A,B) FIXED BINARY;
          IF A < B
             THEN
                RETURN(A);
             ELSE
                RETURN(B);
          END;
      IF N = 1
         THEN
            RETURN(CHANGE/V(1));
         ELSE DO;
            /* DO I = 0 TO CHANGE/V (N)
                  MIN_NUMBER=MIN(I+COINS(N-1,CHANGE-I*V(N)))*/
            MIN_NUMBER = COINS(N-1,CHANGE); /* I=0 case */
            DO I = 1 TO CHANGE/V(N);
                MIN_NUMBER =
                    MIN(MIN_NUMBER,I+COINS(N-1,CHANGE-I*V(N)));
                END;
            RETURN(MIN_NUMBER);
         END;
      END COINS;
   /* Get N denominations */
   DO I = I TO N;
       GET LIST(V(I));
       END;
   PUT SKIP LIST(COINS(N,CHANGE));
   END;
END MAKECHANGE;
```

We are still not through with this problem, since we have assumed the fact that a solution always exists. For example, the recursive relationship assumes that *CHANGE*/*V*(*N*) has a solution for *N* equal to 1. We can fix this up by returning a value of infinity so that another solution will be the minimum. Thus the statement:

```
if N = 1
    then return(CHANGE/V(1));
```

must be altered to:

1. Return *CHANGE*/*V*(1) if *V*(1) divides *CHANGE*
2. Return infinity otherwise

As was the case with the recursive algorithm to compute Fibonacci numbers, the change-making algorithm repeatedly computes intermediate results. Invoking the program to find the minimum number of coins from among the four denominations—1, 5, 10, 20—for a total change of 20 results in the computation shown in Figure 3.7. Note that the calls (1, 10) and (1, 5) are made twice to compute the minimum number of coins of the first denomination necessary to reach the total changes for 10 and 5 respectively.

Exercise 3.11: The above solution still assumes that some solution exists even though we have taken care of the case when CHANGE is not divisible by *V*(1). Modify the program to also print out "No solution exists" if change is not possible (e.g., change for 10 with coins of value 3 and 8).

Exercise 3.12: Under what conditions for the denominations will the "obvious algorithm" mentioned in this section always generate the minimal solution?

Exercise 3.13: Give an example where MAKECHANGE, as described, gives the incorrect answer.

3.4.2 Dynamic Programming Solution

As in the Fibonacci series, dynamic programming can be used to simplify the solution. Wright [75] has proposed such a solution. Rather than repeating the computations of smaller amounts of change, we start by computing the minimum number of coins for the smaller amounts of change until we reach the desired amount.

```
do I = 1 to CHANGE_WANTED;
    Compute the minimum number of coins for CHANGE = I
    end;
```

If we save the minimum number of coins needed for each amount of change from 0 through $I - 1$ in the array *COINS*, then we can compute the minimum number of coins for *CHANGE*=*I* by selecting the smallest number from among:

$$COINS(I-V(1))+1,\ COINS(I-V(2))+1, \ldots, COINS(I-V(N))+1$$

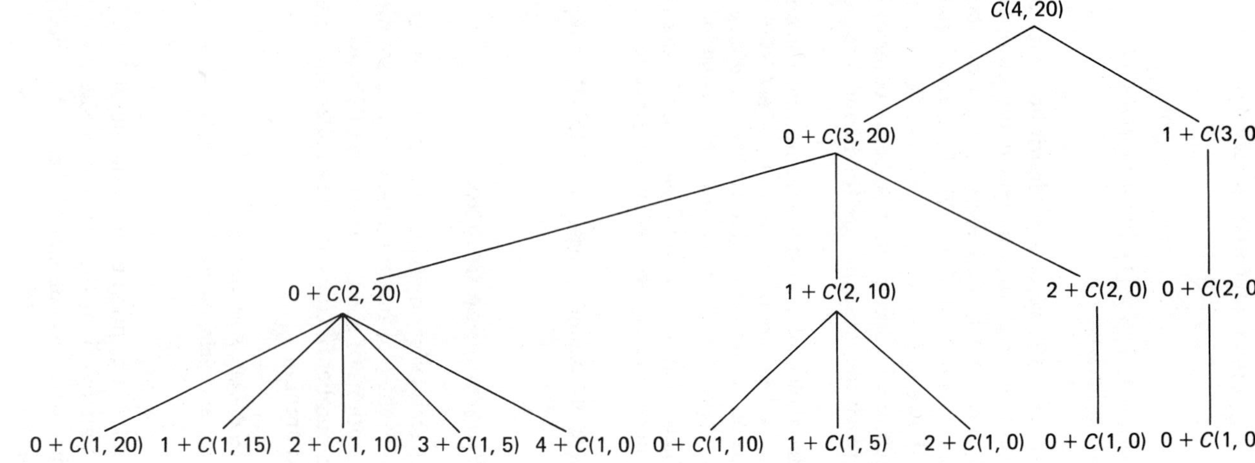

Figure 3.7 Procedure invocations to compute *CHANGE*=20 with four denominations.

where N is the number of different denominations. Obviously the quantity $I - V(J)$ for $1 \leq J \leq N$ must be positive for this computation to occur.

```
/* Compute the minimum number of coins for CHANGE = I */
COINS(I) = 99999;  /* Arbitrary initial value */
  do J = 1 to N;
    if I - V(J) ≥ 0
      then
         COINS(I) = MIN(COINS(I),COINS(I-V(J))+1);
    end;
```

If we again add a definition for MIN and the proper initialization code, we obtain the following solution.

```
MAKECHANGE:PROCEDURE OPTIONS(MAIN);
DECLARE (N,CHANGE) FIXED BINARY;
GET LIST(CHANGE,N);
BEGIN;
  MIN:PROCEDURE(A,B) RETURNS(FIXED BINARY);
      DECLARE (A,B) FIXED BINARY;
      IF A < B
         THEN
            RETURN(A);
         ELSE
            RETURN(B);
      END;
  DECLARE V(N) FIXED BINARY;
  DECLARE COINS(0:CHANGE) FIXED BINARY;
  DECLARE (I,J) FIXED BINARY;
  /* Get N denominations */
  DO I = 1 TO N;
      GET LIST(V(I));
      END;
  COINS(0) = 0;
  DO I = 1 TO CHANGE;
  /* Compute the minimum number of coins for CHANGE = I */
     COINS(I) = 99999;
     DO J = 1 TO N;
        IF I - V(J) ≥ 0
           THEN
              COINS(I) = MIN(COINS(I),COINS(I-V(J))+1);
        END;
     END;
  PUT SKIP LIST(COINS(CHANGE));
  END;
END MAKECHANGE;
```

Now the computation of the minimum number of coins whose values total 20 proceeds as follows:

```
COINS(0)  = 0
COINS(1)  = MIN(99999, COINS(1-1)+1)
COINS(2)  = MIN(99999, COINS(2-1)+1)
   .
   .
   .
COINS(10)  = MIN(99999, COINS(10-1)+1, COINS(10-5)+1,
                 COINS(10-10)+1)
   .
   .
   .
COINS(20)  = MIN(99999, COINS(20-1)+1, COINS(20-5)+1,
                 COINS(20-10)+1, COINS(20-20)+1)
```

Exercise 3.14: Explain how this solution avoids the problem encountered with the previous solution. What if you wanted the change from 99999? Will the program work?

3.5 PATH THROUGH A MAZE

Problem statement: Write a program to find a path through a maze. A maze consists of a rectangular array of cells colored white and black, and has designated entrance and exit cells. Movement from one white cell to an adjacent (horizontally or vertically) white cell is permitted.

The mazes that we are considering are represented by the example in Figure 3.8. For simplicity we assume that all mazes are entered from the upper left corner but may be exited from any location. We leave it as an exercise to modify the program to enter at any cell in the maze.

Mazes typically have multiple paths from the entrance cell, with all but one of them terminating in a dead end. The problem is to find the one path that successfully reaches the exit. Since the basic problem is to search for a solution among several alternatives, two fundamental search strategies, a breadth-first search and a depth-first search, are presented as two different solutions to this problem.

3.5.1 Breadth-first Search Solution

In order to solve this problem, it is first necessary to describe a data structure to represent a maze. We will use a straightforward representation.

If we number each cell of a maze from left to right and from top to bottom, we can let an array *MAZE* represent each white and black cell.

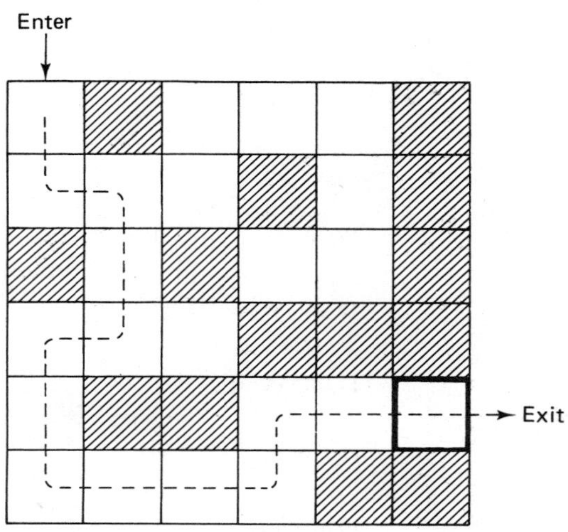

Figure 3.8 Sample maze.

$MAZE(I, J)$ will be given the following values:

- -1 if cell (I, J) is the exit cell
- 0 for all other white cells
- $+1$ for all black cells

The problem reduces to finding a path from $MAZE(1, 1)$ through cell values equal to 0 until the cell value of -1 is found.

An approach towards finding a solution is greatly helped by the following observation: If each white cell is assumed to be connected to its white neighbors by a flexible string, and the maze is lifted via its entrance cell, the maze will fall into a tree structure and a solution will be a path from the entrance node at the root of the tree to the exit node (which may or may not be a leaf node) (Figure 3.9). For this first solution, a breadth-first search will be used.

Conversion of a maze into a tree has several problems which must be considered. In one case, there may be two or more unconnected trees resulting from this operation (e.g., a forest). For example, in Figure 3.8, this would occur if cell (1, 4) were black instead of white. In this case, only the tree containing the root node need be considered since there would not be any way to get to one of the unconnected trees from the entrance cell of the maze.

Two other problems, however, cannot be dismissed so easily. There may be multiple paths to the exit cell, such as if cell (4, 5) in Figure 3.8 were white instead of black. This signifies that the maze has a loop and that the tree is really an undirected graph. Finally there may not even be a path to the exit

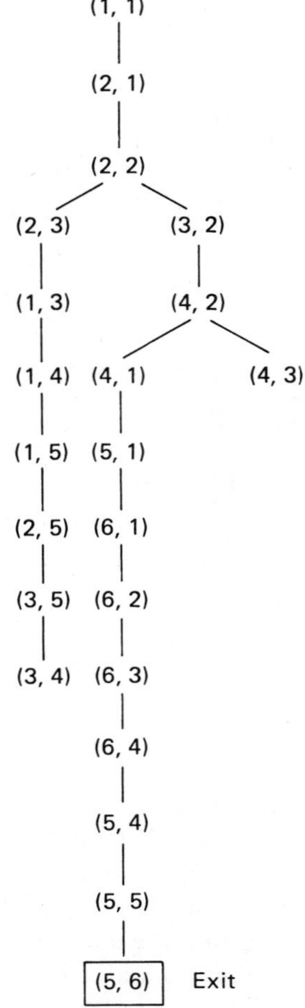

Figure 3.9 Tree structure of maze of Figure 3.8.

node, such as if cell (6, 3) were black in Figure 3.8. Both of these conditions will have to be considered in generating a valid solution to this problem.

The basic breadth-first search examines the tree one level at a time looking for a solution. Using Figure 3.8 as an example, the algorithm first checks whether (1, 1) is a solution. If not, (2, 1) is checked, etc. There may be several possible solutions at the same time. For example, at level 4 both (2, 3) and (3, 2) need to be checked as possible solutions. The maximum number of pending solutions will be three at level 6: (1, 4), (4, 1), and (4, 3).

This fact can also be represented by the maze of Figure 3.10. The number in each white cell represents the number of moves necessary to reach that cell

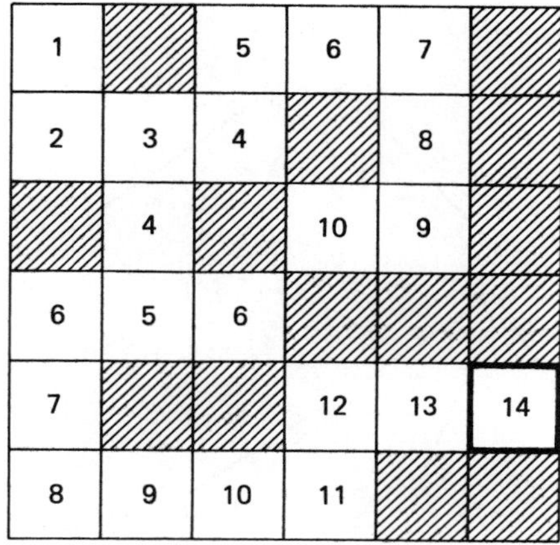

Figure 3.10 Number of moves to reach each cell of maze.

from the entrance cell. Our solution will consist of entering cells in this sequence. We will do this by creating a set *A*1 consisting of the entrance node (1, 1). From *A*1, set *A*2 will be created consisting of all nodes reachable from nodes in *A*1 by one move. Set *A*3 is constructed from nodes in *A*2, etc. This process is continued until the exit node is placed in some *Ai* (signifying a path from (1, 1)), or until it is apparent that there is no solution.

As the algorithm proceeds, however, only two sets are ever in use at any one time. We will call these sets *A* and *B*. Nodes will be taken from set *A*, and all nodes reachable from these nodes will be placed into set *B*. If a solution is not found, then the *B* nodes are copied into *A*, and the process is repeated.

This means that we need information about nodes in a tree. In one such representation, knowledge about a node's father node, left son node, and right brother node is sufficient for recreating the entire tree (Figure 3.11) [Knuth, 68]. We will use this and assume that a data structure called NODE exists for storing the information (Figure 3.12). Once the exit node is reached, it is only necessary to follow the father pointers back to the entrance node in order to determine the path through the maze.

A possible data structure for *NODE* can be the following:

```
declare 1 NODE,
          2 CELLINDEX,
            3 I,             /* Vertical location */
            3 J,             /* Horizontal location */
          2 SON,
          2 BROTHER,
          2 FATHER;
```

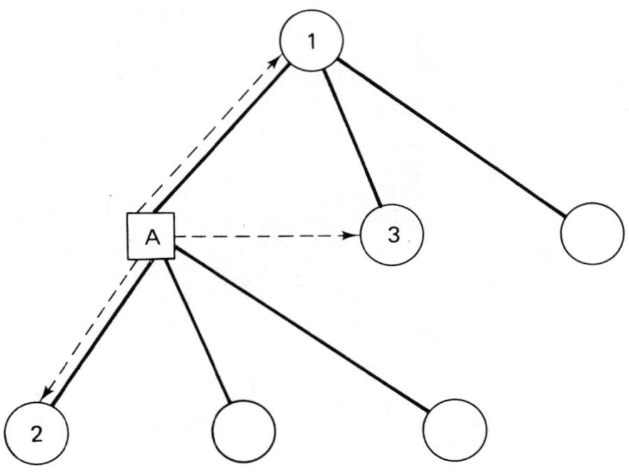

Node 1 = father
Node 2 = left son
Node 3 = right brother

Figure 3.11 Data structures to store tree (e.g., node A in this figure).

NODE INDICES (I, J)	LEFT SON	RIGHT BROTHER	FATHER

Figure 3.12 Data structure representation of a tree.

A utility routine will be needed to locate space for each node and return a pointer to this space, as in:

```
GETNODE: procedure(PTR);
        declare PTR; /* Next node allocated */
        Find location for node to be allocated;
        PTR = node address;
        end GETNODE;
```

For this implementation, *NODE* may be either a large array with *PTR* the index into the array, as in:

```
declare 1 NODE(NUMBER_NODES),
        . . .
```

or *NODE* can be a BASED variable that is allocated when needed and *PTR* is a pointer variable pointing to it as in:

```
declare 1 NODE BASED(PTR),
        . . .
```

Either solution is satisfactory, although the former requires prior knowledge about the number of nodes ultimately needed. For ease in describing this design, the first model for *NODE* will be assumed.

From this discussion, we can write a top-level PDL for this solution as follows:

```
MAZE1 : procedure;
        declare MAZE(M,N);
        declare (A,B) SET OF NODES;
        Initialize MAZE;
        CALL GETNODE(PTR);
        Set NODE(PTR) = (1,1); /* Initial entrance node */
        A = {(1,1)};
        do while(not finished);
                do for all L in A;   /* Create B from A */
                      do for each K = cell reachable from L;
                         call GETNODE(PTR);    /* Save K in set B */
                         Link NODE(PTR) to L;
                         Put NODE(PTR) in B;
                         if K is exit then call FINISHUP; /* Done */
                         end;
                      end;   /* Of transfer of A to B */
                A = B; /* If here, no solution, try next level */
                end;
        end MAZE1;
```

In order to expand this solution, a data structure for a SET OF NODES is needed. Since sets contain NODEs and NODEs are indexed, a set could simply be an array of indexes with a count of the number of elements in it. The SET declarations then expand to:

```
declare 1 A,   /* SET A */
          2 NUMBER INIT(0),
          2 ELEMENT(ELEMENTS_PER_SET);
declare 1 B,   /* SET B */
          2 NUMBER INIT(0),
          2 ELEMENT(ELEMENTS_PER_SET);
```

We are making the implicit assumption that there are never more than ELEMENTS_PER_SET pending nodes for any possible solution. Thus sets *A* and *B* have at most ELEMENTS_PER_SET elements in them.

Exercise 3.15: How can you modify the design to allow sets *A* and *B* to grow arbitrarily large?

In order to execute:

```
Initialize MAZE;
```

it is necessary to read in the input maze. One possible solution is to read in only the white boxes with the exit node last, as in:

```
MAZE = 1;   /* Assume all black boxes */
I = 1; J = 1;   /* Set initial value */
do while (MAZE(I,J) ≠ -1); /* Quit on exit node */
      get LIST(I, J, MAZE(I,J));
      end;
```

Exercise 3.16: The GET statement above assumes that all input data is correct. What are the actual specifications on the data? How can the loop be written to check for these specifications?

In order to expand:

```
Set NODE(PTR) = (1,1);
```

the code is:

```
NODE(PTR).I = 1;
NODE(PTR).J = 1;
NODE(PTR).SON = 0;
NODE(PTR).FATHER = 0;
NODE(PTR).BROTHER = 0;
```

The expansion of

```
A = {(1,1)};
```

is just:

```
A.NUMBER = 1;
A.ELEMENT(1) = PTR;
```

The first major complexity occurs with the expansion of the statement:

```
do while (not finished);
      . . .
      end;
```

We have to consider what finishing means. If there is a solution, then FINISHUP is called, and it will terminate the program. Thus a means is needed to terminate the program if no solution is found.

If there are no loops in the maze, then set A will eventually be empty since all paths will eventually become dead ends. Thus a possibility for the **do** statement is:

```
do while (A not empty);
```

which expands to:

```
do while(A.NUMBER≠0);
```

However, if there are loops in the graph, then *A* will never be empty, since an unending path will always be found.

A way to avoid this is to prevent all loops. In considering nodes for possible inclusion into set *B*, it is not necessary to consider any nodes that have already been visited before since that would mean that there already is a shorter path to that node. We can test for this condition by having an auxiliary array giving this information. We therefore add at the beginning of the program:

```
declare REACHED(M,N) BIT(1);
REACHED = FALSE; /* No nodes reached yet */
REACHED(1,1) = TRUE; /* Entrance node reached */
```

If we update *REACHED*, then the **do while** ($A.NUMBER \neq 0$) will terminate since loops will not be processed.

```
do for all L in A;
```

can be expanded to:

```
do L = 1 to A.NUMBER; /* Each element of A */
   I = NODE(L).I;
   J = NODE(L).J; /* (I,J) is current cell location */
```

The statement:

```
do for all K = cell reachable from L;
```

is more complex. We already know that *MAZE(I,J)* is white. For possible *K*'s, we must consider all adjacent squares at locations $(I-1, J)$, $(I+1, J)$, $(I, J-1)$, $(I, J+1)$. All of these with unreached white entries (or values of 0 in *MAZE*) are valid *K*'s to be added to set *B*.

Exercise 3.17: Why is *MAZE(I, J)* equal to 0 at this point?

Exercise 3.18: What if *I* is equal to 1? In this case $MAZE(I-1, J)$ is a bounds error. How can *MAZE* be declared and initialized to avoid either this problem or the need for special cases to be placed in the code to account for traveling along the border of the maze?

Assume that a valid *K* is at cell (*I*', *J*'). Then the code:

```
Link NODE(PTR) to L;
```

is:

```
/* PTR is address of new node */
/* L is address of father node */
NODE(PTR).I = I';
NODE(PTR).J = J';
NODE PTR).FATHER = L;
NODE(PTR).SON = NULL; /* No sons yet */
NODE(PTR).BROTHER = NODE(L).SON; /* See Exercise 3.19 below */
NODE(L).SON = PTR;
REACHED(I',J')=TRUE;
```

Exercise 3.19: The statement *NODE(PTR).BROTHER* = *NODE(L).SON* requires some explanation. This has the effect:

1. If *PTR* represents the first node reachable from *L*, *NODE(PTR). BROTHER* will be NULL (e.g., no right brother).

2. If *PTR* is not the first node reachable from *L*, *NODE(PTR). BROTHER* will point to *PTR*'s brother.

Show that these statements are true.

```
Put NODE(PTR) in B;
```

is just:

```
B.NUMBER = B.NUMBER+1;
B.ELEMENT(B.NUMBER) = PTR;
```

The code for the procedures FINISHUP and GETNODE will be left as exercises.

Exercise 3.20: Show that this breadth-first search solution will find the minimal path solution to the maze problem.

The solution just presented will work but has a serious practical defect. Once a node is allocated, the allocation remains even if the node represents a cell on a dead end path. We can make this solution more space efficient by returning dead nodes back to the allocation routine via the utility:

```
PUTNODE: procedure(PTR);
```

which frees the *NODE* pointed to by *PTR*. The code will be left as an exercise.

We free node *L* if there is no *K* reachable from *L* in set *A*. At that point in the program, node *L* can be freed since it represents a dead end path. (However, the corresponding element in the array *REACHED* remains TRUE. Why?) In addition, the father of this freed node can also be freed if the freed node has no brothers. (Why is this also true?) A loop can be written to free as many nodes as possible.

With this addition, the only nodes allocated are those on paths from the root to the nodes in set *A*. These all represent still possible paths through the maze. This greatly reduces the size of the array needed for *NODE* storage.

Exercise 3.21: Show that these changes do work as intended.

Exercise 3.22: Using the principles of data abstractions, rewrite this solution so that SETs and the internal structure of NODEs are hidden inside separate modules.

3.5.2 Depth-first Search Solution

The previous solution, while having the advantage of finding the minimal length path through a maze, has the disadvantage of requiring a large data space to store the nodes of the tree representation of the maze. It also represents a parallel solution. The depth-first search solution presented here requires less data space and represents an algorithm that can be used to walk through such a maze.

In a depth-first search, a given path is tried until a leaf node is reached. If that fails, then backtracking is used to find an alternate path. Referring back to Figure 3.9, the path from (1, 1) to (3, 4) will first be traversed. When that fails, the program backs up to node (2, 2) and tries the path to leaf (4, 3). When that fails, the program will back up to (4, 2) and try the successful path to (5, 6).

In order to implement this, the basic algorithm will be to enter a node (cell in the maze) and then move left to the next cell. At this point solve the maze problem from this new cell. If that should fail (either there is no white cell to the left or else the program returns from that cell stating that no solution can be found in that direction), the program will try to move straight ahead. If that fails, then the right direction will be tried. If that also fails, then the program will back up one cell and state that movement in this direction cannot proceed.

Exercise 3.23: Show that this algorithm will eventually cover every white cell in the maze that is connected to the entrance cell.

From this description, two data structures are needed besides the array *MAZE* used in solution 1. As in solution 1, we need the array *REACHED*. Similarly we need to know how a given cell was reached. A stack is useful for this. Similar to the parking problem of this chapter, we can write the following recursive solution to this problem:

```
MAZE2: procedure(LOCI,LOCJ) recursive;
        declare LOCI, LOCJ;  /* Current location in maze */
        declare I,J;         /* Save location in stacked */
                             /* activation record       */
```

```
I = LOCI; J = LOCJ;
REACHED(I,J) = TRUE; /* set cell now visited      */
if MAZE(I,J)=-1 then call FINISHUP; /* done */
if can move to left then call MAZE2(I',J');
                    /* (I',J') is next cell */
if can move straight then call MAZE2(I',J');
if can move right then call MAZE2(I',J');
return;     /* Fail - no solution here */
end MAZE2;
```

This solution has an additional complexity not encountered in solution 4 of the parking problem. Moving left, straight, or right depends upon the direction used to enter a given cell. For example, if node (I, J) is entered from the top (call it north), then left will be to node $(I, J + 1)$, while if (I, J) is entered from the left (call it west), then left will be to node $(I - 1, J)$.

However, in all cases either the value of $+1$ or -1 is added to the I or J index in order to get to the next cell, and the total number of possibilities is finite. The location of the next move depends only upon the entrance direction (north, east, south, or west) and the movement direction (left, straight, or right) (Figures 3.13 and 3.14). Thus a 4 by 3 array can be used to determine

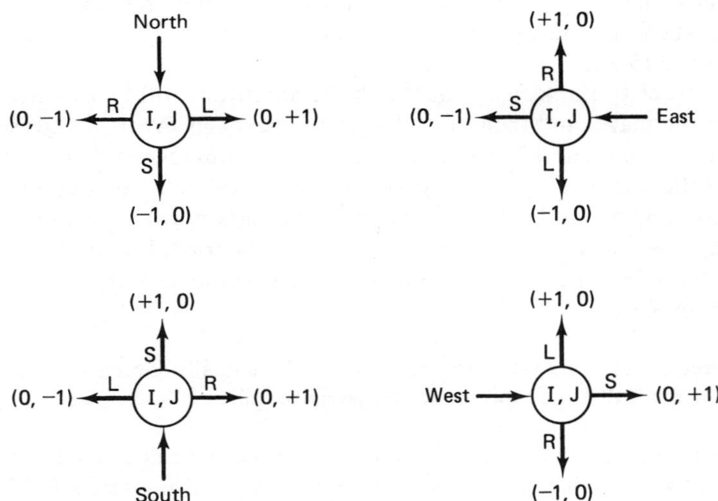

Figure 3.13 Based upon direction cell (I, J) is entered, changes to indices I and J in moving left (L), right (R), and straight (S) to new cell.

the next I location, the next J location, and the direction used to enter the next cell. This is just a finite state technique (Section 2.6.7). These can be described by the following data structures:

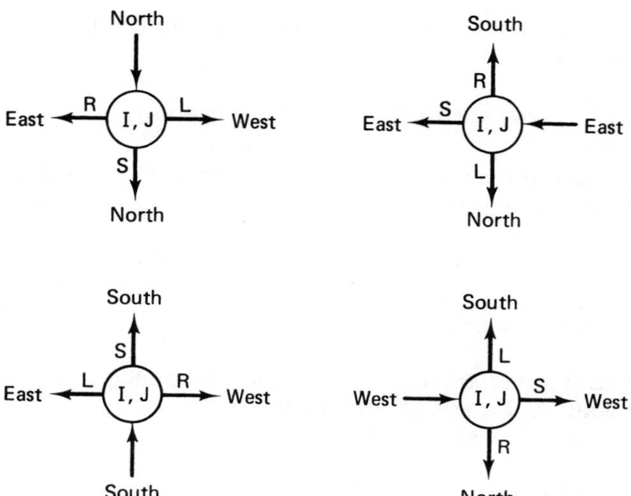

Figure 3.14 Based upon direction cell (I, J) is entered, direction next cell is entered after moving left (L), right (R), or straight (S).

```
declare LEFT INIT(1),
        STRAIGHT INIT(2),
        RIGHT INIT(3),
        NORTH INIT(1),
        EAST INIT(2),
        SOUTH INIT(3),
        WEST INIT(4);
/* For each entry in the following two matrices, */
/*     +1 means to increment index by 1           */
/*     -1 means to decrement index by 1           */
/*      0 means no change in index                */
declare NEXTI(4,3) INIT( /* LEFT STR RIGHT FROM */
                          0,  -1,   0,  /* N */
                         -1,   0,  +1,  /* E */
                          0,  +1,   0,  /* S */
                         +1,   0,  -1), /* W */
    NEXTJ(4,3) INIT( /* LEFT STR RIGHT FROM */
                         +1,   0,  -1,  /* N */
                          0,  -1,   0,  /* E */
                         -1,   0,  +1,  /* S */
                          0,  +1,   0), /* W */
  NEXTDIRECTION(4,3) INIT(4,   1,   2,
                          1,   2,   3,
                          2,   3,   4,
                          3,   4,   1);
```

Thus if cell (I, J) is entered from direction D, the cell to the left of (I, J) will be at location:

$$(NEXTI(D,LEFT)+I,\ NEXTJ(D,LEFT)+J)$$

Similarly for the cell straight ahead or to the right. The new direction (call it D') the left cell is entered by is given by:

$$D' = NEXTDIRECTION(D,LEFT)$$

The solution then becomes:

```
MAZE2: PROCEDURE(LOCI,LOCJ,DIRECTION) RECURSIVE;
        DECLARE LOCI, LOCJ, DIRECTION;
        DECLARE I, J, INEXT, JNEXT, NEWDIRECTION;
        I = LOCI;
        J = LOCJ;
        REACHED(I,J) = TRUE;
        IF MAZE(I,J) = -1
             THEN /* done */
                CALL FINISHUP;
        /* check for move left */
        INEXT = NEXTI(DIRECTION,LEFT)+I;
        JNEXT = NEXTJ(DIRECTION,LEFT)+J;
        IF (MAZE(INEXT,JNEXT)=0) & (REACHED(INEXT,JNEXT)=FALSE)
               /* found next location */
               THEN DO;
                       NEWDIRECTION = NEXTDIRECTION(DIRECTION,LEFT);
                       CALL MAZE2(INEXT,JNEXT,NEWDIRECTION);
                       END;
        /* check for move straight */
        Repeat above code replacing LEFT by STRAIGHT;
        /* check for move right */
        Repeat above code replacing STRAIGHT by RIGHT;
        RETURN; /* fail exit */
        END;
```

Due to the repetitive nature of the above code, the actual movement either left, straight, or to the right could be made into a subroutine. The details of the procedures FINISHUP and modifications needed to print out the stacked routine through the maze are left as exercises.

Exercise 3.24: The array *NEXTDIRECTION* is not really needed since the new direction can be calculated from the entering direction (north, east, south, west) and the exiting direction (left, straight, or right). Make this change to MAZE2.

Exercise 3.25: A recursive solution is not really necessary. Rewrite this solution as a nonrecursive solution which stores the set of nodes in the currently pending path into a stack.

3.6 AIRLINE RESERVATION SYSTEM

Problem statement: Construct an airline reservation system whose input is described below.

```
⟨Commands⟩ ::= ⟨Commands⟩ ⟨Command⟩
             | ε
⟨Command⟩ ::= FLY ⟨Number⟩
            | GROUND ⟨Number⟩
            | SEAT ⟨Number⟩ ⟨Name⟩ ⟨Name⟩
            | CANCEL ⟨Number⟩ ⟨Name⟩ ⟨Name⟩
            | PRINT ⟨Number⟩
```

Each command appears in free format (i.e., any number of blanks between any two fields) in a single line of input. A ⟨Number⟩ contains three digits, and a ⟨Name⟩ contains an arbitary number of alphanumeric characters. Each command produces some output, either an error message indicating an illegal argument or request, or a confirmation of the successful completion of the command. The actions associated with each command are described below:

FLY ⟨Number⟩. The flight numbered ⟨Number⟩ is added to the system. The attempted addition of a duplicate flight is an error.

GROUND ⟨Number⟩. The flight numbered ⟨Number⟩ is deleted from the system. Any passengers on the flight must be removed. The removal of a nonexistent flight is an error.

SEAT ⟨Number⟩ ⟨Name1⟩ ⟨Name2⟩. Add a passenger to the flight numbered ⟨Number⟩. A passenger's name is given by the first letter of ⟨Name1⟩, followed by a blank, followed by ⟨Name2⟩. Passengers' names need not be unique. It is an error to attempt to seat a passenger on a flight that does not exist.

CANCEL ⟨Number⟩ ⟨Name1⟩ ⟨Name2⟩. Remove a passenger from the flight numbered ⟨Number⟩. A passenger's name is given by the first letter of ⟨Name1⟩, followed by a blank, followed by ⟨Name2⟩. It is an error to attempt to seat a passenger on a flight that does not exist or to remove a passenger from a flight on which he is not booked.

PRINT ⟨Number⟩. Print an alphabetized list of the names of the passengers on the flight numbered ⟨Number⟩. An error occurs if the flight does not exist.

3.6.1 Abstraction Solution

Since this system is very dependent upon a data structure to keep track of a set of flights, we will use the concepts of data abstraction to organize our solution. We will hide the representation of the data, a set of flights each with its own set of passengers, in separate modules. The main driver program, which reads and parses commands, will also be a separate module with no knowledge of the representation. When the driver module recognizes a command, a call will be performed to one of the external procedures in the data abstraction module corresponding to the command. This division of the problem will allow us to confine changes in the system to smaller segments of the source code. For example, changes in the syntax of the commands can be handled entirely within the driver module, and changes in the representation (perhaps to improve the performance of the system) are relegated to the data abstraction modules. We begin by developing the driver program to read and parse commands. This program contains a loop that reads, echos, and processes each command. As we shall see, this part of the program does not need any knowledge of the data representation for flights. In fact, once we have finished this module, we can test our system by supplying dummy modules, which merely announce their invocation, for our abstract operations.

```
on ENDFILE (SYSIN) stop;
do while(TRUE);
    Read and write input;
    Parse and process commands;
    end;
```

In order to parse a command, we must determine the type of the command and obtain its arguments. Thus we will need routines to obtain commands, flight numbers, and passenger names. Since the first parameter of each of the commands is a flight number, we can obtain its value before deciding which command to process. Processing a command just involves obtaining the remaining parameters for passenger commands and invoking the appropriate operations to manipulate the set of flights.

```
on ENDFILE (SYSIN) stop;
do while (TRUE);
   get COPY EDIT (CARD) (A(80));
   if GETCOMMAND(CARD,COMMAND)
      then
          if GETNUMBER(CARD,FLIGHT#)
             then
                 do case(COMMAND);
                 \fly\   /* Process FLY */
                     call ADDFLIGHT(FLIGHT#);
```

```
                    \ground\ /* Process GROUND */
                       call REMOVEFLIGHT(FLIGHT#);
                    \seat\ /* Process SEAT */
                       if GETNAME(CARD,NAME)
                          then
                             call ADDPASS(FLIGHT#,NAME);
                          else
                             call ERRORMSG;
                    \cancel\ /* Process CANCEL */
                       if GETNAME(CARD,NAME)
                          then
                             call REMOVEPASS(FLIGHT#,NAME);
                          else
                             call ERRORMSG;
                    \print\ /* Process PRINT */
                       call PRINTPASS(FLIGHT#);
                    end; /* of do case(command) */
               else /* Illegal flight number */
                  call ERRORMSG;
         else /* Illegal command */
            call ERRORMSG;
      end;
```

Each of the procedures GETCOMMAND, GETNUMBER, and GETNAME searches the current input image for the next nonblank field, removes the field from the image (subsequent invocations of these procedures should not return identical values), and checks the validity of the field. Both ill-formed and missing data can cause a field to be invalid. Since these routines have such similar functions, their interfaces should be identical so a user does not have to remember which of the three routines return values and which act by side effect. Therefore, each of the routines accepts two parameters, the card to be examined and an output parameter containing the result of the routine. Each routine also returns a boolean value indicating whether or not valid data is being returned. A procedure named GETWORD is used to remove the next nonblank field of its first argument and return it. The procedure returns the null string if it fails to find a nonblank field.

```
GETCOMMAND:procedure(CARD,COMMAND) returns(BIT(1));
   COMMAND# = GETWORD(CARD);
   if COMMAND# ≠ ''
      then do;
         Check for valid command;
         end;
      else
         return(FALSE);
   end;
```

```
GETNUMBER: procedure(CARD,NUMBER) returns(BIT(1));
  NUMBER = GETWORD(CARD);
  if NUMBER ≠ ''
    then do;
        Check for valid number;
        end;
    else
        return(FALSE);
  end;
GETNAME: procedure(CARD,NAME) returns(BIT(1));
  TEMP = GETWORD(CARD);
  if TEMP ≠ ''
    then do;
        Check for valid name;
        end;
    else
        return(FALSE);
  end;
```

We can finish each of these procedure easily. Unfortunately, the **case** statement only permits selectors that are either all integers or all single characters. Thus, we must chose between a group of nested **if** statements that explicitly checks the returned value against literals representing commands and a **do** loop that compares the returned value with an array of character strings that has been initialized to the string representations of the commands.

```
/* Check for valid command */
if COMMAND# = 'FLY' then COMMAND = FLY;
  else if COMMAND# = 'GROUND' then COMMAND = GROUND;
    else if COMMAND# = 'SEAT' then COMMAND = SEAT;
      else if COMMAND# = 'CANCEL' then COMMAND = CANCEL;
        else if COMMAND# = 'PRINT' then COMMAND = PRINT;
             else
               return(FALSE);
return(TRUE);
```

In order to check for a valid number, we add the condition

```
LENGTH(NUMBER) = 3
```

to our existing **if** statement and check that each digit is in the range '0'. .'9'. We would prefer to check all the digits at one time with the following condition:

```
NUMBER ≥ '000' & NUMBER ≤ '999'
```

but refrain from doing so. (Why?)

```
/* Check for valid number */
do I = 1 to LENGTH(NUMBER);
   if SUBSTR(NUMBER,I,1) < '0' | SUBSTR(NUMBER,I,1) > '9'
     then
        return(FALSE);
   end;
   return(TRUE);
```

As we are not overly concerned with the characters within a name, we simply get the second name and append it to the first letter of the first name followed by a blank.

```
/* Check for valid name */
NAME = SUBSTR(TEMP,1,1) || ' ';
TEMP = GETWORD(CARD);
if TEMP ≠ ''
  then do;
     NAME = NAME || TEMP;
     return(TRUE);
     end;
  else
     return(FALSE);
```

GETWORD removes and returns a nonblank substring from its argument. If the argument does not contain a nonblank substring, the null string is returned. We use two local variables to determine the position of the nonblank field: *I* contains the index of the first nonblank character and *J* contains the index of the first subsequent blank character (or a value greater than the length of the string if no blank follows the substring). Thus we return the $J-I$ characters starting at position *I*.

```
GETWORD:procedure(CARD) returns(CHARACTER (80) VARYING);
   I = Location of first nonblank character;
   if no nonblank character
     then
        return('');
   J = Location of first character past nonblank substring;
   WORD = SUBSTR(CARD,I,J-I);
   CARD = remaining characters of card;
   return(WORD);
   end;
```

The obvious implementation for the remaining abstract instructions carefully avoids substring errors by first making sure that the character being examined is within the argument (i.e., less than or equal to LENGTH(*CARD*)) and only then examining the character to see if it has the desired value.

```
/* I = Location of first nonblank character */
I = 1;
do while (I ≤ LENGTH(CARD));
   if SUBSTR(CARD,I,1) = ' '
     then
        I = I + 1;
     else
        leave;
   end;
if I > LENGTH(CARD) /* no nonblank character */
   then
     return ('');
/* J = Location of first character past nonblank substring */
J = I;
do while (J ≤ LENGTH(CARD));
   if SUBSTR(CARD,J,1) ≠ ' ')
     then
        J = J + 1;
     else
        leave;
   end;
WORD = SUBSTR(CARD,I,J-I);
/* CARD = remaining characters of card */
if J > LENGTH(CARD)
   then
     CARD = '';
   else
     CARD = SUBSTR(CARD,J);
```

Since we cannot be sure that we will find a word on the image, we must make two checks each time we examine a character. First we make sure we are within the string boundaries; then we check the current character to determine if we should examine the next character. We must also be careful in taking SUBSTR(*CARD*,*J*) in those cases where *J*>LENGTH(*CARD*). An alternate solution would involve placing a special, nonblank character on the end of each image. Thus, we need not check that we are within the image when we search for a blank because we must find a nonblank character before we exhaust the image. We must also alter the loop that searches for the next blank character to recognize our new end-of-image character.

```
/* Add end-of-image character */
if SUBSTR(CARD,LENGTH(CARD),1) ≠ ';'
  then
     CARD = CARD || ';';
```

```
/* I = Location of first nonblank character */
I = 1;
do while (SUBSTR(CARD,I,1) = ' ');
  I = I + 1;
  end;
if SUBSTR(CARD,I,1) = ';' /* no nonblank character */
  then
     return('');
/* J = Location of first character past nonblank substring */
J = I;
do while (SUBSTR(CARD,J,1) ≠ ' ' & SUBSTR(CARD,J,1) ≠ ';');
  J = J + 1;
  end;
WORD = SUBSTR(CARD,I,J−I);
/* CARD = remaining characters of card */
CARD = SUBSTR(CARD,J);
```

Now we are ready to develop ADDFLIGHT, REMOVEFLIGHT, ADDPASS, REMOVEPASS, and PRINTPASS. At some point in this process, we must decide on a representation for the flight and passenger information we are saving. There is no need for the driver segment to know about these representations, so we place the representations into separately compiled procedures and make the operations entry points in the procedures as described in Chapter 2. Each of these operations must determine if the flight number passed to it is legal. Therefore, each of these operations calls the procedure FINDFLIGHT, which searches for the flight identified by *FLIGHT#* and returns the location of the *PREVIOUS* and *NEXT* flights in our information structure. (The *NEXT* flight is the one that follows the flight referenced by *PREVIOUS*, so it may or may not be the flight we are seeking.)

```
FLIGHTS:procedure;
ADDFLIGHT:entry(FLIGHT#);
   declare FLIGHT# CHARACTER(*) VARYING;
   PREVIOUS = FIRSTFLIGHT; /* Starting point */
   if FINDFLIGHT(FLIGHT#,PREVIOUS,NEXT)
     then
        put SKIP LIST('ERROR: DUPLICATE FLIGHT');
     else do;
        Insert flight(FLIGHT#);
        put SKIP LIST('OK');
        end;
   put SKIP;
   return;
REMOVEFLIGHT:entry(FLIGHT#);
   PREVIOUS = FIRSTFLIGHT; /* Starting point */
   if ¬FINDFLIGHT(FLIGHT#,PREVIOUS,NEXT)
     then
```

```
            put SKIP LIST('ERROR: NONEXISTENT FLIGHT');
         else do;
            Delete flight(FLIGHT #);
            put SKIP LIST('OK');
            end;
      put SKIP;
      return;
   PRINTPASS:entry(FLIGHT #);
      PREVIOUS = FIRSTFLIGHT; /* Starting point */
      if FINDFLIGHT(FLIGHT #,PREVIOUS,NEXT)
         then do;
            List people(FLIGHT #);
            put SKIP LIST('OK');
            end;
         else
            put SKIP LIST('ERROR: NONEXISTENT FLIGHT');
      put SKIP;
      return;
   ADDPASS:entry(FLIGHT #,NAME);
      declare NAME CHARACTER(*) VARYING;
      PREVIOUS = FIRSTFLIGHT; /* Starting point */
      if FINDFLIGHT(FLIGHT #,PREVIOUS,NEXT)
         then do;
            Insert person(FLIGHT #,NAME);
            put SKIP LIST('OK');
            end;
         else
            put SKIP LIST('ERROR: NONEXISTENT FLIGHT');
      put SKIP;
      return;
   REMOVEPASS:entry(FLIGHT #,NAME);
      PREVIOUS = FIRSTFLIGHT; /* Starting point */
      if FINDFLIGHT(FLIGHT #,PREVIOUS,NEXT)
         then
            Delete person(FLIGHT #,NAME);
         else do;
            put SKIP LIST('ERROR: NONEXISTENT FLIGHT');
            put SKIP;
            end;
      return;
   end;
```

In order to further refine ADDFLIGHT and REMOVEFLIGHT, we must decide on a representation for flights. We pick an unordered linked list whose first element is referenced by *FIRSTFLIGHT*. *FIRSTFLIGHT* is declared to be STATIC, so that its value and storage persist between operation invocations.

```
declare 1 FLIGHT BASED(FLIGHTPTR),
          2 NUMBER CHARACTER(3) VARYING,
          2 PASSENGER POINTER,
          2 LINK POINTER;
declare FIRSTFLIGHT POINTER STATIC INITIAL(NULL);
```

In adding or deleting a flight, we are presented with a decision similar to the one we made for processing input images. Either we must know when we are adding the first flight to the list of flights (so we make *FIRSTFLIGHT* reference it rather than some other flight's *LINK* field) and removing the first flight from the list (so we set *FIRSTFLIGHT* rather than *PREVIOUS*⟶*LINK* to point to the remainder of the flight list) or we must always have one flight in the list (whose flight number does not conflict with any other flight's number). We prefer the second alternative and add another entry point named INITFLIGHTS that is invoked by the driver module before any commands are processed. (We could have each operation check that INITFLIGHTS had already been invoked, but this would add code and run-time overhead to each of the operations.) INITFLIGHTS causes a flight with the fictitious "number" XXX to be added to our list of flights.

```
INITFLIGHTS:entry;
  call GETFLIGHT('XXX',FIRSTFLIGHT);
  return;
```

GETFLIGHT allocates and initializes an object of type FLIGHT, returning a reference to the object through its second parameter.

```
GETFLIGHT:procedure(FLIGHT#,PTR);
  ALLOCATE FLIGHT SET(PTR);
  PTR⟶NUMBER = FLIGHT#;
  Initialize passenger list;
  PTR⟶LINK = NULL;
  end;
```

We can now finish the operations for inserting and deleting flights by making the following refinements. The modifications to the representation for flights are pictured in Figures 3.15 and 3.16.

```
/* Insert flight */
call GETFLIGHT(FLIGHT#,FLIGHTPTR);
FLIGHTPTR⟶LINK = NEXT; /* NEW FLIGHT⟶NEXT FLIGHT */
PREVIOUS⟶LINK = FLIGHTPTR; /* PREVIOUS FLIGHT⟶NEW FLIGHT */
/* Delete flight */
FLIGHTPTR = NEXT⟶LINK; /* FLIGHTPTR⟶FLIGHT AFTER NEXT */
call FLUSHPEOPLE(NEXT⟶PASSENGER);
free NEXT⟶FLIGHT;
PREVIOUS⟶LINK = FLIGHTPTR; /* PREVIOUS⟶FLIGHT AFTER NEXT */
```

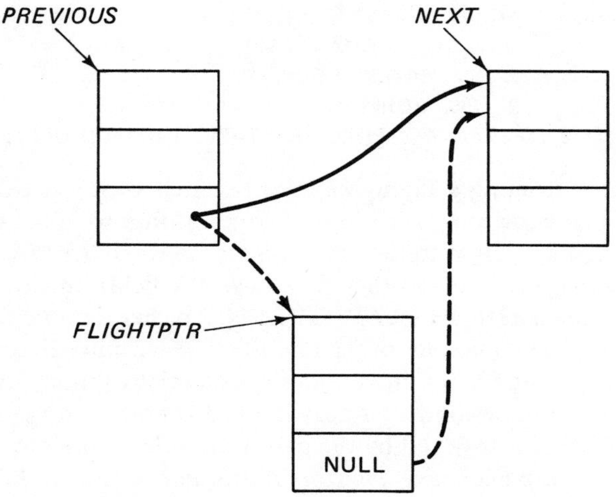

Figure 3.15 Inserting a new flight.

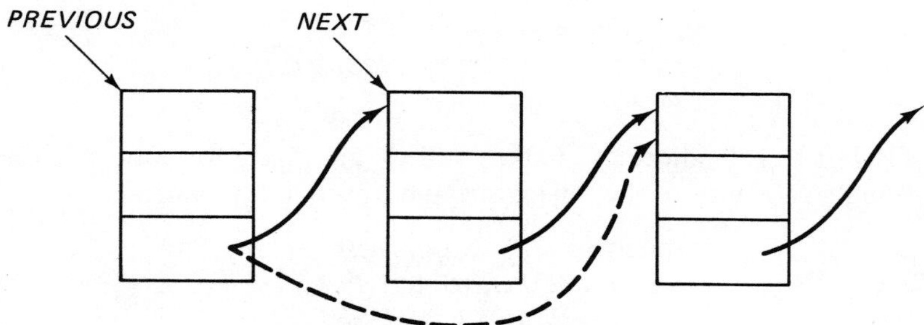

Figure 3.16 Deleting a flight.

In implementing FINDFLIGHT, we start with *PREVIOUS* referencing our first flight and set *NEXT* to point at the next flight (possibly NULL). We can do this because we are sure there is at least one flight initially. We move both pointers along until either we find a match (*NEXT*⟶*NUMBER* = *FLIGHT#*) or no more flights remain to be examined (*NEXT* = NULL).

```
FINDFLIGHT:procedure(FLIGHT#,PREVIOUS,NEXT) returns(BIT(1));
  FOUND = FALSE;
  NEXT = PREVIOUS⟶LINK;
  do while (NEXT ≠ NULL & ¬FOUND);
     if NEXT⟶NUMBER = FLIGHT#
       then
          FOUND = TRUE;
```

```
            else do;
               PREVIOUS = NEXT;
               NEXT = NEXT——>LINK;
               end;
         end;
      return(FOUND);
      end;
```

We now finish developing the operations that deal with passengers by turning the remaining abstract instructions into call statements. Instead of adding the representation for passengers and the instructions for manipulating it to the FLIGHTS procedure, we again set up a new separately compiled procedure, PASSENGERS, with the operations INSERTPERSON, DELETEPERSON, LISTPEOPLE, and FLUSHPEOPLE. This allows us to hide the representations of flights and passengers from one another. By freezing interface information (all operations in PASSENGERS accept a pointer to a flight's passenger list), we limit the scope of changes to either the representation or operations of flights and passengers to their respective modules. Of course, if any changes modify the interface information, we must make changes to both modules.

Each flight has an ordered linked list of the names of its passengers. The list is kept ordered because we need to produce an alphabetized list of passenger names in response to each PRINT command. Rather than sort the list for each PRINT request, INSERTPERSON and DELETEPERSON maintain the list in sorted order. Since the code for the passenger operations is similar to that for the flight operations, we skip its development and show the completed program below. The major differences between the FLIGHTS and PASSENGERS modules are in FINDPERSON and GETPERSON. In FINDPERSON, we search for a passenger name only until we either find it or encounter a lexically greater name. Unlike GETFLIGHT, GETPERSON must be an entry point because it is called from GETFLIGHT to initialize the passenger list for a flight with a passenger with an empty name. Thus, because we invoke GETPERSON from within INSERTPERSON in the PASSENGER module, we must declare GETPERSON to be recursive.

```
DRIVER:PROCEDURE OPTIONS(MAIN);
DECLARE TRUE BIT(1) INITIAL('1'B);
DECLARE FALSE BIT(1) INITIAL('0'B);
DECLARE FLY FIXED BINARY INITIAL(1);
DECLARE GROUND FIXED BINARY INITIAL(2);
DECLARE SEAT FIXED BINARY INITIAL(3);
DECLARE CANCEL FIXED BINARY INITIAL(4);
DECLARE PRINT FIXED BINARY INITIAL(5);
DECLARE CARD CHARACTER(81) VARYING;
DECLARE COMMAND FIXED BINARY;
DECLARE (FLIGHT#,NAME) CHARACTER (80) VARYING;
```

```
ERRORMSG:PROCEDURE;
   PUT SKIP LIST('ERROR: RE–TRY COMMAND');
   PUT SKIP;
   END;
GETWORD:PROCEDURE(CARD) RETURNS(CHARACTER(80) VARYING);
   DECLARE CARD CHARACTER(*) VARYING;
   DECLARE WORD CHARACTER(80) VARYING;
   DECLARE (I,J) FIXED BINARY;
   /* Insert end-of-image character */
   IF SUBSTR(CARD,LENGTH(CARD),1) ≠ ';'
      THEN
          CARD = CARD || ';';
   /* I = Location of first nonblank character */
   I = 1;
   DO WHILE (SUBSTR(CARD,I,1) = ' ');
       I = I + 1;
       END;
   IF SUBSTR(CARD,I,1) = ';' /* no nonblank character */
      THEN
         RETURN('');
   /* J = Location of first char past nonblank substring */
   J = I;
   DO WHILE (SUBSTR(CARD,J,1) ≠ ' ' & SUBSTR(CARD,J,1) ≠ ';');
       J = J + 1;
       END;
   WORD = SUBSTR(CARD,I,J–I);
   /* CARD = remaining characters of card */
   CARD = SUBSTR(CARD,J);
   RETURN(WORD);
   END;
GETCOMMAND:PROCEDURE(CARD,COMMAND) RETURNS(BIT(1));
   DECLARE CARD CHARACTER(*) VARYING;
   DECLARE COMMAND FIXED BINARY;
   DECLARE COMMAND# CHARACTER(80) VARYING;
   COMMAND# = GETWORD(CARD);
   IF COMMAND# ≠ ''
      THEN DO; /* Check for valid command */
          IF COMMAND# = 'FLY' THEN COMMAND = FLY;
          ELSE IF COMMAND# = 'GROUND' THEN COMMAND = GROUND;
          ELSE IF COMMAND# = 'SEAT' THEN COMMAND = SEAT;
          ELSE IF COMMAND# = 'CANCEL' THEN COMMAND = CANCEL;
          ELSE IF COMMAND# = 'PRINT' THEN COMMAND = PRINT;
          ELSE RETURN(FALSE);
          RETURN(TRUE);
          END;
      ELSE
          RETURN(FALSE);
   END;
```

```
GETNUMBER: PROCEDURE(CARD,NUMBER) RETURNS(BIT(1));
  DECLARE (CARD,NUMBER) CHARACTER(*) VARYING;
  DECLARE I FIXED BINARY;
  NUMBER = GETWORD(CARD);
  IF NUMBER ≠ '' & LENGTH(NUMBER) = 3
    THEN DO; /* Check for valid number */
       DO I = 1 TO LENGTH(NUMBER);
          IF SUBSTR(NUMBER,I,1) < '0' | SUBSTR(NUMBER,I,1) > '9'
            THEN
               RETURN(FALSE);
          END;
       RETURN(TRUE);
       END;
    ELSE
       RETURN(FALSE);
  END;
GETNAME: PROCEDURE(CARD,NAME) RETURNS(BIT(1));
  DECLARE (CARD,NAME) CHARACTER(*) VARYING;
  DECLARE TEMP CHARACTER(80) VARYING;
  TEMP = GETWORD(CARD);
  IF TEMP ≠ ''
    THEN DO; /* Check for valid name */
       NAME = SUBSTR(TEMP,1,1) || ' ';
       TEMP = GETWORD(CARD);
       IF TEMP ≠ ''
         THEN DO;
            NAME = NAME || TEMP;
            RETURN(TRUE);
            END;
         ELSE
            RETURN(FALSE);
       END;
    ELSE
       RETURN(FALSE);
  END;
ON ENDFILE (SYSIN) STOP;
CALL INITFLIGHTS;
DO WHILE (TRUE);
  GET COPY EDIT (CARD) (A(80));
  IF GETCOMMAND(CARD,COMMAND)
    THEN
       IF GETNUMBER(CARD,FLIGHT#)
         THEN
            DO CASE(COMMAND);
               \1\  /* Process FLY */
                  CALL ADDFLIGHT(FLIGHT#);
               \2\  /* Process GROUND */
                  CALL REMOVEFLIGHT(FLIGHT#);
```

```
                    \3\  /* Process SEAT */
                       IF GETNAME(CARD,NAME)
                         THEN
                            CALL ADDPASS(FLIGHT#,NAME);
                         ELSE
                            CALL ERRORMSG;
                    \4\  /* Process CANCEL */
                       IF GETNAME(CARD,NAME)
                         THEN
                            CALL REMOVEPASS(FLIGHT#,NAME);
                         ELSE
                            CALL ERRORMSG;
                    \5\  /* Process PRINT */
                       CALL PRINTPASS(FLIGHT#);
                    END; /* of do case(command) */
              ELSE /* Illegal flight number */
                 CALL ERRORMSG;
         ELSE /* Illegal command */
            CALL ERRORMSG;
   END;
FLIGHTS:PROCEDURE;
DECLARE TRUE BIT(1) INITIAL('1'B);
DECLARE FALSE BIT(1) INITIAL('0'B);
DECLARE 1 FLIGHT BASED(FLIGHTPTR),
          2 NUMBER CHARACTER(3) VARYING,
          2 PASSENGER POINTER,
          2 LINK POINTER;
DECLARE FIRSTFLIGHT POINTER STATIC;
DECLARE (PREVIOUS,NEXT) POINTER;
FINDFLIGHT:PROCEDURE(FLIGHT#,PREVIOUS,NEXT) RETURNS(BIT(1));
 /* Search the list of flights for one numbered 'flight#' */
 /* starting with the flight referenced by PREVIOUS.      */
 /* If such a flight is found:                            */
 /*   PREVIOUS refers to the flight before it             */
 /*   NEXT refers to the flight found                     */
 /*   The function returns the value TRUE                 */
 /* If no such flight exists:                             */
 /*   NEXT = NULL                                         */
 /*   The function returns the value FALSE                */
 DECLARE FLIGHT# CHARACTER(*) VARYING;
 DECLARE (PREVIOUS,NEXT) POINTER;
 DECLARE FOUND BIT(1);
 FOUND = FALSE;
 NEXT = PREVIOUS——>LINK;
 DO WHILE (NEXT ≠ NULL & ¬FOUND);
    IF NEXT——>NUMBER = FLIGHT#
       THEN /* A match */
          FOUND = TRUE;
```

```
        ELSE DO; /* Get next flight */
           PREVIOUS = NEXT;
           NEXT = NEXT——>LINK;
           END;
      END;
  RETURN(FOUND);
  END;
GETFLIGHT:PROCEDURE(FLIGHT#,PTR);
   /* Allocate and initialize objects of mode FLIGHT to    */
   /* (flight#,GETPERSON(''),NULL). Return reference */
   /* to object in PTR                                     */
   DECLARE FLIGHT# CHARACTER(*) VARYING;
   DECLARE (PTR,PREVIOUS,NEXT) POINTER;
   ALLOCATE FLIGHT SET(PTR);
   PTR——>NUMBER = FLIGHT#;
   PTR——>PASSENGER = GETPERSON('');
   PTR——>LINK = NULL;
   END;
ADDFLIGHT:ENTRY(FLIGHT#);
   DECLARE FLIGHT# CHARACTER(*) VARYING;
   PREVIOUS = FIRSTFLIGHT; /* Starting point */
   IF FINDFLIGHT(FLIGHT#,PREVIOUS,NEXT)
      THEN
         PUT SKIP LIST('ERROR: DUPLICATE FLIGHT');
      ELSE DO; /* Insert flight */
         CALL GETFLIGHT(FLIGHT#,FLIGHTPTR);
         FLIGHTPTR——>LINK = NEXT; /* NEW FLIGHT——>NEXT FLIGHT */
         PREVIOUS——>LINK = FLIGHTPTR; /* PREVIOUS——>NEW FLIGHT */
         PUT SKIP LIST('OK');
         END;
   PUT SKIP;
   RETURN;
REMOVEFLIGHT:ENTRY(FLIGHT#);
   PREVIOUS = FIRSTFLIGHT; /* Starting point */
   IF ¬FINDFLIGHT(FLIGHT#,PREVIOUS,NEXT)
      THEN
         PUT SKIP LIST('ERROR: NONEXISTENT FLIGHT');
      ELSE DO; /* Delete flight */
         FLIGHTPTR = NEXT——>LINK; /* Point to flight after next */
         CALL FLUSHPEOPLE(NEXT——>PASSENGER);
         FREE NEXT——>FLIGHT;
         PREVIOUS——>LINK=FLIGHTPTR;
                                  /*PREVIOUS——>FLIGHT AFTER NEXT*/
         PUT SKIP LIST('OK');
         END;
   PUT SKIP;
   RETURN;
```

```
PRINTPASS:ENTRY(FLIGHT#);
   PREVIOUS = FIRSTFLIGHT; /* Starting point */
   IF FINDFLIGHT(FLIGHT#,PREVIOUS,NEXT)
      THEN DO;
          CALL LISTPEOPLE(NEXT—>PASSENGER);
          PUT SKIP LIST('OK');
          END;
      ELSE DO;
          PUT SKIP LIST('ERROR: NONEXISTENT FLIGHT');
          END;
   PUT SKIP;
   RETURN;
ADDPASS:ENTRY(FLIGHT#,NAME);
   DECLARE NAME CHARACTER(*) VARYING;
   PREVIOUS = FIRSTFLIGHT; /* Starting point */
   IF FINDFLIGHT(FLIGHT#,PREVIOUS,NEXT)
      THEN DO;
          CALL INSERTPERSON(NEXT—>PASSENGER,NAME);
          PUT SKIP LIST('OK');
          END;
      ELSE DO;
          PUT SKIP LIST('ERROR: NONEXISTENT FLIGHT');
          END;
   PUT SKIP;
   RETURN;
REMOVEPASS:ENTRY(FLIGHT#,NAME);
   PREVIOUS = FIRSTFLIGHT; /* Starting point */
   IF FINDFLIGHT(FLIGHT#,PREVIOUS,NEXT)
      THEN
          CALL DELETEPERSON(NEXT—>PASSENGER,NAME);
      ELSE DO;
          PUT SKIP LIST('ERROR: NONEXISTENT FLIGHT');
          PUT SKIP;
          END;
   RETURN;
INITFLIGHTS: ENTRY;
  /* Add dummy flight so one always exists */
  CALL GETFLIGHT('XXX',FIRSTFLIGHT);
  RETURN;
END;
PASSENGERS:PROCEDURE RECURSIVE;
DECLARE TRUE BIT(1) INITIAL('1'B);
DECLARE FALSE BIT(1) INITIAL('0'B);
DECLARE 1 PERSON BASED,
          2 ID CHARACTER(80) VARYING,
          2 NEXTP POINTER;
DECLARE (PTR,NEXT,PREVIOUS) POINTER;
```

```
FINDPERSON:PROCEDURE(NAME,PREVIOUS,NEXT);
  /* Search the list referenced by PREVIOUS for a passenger */
  /* names NAME.                                             */
  /* If such a passenger is found:                           */
  /*   PREVIOUS references the preceding passenger           */
  /*   NEXT refers to the passenger found                    */
  /* If no such passenger exists:                            */
  /*   NEXT = NULL                                           */
  DECLARE NAME CHARACTER(*) VARYING;
  DECLARE (PREVIOUS,NEXT) POINTER;
  DECLARE QUIT BIT(1);
  QUIT = FALSE;
  NEXT = PREVIOUS——>NEXTP;
  DO WHILE (NEXT ≠ NULL & ¬QUIT);
      IF NEXT——>ID = NAME
         THEN /* A match */
             QUIT = TRUE;
         ELSE DO; /* Get next passenger */
             PREVIOUS = NEXT;
             NEXT = NEXT——>NEXTP;
             END;
      END;
  END;
GETPERSON:ENTRY(NAME) RETURNS(POINTER);
   /* Allocate and initialize object of mode PERSON to */
   /* (NAME,NULL) and return pointer to object.        */
   DECLARE NAME CHARACTER(*) VARYING;
   ALLOCATE PERSON SET(PTR);
   PTR——>ID = NAME;
   PTR——>NEXTP = NULL;
   RETURN(PTR);
INSERTPERSON:ENTRY(FLIGHTPTR,NAME);
   /* Insert passenger named NAME on flight list referenced */
   /* by FLIGHTPTR.                                         */
   DECLARE FLIGHTPTR POINTER;
   PREVIOUS = FLIGHTPTR; /* Points to first passenger *1
   CALL FINDPERSON(NAME,PREVIOUS,NEXT);
   PREVIOUS——>NEXTP = GETPERSON(NAME); /* PREVIOUS——>NEW */
   PREVIOUS = PREVIOUS——>NEXTP;
   PREVIOUS——>NEXTP = NEXT; /* NEW——>NEXT */
   RETURN;
DELETEPERSON:ENTRY(FLIGHTPTR,NAME);
   /* Delete passenger named NAME on flight list referenced by */
   /* FLIGHTPTR.                                               */
   PREVIOUS = FLIGHTPTR; /* Points to first passenger */
   CALL FINDPERSON(NAME,PREVIOUS,NEXT);
```

```
   IF NEXT ≠ NULL
      THEN DO; /* Remove passenger */
          PTR = NEXT——>NEXTP; /* Passenger after next */
          FREE NEXT——>PERSON;
          PREVIOUS——>NEXTP=PTR;
                                   /*PREVIOUS——>PASSENGER AFTER NEXT*/
          PUT SKIP LIST('OK');
          END;
      ELSE
          PUT SKIP LIST('ERROR: NONEXISTENT PASSENGER');
   PUT SKIP;
   RETURN;
LISTPEOPLE:ENTRY(FLIGHTPTR);
  /* Print passenger list of flight referenced by FLIGHTPTR */
  PTR = FLIGHTER——>NEXTP; /* Skip null passenger */
  DO WHILE (PTR ≠ NULL); /* More passengers */
      PUT SKIP LIST(PTR——>ID);
      PTR = PTR——>NEXTP; /* Next passenger */
      END;
  RETURN;
FLUSHPEOPLE:ENTRY(FLIGHTPTR);
  /* Remove all passengers from flight referenced by FLIGHTPTR */
  PTR = FLIGHTPTR;
  DO WHILE (PTR ≠ NULL); /* More passengers */
      NEXT = PTR——>NEXTP; /* Next passenger */
      FREE PTR——>PERSON;
      PTR = NEXT;
      END;
  RETURN;
END;
```

3.6.2 More Efficient Solution

If we have a large number of flights, the response to requests in our system may be unacceptably slow. In the worst case, any request may cause us to search through all the flights in our system. We could sort our linked list of flights by flight number, but this would not improve the worst-case performance of our system. Changing our representation for flights from a list to a tree may make searching more efficient. The new representation for flights is shown below:

```
declare 1 FLIGHT BASED(FLIGHTPTR),
          2 NUMBER CHARACTER(3) VARYING,
          2 PASSENGER POINTER,
          2 LEFT POINTER,
          2 RIGHT POINTER;
```

A balanced binary tree of 15 flights is shown in Figure 3.17. To find a particular flight, we start at the root node and compare its number to that of the flight for which we are searching. If the number of the root node is greater

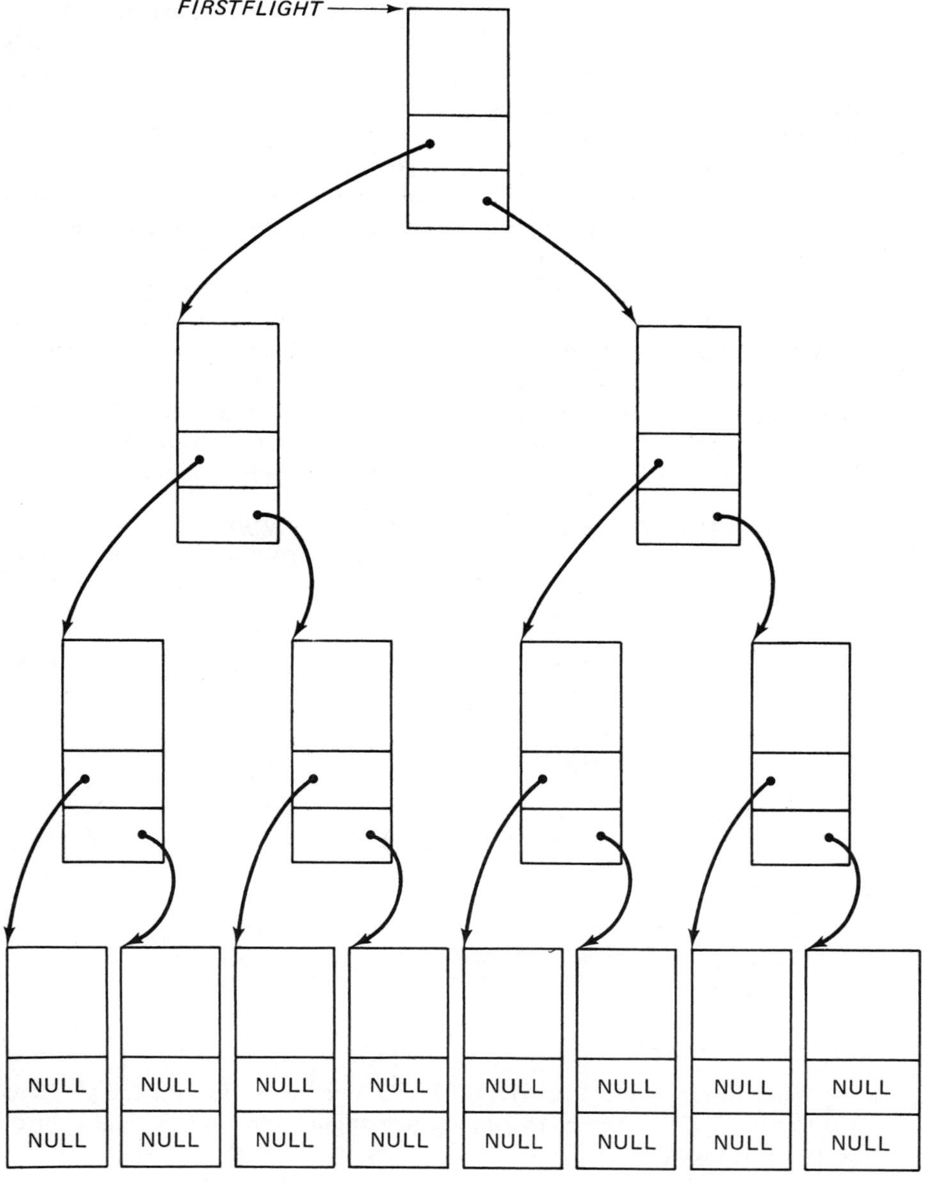

Figure 3.17 Balancing binary tree with 15 flights.

than the desired flight number, we continue searching the subtree referenced by the *LEFT* pointer of the root node. If the number of the root node is less than the desired flight number, we continue searching the right subtree of the root node. In the worst case, we need four comparisons either to find the flights at the leaves of the tree or determine that the flight for which we are searching is not in the tree. In general, a balanced binary tree with $N - 1$ nodes has $\log_2 (N)$ levels. Thus, we need no more than $\log_2 (N)$ comparisons to locate any flight. However, if a series of flights with increasing flight numbers is added to our system, the binary tree effectively becomes an ordered linked list. (See Figure 3.18.)

We claimed that the advantage of structuring our system as we did in the first solution is that changes in the representations of flights and passengers that did not affect interfaces would be confined to their respective modules. Let us see if this is indeed the case.

FINDFLIGHT undergoes the most radical changes, becoming a recursive procedure that still returns *PREVIOUS* pointing to the preceding flight, *NEXT* either pointing to the flight found or NULL, and a binary indication of the success of the search. On entry to FINDFLIGHT, we assume that *PREVIOUS* references the root of the subtree to be searched. The subtree is not empty, and the root node does not contain the flight number we are seeking. Thus, INITFLIGHTS must still insert its dummy flight.

```
FINDFLIGHT:procedure(FLIGHT#,PREVIOUS,NEXT)
                                        returns(BIT(1)) recursive;
 if PREVIOUS——>NUMBER > FLIGHT#
   then /* NEXT——>left subtree */
      NEXT = PREVIOUS——>LEFT;
   else /* NEXT——>right subtree */
      NEXT = PREVIOUS——>RIGHT;
 if NEXT = NULL
   then /* No subtree to search */
      return(FALSE);
   else /* Search NEXT——>subtree */
      if NEXT——>NUMBER = FLIGHT#
        then /* A match */
           return(TRUE);
        else do; /* PREVIOUS——>subtree to search */
           PREVIOUS = NEXT;
           return(FINDFLIGHT(FLIGHT#,PREVIOUS,NEXT));
           end;
 end;
```

When inserting a flight, ADDFLIGHT must now examine the previous flight to determine whether to add the new flight as the left or right subtree of the previous flight.

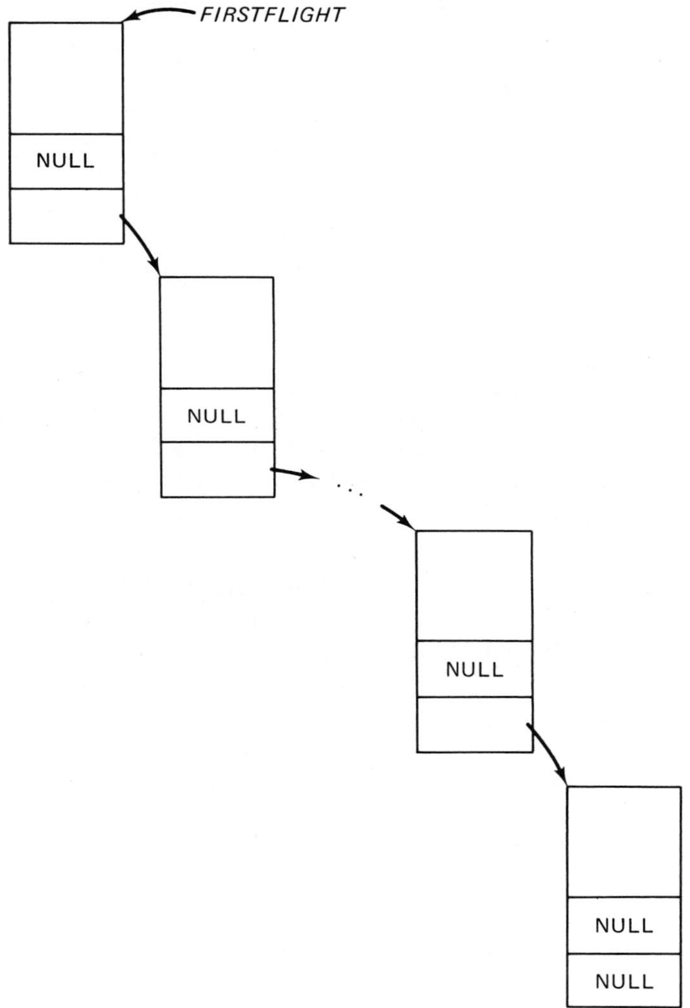

Figure 3.18 Unbalanced binary tree.

```
ADDFLIGHT:entry(FLIGHT#);
   PREVIOUS = FIRSTFLIGHT; /* Starting point */
   if FINDFLIGHT(FLIGHT#,PREVIOUS,NEXT)
     then
        put SKIP LIST('ERROR: DUPLICATE FLIGHT');
     else do;
        call GETFLIGHT(FLIGHT#,FLIGHTPTR);
```

```
        if PREVIOUS——>NUMBER < FLIGHT#
           then /* Add as left subtree */
              PREVIOUS——>LEFT = FLIGHTPTR;
           else /* Add as right subtree */
              PREVIOUS——>RIGHT = FLIGHTPTR;
        put SKIP LIST('OK');
        end;
   put SKIP;
   return;
```

GETFLIGHT must now initialize two pointers, *LEFT* and *RIGHT*, to NULL.

```
GETFLIGHT:procedure(FLIGHT#,PTR);
   allocate FLIGHT SET(PTR);
   PTR——>NUMBER = FLIGHT#;
   PTR——>PASSENGER = GETPERSON('');
   PTR——>LEFT = NULL;
   PTR——>RIGHT = NULL;
   end;
```

The alterations to REMOVEFLIGHT are left as an exercise. However, once they are completed, our system should be ready to run with no changes to either the DRIVER or PASSENGERS procedures.

4 Design of a Single-language Multiprogramming System

4.1 INTRODUCTION

4.1.1 Purpose and Type of System

The operating system described in this chapter is designed to run user programs that are written in a *single high-level language* and submitted in a *batch* mode. This single-language operating system is called *SLOS* for brevity. The objectives of SLOS are to provide fast turnaround of jobs and to run them as economically as possible. To accomplish this, jobs are serviced on a first-come, first-served basis and *share* the system's resources with other jobs and parts of the operating system.

SLOS processes jobs in a *multiprogrammed* fashion; that is, several executing jobs reside in main store at the same time, if possible. All jobs are *spooled* on input and output. Thus, each job is initially written on auxiliary storage, performs all input-output (IO) through virtual IO regions on auxiliary storage, and stores its final output on auxiliary storage from whence it is printed. It is assumed that the reader has had a first course in operating systems e.g., [Shaw, 74].

4.1.2 Design Methodology

The system is designed as a hierarchy of *abstract* or *virtual machines* [Dijkstra, 68b]. The lowest level in the hierarchy is the computer hardware; each succeeding level defines a (virtual, abstract) machine in terms of the facilities (machines) at lower levels. Directly above the machine hardware, an operating system's *nucleus* or *kernel* is provided; the nucleus contains primitive operations and data structures that are used for the management of processes and resources. The remaining levels, representing the principal parts of SLOS, are realized mainly as a set of interacting *processes.*

The design is described in the software design language presented in Chapter 2. This type of language is not only a good design and documentation notation, but is also a possible implementation language; with the possible exception of the SLOS nucleus, which must be in direct contact with much of the hardware, the operating system is most conveniently coded in such a higher level systems programming language.

The design is first developed in a *top-down* manner, leading from general specifications on *what* the system does to program and data details on *how* it performs its functions. The next section describes the global organization and tasks of the hardware, language processor, and operating system complex. Section 4.3 then presents in detail the user interface, including the simple job control language and output listing formats. At this point, the SLOS design is continued from the *bottom up*, starting with the nucleus in Section 4.4 and followed by interrupt and input-output processes in Section 4.5. The next section discusses the file structures employed throughout SLOS, including the input spool, active job, output spool, accounting, and measurement files. It is then logically possible to consider the local and global strategies for scheduling and allocating principal resources, such as the central processor, main and auxiliary storage, buffers, processes, and jobs; Section 4.7 develops these policies. The major higher level processes, such as the job Supervisor, Loader, Spoolin, and Spoolout, are then elaborated in Section 4.8. Following this is a description of the file system that performs filing services for all other processes. Finally, Section 4.10 is concerned with software probes for system performance measurement.

This order of presentation was selected because it approximates the order in which the system was designed by the author. The actual design process consisted of several iterations through a mixture of top-down and bottom-up specifications of SLOS components.

4.2 SYSTEM OVERVIEW

4.2.1 Hardware Components

The underlying computer is assumed to have the conventional components and organization shown in the block diagram of Figure 4.1. This represents a small- to medium-size installation, including a minicomputer system. This machine could also be a virtual hardware system that is simulated and/or emulated by a larger computer; SLOS would then be a *subsystem* running

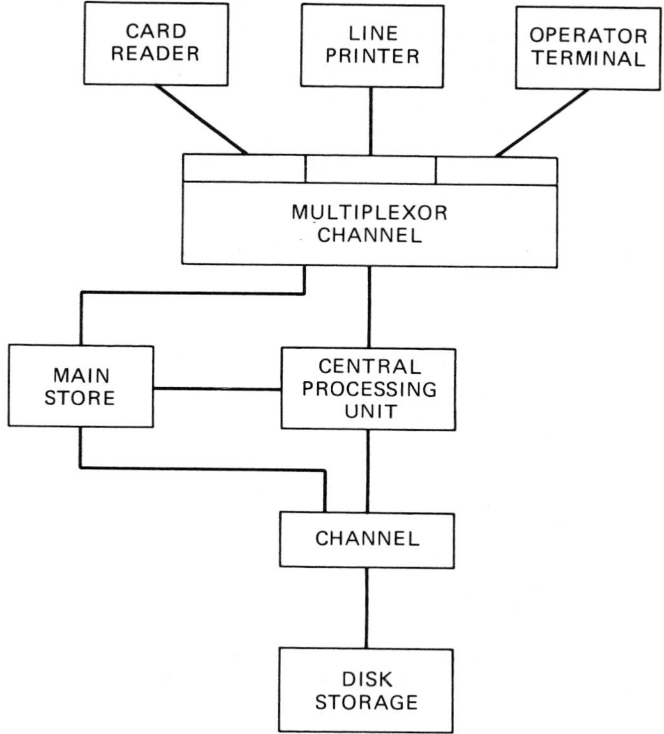

Figure 4.1 Hardware components.

under the control of a host operating system. The hardware is a minimal configuration. It would have to be augmented by magnetic tape drives, removable disks, or a communication line to another computer so that software development, system maintenance, and recovery from catastrophic failures can be conveniently done.

Main store is a standard random access memory divided into addressable cells (words or bytes); it may be read or written by either the central processing unit or by an input-output channel. *Auxiliary storage* consists of a fixed-head *disk*, where each head can access a *track* of information. Tracks are divided into a fixed number of *sectors*; the sector is the smallest addressable area on the disk. We assume that the disk contains t tracks, s sectors per track, and w cells of storage per sector. Typical values for t, s, and w are $t = 250$, $s = 100$, and $w = 400$, giving a capacity of 10^7 cells. A sector is addressed by a [track number, sector number] pair.

The card reader, line printer, and operator terminal share a multiplexor channel that is treated as three separate channels. Disk storage is connected through its controller to a separate channel. A channel is either *busy* or *free*, and its status is stored in CPU-accessible registers. At the completion of an IO operation, the channel sets an IO interrupt register that will cause the CPU to be *interrupted* (unless the IO interrupt is masked).

The central processing unit (*CPU*) has a standard program state word (*PSW*) that is used for storing and restoring processor states. In addition to the instruction counter and other registers, the state word contains bit masks that permit the IO and timer interrupts to be selectively inhibited. An IO operation is initiated by the CPU with the instruction:

startio(c, op, S, D, n);

where:

- c is the channel number.
- op is the operation (e.g., read or write).
- S is the source address of the data to be transmitted (e.g., device address, main store location, or disk sector address).
- D is the destination address.
- n gives the number of cells involved.

There are two timing mechanisms in the CPU. The *interval timer* decrements a timer register with a fixed frequency; the timer interrupt is raised when the register becomes zero. There is also a *time-of-day clock* which can be read through a register. Both clocks may be set by software.

4.2.2 User Job Flow

One way to understand and infer the operating system requirements is to consider the flow or path of a user job as it moves through its various phases. In a standard batch multiprogramming system, a user job, say *J*, is submitted on cards and flows through a number of processing phases as specified by the *flows* [Shaw, 75a] [Shaw, 78] of Figure 4.2:

1. *Input spooling*. *J* is read into main storage and placed on auxiliary storage in an incremental manner. At this time, *J*'s accounting record is verified (a "credit" check) and resource requirements for the execution of *J* are extracted; the latter information includes main storage, estimated CPU time, and input (card)/output (printer) usage. *J* becomes known to the system by storing its characteristics in a *job table*.

2. *Run*. Eventually *J* is selected for loading and execution, and enters the run phase. Main-storage buffers for performing input-output (IO) are established, and files are opened for *J*'s virtual card reader and line printer. The source program will be executed directly by an *interpreter* so that *J* is now ready to start execution. A process corresponding to *J*, say *j*, is created

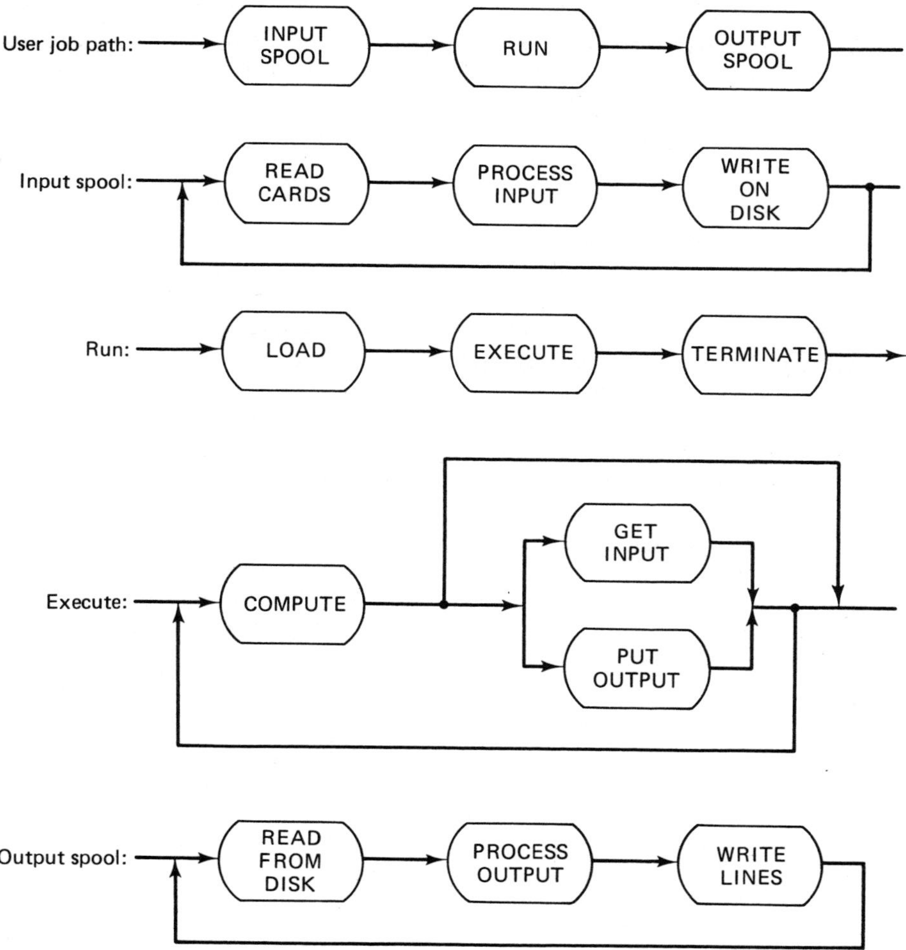

Figure 4.2 Path of a user job.

to represent *J* during its execution. After *j* is allocated the CPU by the process scheduler, the source program is interpreted a statement at a time. Whenever *j* requests an input record (the next "card") or produces output (the next printer "line"), the IO is performed through a virtual card reader or line printer, respectively, on the disk. *j* may lose the CPU while it is waiting for IO completion or due to preemption by a higher priority process. In general, *j* will share the CPU with a number of other processes during its execution.

Process *j* will terminate either naturally or as a result of an error condition. At this point, the process *j* is destroyed, its main storage is released, and the final resource usage record for the job is stored on disk.

3. *Output spooling*. *J*'s output file is read from disk and printed on the line printer. The job has now been completely processed. *J*'s job files are then destroyed, and the auxiliary storage space dedicated to *J* is freed.

4.2.3 Single-language Interpreter and User Workspaces

In the preceding job flow description, no mention was made of several common tasks associated with the high-level language processing in many systems; these may include compiling the source program into an object program, relocation and linking of object programs, loading the language processor, and loading the language run-time support. The SLOS system is relatively simple (but still practical) in this respect. The language processor is an *interpreter*; thus user source programs are "executed" directly. For efficiency, a *single* copy of the interpreter is permanently resident in main storage and is shared by all user programs.

Each executing user job—more precisely, the process associated with the job (process *j* in the last section)—will have a *workspace* in main store containing its source program and any required data areas. These workspaces are of *variable* length, depending on the requirements of each program, and occupy a *contiguous* area of main storage. A major responsibility of SLOS is to manage these variable-length contiguous workspaces. The allocation of main store to the operating system, language interpreter, and several user workspaces is illustrated in Figure 4.3; in the figure, there are three workspaces, i.e., three jobs have been loaded for execution.

4.2.4 The Operating System

Process structure

In the multiprogramming environment of SLOS, a variable number of user jobs may be flowing through the system concurrently. Input spooling constitutes a "critical section" activity in that at most one job may be in this phase at any time; this exclusiveness is necessary because there is only *one* device for initially reading the batched job input—the card reader—and a job must be read in its entirety before starting to read the next one. Similarly, output spooling to the serial line printer is performed by one job at a time until completion. It is not practical to load more than one job from disk at the same time, but several jobs may be in execution simultaneously. Finally, input spooling of one job, loading of another job, output spooling of a third, and the execution of several others can all be performed concurrently from

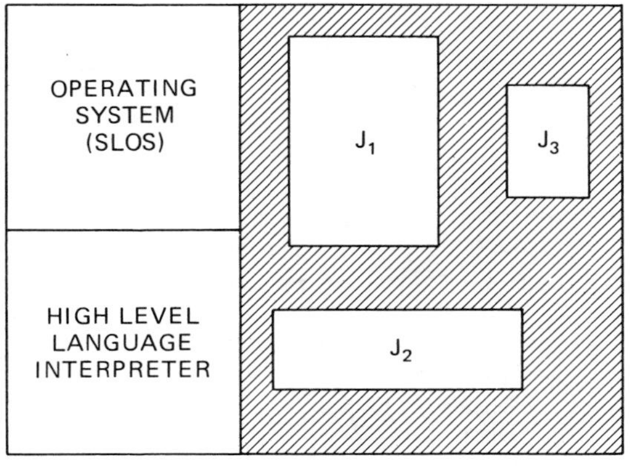

J_i: Workspace for job J_i

Free space

Figure 4.3 Main-store allocation.

a logical point of view. This multiprocessing is implemented on the single central processor by switching control when a process must wait for a resource, such as main storage or an input-output signal, to be available or when higher priority processes become ready.

The SLOS operating system that controls the flow of user jobs has the process structure given in Figure 4.4. This organization was selected because each of its components can easily be identified with one or more distinct *functional* requirements of the system, leading to a modular and straightforward design and implementation. The U_i represent the user processes corresponding to the execution by the interpreter of each job. The *Loader* is responsible for loading a job—the source program—from disk to main storage. Controlling the Loader and U_i is the *Job Supervisor* process that selects the next job to be loaded, creates and initiates the U_i processes, and terminates job execution.

Spoolin and *Spoolout* handle input and output spooling, respectively; these processes directly communicate with the *Card Reader* and *Line Printer Drivers* that are responsible for initiating and controlling the peripheral devices. The computer operator communicates with SLOS through the *Operator Terminal Driver* that is directly connected to the machine terminal. The *Operator Communication* process implements one- and two-way conversations with the terminal to provide such services as updating of user accounting records, retrieval of systems performance statistics, and displaying of current activities and queues.

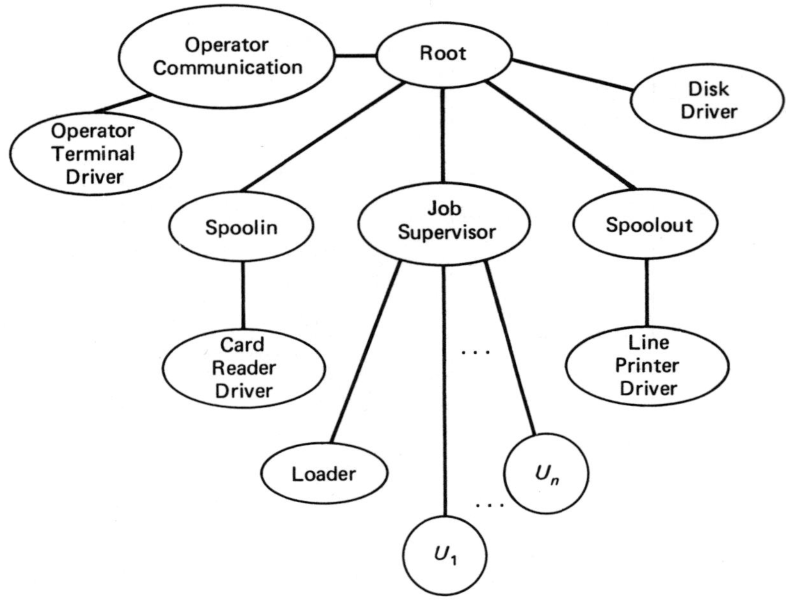

Figure 4.4 Process structure.

The creation, storage, retrieval, and deletion of all files on disk storage are done by File System routines invoked by SLOS processes. Permanent files are maintained for accounting records and systems performance statistics, while temporary files are dynamically established and terminated for user jobs and their output. The File System routines perform disk IO through the *Disk Driver*. At the root of the process tree is the *Root* process. Root is the creator of all other SLOS components and also serves as an "idle" process when all other processes are blocked (but not deadlocked!).

Virtual machine hierarchy

The processes and routines of SLOS define a hierarchy of virtual machines. The levels or layers of these machines are presented in Figure 4.5. The hierarchy is useful because it explicitly exhibits some of the dependencies that exist among the various components and, consequently, simplifies the design, construction, debugging, and understanding of the system.

The first level of software, the SLOS nucleus, implements processes and some basic resources, such as messages, locks, and storage. The next layer, consisting of the IO device driver processes and interrupt-handling "pseudo" processes, is constructed using the facilities of the nucleus level. Above these two software layers is the file system; all processes that are higher in the hierarchy can assume the availability of disk-filing services. Most of the SLOS

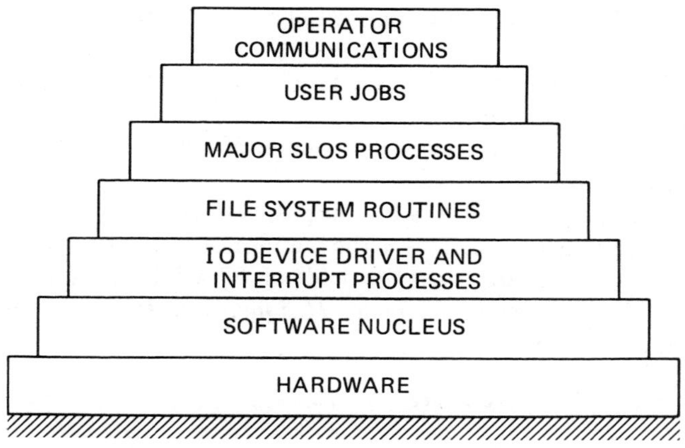

Figure 4.5 Virtual machine hierarchy.

processes appear next in the ordering; they define an operating system machine capable of running the user jobs that, in turn, are logically situated one level higher. The operator processes are placed at the top of the hierarchy, since the operator should be able to access all virtual machines in the system.

4.3 THE USER INTERFACE

A user of SLOS prepares a job on cards and submits it to the system operator who places the job in the batch queue of the card reader. After the job is run, the user receives hard copy output produced by the line printer. In this section, the format and contents of the job input and output are described. Job input and output are stored internally (on the disk) in two files: an *input spool file* and an *output spool file*, respectively.

4.3.1 Job Input

Unfortunately, a nonstandard part of any operating system is the *job control* or *command language* employed by the user to describe his job. In SLOS (and other similar systems), a user job contains control, program, and data cards in the following order: Job card, Source Program, End-of-Program card, Data cards, and End-of-Job card.

1. The following six entries appear on the job card. These are sufficient to describe a job to SLOS:

(a) $JOB. This specifies the type of card. It informs the input spooler of the start of a new card deck.

(b) Job Id. This is a user-defined character string that identifies the job.

(c) Account Number. This is a number, associated with the user, that identifies his accounting records.

(d) Time Estimate. This is an estimate of maximum CPU time to be used by the job.

(e) Line Estimate. This is the output estimate.

(f) Storage Estimate. This is the amount of main storage required.

If *JC* designates a Job card, then the fields of *JC* will be referenced with the notation *JC.Id*, *JC.Account*, *JC.Time*, *JC.Line*, and *JC.Store*, and can be defined by the structure:

```
declare 1 JC,
          2 Id,
          2 Account,
          2 Time,
          2 Line,
          2 Store;
```

2. The Source Program contains the program in symbolic form.
3. The End-of-Program card acts as a terminator for the source program and as the start of data cards, if any are present. This card contains the string $EOP.
4. The Data cards are the input data for the source program and are optional.
5. A job is terminated by the End-of-Job card, which has the entry $EOJ.

The particular format for the simple job control or command language defined by the '$' cards is somewhat arbitrary here. The important requirements are that the system be able to easily distinguish the commands from source program and data and that sufficient information is provided to identify and run the jobs. For example, each item can be separated by commas or can be in fixed columns on the $JOB card. Such details will not be specified.

4.3.2 Job Output

The job output file, which is written on the line printer and given to the user, contains, in order, an accounting header, the original source program and any errors, the output produced by the user program's "write" statements, and a job terminator. The accounting header includes the items: Job Id, Account Number, amount charged to the account for running the job, the number of CPU time units used, the number of input cards read, and the number of output lines printed. The date and time are also recorded.

During interpretation of the source program, any errors in syntax will be interspersed with the source program output. The job terminator record reproduces the Job Id and Account Number and specifies the reason for job termination; the latter may be normal termination, syntax errors, detectable run-time errors such as divide by zero, and job has exceeded its CPU time or output line estimate.

4.4 THE NUCLEUS

The SLOS nucleus provides a uniform set of data structures and primitive operations for the management of all processes and resources. This nucleus is a restricted version of the one described in Shaw [74, Chapter 7], [75b].

4.4.1 Process Management Kernel

The "state" of a process is completely characterized by its data structure, called a *process descriptor*. All process descriptors have the same general form and function, as shown in Table 4.1. The *Status* field is interpreted as follows. A process executing on the CPU is said to be in *running* status, processes that are eligible to run as soon as the CPU is made available to them are *ready*, and processes that are waiting for requested units of a resource to be allocated are defined as *blocked*. If a process is ready or running, it is linked through the *Ready List*. Otherwise, it is on a *Wait List* associated with the resource upon which the process is blocked; in this case, data passed with the resource request is stored in *BlockedData*. More details on the structure of the Ready and Wait Lists are given in Sections 4.4.2 and 4.4.4.[1]

TABLE 4-1 Process Data Structure

```
declare 1 Process_Descriptor,
          2 Status,     /* running, ready, or blocked */
          2 List,       /* ready or wait list linkage */
          2 BlockedData,  /*  when blocked */
          2 PSW,               /* Program Status Word, */
                           /* when process is not running */
          2 Priority,
          2 CPUtimeleft,
          2 Workspace,  /* user main storage */
          2 JobFile;    /* user job file */
```

[1]The Status field is redundant since status can also be determined from the List field; the Status field is included for efficiency.

The *time* field is used for accounting purposes and to ensure that an errant user process does not totally monopolize the system. For user processes that represent user jobs during their execution, the *Workspace* field gives the workspace address and length while the *JobFile* entry points to the file of the corresponding user job.

User processes are *temporary*; as new jobs enter and leave the system, the associated processes are created and destroyed. All other SLOS processes are *permanent*. Two primitive operations, *CreateProcess* and *DestroyProcess*, are used to establish and terminate, respectively, the temporary user process. Both routines must be *noninterruptable* because they interrogate and update central SLOS data that is shared by several concurrent processes. *CreateProcess* creates a new process by constructing a new process descriptor; *DestroyProcess* returns the descriptor to the nucleus "descriptor space." These procedures are described in Figure 4.6. Note that processes are referenced by their descriptors and that, for simplicity, pointer variables are not used in the program descriptions.

```
CreateProcess: procedure(maxCPUtime, workspace, file);
/* Create a new user process and return its descriptor. */
   pd = GetNewProcessDescriptor; /* Allocate from descriptor */
                                 /* space. */
   pd.CPUtimeleft = maxCPUtime;
   pd.Workspace = workspace; /* workspace=(length,baseaddr) */
   pd.JobFile = file;
   pd.Priority = userpriority; /* All users have same */
                               /* priority. */
   pd.Status = 'ready';
   call ReadyList_Insert1(pd.List); /* Link pd through its List */
                                    /* field to the ready      */
                                    /* list.                   */
   pd.PSW = InterpreterInitialState; /* Start with initial */
                                     /* state of language */
                                     /* interpreter.      */
   end CreateProcess;

DestroyProcess: procedure(pd);
/* Destroy process with descriptor pd. */
   call DeleteFromList(pd.List); /* Remove from Ready/Wait list */
   call PutDescriptor(pd); /* Return pd to descriptor space. */
   end DestroyProcess;
```

Figure 4.6 Process primitives.

Descriptor space consists of $t + p$ blocks of storage, where t is the maximum number of temporary processes and p is the number of permanent processes. Thus, the system can execute no more than t jobs (equivalently, job processes) at any time; in other words, the *multiprogramming* level is t.

4.4.2 Resource Management Kernel

Resources consist of *reusable* hardware and software resources, such as main and auxiliary storage and locks associated with critical sections, and *consumable* resources, such as interprocess messages and wakeup signals caused by interrupts. Abstractly, a resource is *any* entity on which a process can be blocked. The state and allocation strategy of each resource is defined in a *resource descriptor*. It is convenient to specify a standard descriptor format that applies to all resources, as shown in Table 4.2. An instance of this data structure is declared for each resource *class*.

TABLE 4-2 Resource Data Structure

Available List	:	free units
Wait List	:	blocked processes
Allocator	:	allocation routine

For reusable resources, the *Available List* contains the free units of the resource that are currently available for allocation to a requesting process. In the case of consumable resources, this list stores those units (messages) that have been produced (sent) but not yet consumed (received). The *Wait List* field is a *queue* header pointing to a doubly linked list (possibly empty) of processes blocked on the resource; blocked processes are linked through the process descriptors. *Each* list has associated routines for inserting an element and for removing an element. The *Allocator* is a boolean function that attempts to match available units to requests for the resource. For the resource named R, it has the call: R_Allocator (k, PD); Allocator returns TRUE if an allocation is made and FALSE otherwise; if TRUE is returned, then $PD(i)$, $i = 1, \ldots, k$ point to the processes (descriptors) whose requests have been satisfied.

All SLOS resources are permanent and are "created" at the time that the system is generated.[2] Two primitive operations, *Get* and *Put*, are employed to obtain and free resources, respectively. A process wishing to acquire one or more units of the resource R issues the request: **call** R_Get(m), where m contains the data of the Get, such as the number of units requested and the location in which the details of the resulting allocation are to be placed when the request is satisfied. The requesting process, say cp, is placed in *blocked* status until the allocation is made; the state of cp is saved in the process descriptor. The Put operation either returns a reusable resource that had previously been acquired (through a Get) or produces a consumable

[2]Because of the relative simplicity of the user environment (single language, interpreter, no user-created files, predetermined resource needs), it is neither necessary nor efficient to include temporary resources that are dynamically created and destroyed at run time.

resource (message). Put may cause a process that was previously blocked on the resource to be awakened and made ready. The release of a resource R is performed by the call: **call** R_Put(*m*), where *m* gives the specifics of the freed resource.

Get and Put are described in the programs of Figure 4.7. (These primitives are simplified versions of the general Request/Release operations presented in Shaw [75b].) As with the process primitives, both of these operations must be logically indivisible; for the case of a single CPU system, disabling the interrupts for the duration of the operations is sufficient to ensure the indivisibility. The process scheduler, *Scheduler*, is invoked conditionally by both Get and Put. It has the task of allocating the CPU to ready processes.

4.4.3 Resource Definitions

Each resource class used in SLOS will be selected from a set of generic resources that are defined in this section.

```
Get: procedure(m);
/* Let the caller of Get, the current process, be cp. */
/* Block cp and insert m into BlockedData. */
      cp.Status = 'blocked';
      cp.BlockedData = m;
      call WaitList_Insert(cp.List); /* Link cp to Wait List */
                                     /* of resource. */
      /* Invoke allocator for resource. */
      if Allocator(k, PD)
          then do; /* Get is satisfied. Make cp running again. */
          cp.Status = 'running';
          call ReadyList_Insert2(cp.List);
               /* Insert cp at top of list at its priority. */
          end;
      else /* Get is not satisfied. Find another process. */
           call Scheduler;
      end Get;
Put: procedure(m);
/* Add m to Available List and call Allocator. */
      call AvailList_Insert(m);
      if Allocator(k,PD)
          then do i = 1 to k; /* Make processes ready. */
          PD(i).Status = 'ready';
          call ReadyList_Insert1 (PD(i).List);
               /* Insert PD(i) at bottom of list */
               /* at its priority. */
          end;
      call Scheduler; /* Select highest priority */
                  /* ready process. */
      end Put;
```

Figure 4.7 Get and Put resource primitives.

1. *Directed Messages.* All consumable resources will be directed messages with the following Get/Put conventions:

(a) M_Get(m); A message of class M is requested. The parameter m contains two fields $m = \langle sender, message \rangle$; when the Get is satisfied, *sender* will identify the process that sent (Put) the message while the second field will contain the actual message.

Equivalently, m is the structure:

```
declare 1 m,
          2 sender, /* message sender */
          2 message; /* message sent */
```

(b) M_Put(m); A message of class M is sent. $m = \langle receiver, message \rangle$, where the first element identifies the intended receiver of the message and the second field points to the message.

The available units data structure is a bounded list of triples: $\langle sender, receiver, message \rangle$, linked in *FIFO order* (first-in, first-out). Figure 4.8 outlines the allocator for directed messages. All explicit process-to-process communication occurs through resources of this type.

```
M_Allocator: procedure(k, PD) returns(BIT);
     alloc = FALSE; k = 0; /* Initialize. */
     W = M_WaitList_First( ); /* first process on wait list */
     do while(¬null(W)); /* Loop through waiting processes. */
          A = M_AvailList_First( ); /* first available message */
          do while(¬null(A));
               if W = A.receiver /* Match found. */
                    then do;
                    W.BlockedData = [A.sender,A.message];
                    call M_AvailList_Delete(A);
                    alloc = TRUE;
                    k = k+1; PD(k) = W;
                    call M_WaitList_Delete(W);
                    end;
               A = M_AvailList_Next(A);
               end;
          W = M_WaitList_Next(W);
          end;
     return(alloc);
     end M_Allocator;
```

Figure 4.8 Directed message allocator.

2. *Locks.* A lock is a single unit reusable resource that is employed to protect a data area that must be accessed on a serial basis only. Locks will be used to surround the *critical sections* of code that access the data areas. The protocol and Get/Put conventions are:

```
call L_Get;          /* Get lock L.3 */
Critical section of code;
call L_Put;          /* Unlock L. */
```

For each lock *L*, the available units is described by a boolean flag, say *L.Lock*, which is set TRUE if the lock has been allocated and FALSE otherwise. The generic allocator for locks is given in Figure 4.9. Note that the lock is implemented as a *binary semaphore* [Shaw, 74] with no check on whether the lock protocol is violated. *L.Lock* is set FALSE by the AvailList_Insert in Put.

```
L_Allocator: procedure(k, PD) returns(BIT);
    if L.lock | empty(L.WaitList)
        then return(FALSE);
    else do; /* L.lock is false. */
        W = L_WaitList_Remove( );
        L.lock = TRUE;
          /* equivalent to L_AvailList_Delete( ) */
        k = 1; PD(1) = W;
        return(TRUE);
        end;
    end L_Allocator;
```

Figure 4.9 Lock allocator.

3. *Storage Blocks.* Main and auxiliary storage will be allocated in terms of resource units called *blocks*. For auxiliary storage, a block will correspond to a disk *track*. The user workspace area of main storage will be divided, for allocation purposes, into *n* blocks, where, for example, $n = 100$ and block size is 400 cells. The available units is most easily specified by a *bit map* $b_0b_1...b_{n-1}$, where *n* is the number of blocks and $b_i = 1$ if block *i* is free and 0 if it is allocated. The allocators are then straightforward and can use simple masking, shifting, and bit-testing operations on the bit maps.[4] Blocks of reusable storage are obtained and released with the calls:

(a) **call** MAINSTORE_Get(*m*);
where *m* is the structure:

```
declare 1 m,
          2 k, /*number of contiguous blocks */
          2 base_adr;  /* first addr allocated */
```

[3]When the argument fields of the Get and Put procedures are not used, they will be omitted.

[4]Other schemes, such as linked lists of free-space headers and/or boundary tags [Shaw, 74], are unnecessarily complex for our application. Section 2.6.8 presents some other storage strategies that can be used.

k contiguous blocks of main storage are requested. When the Get is granted, *base_adr* will point to the address of the first block allocated.

```
call MAINSTORE_Put(⟨k,base_adr⟩);
```

The k blocks starting at *base_adr* are freed.

(b) **call** DISKSTORE_Get(m);
where m is declared to be:

```
declare   1 m,
            2 k, /*number of tracks*/
            2 Track( ); /* track numbers */
```

k tracks of disk are requested; the tracks need not be contiguous. On return from the Get, *Track*(i), $i = 1, \ldots, k$ contain the addresses of the k allocated tracks.

```
call DISKSTORE_Put(⟨k,Track( )⟩);
```

The k disk tracks, *Track*(i), $i = 1, \ldots, k$ are liberated.

4.4.4 Process Scheduling

All of the SLOS and user processes compete for the CPU. In order to control the allocation of the vital CPU resource, we predefine a scheduling priority for each process. This priority component of the process descriptor is used by the Scheduler to ensure that the *highest* priority ready process receives the CPU. In the case of highest priority ties, it is reasonable to schedule the tied processes on a FIFO basis. The selection of priorities will be discussed in Section 4.7.1.

Our scheduling policy is *preemptive* in that an important (high priority) process that becomes ready after being blocked will preempt the CPU from a lower priority running process. The Scheduler need only be invoked within Get and Put and by interrupt-handling pseudo processes (Section 4.5). The Scheduler algorithm is given in Figure 4.10. Note that the "CPUstate" saved for the current process cp actually must have its instruction counter field point to the *return* address of Scheduler in order for cp to properly resume execution later.

The *Ready List* is a linked list of processes in priority order. A convenient data structure for this list is described in detail in Chapter 7 of Shaw [74].

Exercise 4.1: The algorithms presented in Sections 4.4.2, 4.4.3, and 4.4.4 assume the availability of a number of list-processing routines for accessing

```
Scheduler: procedure;
/* Give CPU to highest priority ready process. */
    hp = ReadyList_First( ); /* highest priority ready */
                             /* process                 */
    /* Let cp be the calling process. */
    if cp.Status='running'
        then do;
        if hp.Priority ≤ cp.Priority then EXIT;
        cp.Status = 'ready';
            /* cp will be pre-empted by hp. */
        end;
    /* Update descriptor of cp. */
    cp.CPUtimeleft = intervaltimer;
    cp.PSW = CPUstate;
         /* CPUstate = 'return' state of scheduler */
    /* Give CPU to hp. */
    hp.Status = 'running';
    intervaltimer = hp.CPUtimeleft; /* Load timer. */
    LoadCPUstate(hp.PSW); /* Exit from Scheduler to hp. */
    end Scheduler;
```

Figure 4.10 Process scheduler.

and updating Wait Lists, Available Lists and the Ready List. Give a detailed design for the data structures of these lists and for their associated accessing procedures.

Exercise 4.2: Give PDL procedures for the MAINSTORE and DISK-STORE allocators described in this section.

4.5 INTERRUPTS AND INPUT-OUTPUT

4.5.1 Interrupt and Trap Handling

Interrupts can be generated by the IO channels and by the hardware timer. The basic tasks of an interrupt handler are to gracefully store the state of the interrupted process and to send a message to a system service process that is waiting for the interrupt. To provide these facilities in a clean fashion, we associate a *pseudo process* ps_I and a message class X_I with each interrupt I. ps_I performs the tasks of the interrupt handler and is *directly* connected to the hardware interrupt; the actions of ps_I are:

1. Save state of interrupted process *cp* in its descriptor.
2. Place *cp* in ready status.
3. Decode interrupt into a message, *message*.
4. Issue **call** X_I_Put($\langle$*serviceprocess*, *message*$\rangle$);
5. Call the Scheduler, just in case Put did not.

A pseudo process *always* relinquishes the CPU at the end of the interrupt-handling sequence so that either the service process or the interrupted process continue execution.

Traps are internal forced transfers of control within a process that often signify errors in programming (e.g., register overflow or divide by zero). These are treated in a different manner than interrupts. It is assumed that traps will only occur within user processes and that they will be serviced by the high-level language interpreter. The trap handlers, i.e., the code directly connected to the traps, will simply:

1. Save the state of the current process in its descriptor
2. Transfer control to a fixed location in the interpreter

The interpreter may terminate execution in the case of error traps, or may service the request in the case of executive requests or supervisor calls (e.g., open a file or return time of day).

4.5.2 Input-Output Device Driver Processes

Input-output and interrupt-handling represent the lowest level applications of the process and resource kernels. For *each* input-output device—card reader, line printer, disk unit, and operator's console—we define a software *driver* process that is responsible for honoring input-output requests. With this convention, the entire system can be specified in terms of logical asynchronous processes. The protocol for performing input-output is illustrated in Figure 4.11.

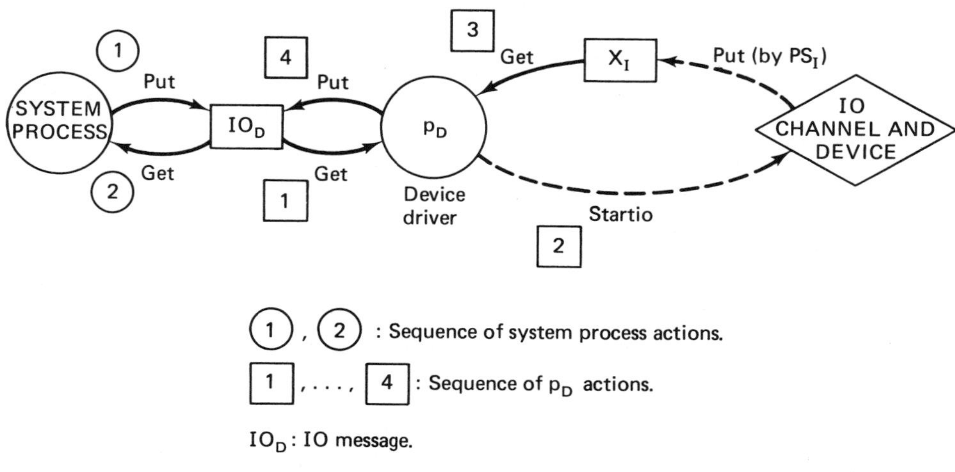

Figure 4.11 Input-output sequence.

To perform an input-output operation on device *D*, a message of type *IOD* is released to the driver process for that device, say *PD*: **call** IOD_Put (⟨*PD*, *IOparams*⟩); . The *IOparams* field may include parameters such as buffer addresses, read or write indicators, and number of cells to be transmitted, depending on the particular device. At some later time, a completion message is requested from *PD*: **call** IOD_Get(⟨*PD*, *completionmessage*⟩);.

An IO driver *PD* is a cyclic process that provides a logical message interface between the processes in the system and the hardware signals of both the IO device *D* and the interrupts generated through its connecting channel. Figure 4.12 contains the code for the disk-driver process. The other drivers have a similar form. Note that it is assumed that device-end and channel-end interrupts are synonymous and that IO errors do not occur. To handle errors in IO transmission, we might repeat the operation several times and return an error message if still unsuccessful.

```
DiskDriver:procedure;
    do while(TRUE); /* Cycle forever. */
        call DISKIO_Get(⟨sender, ⟨buffer,sector,rw,
                cellcount⟩⟩); /* Get next record. */
        if rw='read' then /* read command */
            startio(channel4,read,sector,buffer,cellcount);
        else /* write command */
            startio(channel4,write,buffer,sector,cellcount);
        call DISKINT_Get(⟨ps,interruptcause⟩);
                /* Wait for IO interrupt. */
        call DISKIO_Put(⟨sender,interruptcause⟩);
                /* Notify sender. */
        end;
    end DiskDriver;
```

Figure 4.12 Disk-driver process.

4.6 FILE STRUCTURES

4.6.1 Job Tables and Files

Each user job in the system is represented by an entry in a *job table*. All accounting and resource records are temporarily maintained in this table for the duration of the job—from the time it is recognized by the input spooling phase until it has been terminated and all of its resources released. Table 4.3 describes the contents of each job table entry. Each *Diskaddress* field contains $N + 1$ elements: (*N*, *Trackaddress*(*i*), $= 1, \ldots, N$), where *N* is the number of tracks allocated to the file and *Trackaddress*(*i*) gives the address of the *i*th allocated disk track. These fields will be referenced as *F.N* and *F.Trackaddress*(*i*), for the file *F*.

TABLE 4-3 Job Table Descriptor

```
declare 1 JT,
          2 Identification,
               3 JobID,
               3 AccountNumber,
          2 ResourceClaim,
               3 MaxCPUtime,
               3 MaxOutLines,
               3 MainStore,
          2 ResourceUse,
               3 CPUtime,
               3 Input, /* cards */
               3 Output, /* lines */
          2 TerminationCause,
          2 Files,
               3 Source, /* source program */
                    4 Diskaddress,
                         5 N,
                         5 Trackaddress(*),
               3 InputData,
                    4 Diskaddress,
                         5 N,
                         5 Trackaddress(*),
               3 OutputLines,
                    4 Diskaddress,
                         5 N,
                         5 Trackaddress(*);
```

The job table is included in the *descriptor* for user job files. Three types of *sequential* user job files are maintained:

1. *Input spool.* These contain the spooled-in source program and data input for each job that has entered the system but has not yet been selected for loading and execution.
2. *Output spool.* After a job has been run, all of its output is stored in the Output Spool file for subsequent printing.
3. *Active job.* A file is *active* ("open") when it is ready for reading and writing. Job files become active at the time a job is selected for loading and remain active until execution is terminated; they are also active *during* input and output spooling.

While a user job file is most conveniently treated as belonging to one of the above three types, it actually represents the same file as it changes status during job processing. The file classification is reflected by its position in the *file directory.*

SLOS has two other files. An *Accounting* file stores accounting information for each user (Account Number). It is used for credit checking when a job enters the system and for billing purposes. The components of an accounting record are given in Table 4.4. A systems *Measurement* file contains daily and monthly statistics on systems performance, including job measurements and resource utilization.

TABLE 4-4 Accounting Record

```
declare 1 ad,  /* accounting descriptor */
          2 Name,
          2 AccountNumber,
          2 RemainingDollars,  /* in account */
          2 DollarsSpent,      /* spent this month */
          2 Runs,              /* runs this month */
          2 LastActivity;      /* date of last run */
```

4.6.2 Directory Structure

The file directory is organized as a multilevel *tree* with the files as leaves. Figure 4.13 gives a schematic of the complete directory organization. The *master* directory contains five entries, one for each type of file. For user job files, the master directory entry points to a linked chain of descriptor addresses; these, in turn, point to the descriptors of each file, which point to the actual files. The master directory points to the descriptor itself in the case of the Accounting and Measurement files.

All files reside on disk storage, but most of the directory is kept permanently in main store for more efficient access. In particular, the master directory, descriptor chains, and descriptors for Active, Accounting, and Measurement files will be stored in main memory. Descriptors for Input Spool and Output Spool files are retained on disk since there is potentially a large number of these files and their descriptors would consume too much main storage.

4.6.3 File Descriptors

The descriptor associated with each file contains the information required by the file system procedures in order to access the file. *The job table entry is part of the descriptor for all user job files.* In the case of Active job files, additional data is necessary for reading and writing. These items include buffers and logical and physical record pointers; it is assumed that several *logical* records (card or line images) comprise a *physical* record and that a physical record is one disk sector in length. Each active input or output file *F* will then have the following descriptor components in addition to the Job Table (Table 4.3):

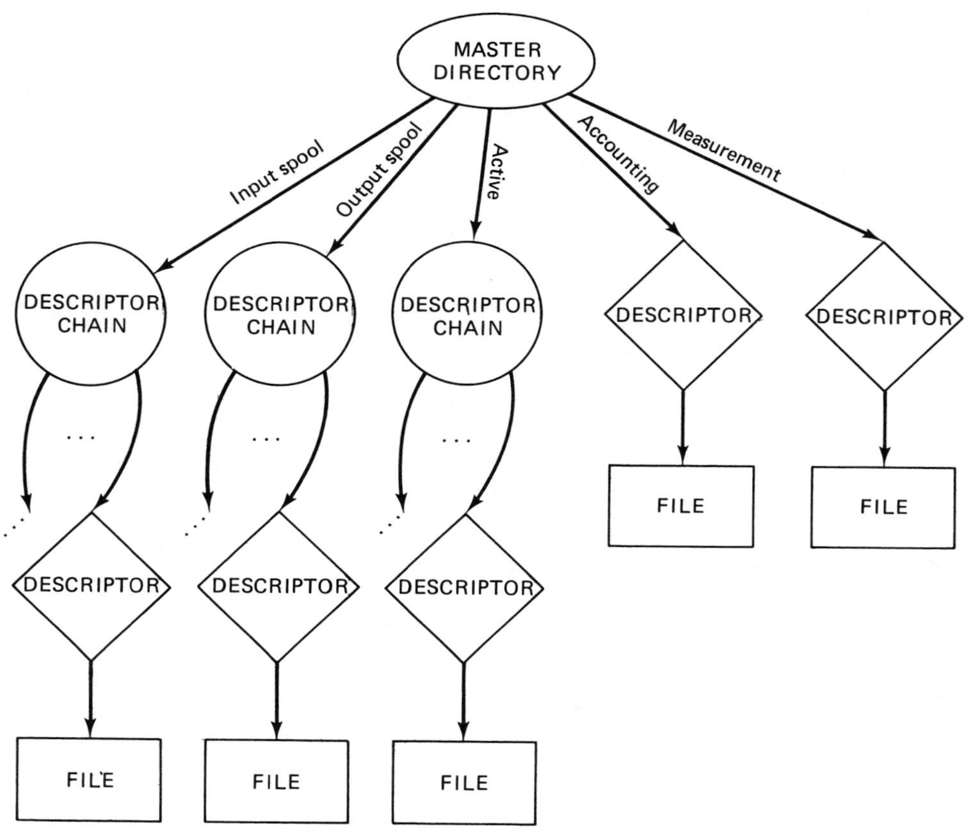

Figure 4.13 Directory tree structure.

```
2  Files,
 3  InputData,
    4  DiskAddress,        /* start of file */
    4  DiskBuffer,         /* ID of buffer in main store */
                              /* used for reading */
    4  NextPR,             /* [track,sector] of next */
                              /* physical record */
    4  NextLR,             /* index into DiskBuffer */
                              /* of next record */
    4  LRlength,           /* logical record length */
 3  OutputLines, . . .      /* same as above */
```

The Accounting file descriptor will contain the address of the Accounting file, assumed to be, say, one track at most in length, and a disk buffer address. Because of the relatively small size of each record, several records can fit into one sector. A particular record can be addressed by a pair $[s, i]$, denoting the ith record in sector s. Hash coding methods are convenient for organizing the record addresses in this file; the *sector* corresponding to a given account will be obtained by applying an appropriate hashing function to the *account number*. The Measurements file descriptor contains a disk buffer address and the addresses of the three components of this file: a daily job and resource utilization log, month-to-date user job measurements, and month-to-date resource utilization.

4.7 SCHEDULING AND ALLOCATION POLICIES

This section is concerned with scheduling strategies for jobs, processes, IO buffers, and main and auxiliary storage. The objectives are to provide efficient service and, at the same time, to avoid deadlock and starvation problems.

4.7.1 Job and Process Scheduling

The Input Spool files will normally contain several spooled-in jobs. The *job scheduling* policy determines which one is selected next for loading and execution. This is perhaps the highest level policy decision of SLOS. The Job Supervisor process, which is responsible for next job selection, will choose on a *FIFO* basis initially since it is the easiest to implement, is generally recognized as being fair, and guarantees that every job will eventually be selected. The major disadvantage of FIFO is that systems resources, such as storage, IO, and the CPU, may be inefficiently used, resulting in decreased throughput and *average* turnaround time.

Example. Suppose the Input Spool file contains in FIFO order, four jobs J_1, J_2, J_3, and J_4, requesting workspaces of size W_1, W_2, W_3, and W_4 respectively. Assume that $W_1=W_2$, $W_3=W_4$, $W_1 \ll W_3$, and that W_1+W_3 is equal to the total main storage size. Given that there are no other jobs in the system, and that the run times of each job are approximately the same, FIFO job scheduling would result in the multiprogrammed execution of J_1 and J_2 together, followed by the execution of J_3 and then J_4. However, a more efficient strategy is to run a small job with a large one, i.e., first run J_1 and J_3 together and then execute J_2 and J_4 together.

By isolating the job scheduling mechanism within a small part of the Job Supervisor, it will be possible to change this FIFO policy in the future if warranted. The FIFO policy is easily implemented: The descriptor chain for Input Spool files (Section 4.6.2) is organized as a FIFO queue, and a lock is used to protect the table during scheduling.

The efficient use of systems resources depends to a large extent on how wisely the CPU is allocated to competing processes. The priority preemptive scheduler permits control of the scheduling policy through the selection of priorities. Table 4.5 lists the relative priorities for all SLOS processes.

TABLE 4-5 Relative Priorities of Processes

Highest Priority	IO Device Drivers
	Operator Communication
	Job Supervisor, Loader
	Spoolin, Spoolout
	U_i
Lowest Priority	Root

The IO device drivers are given the highest priority since it is desirable to keep the devices as busy as possible and since user and system processes are often waiting for IO completion messages. The importance of the human machine operator is recognized by giving the second highest priority to the Operator Communication process; in this way, external control of the system through the operator can be effected with a minimum of delay. The Job Supervisor and Loader are next on the scheduling list since they are responsible for user job initiation and termination and should be expected to perform these tasks whenever possible. Below these are the Spoolin and Spoolout processes; because they are expected to be IO bound, they are given a higher priority than the user processes. The second lowest priority level is assigned to user processes because we do not want a compute-bound user process to monopolize the system and prevent overlapped IO and central processing. When the system has nothing else to do, the Root process is run as an "idle" process; thus it receives the lowest priority.

Starvation is a situation wherein a process or job may be indefinitely prevented from making progress (e.g., blocked indefinitely or indefinitely in ready status or indefinitely in the Input Spool file) even though it is *logically* possible to do so. The FIFO policies on job scheduling and message allocations prevent starvation since FIFO guarantees eventual service (provided deadlock does not occur). However, a priority scheduling system may prevent lower priority processes from ever running. The only process for which starvation is desirable is the Root process. For the others, it is necessary that progress be guaranteed, despite their differing priorities.

The Operator Communication process is the only one that can starve the system. It can starve the system in the unlikely and ridiculous case when it is continuously active; this occurs if the operator is almost *continuously* sending and receiving messages and the Operator Communication process consumes virtually all of the CPU cycles. None of the other SLOS processes can starve without causing the remaining ones to be *blocked*. For example, if Spoolout is starved, then eventually the disk will fill with Input Spool, Active, and Output Spool files; the remaining processes will then be blocked waiting for disk space to be released (by Spoolout).[5] In this situation, the starved process will be the only "ready" one (in addition to Root and, possibly, the Operator Terminal Driver and Operator Communication process) and will eventually get scheduled; thus the starved process becomes unstarved and we have a contradiction. A particular user process cannot starve since all user processes are scheduled on a FIFO basis within their priority. If all user processes are starved, then eventually Spoolin will either run out of new jobs or fill the disk and Spoolout will print all available output and have nothing to do. Thus, user processes will be the only ones ready. In this way, the system is self-regulating.

4.7.2 IO Buffering Methods

In order to maintain a maximum degree of IO activity and a high degree of *concurrent* execution of the three processors in the system (multiplexor channel, disk channel, and the CPU), all input-output is buffered via software through main storage buffer areas. Buffering is implemented with directed message resources.

1. *Card reader and input spooling*. A ring of n buffers ($n \geq 2$), each of size one card record (e.g., 80 bytes), will be used for card input. A class of directed messages, CARDIO, with an initial "allocated" units of n empty messages is defined. The card *consumer* process, Spoolin, initially sends n messages to the card *producer* process, CardReaderDriver. Subsequently, Spoolin obtains the next full card buffer with:

```
call CARDIO_Get(⟨CardReaderDriver,buffer⟩);
```

After the buffer has been "emptied," Spoolin issues:

```
call CARDIO_Put(⟨CardReaderDriver,buffer⟩);
```

where *buffer* points to an 80-byte buffer area in main storage. Space for the n buffers is allocated at system load time. Assume that the buffer addresses are stored in the table *CardBuffer*(0), . . . , *CardBuffer*($n-1$), where *CardBuffer*(i) contains the address of buffer i. Then, Spoolin performs the initial N Put's with the code:

[5]This assumes a continual stream of jobs; otherwise, the disk may not fill, but a similar blocking situation will eventually occur.

```
do I = 0 to n-1 ;
    call CARDIO_Put(⟨CardReaderDriver,CardBuffer(I)⟩) ;
    end ;[6]
```

2. *Line printer and output spooling.* IO buffering for printer output is designed in a similar manner as the card input. Here a ring of m buffers ($m \geq 2$), each of sufficient size to contain one print line, is provided by a directed message class, LINEIO. Assume that the print buffers are addressed by the array elements *LineBuffer*(0), . . . , *LineBuffer*($m-1$); m messages with these addresses are initially sent to the Spoolout process. Spoolout then requests an empty line buffer by:

```
call LINEIO_Get (⟨LinePrinterDriver, buffer⟩) ;
```

Spoolout sends a full line buffer to the Line Printer Driver with:

```
call LINEIO_Put(⟨LinePrinterDriver, buffer⟩) ;
```

3. *Disk buffers.* Requests for disk input and output originate from all SLOS and user processes except the IO drivers. *Each* open file (Active files, Accounting, and Measurement) is allocated a main storage disk IO buffer equal to the length of a disk sector. For this purpose, a pool of k buffers is available, where k is the maximum number of files that may be open at the same time; a lock protects the pool during the request and release of buffers. The buffer address is stored in the file descriptor and is used directly by the Disk Driver for IO.

Single buffers, rather than double buffers, a variable number of buffers, or some more elaborate scheme, were chosen for each file involved in disk IO for several reasons. First, the buffers consume a large amount of main storage space and, from that point of view, it is desirable to use as few as possible. Second, a form of double buffering is still possible because there are usually many logical records in a physical one; thus, it is possible to read or write "ahead" once the last logical record of a buffer is read or written. Finally, since there will be a relatively large number of open files under normal running conditions, each file with its own IO buffer, it is unlikely that the lack of buffer space will be the cause of blocking in the Disk Driver or of too much undesirable Root process activity.

4.7.3 Storage Policies

All blocks of *main* store required by a user process are obtained at the same time with one MAINSTORE_Get operation. For *disk* storage, the allocation policy is more complex because the storage needs of a user job

[6]Note that the Put/Get IO sequences here are a variation of the general theme presented in Section 4.5.2.

file are not known in advance; a *dynamic* scheme is necessary here, but care must be taken to avoid *deadlock*.

Deadlock is possible in the system if there is some legitimate sequence of Gets and Puts on the resources such that a subset of the processes becomes *permanently* blocked. The blocked processes are waiting on Gets which can *never* be satisfied because the only processes capable of freeing the required resources are themselves blocked. SLOS can easily deadlock if disk tracks are allocated dynamically without any restrictions. For example, suppose that the disk becomes full with Input Spool and Active files (*no* Output Spool files). This situation can arise after a slow compute-bound job that consumes *all* of main store workspace is run; several user jobs may subsequently be loaded and initiated. It is then possible for the Spoolin process to be blocked waiting for another track to store a job, all user processes to be blocked waiting for tracks to place output, and Spoolout to be blocked waiting for a job to be completed; in this state, the system is deadlocked.

To prevent deadlock on disk tracks and, at the same time, not excessively overallocate disk space, the following policy is imposed. The strategy will ensure that it is always possible to have at least one Output Spool file. The Spoolin process will be permitted to dynamically Get disk tracks for Input Spool files, one track at a time, but only up to a specified maximum number of tracks. In particular, the Source and Input Data files may only occupy m tracks:

$$m = maxtracks - maxlineouttracks,$$

where *maxtracks* is the number of disk tracks available for user job files and *maxlineouttracks* is the size of the maximum permissible Output Lines file. When a job is *loaded* for execution, *all* of its remaining required disk space will be allocated with a single DISKSTORE_Get; the Line Estimate on the user Job card will be used to estimate the number of tracks needed for the Output Lines file.

Exercise 4.3: Instead of obtaining all of the remaining required disk space at load time, an alternate strategy would be to allocate tracks dynamically for output, one at a time, until the number of free tracks remaining was *maxlineouttracks*. At that time, pick one process to continue and block all others. Since users usually overestimate output, this may allow greater disk utilization. Compare this dynamic strategy with the static deadlock prevention method presented in the text (e.g., in terms of design complexity and expected systems performance).

4.8 PROCESS ELABORATION

The file structures, nucleus, and resource management policies of SLOS have been fully specified. Each of the processes previously outlined in Section 4.2.4 are now designed in detail.

4.8.1 Job Supervisor

The Job Supervisor (JS) is the logical center of the system. It has two essential functions: to initiate the loading and execution of user jobs and to terminate user jobs. In performing these tasks, the JS process must communicate with most of the other SLOS processes; the communication paths are outlined in Figure 4.14.

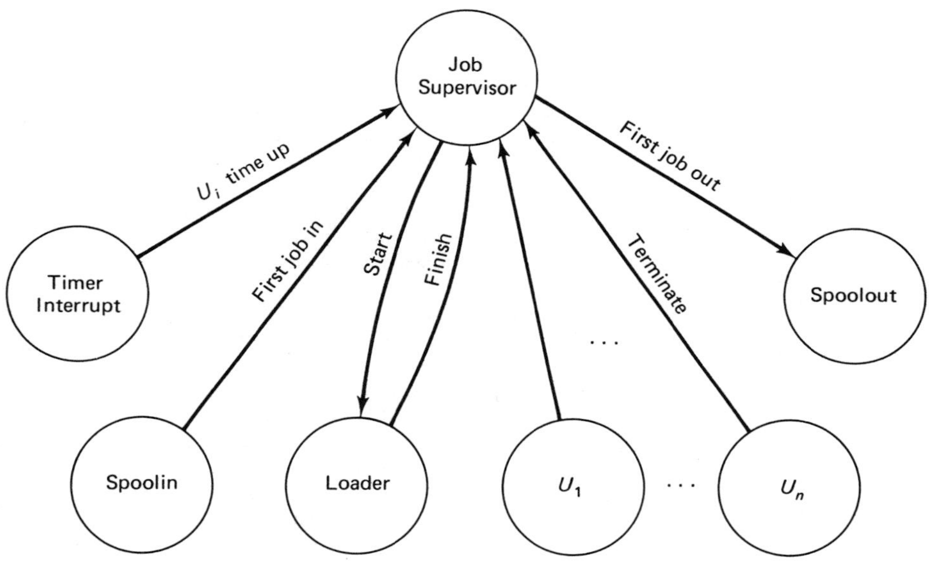

Figure 4.14 Job supervisor communications.

A user job passes through JS as follows: first, JS selects the next user job, say *j*, (job scheduling) and sends a message to the Loader. After the Loader has loaded *j* and acquired the necessary resources and files for *j*, JS again receives control and creates a process U_j for *j*. U_j eventually terminates either explicitly or implicitly. Explicit termination occurs when U_j sends a normal or abnormal termination message to JS; implicit termination is caused by a timer interrupt indicating that U_j has exceeded its maximum CPU time. U_j is destroyed and its main storage released. JS then invokes a File System routine to close the job file. Finally, the job is ready for output spooling and the job file is inserted into the Output Spool queue.

Figure 4.15 contains the algorithm for the Job Supervisor process. The process is designed as a cyclic process that responds to messages originating from Spoolin, Loader, the timer-interrupt pseudo process, and any job process U_i. A single message class, JOBSUP, is employed for this communication.

```
JobSupervisor:procedure;
    Initialization code;
    do while(TRUE); /* Cycle forever. */
        call JOBSUP_Get(<sender,message>);
        do case(sender);
            \Spoolin\ /* First job is in */
                        /* Input Spool file. */
                    /* message is empty. */
                do;
                call ISLOCK_Get; /* Lock directory. */
                jda = InputSpool_Remove( );
                        /* Retrieve descriptor address. */
                call ISLOCK_Put;
                call JOBSUP_Put(<Loader,jda>);
                        /* Wake up loader. */
                end;
            \Loader\ /* Loader has completed loading */
                        /* a job and opening its files */
                        /* for IO.   */
                /* message = <fd,workspace> where */
                    /* fd is descriptor of active job */
                    /* file and workspace is main   */
                    /* storage for user process. */
                do;
                call CreateProcess(fd.maxCPUtime,workspace,
                        fd); /* Create job process. */
                /* Initiate loading of next job, */
                    /* if possible. */
                call ISLOCK_GET; /* Lock Input */
                                    /* Spool descriptors. */
                jda = InputSpool_Remove( );
                        /* Get descriptor disk address. */
                if null(jda) then /* no jobs waiting */
                    JSwaiting = TRUE;
                else call JOBSUP_Put(<Loader,jda>);
                call ISLOCK_Put;
                end;
            \U_i\ /* Sender U_i has explicitly requested */
                  /* a normal or abnormal job */
                  /* termination or timer interrupt */
                  /* occurs during U_i execution. */
                /* message contains termination cause. */
                /* Terminate the job. */
                do;
                jd = sender.JobFile; /* jobfile descriptor */
                jd.TerminationCause = message;
                jd.CPUtime = jd.MaxCPUtime
                                - sender.CPUtimeleft;
                /* Call File System routine to empty */
                   /* output buffers and clean up any */
                   /* pending IO. */
                   call CleanupIO(sender);
```

Figure 4.15 Job supervisor process.

```
                        /* Free workspace storage */
                            /* and destroy the process. */
                        call MAINSTORE_Put(sender.Workspace);
                        call DestroyProcess(sender);
                        /* Remove file from Active File List. */
                        call AFLOCK_Get;
                        call Active_Delete(jd);
                        call AFLOCK_Put;
                        /* Close the file, returning disk */
                            /* address of descriptor. */
                        jda = Close(jd);
                        /* Add file to Output Spool. */
                        call OSLOCK_Get;
                        call OutputSpool_Insert(jda);
                        if SOwaiting then
                            do; SOwaiting = FALSE;
                            call JOBSUP_Put(<Spoolout>);
                            end;
                        call OSLOCK_Put;
                        end;
                    end; /* do case */
                end; /* do while */
            end JobSupervisor;
```

Figure 4.15 *(Cont.)*

A "first job in" message is sent by Spoolin whenever it has completed spooling in a first job to the Input Spool file and finds the *JSwaiting* flag TRUE. The Loader transmits a "finish" message after it has loaded a job; JS creates the job process, and selects another job to be loaded, if one is available. A lock, ISLOCK, is used to ensure the integrity of the Input Spool file during job selection. A message from a user process or the timer interrupt initiates job termination. After the job is moved from the Active file to the Output Spool file, a "first job out" message is sent to Spoolout if it was waiting, as indicated by the *SOwaiting* flag. The locks, AFLOCK and OSLOCK, protect the Active and Output Spool directories during updating. This design of the Job Supervisor terminates jobs quickly and loads new jobs as soon as possible.

Exercise 4.4: Discuss the details of the interrupt-handling pseudo process for the *timer* (Sections 4.5.1 and 4.8.1).

4.8.2 Loader

Loader is a cyclic process with relatively straightforward logic (Figure 4.16). Upon receiving the disk address of a job descriptor from the Job Supervisor, it opens the job file. The Open procedure is a File System routine

```
Loader:procedure;
      do while(TRUE); /* Cycle forever.*/
            call JOBSUP_Get(⟨sender,jda⟩);
                  /* Get disk address jda of */
                        /* descriptor for next job. */
            jd = Open(jda); /* Open file. jd is descriptor. */
            call MAINSTORE_Get(⟨jd.MainStore,baseaddr⟩);
                  /* Get workspace for job. */
            /* Load source program from disk to workspace. */
            a = baseaddr;
            do while(¬endoffile(jd.Source));
                  call ReadNextRecord(jd.Source,a);
                  a = a+cardlength;
                  end;
            /* Add file to active list. */
            call AFLOCK_Get;
            call Active_Insert(jd);
            call AFLOCK_Put;
            /* Notify Job Supervisor that loading is complete. */
            /* Transmit descriptor and workspace as message. */
            call JOBSUP_Put(⟨JobSupervisor, ⟨jd,
                        ⟨jd.MainStore,baseaddr⟩⟩⟩);
            end;
      end Loader;
```

Figure 4.16 Loader.

that activates the file for IO. Its main purpose is to establish a properly initialized descriptor for the file in main memory; as part of the deadlock prevention policy mentioned in Section 4.7.3, the Open routine also gets the disk space required for the Output Lines file.

Next, the necessary main storage workspace is obtained. The source program is then loaded into the workspace, using repeated calls to the File System routine, ReadNextRecord, for input from the disk. The job file is linked into the Active file directory, and the Job Supervisor is finally notified that loading is completed.

4.8.3 User Processes

The user processes U_i use the SLOS File System for input-output services on their virtual card readers and line printers. When the job file is opened by the Loader (Section 4.8.2), all three files—Source Program, Input Data, and Output Lines—are made ready for IO; the Input Data file of a job is thus prepared for reading and the Output Lines file for writing. Consequently, at the time the corresponding job process is created (Section 4.8.1), the File System is ready to receive IO requests. To perform a (virtual) card read operation, U_i (the high-level language interpreter) issues the call:

```
call ReadNextRecord(File.InputData,area)
```

where *file* is the descriptor for the job file corresponding to U_i and *area* is the main store address into which the record is to be stored. Similarly, an output line is (virtually) printed by U_i through the File System call:

```
call WriteNextRecord(file.OutputLines, area)
```

where *area* is the main store address containing the line to be printed. Prior to issuing the WriteNextRecord, the output lines count, *file.Output*, is incremented; if the count exceeds *file.MaxOutLines*, the process is terminated.

Process termination can be initiated by U_i by sending an appropriate message to the job supervisor process:

```
call JOBSUP_Put(⟨JobSupervisor,cause⟩);
call JOBSUP_Get(⟨JobSupervisor⟩);
```

cause is a message containing the reason for termination; for example, *cause* may denote normal end, divide by zero, or a syntax error. U_i is destroyed either before it issues the following Get or while it is blocked.

4.8.4 Spoolin

The basic task of the Spoolin process is to read user jobs from cards and place them on the disk. At the same time, it performs a number of important auxiliary functions, including verification of accounting records, creation of job table entries (job descriptors), and handling of gross errors in user control cards. Inevitably, users can be expected to omit and interchange control cards when submitting their jobs. The SLOS policy will be to "flush" the job and produce an output record indicating the error.

Figure 4.17 contains the Spoolin process and is largely self-explanatory. At its "home" position, Spoolin expects a $JOB card and uses the data therein to construct a job descriptor in *sd*. A job file is created and the account is verified. Following this initialization, the source and data cards are transferred to the disk and the file is closed. The boolean procedures, CONTROL CARD, EOP, and EOJ test for control($), $EOP, and $EOJ cards, respectively. The job is then linked into the Input Spool file; if the Job Supervisor was waiting for a first Input Spool job to be available (*JSwaiting* = TRUE), a JOBSUP message is transmitted. The deadlock prevention policy on disk tracks (Section 4.7.3) is implemented in the file system routines CreateFile and WriteNextRecord.

When a job must be flushed due to accounting or control card errors, the procedure FlushJob is invoked.[7] FlushJob closes the file and adds it to the Output Spool queue; if the Spoolout process is waiting for a first job

[7]The code for handling job card errors (JobCardErrorCheck in the program) and programs or data files that are too large for the system (SourceProgramLengthCheck and DataLengthCheck) is left as an exercise.

```
Spoolin: procedure;
     Initialization code;
     do while(TRUE); /* Cycle forever. */
          /* Get first card of next job ($JOB). */
          s: do while(¬jobcard(card));
               call CARDIO_Get(⟨CardReaderDriver, card⟩);
               end;
          call JobCardErrorCheck;
                    /* Flush job if job card error. */
          /* Fill in job table entries in */
          /* Spoolin descriptor sd. */
          sd.JobID = card.ID;
          sd.AccountNumber = card.Account;
          sd.maxCPUtime = card.Time;
          sd.maxoutlines = card.Line;
          sd.MainStore = card.Store;
          sd.CPUtime=0;
          sd.Input = 0;
          sd.Output = 0;
          call CreateFile(sd); /* File for job */
          /* Read and verify accounting record. */
          call ReadAccountingRecord(card.Account,
                    found);
          if ¬found then /* No accounting record */
               do;
               call FlushJob ('No account');
               goto s; /* Repeat Spoolin cycle. */
               end;
          if ad.RemainingDollars≤0 then
               /* ad is account descriptor. */
               /* insufficient funds for job */
               do;
               call FlushJob('No money in account');
               goto s; /* Repeat Spoolin cycle. */
               end;
          /* Read in source program. */
          call CARDIO_Get(<CardReaderDriver, card>);
          do while(¬controlcard(card));
               call WriteNextRecord(sp.Source,card);
               call CARDIO_Get(⟨CardReaderDriver,card⟩);
               call SourceProgramLengthCheck;
                    /* Flush if program too long. */
               end;
          if ¬eop(card) then /* Expecting end of program */
               do;
               call FlushJob('Expecting $EOP');
               goto s;
               end;
          call WriteEnd(sd.Source); /* Wrap up */
                                        /* source file. */
          /* Read in data cards, if any. */
          call CARDIO_Get(⟨cardReaderDriver,card⟩);
```

Figure 4.17 Spoolin.

```
            do while(¬controlcard(card));
                  call WriteNextRecord(sp.InputData,card);
                  call CARDIO_Get(〈CardReaderDriver,card〉);
                  sd.Input = sd.Input+1;
                  call DataLengthCheck;
                  /* Flush if too much data. */
                  end;
            if ¬eoj(card) then /* Expecting end of job */
                        do;
                        call FlushJob('Expecting $EOJ');
                        goto s;
                        end;
            call WriteEnd(sd.InputData);
                  /* Wrap up data file. */
            jda = Close(sd);
                  /* Close file and return disk address. */
            /* Add file to Input Spool file queue. */
            call ISLOCK_Get;
            call InputSpool_Insert(jda);
            if JSwaiting then
                  do;
                  JSwaiting = FALSE;
                  call JOBSUP_Put(〈JobSupervisor〉);
                  end;
            call ISLOCK_Put;
            end; /* Cycle forever */
      end Spoolin;

FlushJob: procedure(tc);
      sd.TerminationCause = tc; /* Set message. */
      if tc='Expecting $EOP' then
            call WriteEnd(sd.Source);
      else if tc='Expecting $EOJ' then
            call WriteEnd(sd.InputData);
      jda = Close(sd); /* Close file and return disk address. */
      /* Add file to Output Spool queue. */
      call OSLOCK_Get;
      call OutputSpool_Insert(jda);
      if SOwaiting then
            do;
            SOwaiting = FALSE;
            call JOBSUP_Put(〈Spoolout〉);
            end;
      call OSLOCK_Put;
      if tc='No account' | tc='No money in account'
      then card = blank;
      /* card contains job card for flushed job. */
      end FlushJob;
```

Figure 4.17 *(Cont.)*

(*SOwaiting* = TRUE), a JOBSUP message is sent. Flushjob returns to the beginning of the Spoolin cycle after it has completed its work.

Exercise 4.5: Suppose there is only one buffer available for card input ($n = 1$ in first part of Section 4.7.2). Do the CardReaderDriver and Spoolin processes still interact correctly? How would this change affect SLOS performance?

4.8.5 Spoolout

The Spoolout process is outlined in Figure 4.18. It first retrieves the next file in the Output Spool list; if the list is empty, Spoolout sets its waiting flag (*OSwaiting*) and waits for a JOBSUP message, sent by either the Job Supervisor process or Spoolin. (The **while** loop is used to avoid repeating the ⟨lock, Remove, unlock⟩ sequence.) The file descriptor is then read into the permanent Spoolout descriptor *od*, with the File System command Open.

At this point, the process is ready to produce output records to the line printer driver, in the order described in Section 4.3.2. The job charges are computed with some costing function *f* that is supplied by the computer center management; in general, the cost of a job will be some function of the resources used by it. The job header record is then moved into a print buffer and transmitted to the Line Printer Driver process. The details of the header record creation are straightforward and will not be elaborated further. The next steps update the accounting record for the job in the Accounting file (Section 4.6.1). If the job was terminated by the Spoolin process, control is transferred to location *t*, which bypasses the source program and output line listing. Otherwise, the main part of the output is printed. The GetandPrint(*file*) causes repeated execution of the sequence:

```
call  LINEIO_Get(⟨LinePrinterDriver, buffer⟩);
call  ReadNextRecord(file, buffer);
call  LINEIO_Put(⟨LinePrinterDriver, buffer⟩);
```

until an endoffile(*file*) is reached.

The last line, the job terminator, is printed at the statement labeled *t*; the code for printing this record is not specified in detail. The final step is to destroy the file, releasing its disk space.

4.8.6 Operator Communication

The operator at the console can initiate two-way messages for the following purposes:

1. Find the status of a particular job
2. Add and delete accounts and dollar amounts from the Accounting file

```
Spoolout: procedure;
    Initialization code;
    do while(TRUE); /* Cycle forever. */
        /* Get next job from Output Spool file. */
        jda = nil;
        do while(null(jda));
            /* Loop done once or twice only. */
            call OSLOCK_Get;
            jda = OutputSpool_Remove( );
            if ¬null(jda) then
                call OSLOCK_Put;
            else do;
                OSwaiting = TRUE;
                call OSLOCK_Put;
                call JOBSUP_Get(⟨sender⟩);
                    /* Wait for first job out. */
                end;
            end;
        call Open(jda); /* Read descriptor into Spoolout */
                                /* descriptor storage, od. */
        /* Write output header. */
        call LINEIO_Get(⟨LinePrinterDriver,
                        buffer⟩); /* Get buffer. */
        JobCost = f(od.MainStore, od.CPUtime,
                    od.Input,od.Output); /* Compute charges. */
        /* Produce output header and put into buffer. */
        call LINEIO_Put(⟨LinePrinterDriver,
                        buffer⟩); /* buffer to printer */
        if od.TerminationCause ≠ 'No Account'
            then do;
            /* Update accounting record for job. */
            call ReadAccountingRecord(sd.AccountNumber);
            /* ad is accounting record descriptor. */
            ad.RemainingDollars=ad.RemainingDollars−JobCost;
            ad.DollarsSpend=ad.DollarsSpent+JobCost;
            ad.Runs=ad.Runs+1;
            ad.LastActivity = DateToday;
            call WriteAccountingRecord;
            if od.TerminationCause is not in
                {'No Money in Account',
                 'Expecting $EOP',
                 'Expecting $EOJ'} then do;
                /* Print program and output. */
                call GetandPrint(od.Source);
                call GetandPrint(od.OutputLines);
                end;
            end;
        t:  Print job terminator record with cause;
        /* Destroy file, releasing its disk space. */
        call DestroyFile(od);
        end;
    end Spoolout;
```

Figure 4.18 Spoolout.

3. Print systems measurements and the daily job log from the Measurements file
4. Type out the number of jobs in each of the Input Spool, Active, and Output Spool queues
5. Determine the current allocation of resources, such as disk and main store

In addition, one-way messages from SLOS to the operator may be sent to notify the operator of various conditions requiring operator attention; these include running out of paper on the line printer, excessive IO errors on the disk, and card reader errors. The operator process is a cyclic message handler, driven primarily by IO messages from the Operator Terminal Driver. The details of this process are left as an exercise.

Exercise 4.6: Design the Operator Communication process. (See pp. 73–78 of Shaw [74] for the global design of a many-process system that might perform a similar set of functions.) Note that the associated data structures (e.g., the Input Spool queue) must be locked by this process during reading and updating in order to obtain consistent results. It is also necessary to expand the IO driver processes to respond to IO conditions that require operator handling.

4.8.7 The Root Process

When the system is initially loaded, the Root process is implicitly created and activated. It creates its own descriptor, inserts itself on the Ready List, sets the starting value of the time-of-day clock, creates the remaining SLOS processes, invokes the process Scheduler, and then enters an idle loop:

```
do while(TRUE);
        /* Do nothing */
        end;
```

The process descriptor for *Root* is initialized with:

```
Root.CPUtimeleft = w;   /*a very large integer*/
Root.Priority = lowestpriority;
Root.Status = 'running';
```

Note that the CPU *idle* time during the running of SLOS is approximately equal to *w* — *Root.CPUtimeleft* and that elapsed time can easily be obtained from the time-of-day clock.

Exercise 4.7: Instead of doing nothing, this idle loop can be used to monitor system performance, estimate resource utilization, and provide extra services, since it is "free time" not usable by any other process. Give a detailed list of tasks that may be performed by the idle loop.

Exercise 4.8: Suppose that all SLOS processes have the *same* priority. What effect will this have on system performance? How should the idle loop of the Root process be changed so that Root does not starve the rest of the system?

4.9 FILE SYSTEM ROUTINES

The File System performs an extensive number of services for almost every process of SLOS. It is convenient to group these services into three areas, according to the tasks they perform: directory manipulation, initialization and termination, and read/write. Table 4.6 lists the main File System routines in each subgroup and the processes that invoke them.

TABLE 4-6 File System Routines and Callers

Name of Routine	Calling Processes
1. Directory Manipulation	
Userjobfile_Insert	JobSupervisor, Loader, Spoolin
Userjobfile_Remove	JobSupervisor, Spoolout
Active_Delete	JobSupervisor
2. Initialization and Termination	
CreateFile	Spoolin
Open	Loader, Spoolout
DestroyFile	Spoolout
Close	JobSupervisor, Spoolin
3. Read/Write	
ReadNextRecord	Loader, U_i, Spoolout
WriteNextRecord	U_i, Spoolin
CleanupIO	JobSupervisor
WriteEnd	Spoolin
ReadAccountingRecord	Spoolin, Spoolout
WriteAccountingRecord	Spoolout

4.9.1 Directory Manipulation

The Insert, Remove, and Delete routines access and update the directory by manipulating the linked chain of descriptor addresses that point to the particular user job file type (Input Spool, Active, or Output Spool). Insert and Remove treat the chains as FIFO queues. file_Insert(*da*) inserts the descriptor address *da* at the tail or end of the list for *file* while file_Remove( ) removes and returns the first or head element. Active_Delete(*da*) removes the element *da* from the Active file directory. These are conventional list processing routines and their details will not be presented.

4.9.2 Initialization and Termination

CreateFile creates a newfile in the system by obtaining an initial track of disk space for the Source file of the new job and initializing the file descriptor for IO (Figure 4.19). The routine PreventDeadlock ensures that the CreateFile caller, Spoolin, does not consume a dangerous amount of disk space (Section 4.7.3); if the number of tracks allocated to Source and Input Data files (denoted by *allocatedspace* in the program) is equal to *m*, the maximum

```
CreateFile: procedure(sd);
/* sd contains the permanent Spoolin descriptor. */
    call PreventDeadlock;
    call DISKSTORE_Get(<1,Track>);
        /* Get first track for Source file. */
    /* Initialize disk address fields of file descriptor. */
        /* (Section 4.6.1). */
    sd.Source.N = 1; /* N is number of tracks in file. */
    sd.Source.Trackaddress(1) = Track(1);
    sd.InputData.N = 0;
    sd.OutputLines.N = 0;
    /* Initialize physical and logical record pointers */
        /* (Section 4.6.3). */
    sd.Source.NextPR = [Track(1), d+1];
        /* Descriptor is stored in first d sectors. */
    sd.Source.NextLR = 0;
    sd.InputData.NextLR = 0;
    sd.OutputLines.NextLR = 0;
    sd.InputData.NextPR = [1,1];
    sd.OutputLines.NextPR = [1,1];
    end CreateFile;

PreventDeadlock: procedure;
/* Block Spoolin if source and input data files occupy too */
    /* much of disk space. */
    call DEADLOCK_Get;
    allocatedspace = allocatedspace + 1;
    if allocatedspace>m then
        do;
        SIwaiting = TRUE;
        call DEADLOCK_Put;
        call DL_Get(<Spoolout>);
        end;
    else call DEADLOCK_Put;
    end PreventDeadlock;
```

Figure 4.19 Creating a file.

permissible, Spoolin is blocked until Spoolout releases some disk space. The directed message class DL provides the communication between Spoolin and Spoolout, while the lock, DEADLOCK, guarantees the integrity of the data items *allocatedspace* and *SIwaiting* when they are accessed or updated by these processes. The basic tasks of DestroyFile, given in Figure 4.20, are to release the disk space of the file and to wake up Spoolin if it was blocked due to the deadlock prevention policy.

```
DestroyFile: procedure(od);
/* od is the permanent Spoolout descriptor. */
    /* Determine tracks to be liberated */
    do I = 1 to od.Source.N;
        Track(I) = od.Source.Trackaddress(I);
        end;
    t = od.Source.N; /* t is number of tracks to free. */
    do I = 1 to od.InputData.N;
        Track(t+1)=od.InputData.Trackaddress(I);
        end;
    u = t + od.InputData.N;
    /* u = number of Source and Input Data tracks */
    do I = 1 to od.OutputLines.N;
        Track(u+I) = od.OutputLines.Trackaddress(I);
        end;
    t = u + od.OutputLines.N;
    /* t = total tracks to free */
    /* Release the space. */
    call DISKSTORE_Put(<t,Track>);
    /* Check if Spoolin is waiting on deadlock prevention. */
    call DEADLOCK_Get;
    allocatedspace = allocatedspace-u;
    if SIwaiting then
        do;
        SIwaiting = FALSE;
        call DL_Put(<Spoolin>);
        end;
    call DEADLOCK_Put;
    end DestroyFile;
```

Figure 4.20 Destroying a file.

The procedure for opening a file, Open, reads the file descriptor from disk into main store and initializes the file record pointers in preparation for IO. Figure 4.21 contains the code for this File System function. The routine could be broken into two procedures, OpenbyLoader and OpenbySpoolout, since the code for each caller is disjoint; however, because the tasks are similar, they have been combined in a single procedure. The Loader (in the Open procedure) first retrieves main store space for the descriptor and reads the file descriptor from disk. Two buffers for disk IO are then obtained. An

```
Open: procedure(jda) returns(File Descriptor);
/* jda is the disk address of file descriptor. */
    do case (caller);
        \Loader\ /* Loader is opening file for execution. */
            do;
            /* First get main store space for descriptor. */
            call AFLOCK_Get;
            jd = GetActiveFileDescriptor;
            call AFLOCK_Put;
            /* Read file descriptor from disk into jd. */
            call DISKIO_Put(⟨DiskDriver,
                ⟨ja, jda, 'read', descriptorlength⟩⟩);
            call DISKIO_Get(⟨DiskDriver,mess⟩);
                /* Wait for disk to complete. */
            /* Get input and output buffers for file. */
            call BFLOCK_Get;
            jd.Source.DiskBuffer = GetDiskBuffer;
            jd.InputData.DiskBuffer = jd.Source.DiskBuffer;
            jd.OutputLines.DiskBuffer = GetDiskBuffer;
            call BFLOCK_Put;
            /* Allocate disk space for Output Lines file */
                /* using estimating function g. */
            jd.OutputLines.N = g(jd.Maxoutlines);
            call DISKSTORE_Get(⟨jd.OutputLines.N,
                jd.OutputLines.Trackaddress⟩);
            /* Initialize physical and logical record */
                /* pointers. */
            jd.Source.NextPr = [jd.Source.Trackaddress(1),
                    d+1];
            if jd.InputData.N≠0 then
                jd.InputData.NextPR = [jd.InputData.
                    Trackaddress(1), 1];
            jd.OutputLines.NextPR = [jd.OutputLines.
                Trackaddress(1),1];
            jd.Source.NextLR = 0;
            jd.InputData.NextLR = 0;
            jd.OutputLines.NextLR = 0;
            return(jd);
            end;
    \Spoolout\
        /* Spoolout is opening file for output spooling. */
            do;
            /* Read file descriptor from disk */
                /* into Spoolout descriptor od. */
            call DISKIO_Put(⟨DiskDriver, ⟨od, jda, 'read',
                    descriptorlength⟩⟩);
            call DISKIO_Get(⟨DiskDriver, mess⟩);
                /* Wait for IO. */
            /* Initialize physical and logical record */
                /* pointers. */
```

Figure 4.21 Opening a job file.

```
        od.Source.NextPR = [od.Source.
            Trackaddress(1),d+1];
        if od.OutputLines.N≠0 then
            od.OutputLines.NextPR =
                [od.OutputLines.Trackaddress(1),1];
        od.Source.NextLR = 0;
        od.OutputLines.NextLR = 0;
        return(od);
        end;
    end;
end Open;
```

Figure 4.21 *(Cont.)*

input buffer is shared by the Source file and Input Data file, and an output buffer is allocated for the Output Lines file; these buffers are used by the Loader and by a (later-created) user process. Spoolout has a permanent main store descriptor and disk IO buffer so that it is not necessary to allocate these during the Open.

The Close procedure is responsible for storing the file descriptor on disk and is invoked by the Job Supervisor and Spoolin processes after all file IO is completed. It has the call: *jda* = Close(*jd*), where *jd* is a file descriptor and the returned value, *jda*, is the disk address of the descriptor. In the case where the Job Supervisor is the caller, the Close routine will also release the Active file descriptor space in main store and return the file's IO buffers to the buffer pool. The code for Close is left as an exercise.

4.9.3 Read and Write Routines

Job files are read and written, at the *logical record* level, by ReadNext-Record and WriteNextRecord, respectively. The WriteNextRecord routine is outlined in Figure 4.22. If the disk buffer associated with the file is being written to disk, the invoking process blocks on the DISKIO_Get until the buffer has been emptied. The logical record to be written is then transferred to the buffer by the Move procedure, and the logical and physical record pointers are updated. If the disk buffer is not full (and consequently, not being written), the logical record is moved to the next sequential free area in the buffer and the logical record pointer incremented. At this point, it is possible that the buffer is full and can be written onto the disk. A new track is required if the previous write filled the current track or if this is the first write on an Input Data or Output Lines file; this test is made in the New-TrackNeeded procedure (not detailed) by examining *NextPR*. After a new track is returned by FindDiskTrack, *NextLR* is set to indicate that the buffer is not available due to writing and a 'write' message is sent to the Disk Driver process.

```
WriteNextRecord: procedure (file, area);
/* Write next logical record from area into file. */
      if File.NextLR = -1 then
          /* Disk buffer is being written to disk. */
          do;
          call DISKIO_Get(⟨DiskDriver, mess⟩);
               /* Wait for completion. */
          call Move(area, File.DiskBuffer, 0, File.LRlength);
          File.NextLR = File.LRlength; /* second record */
          File.NextPR.sector = File.NextPR.sector+1;
          end;
      else /* Disk buffer is not yet full. */
           do;
           call Move(area, File.DiskBuffer, File.NextLR,
                     File.LRlength);
           File.NextLR=File.NextLR+File.LRlength;
           if File.NextLR+File.LRlength>sectorlength
               then do; /* Disk buffer is now full. Write it. */
               if NewTrackNeeded(file) then
                     /* Get the next disk track. */
                     do;
                     tr = FindDiskTrack(file);
                     File.NextPR = [tr, 1];
                     end;
               File.NextLR = -1; /* Set for disk writing. */
               call DISKIO_Put(⟨DiskDriver,
                     ⟨File.DiskBuffer, File.NextPR, 'write',
                     sectorlength⟩⟩);
               /* overlapped IO */
               end;
           end;
      end WriteNextRecord;

FindDiskTrack: procedure(file) returns(diskaddress);
      do case(caller);
            \Ui\ /* Tracks have previously been allocated. */
                return(NextTrack(files));
                /* Linear search through Trackaddress of file. */
            \Spoolin\ /* Tracks are allocated dynamically. */
                do;
                call PreventDeadlock; /* See Figure 4.19. */
                call DISKSTORE_Get(⟨1, Track⟩);
                File.N=File.N+1;
                File.Trackaddress(File.N)=Track(1);
                return(Track(1));
                end;
            end;
      end FindDiskTrack;
```

Figure 4.22 Write a file record.

The FindDiskTrack procedure returns the next disk track for writing the file either by searching the file descriptor for the next track or by invoking the disk storage allocator. The first method is used when some user process U_i is the caller since all tracks have already been allocated and are identified in the track address fields of the descriptor. When Spoolin needs the track, a deadlock prevention and disk allocation method, similar to that used in the CreateFile routine, is applied.

The procedure ReadNextRecord(*file*, *area*) transfers the next logical record of the *file* into the main storage locations designated by *area*. It will also read ahead to some extent by initiating a disk read whenever the last logical record is moved from the disk buffer. However, if it reaches the end of the file, ReadNextRecord will return an end of file indicator and continue to do so on all subsequent calls. (The endoffile( ) routine in the Loader and Spoolout descriptions test for this indicator.)

WriteEnd is used by Spoolin to empty the disk buffer after the last WriteNextRecord has been performed for the file. It writes an end-of-file marker at the end of the file and ensures that the last buffer is written. A track allocation is occasionally required for the last record. CleanupIO, called by the Job Supervisor when it is terminating a user process, must perform some of the same tasks as WriteEnd. In addition, CleanupIO also has the rather messy responsibility of intercepting IO messages directed from the Disk Driver to the U_i. The details of these routines, along with ReadAccountingRecord, WriteAccountingRecord, and the File System routines for accessing the Measurements files, are left as exercises.

Exercise 4.9: A number of File System routines were not specified in the above section. Give a more detailed design of the ReadNextRecord, WriteEnd, and CleanupIO routines in our PDL language. Design the routines ReadAccountingRecord and WriteAccountingRecord.

4.10 PERFORMANCE MEASUREMENTS

Measurements of user job characteristics and resource utilization are necessary for recording, evaluating, and modifying the performance of the SLOS system. The software for obtaining this information and storing it in the Measurements file will not be specified. Instead, this section will identify some of the data that should be in the file and briefly discuss where and how to obtain the data.

Most of the useful job information, such as statistics on run time, IO times, IO device utilization, and storage consumption, can be obtained from the job tables directly. The principal measurement that is missing is job turnaround time, defined here as the difference between the time that the last line of a job was printed by Spoolout and the time that the first card was read by Spoolin; these times could easily be obtained from the time-of-day clock and stored in the job table. Updating of a daily job log and month-to-date user job statistics can be done conveniently by a measurements routine that is invoked by Spoolout.

The data for deriving CPU utilization statistics is directly available from the *CPUtimeleft* fields of the process descriptors and the time-of-day clock; from this information, one can determine the relative and absolute times spent by each of the system processes and user processes. Channel usage may be approximated either by counting the number of IO operations on each device or by recording the times between a startio in a driver process and the subsequent IO interrupt.

Somewhat more complex methods are required for determining statistics on the multiprogramming level (number of user jobs in execution), main store (workspace) and disk space usage, number of user job files, and lengths of waiting queues on the message, lock, and storage resources. A sampling technique would be appropriate here. At sufficiently small time intervals (perhaps changed dynamically with the aid of a random number generator), a measurements procedure, the sampling routine, is called to read the current values of the above items. The sampling routine could be invoked by a process, such as the Job Supervisor, that is guaranteed to be frequently running.

Exercise 4.10: Design a subsystem for measuring, storing, and retrieving data on user job characteristics and resource utilization.

4.11 CONCLUSIONS

The preceding sections have described the design of a single-language batch multiprogramming system that could be implemented on a variety of computers. For brevity, several necessary or convenient parts that should appear in a practical system of this type were not included. In this section, some of these omissions are listed and several implementations related to SLOS are mentioned.

Any computer system will occasionally fail because of both hardware malfunctions and, unfortunately, software errors. Modules for reloading the SLOS system and, if possible, recovering from these inevitable failures are thus necessary. Similarly, a mechanism for initially loading SLOS must be designed. The machine operator would be involved in the above procedures, as well as in the tasks outlined in Section 4.8.6. From the user's point of view, SLOS would be enhanced considerably if a permanent file system were available for user programs and data.

Some, but not all, components of SLOS have been implemented, and there exist operating systems with similar designs. In particular, Reference

[Shaw, 75b] describes the implementation of a more generalized version of the nucleus, interrupt handlers, and IO device drivers given in Sections 4.4 and 4.5. The multiprogramming system presented in Shaw and Weiderman [71] has a similar, but more simplified, process structure. Finally, the experimental time sharing system of Wilkinson [75] is built upon the kernel of Shaw [75b] with dynamic user processes.

Exercise 4.11: Implement the SLOS system and the high-level language interpreter. One of the most important and *first* tasks to be done is to construct a *debugging* system that produces traces, including system data structures and resource and process descriptors, in readable form.

4.12 ACKNOWLEDGMENTS

I am grateful to Ram Rao and Marvin Zelkowitz for their comments and suggestions on the design. This work was supported in part by the National Science Foundation, Grant MCS75-19480.

5 Design of a Compiler

5.1 COMPILER DESIGN

After 20 years of experience in building compilers, we now have a good idea of how compilers are constructed. Even so, there is still a great deal of flexibility in the basic organization of this important piece of software. Compilers are designed with varying goals in mind, and the resulting organization often reflects those goals. This chapter describes the step-by-step process of implementing one compiler. When assumptions must be made, an explanation will be given as to why, and what alternate strategies exist. The compiler described in this chapter is relatively simple and has been implemented as a PL/1 program of approximately 900 statements, and so it is suitable as a student term project.

When students first learn how to program, there is usually an air of mystery surrounding the compiler. Source programs are read by the compiler, and magically, the program executes and produces results—sometimes correct ones, but more often ones not so correct. What is important to realize is that the computer itself cannot execute directly these programs written in languages like FORTRAN, BASIC, or PL/1. The computer only executes very primitive instructions such as moving information from one location to another or adding together the contents of two different locations. It is the purpose of the compiler to transform the source program into a format understandable to the primitive computer.

For example, the simple PL/1 statement $X = Y + Z$ will have to be translated to a sequence of instructions similar to the following:

> Access location containing variable *Y*.
> Access location containing variable *Z*.
> Add together *Y* and *Z*.
> Move result to location containing variable *Z*.

Later we will describe the structure of this computer in greater detail.

This discussion points out two important points about compiling: (1) A source program (written in some programming language) is simply a string of characters (e.g., a deck of 80 column cards) that is read by the compiler and translated into a format that is directly executable by the computer, and (2) a compiler is simply another program that reads in certain character strings (the source program) and outputs another character string (the machine language program).

In order to simplify the designs of a compiler, a general structure has evolved. Essentially all compilers fit into this general framework. It is the purpose of this chapter to describe some of these models and how they can be used to create a running piece of software.

All compilers consist of three basic components: lexical analysis, syntactic analysis, and code generation. The first two of these lend themselves nicely to formal models, while the third does not have as clear a definition.

Since a compiler simply reads in a long character string and converts it to another string, the *lexical analysis* phase aids in shortening this process. Rather than viewing a program as a sequence of unconnected symbols, lexical analysis breaks the source program down into chunks, called *tokens*. These units are the special words in the language (e.g., IF, DO, BEGIN, etc.), variable names, constants, and operators (e.g., * and +). They are considered as single entities rather than separate groups of symbols.

After breaking a program into tokens, the *syntactic analysis* phase determines if the tokens fit together in the correct order, called parsing. For example, for an IF statement, which may have the format:

```
IF expression THEN statement;
```

syntactic analysis insures that the IF token is followed by a valid expression, which is followed by the THEN token, which is followed by a valid statement, which is followed by a valid semicolon token.

The final process is the *code generation* process which takes the output of syntactic analysis and creates executable machine language from it. Some formal models have been developed; however, in most production compilers the process is only semiautomatic, and no theory yet developed includes all of the code generation process. Implementing a good code generator is still somewhat of an art; however, the chapter describes some general techniques that can be used to eliminate much of the mystery surrounding this process.

Although all compilers consist of the same three basic components, they can be put together in many different ways. Figure 5.1 gives three basic designs. In Figure 5.1(a), the scanner reads a source program and writes it out as a file of tokens. The parser reads the file and produces a file consisting of the parsed program in some other form, such as postfix. Finally the code generator reads this postfix file and produces the generated object code.

This compiler is a three-pass compiler since the program is read three times (original source, token file, and postfix file). It should be immediately obvious that this organization does not lead to a particularly fast compiler, since file operations are usually slow in most computer systems.

However, this organization does have important advantages. Perhaps the most important is the relative independence of each phase. The phases are linked only by the data files. Each pass can be designed independently of the others. This independence is important if portability is a requirement. If the compiler generates code for machine X, and code for machine Y is needed, then only the code generation phase need be modified. As long as the new code generator can generate code from the same postfix file as the original compiler, no changes need to be made to the first two passes.

Similarly, if it is desired to alter the source language, then only the scanner (or maybe the parser) needs to be modified. As long as the same postfix is produced, the code generator is invariant.

This organization is also relevant where space is at a premium, such as in a minicomputer. Since each phase is executed independently of the others, any given phase is relatively small. In fact, in minicomputers with small memories, it is not uncommon to run several programs through the scanner, load the parser and run several programs through it, and repeat this process until compilation has been completed.

On the other hand, if compilation speed is important, a one-pass organization (Figure 5.1(b)) may be used. In this case, the parser is the main driving routine with the scanner and code generator being subroutines or coroutines. The parser calls the scanner for tokens until it produces the next postfix symbol. The parser then calls the code generator to generate code for that piece of program.

This organization is obviously efficient since only one pass of the program needs to be made and no file operations are necessary. However, this organization also has some drawbacks. For one, the code that is produced is generally not optimal. For example, the statement

```
GOTO label;
```

may pose problems since *label* may not have been seen as yet and it is difficult to generate code. Also, in:

```
A+(B+C);
D=(B+C)+(E+F);
```

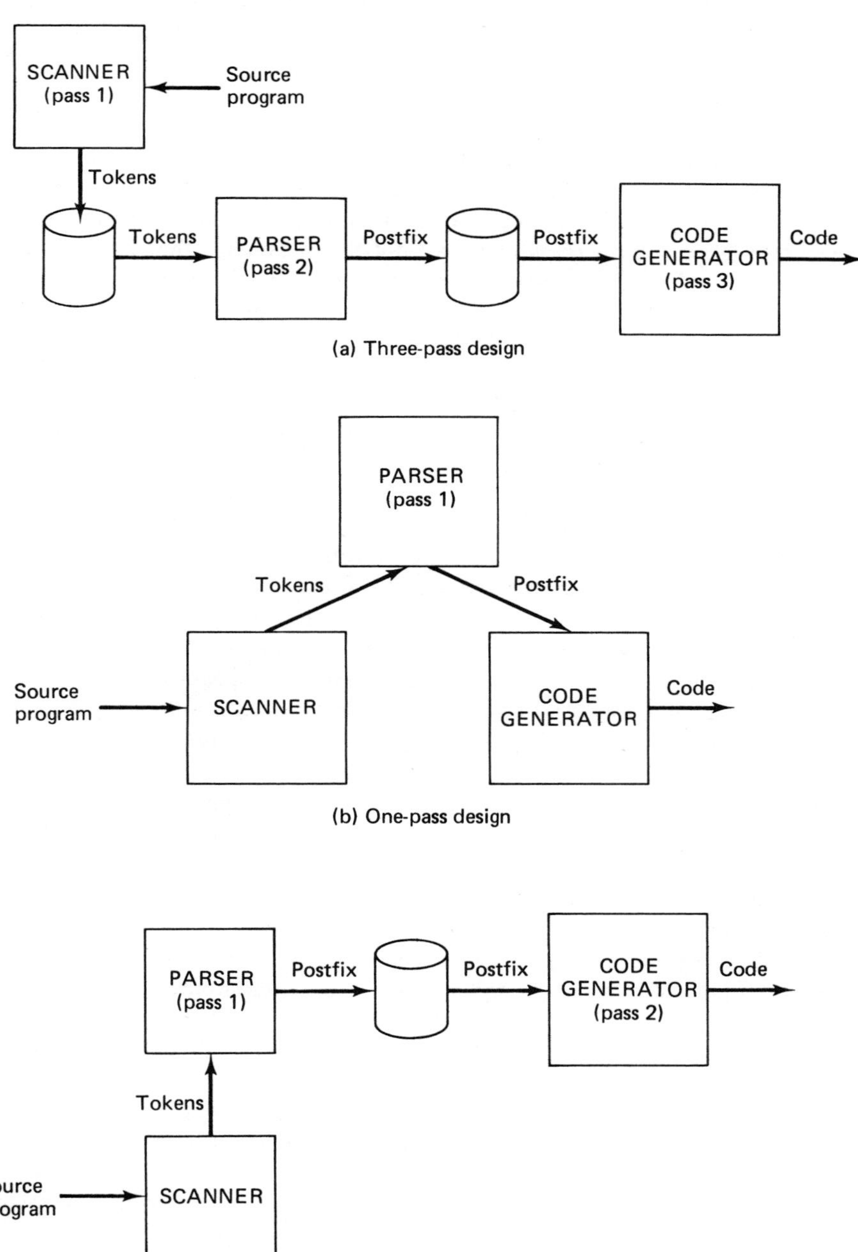

Figure 5.1 Compiler organizations.

the compiler may generate more efficient code if it transforms the statements into:

```
A=(B+C);
D=A+(E+F);
```

However, in a one-pass organization, it may have already lost some of the necessary information to optimize the code by the time it scans $(E + F)$.

Since the entire compiler is in memory, a one-pass organization will generate large compilers, which may not fit on systems that have memory constraints. If efficient code is a requirement, the three-pass organization may be more practical. For example, an optimization phase may be inserted between the parser and the code generator. This phase would read a postfix file and produce a new postfix file which represented an equivalent, but more efficient, program. Since the output of this optimizer is also a postfix file, the same code generator can be used. In fact, optimization could be a user option: if rapid compile time is needed, the optimizer could be ignored; if rapid execution time is needed, the optimizer could be inserted between the parser and code generator.

We are not quite done with the various organizations. Figure 5.1(c) represents a cross between the one- and three-pass schemes already described. This figure describes the "classical" two-pass compiler. In this case, the parser calls the scanner for tokens and then produces a file giving the postfix for the program. A code generator reads this file and produces code.

This organization has the advantage of being relatively efficient—only two passes are needed (source program and postfix file). In addition, such problems as the forward GOTO mentioned previously are handled since the forward label has been seen by the first pass before the second pass generates code for it. It also permits the inclusion of a separate optimization phase if desired.

Figure 5.1 does not represent all possible compiler organizations. Variations on these are possible. The reader should realize that all three are "correct" for some applications and inefficient for others.

Before continuing, we should clearly define what we mean by a compiler. For the first FORTRAN compiler this was easy. Computers were standard pieces of hardware, such as the IBM 704 or 709, with fixed machine language instructions. The problem reduced to converting the FORTRAN source code into an equivalent machine language program.

However, today the situation is more complex. Although many machines still have the fixed architecture of the earlier machines, many others are implemented using a microprogrammed central processor. That means that new machine language instructions can be created by rewriting the microcode. While the addition of these new instructions is often left to the manufacturer of the computer, several machines, especially minicomputers, have user- "writeable" microcode so that users can create their own instructions. In the future, this may complicate the compiler writer's problem since the compiler may need the flexibility of altering the code that it generates depending upon application.

Another problem is that families of similar, but not identical, machines exist. The IBM 360/370 family is one such example. While all of these computers have a common base set of instructions, the larger and newer machines have additional operations. Since compilers are expensive to build, should a compiler be written to generate unique code for each model or only generate code for the base instruction set and hence not generate optimal code for programs which execute on the larger machines?

An alternative strategy to compilation is a program, typically called an *interpreter*, that immediately executes a given source statement. For example, given the statement:

```
X=Y+Z
```

rather than generating code to compute the value of $Y + Z$ and then storing it into the area reserved for X, an interpreter would access the values of Y and Z, add them together, and then store that value into the area set aside for the variable X.

As we shall see later, an interpreter has the same general characteristics as a compiler. The source program must first be scanned and the individual tokens of a statement identified. This requires a scanner and parser similar to that used in a compiler. The code generator, rather than generating code to perform some operation, will directly perform that operation. Since the interpretation phase is often simpler than the code generation phase, interpretation is often used where execution speed is not of prime importance.

So much for easy generalizations: the "real-world" situation is not nearly as textbook perfect. Often an interpreter will perform some analysis of the program before execution in order to improve execution efficiency. An interpreter may have the organization of Figure 5.1(a) or 5.1(c); that is, the program may first be parsed into some internal form and this internal form executed. This avoids rescanning statements that are repeatedly executed, such as within a DO loop. However, what is this intermediate text? Is it the postfix output by a parser, is it an assembly language for a real or hypothetical computer which the interpreter simulates, or is it some other form? All these techniques have been used. Since the IBM 360/370 series computer is a microprogrammed machine, it has been said that all IBM compilers are really interpreters generating code for a hypothetical machine with the hardware simulating that machine using the microcoded instruction set. Because of this ambiguity, the term "interpreter" will generally be avoided in this chapter.

When there were only a few large, expensive machines, a programmer would design and implement a program on the same machine; however, the situation is quite different today. Frequently, machines are sold for special applications, such as a small process control machine to automate an assembly line. Since this small machine has only a limited set of functions, it is frequently bought without any peripherals, such as disk drives or tapes, and frequently comes with just sufficient memory to execute the desired tasks. There may not be sufficient space in which to develop the programs, or the machine may be too slow for program preparation. To enhance these systems with additional facilities just for program preparation may not be economically feasible.

This example, and others like it, have led to the concept of a *cross compiler*. A cross compiler is a compiler which executes on one machine and generates code for another, such as using a large-scale computer to generate code for a small minicomputer.

This concept may be mindboggling at first until it is realized what a compiler really does. It is simply a program that reads in a stream of characters (the source program) and converts it to a stream of bits (machine language instructions). This machine language is then output as the compiled program in some standard file format recognized by the operating system as a compiled program. In IBM terminology this would be an *object deck* which is read by the *Linkage Editor* before execution; in Univac terms, this would be a *relocatable element* which is read by the *Collector*. The term *Loader* is also used. Although the terms differ, the concepts are similar.

Note that this description shows that a compiler is not really part of an operating system, but is like any other program written by a user. The system would function quite well were the compiler deleted from the system library. However, it is an important user program since it is used quite frequently.

Since the compiler transforms the source program into a set of bits, there is no reason why the bits have to be interpreted by the local operating system. The compiler could just as easily generate a magnetic tape containing the output recognizable by some other computer system. Since it is compiling from one machine to another, the term cross compiler is now used.

We are not quite finished with this range of options. Frequently, a compiler is needed quickly and with minimal development cost. Therefore shortcuts are taken. Since assemblers exist on all machines, it is sometimes faster to convert the source program into an equivalent assembly language program and then use the assembler to finish the compilation process. (In fact, the first FORTRAN compiler used this technique.)

A related technique is to translate a program into a program in some other language. For example, if a new language is invented (e.g. WHIZBANG), and a program is written to convert WHIZBANG programs into FORTRAN, then the usual FORTRAN compiler can be used to compile this program. Since FORTRAN will perform most of the program analysis, much of the development cost is saved at an increase of complexity in using the new language. Usage costs will rise since users must first convert their programs from WHIZBANG to FORTRAN, and then convert the FORTRAN to machine language.

In addition, if this translation program from WHIZBANG to FORTRAN is itself written in FORTRAN, then this translator can be run on any system that has FORTRAN. Therefore, with the cost of only one translator, the language has been implemented on any system with a FORTRAN compiler—an almost universal condition.

All of this taken together means that the term "compiler" is not altogether appropriate. In general the term "translator" is gaining acceptance. By *translator* we mean any program which converts a string of characters (called the source program) into a string of characters (called the object program). The output of this process can be a machine language program for the same or different machine, or a source language program in some other language. It may also be output in some other form usable by that system. In the remainder of this chapter, we shall use the term "compiler" to mean the classical translation from source program to machine language. If the concept described applies to all variations of the translation process, the term "translator" will be used.

5.2 BACKGROUND

Several aspects of compiler design are based upon formal theories of languages. In this section the concepts of grammars, finite state automata, and postfix notation will be described.

5.2.1 Grammars and Languages

As described in Section 5.1, a compiler is simply a translator from some source programming language, such as FORTRAN, to some object language, such as machine language for some computer. However, what is a language, and how can it be defined?

Syntax and semantics

In describing a language, there are two aspects to consider: its syntax and its semantics. Loosely speaking, the *syntax* of a language is what it looks like, while the *semantics* is what it means. For example, the sentence "The boy drank the milk" is a valid English sentence since it consists of a subject, verb, and direct object and has a valid meaning due to the usual understanding of the words of the sentence.

On the other hand, the sentence "The milk drank the boy" has the same syntactic structure of subject, verb, direct object, yet has no meaning according to everyday usage. Thus "syntactically," both statements are the same, but "semantically" one has a meaning while the other does not.

As another example, consider these sentences: "The girl hit the ball" and "The ball hit the girl." In this case both statements are syntactically similar and both have semantic meanings. However, "hit" is used differently in each. In the first, "girl" is the action to cause "hit," while in the second it can be assumed that some other party caused the action and the ball was only the object of that action (e.g., "The boy hit the ball which hit the girl"). Thus, "hit" has an ambiguous interpretation if based purely on syntax.

It should be clear that syntax alone is insufficient for extracting the meaning of a computer program; semantics must be included. However, while we know a great deal about syntax, programming language semantics is still an evolving topic. Fortunately, for the most part, we can separate these two ideas.

Grammars and languages

In the preceding paragraphs the principal ideas of language syntax have already been introduced. A sentence was simply a string of words that were written in a certain order. We also used special terms (e.g., subject, verb, etc.) to refer to certain classes of those words. We also stated that those special words had to be in a special order in order to be valid (e.g., subject-verb-direct object). These ideas have been formalized via the concept of a grammar, which we will use as our fundamental model for a programming language. A language will simply be all of the sentences that a specific grammar will allow. Thus, instead of describing English as a set of words and an infinite set of sentences, we can describe it more succinctly as a set of words and a set of rules for writing (syntactically) correct sentences.

In order to talk about grammars and languages, certain terms must be defined. A *vocabulary* (also called an *alphabet*) is a finite set of symbols. For English sentences the vocabulary would be the set of English words, for English words the vocabulary would be the 26 letters of the alphabet, and for a computer language, the vocabulary would be the 26 letters, 10 digits, and several special symbols such as (,), ., $+$, $-$, $\times$, /, and $=$. For any language there will always be an underlying vocabulary from which to choose symbols.

A *string* (or *sentence*) over a vocabulary V is a sequence of symbols, not necessarily distinct, belonging to V. Thus if V is the set of 3 elements $\{a, b, c\}$, then all of the following are strings over V: a, b, c, aa, ab, abc, $aaabbcccc$. We shall use the notation $|w|$ to mean the length, or number of elements, in the string w. Thus $|abc|$ is 3 and $|a|$ is 1. If V is a set, $|V|$ will be the number of elements in the set V. In the previous example, $|V|$ is 3. If $|A|$ is zero for a set A, we shall call it the null set ($\varnothing$).

If A is an alphabet, then A^* is all of the finite strings over A. For example, if A is the set $\{0, 1\}$, then A^* will contain 0, 1, 00, 11, 01, 10, 000 and any other string consisting of only 0s or 1s. However, there is one other string we must consider. Assume w is a string of one symbol, and that symbol is removed. What remains? w is still a string, but it contains no symbols in it, and $|w|$ is zero. We shall call this special string ϵ. Note that ϵ, $\{\epsilon\}$, and $\varnothing$ are all different. $\varnothing$ is a set with no elements, ϵ is a valid string, and $\{\epsilon\}$ is a set with one element, the element ϵ.

A little reflection should reveal that since A^* contains all finite strings of elements of A, A^* contains ϵ, even if A did not. We shall use A^+ to mean all strings of length 1 or more (thus excluding ϵ).

Given a vocabulary, we can now talk about a language. A *language* L over a vocabulary V is a subset of V^*. However, which subset? This is the purpose of a grammar. A grammar imposes a structure upon the vocabulary so that only certain strings in V^* are valid sentences.

The notation that will be used will be called *BNF* or *Backus-Naur Form*. This notation was first used in the report defining the language ALGOL-60. John Backus was a major author of the report, and Peter Naur was chairman of the committee that defined the language.

When we state that a sentence is a subject followed by a verb followed by a direct object, we can represent that in BNF as:

```
⟨SENTENCE⟩  ::=  ⟨SUBJECT⟩  ⟨VERB⟩  ⟨DIRECT OBJECT⟩
```

In BNF, symbols enclosed in brackets (⟨, ⟩) are the syntactic classes, and this rule states the syntactic structure of the syntactic class ⟨SENTENCE⟩.

Each of the rightmost three syntactic classes can be further broken down into other syntactic classes or into words of our language. One set of possibilities is the following:

```
⟨SUBJECT⟩  ::=  the girl
⟨VERB⟩        ::= hit
⟨DIRECT OBJECT⟩  ::=  the ball
```

We can then state that "the girl hit the ball" is a sentence since "the girl" is a ⟨SUBJECT⟩, "hit" is a ⟨VERB⟩, and "the ball" is a ⟨DIRECT OBJECT⟩.

Many other sets of rules are possible. For example, the syntactic class ⟨SUBJECT⟩ could be defined as follows:

```
⟨SUBJECT⟩   ::=  ⟨ARTICLE⟩ ⟨NOUN⟩
⟨ARTICLE⟩   ::=  the
⟨NOUN⟩      ::=  girl
⟨NOUN⟩      ::=  boy
⟨NOUN⟩      ::=  bat
```

In this case, three different sentences are possible:

1. the girl hit the ball
2. the boy hit the ball
3. the bat hit the ball

All are generated by our syntactic rules, since each consists of a ⟨SUBJECT⟩ (consisting of ⟨ARTICLE⟩ followed by ⟨NOUN⟩, ⟨VERB⟩, and ⟨DIRECT OBJECT⟩.)

As a bit of shorthand notation, the three rules concerning ⟨NOUN⟩ can be abbreviated as:

⟨NOUN⟩ ::= girl | boy | bat

which is read "A ⟨NOUN⟩ is 'girl' or 'boy' or 'bat'."

This notation is the main vehicle for defining a grammar. Certain objects (the, girl, boy, bat, hit, ball) form the vocabulary and will be called *terminal* symbols, while other objects (⟨NOUN⟩, ⟨ARTICLE⟩, ⟨SUBJECT⟩, ⟨VERB⟩, ⟨DIRECT OBJECT⟩) form the syntactic classes and will be called *nonterminal* symbols. The syntactic BNF rules will be called *productions* and may be written as $A \longrightarrow B$ instead of using ::= and angle brackets when the meaning is clear.

More formally, a *grammar* is a quadruple (N, T, P, S), where:

N is a finite vocabulary called the *nonterminals*.
T is a finite vocabulary called the *terminals*.
P is a set of *production rules*.
S is an element of N and is called the *start symbol*.

There is the additional provision that $N \cap T = \varnothing$. That is, no symbol is both a terminal and a nonterminal.

Intuitively, we already know how productions are used to form sentences. Let us formalize this notion. If AXB is a string and $X \longrightarrow C$ is a production, then the string ACB is *derivable* from AXB and we write $AXB \Rightarrow ACB$. Similarly, if $A \Rightarrow B$ and $B \Rightarrow C$, we can write $A \overset{*}{\Rightarrow} C$ and state that C is derived from A in one or more steps. If S is the start symbol, then if $S \overset{*}{\Rightarrow} A$, then A is called a *sentential form* and $S \Rightarrow U \Rightarrow V \Rightarrow W \Rightarrow \ldots \Rightarrow A$ is called a *derivation*.

If $S \overset{*}{\Rightarrow} xAy \overset{*}{\Rightarrow} xBy$ is a derivation, then B is called a *phrase* of the string xBy (i.e., it is the symbols replaced by the application of the rule $A \overset{*}{\Rightarrow} B$). If there is a production $A \longrightarrow B$, then B is called a *simple phrase*.

From our previous example, we can define a grammar as follows. The grammar is the quadruple (N, T, P, S), where:

$$N = \{S, B, V, D, M, A\}$$

$$T = \{\text{the, girl, boy, bat, ball, hit}\}$$

$$\begin{aligned} P = \{&S \longrightarrow BVD \\ &B \longrightarrow AM \\ &A \longrightarrow \text{the} \\ &M \longrightarrow \text{boy} \mid \text{girl} \mid \text{bat} \\ &V \longrightarrow \text{hit} \\ &D \longrightarrow \text{the ball}\} \end{aligned}$$

(Note that B stands for our previously called ⟨SUBJECT⟩, V is ⟨VERB⟩, D is ⟨DIRECT OBJECT⟩, A is ⟨ARTICLE⟩, and M is ⟨NOUN⟩.)

With our definition of "derives," many strings are derivable from the special start symbol. Some of these are:

BVD	the girl VD	BV the ball
B hit D	the boy hit D	the boy V the ball

the boy hit the ball
the girl hit the ball
the bat hit the ball

The only ones of interest are the last three consisting of only terminal symbols. A little thought will reveal that these are the only possible sentences which can be derived from the given start symbol using only the given rules. Therefore, given a grammar G $= (N, T, P, S)$, a *language L* over G (written L(G)) is the set of all strings over T^* derivable from S. That is,

$$\text{L(G)} = \{w \mid S \overset{*}{\Longrightarrow} w,\ w \epsilon T^*\}$$

We have still left one aspect in defining a grammar quite vague. That is in the definition of a production. Several possibilities exist, and each leads to a different class of grammar. Let G $= (N, T, P, S)$ be a grammar.

REGULAR (type 3). In this case, all productions of P are of the format: $A \longrightarrow Bc$ or $A \longrightarrow c$, where $A, B \epsilon N$ and $c \epsilon T$. Regular grammars are good models for the scanner phase of a compiler.

CONTEXT FREE (type 2). In this case, all productions of P are of the form $A \longrightarrow w$, where $w \epsilon (N \cup T)^*$ and $A \epsilon N$. This class describes most compiled languages and will be the main focus of this chapter.

CONTEXT SENSITIVE (type 1). In this case, all productions are of the format $A \longrightarrow B$, where $A \epsilon N^+$, $B \epsilon (N \cup T)^*$, and $|A| \leq |B|$. That is, all rules are length-nondecreasing.

UNRESTRICTED (type 0). In this case, all productions are of the format $A \longrightarrow B$ with $A \epsilon (N \cup T)^+$ and $B \epsilon (N \cup T)^*$.

Type 0 and type 1 languages are not practical for compiler writing, and will not be considered further in this book.

Parsing

Consider the grammar $\text{G}_1 = (\{S\}, \{0, 1\}, P, S)$, where

$$\begin{aligned} P = \{S &\longrightarrow 0S, \\ S &\longrightarrow 1S, \\ S &\longrightarrow 0, \\ S &\longrightarrow 1\} \end{aligned}$$

Intuitively, it should be clear that the language generated by G_1 consists of all binary strings. Thus, the string 0101 can be derived from S by the following derivation:

$$S \Longrightarrow 0S \Longrightarrow 01S \Longrightarrow 010S \Longrightarrow 0101$$

This can be displayed pictorially by a *derivation tree* (Figure 5.2). In this case, each leaf node is a terminal, each nonleaf is a nonterminal, and the set of arcs leaving a node represent one step in the derivation.

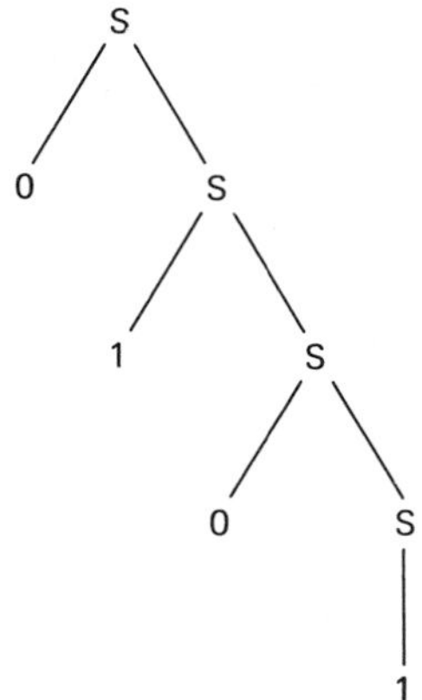

Figure 5.2 Derivation tree of 0101.

We can look at this derivation tree from two perspectives. Starting at the top (S), what strings can be generated by applying rules of the grammar? This is often called the *string generation* problem and is the viewpoint from the theoretical point of view in looking at properties of languages.

In compiling, we are often more interested in the other approach: given a program (a string), is it in the language? That is, can a derivation tree, starting with the start symbol, be generated for this string? This is usually referred to as the *string recognition* problem, although it is essentially the same as the string generation problem. We shall use the term *parse* to refer to the recognition problem and *derivation* to refer to the generation problem.

Consider the grammar $G_2 = (\{S, T\}, \{0, 1\}, P, S)$, where

$$P = \{S \longrightarrow TS \mid 0 \mid 1$$
$$T \longrightarrow 0 \mid 1\}$$

By studying G_1 and G_2, the following two facts should be clear:

1. G_1 and G_2 generate the same language.
2. Derivations in G_1 are unique, but derivations in G_2 are not.

For example, the string 01 has the following two derivations in G_2:

1. $S \Rightarrow TS \Rightarrow 0S \Rightarrow 01$
2. $S \Rightarrow TS \Rightarrow T1 \Rightarrow 01$

However, both derivations have the same derivation tree (Figure 5.3). Therefore, it would be useful to consider them the same. To do this, the concept of a leftmost derivation has been introduced. $xAy \Rightarrow xBy$ is one step in a *leftmost* derivation if B is the *handle* (i.e., leftmost simple phrase) of xBy.

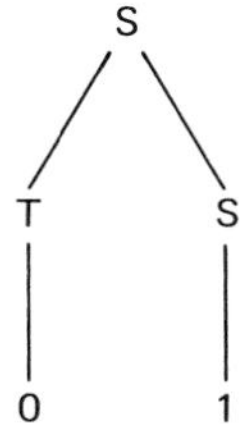

Figure 5.3 Derivation tree of 01.

Using this definition, derivation (1) above is not a leftmost derivation, while derivation (2) is. This is due to the last step in each ($0S \Rightarrow 01$ in (1) and $T1 \Rightarrow 01$ in (2)). The leftmost phrase is the first 0.

Unfortunately, leftmost derivations may not be unique. While grammars G_1 and G_2 both generate unique derivation trees for any string (and hence have unique leftmost derivations), grammars are possible which do not have these properties. Consider G_3 defined as follows:

$$G_3 = (\{S\}, \{0, 1\}, P, S)$$
$$P = \{S \longrightarrow SS \mid 0 \mid 1\}$$

In this case, strings have multiple leftmost derivations. For example, the string 011 has two distinct leftmost derivations:

1. $S \Rightarrow SS \Rightarrow 0S \Rightarrow 0SS \Rightarrow 01S \Rightarrow 011$
2. $S \Rightarrow SS \Rightarrow SSS \Rightarrow 0SS \Rightarrow 01S \Rightarrow 011$

These correspond to the two distinct derivation trees of Figure 5.4.

We shall call a grammar *ambiguous* if there is some string generated by that grammar with two distinct leftmost derivations. As shown, G_3 is ambiguous due to the two derivations for 011.

We shall call a language *inherently ambiguous* if every grammar generating the language is ambiguous. Note that the language generated by G_3 is not inherently ambiguous since G_1 and G_2 both generate the same language,

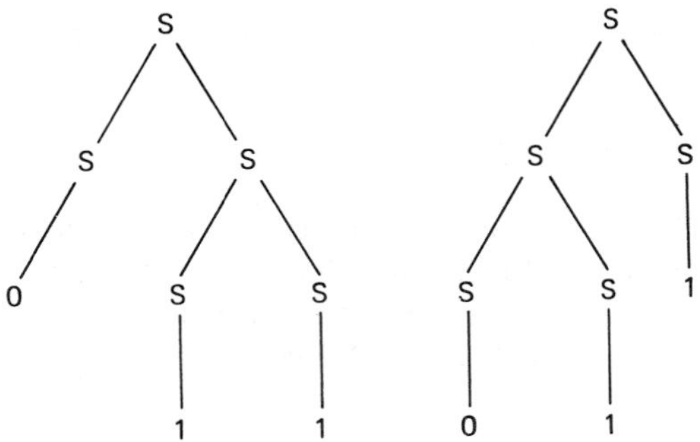

Figure 5.4 Two derivation trees for 011 in grammar G_4.

and neither is ambiguous. Ambiguity is not a desirable property in a language, since that would mean that a program has two distinct interpretations.

5.2.2 Finite State Automata

Consider the set consisting of "any number of zeros." Is ϵ in this set? In order to avoid such ambiguities, more formal notations have been developed. One such notation is the concept of a *state diagram.*

The example just described is pictured in Figure 5.5. In this diagram each arc is labeled with a symbol, and control passes from node to node beginning at the node containing the input arc and moves to succeeding nodes depending upon the input string of characters. A string is accepted if control ends in a final node (one with a double circle).

Thus in Figure 5.5, control begins at *A* and remains there as long as only zeros are input. Any 1 takes control to the node labeled *DEAD*, and once there, control can never return to the final node. This diagram clearly answers the question of whether ϵ is in the set. Clearly it is, since control begins in a final state, so no input (e.g., ϵ) leaves control in a final state. If at least one zero were required, then Figure 5.6 could be used to model that set. Here, at least one zero is needed to take control into final state B.

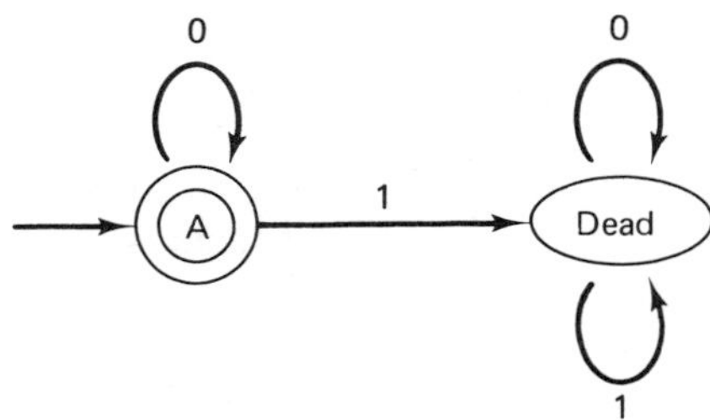

Figure 5.5 State diagram for 0^n, $n \geq 0$.

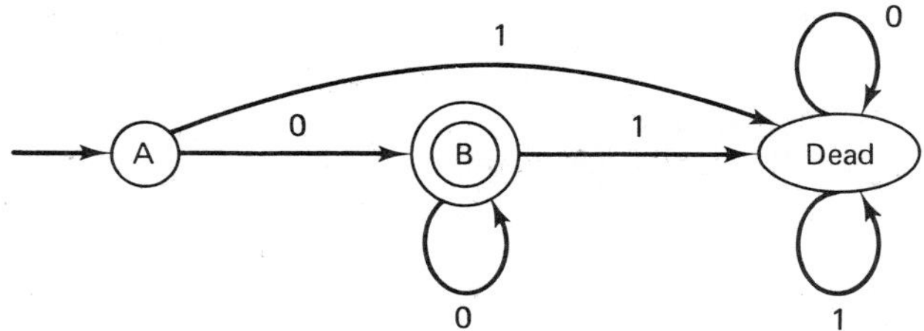

Figure 5.6 State diagram for 0^n, $n \geq 1$.

State diagrams are useful for modeling many types of repetitive strings (e.g., all digits, all letters, etc.) and are useful to model the scanner phase of a compiler.

Rather than considering informal state diagrams, we shall consider a more mathematical model called a *finite state automata*; however, the comparison between the two will be quite evident. From Figures 5.5 and 5.6 we see that a state diagram has five basic components: a set of nodes, a set of arcs, a set of labels attached to each arc, a starting node, and some (zero or more) terminal nodes. We can abstract this by defining a finite state automata as a 5-tuple of these objects.

A *finite state automata* is a 5-tuple (S, I, d, s, F), where:
S is a finite set called the *states*.
I is a finite set called the *alphabet*.
d is a function from $S \times I$ into S. This is the transformation function that takes control from a given state and input symbol to a new state (i.e., the arcs of the state diagram).
s is the *start state* and is in S.
F is a subset of S and is called the *final set*.

We can write $d(a, i) = b$ to mean that if control is in state a and input i is read, control moves to state b (e.g., control follows the arc labeled i from node a to node b in the state diagram).

As an example, Figure 5.6 can be defined by the finite automata M as follows:

$$\text{M} = (S, I, d, A, F)$$

where

$$S = \{A, B, C\}$$
$$I = \{0, 1\}$$
$$F = \{B\}$$
$$d(A,0)=B \quad d(A,1)=C \quad d(B,0)=B \quad d(B,1)=C$$
$$d(C,0)=C \quad d(C,1)=C$$

Although d is only defined on a single input symbol, we can extend the definition in an obvious way. For string xv, with $x \epsilon I$, we recursively define d as follows:

$$d(a, xv) = d(d(a, x), v)$$

That is, move from a based upon the initial input x, and then move according to string v. This definition just says to move one node at a time, based upon successive inputs.

With this extension, we now define the language accepted by a finite automata. For automata $\mathrm{M} = (S, I, d, s, F)$, the *language* accepted by M (called T(M)) is defined as:

$$\mathrm{T(M)} = \{w \mid w \epsilon I^*,\ d(s,w) \epsilon F\}$$

That is, the language is all strings that move from the start state s to some final state in F.

As a second example, consider the state diagram for all strings consisting of an even number of 0s and an even number of 1s. We can construct this if we recognize the following facts:

1. As a string is read, either an even number of 0s or an odd number of 0s have already been seen.
2. Similarly, the string contains either an even number or an odd number of 1s.
3. Facts (1) and (2) above are independent of each other.

These ideas permit the solution represented by Figure 5.7. The upper two nodes (A, B) represent an even number of 1s, and the lower two nodes (C, D) represent an odd number. Each one takes control from A or B to C

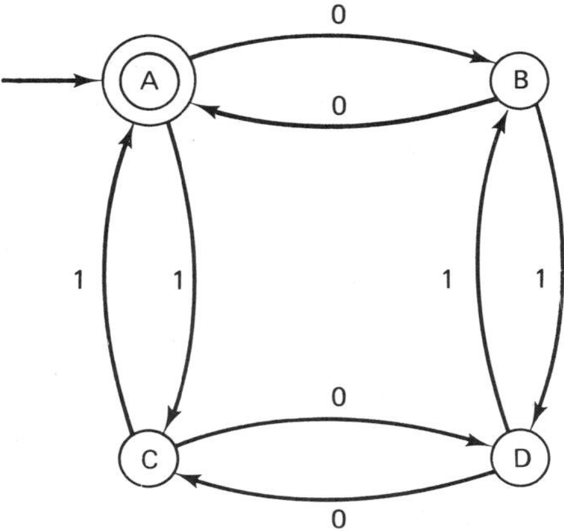

Figure 5.7 State diagram for strings with an even number of 0s and 1s.

or D, or vice versa. Similarly A and C represent an even number of 0s and B and D represent an odd number.

A finite state automata to accept this set can be created almost directly from the state diagram. One such automata is the 5-tuple (S, I, d, s, F), where:

$$S = \{A, B, C, D\}$$
$$I = \{0, 1\}$$
$$F = \{A\}$$
$$s = A$$
$$d(A,0)=B \quad d(A,1)=C$$
$$d(B,0)=A \quad d(B,1)=D$$
$$d(C,0)=D \quad d(C,1)=A$$
$$d(D,0)=C \quad d(D,1)=B$$

Note that the final set need not be limited to a single node. If we want to modify Figure 5.7 to accept all strings consisting of either an even number of 0s and an even number of 1s or an odd number of 0s and an odd number of 1s, then one possible solution is Figure 5.8, which produces an automata similar to the previous example with the only change being that the final set is now $\{A, D\}$.

Nondeterministic finite state automata

So far all state diagrams have exhibited a common property: from any node there was an arc leaving that node for all symbols in the alphabet. This is required in a finite automata since the definition of the function d is a

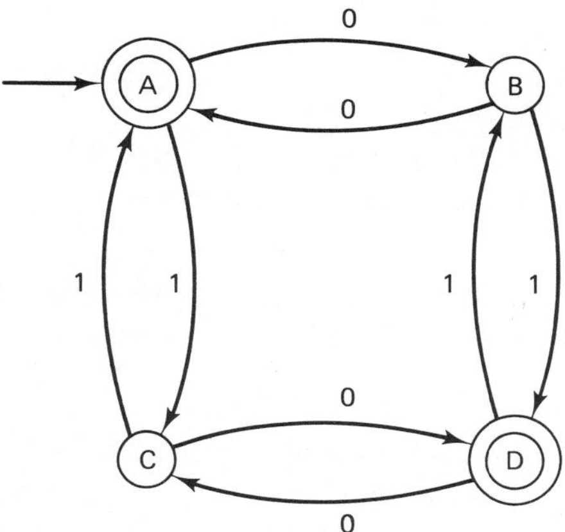

Figure 5.8 State diagram for strings with an even number of 0s and 1s, or an odd number of 0s and 1s.

function from $S \times I$ into S, thus it is defined for all S and I. However, this sometimes clutters up the diagram. Referring back to Figure 5.5, we see that the purpose of the state labeled *DEAD* was to simply provide a node to transfer to upon reading an illegal input.

Figure 5.9 reproduces this state diagram without such a dead state. This represents that a string will be accepted if there is "some" path from the start state to a final state. Figure 5.9 shows that this occurs as long as only 0s are input. If there is no possible transfer from a given node on a given input, we say that the automata halts and rejects the input. In addition, since we are interested in possible paths to a final state, we can also consider the case where there is more than one arc labeled with the same symbol. The automata is said to nondeterministically choose one of these arcs. Such an automata is called a *nondeterministic finite state automata.*

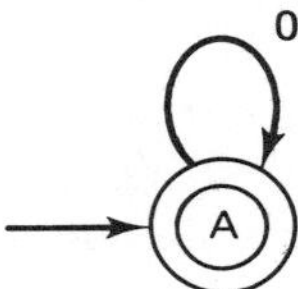

Figure 5.9 Nondeterministic state diagram for 0^n, $n \geq 0$.

This form of automata can be used to describe sets in an easier manner than with the (deterministic) finite state automata. Comparing Figures 5.5 and 5.9 gives one such example.

Just as in the previous section, we can formalize the notion of a nondeterministic finite state automata. A *nondeterministic finite state automata* is a 5-tuple (S, I, d, s, F), where:

S is a finite set of *states.*
I is a finite *alphabet.*
s is in S and is the *start state.*
F is a subset of S and are the *final states.*
d is a function that takes states in S and symbols in I and maps them into subsets of S.

As stated previously, although nondeterministic automata are easier to write for a given set and seemingly add increased numbers of sets to the class of languages accepted, they are in reality the same sets. This can be proven by the following discussion.

Both models have a finite information content. In the deterministic case, only knowledge of the current state is necessary to move from state to state. The past and how one arrived at a certain state is irrelevant. Similarly, in the nondeterministic case, it is only necessary to know in what possible states you could possibly be. Again this is a finite number, and is just the set of subsets of states. Thus a deterministic finite state automata will be equivalent to a nondeterministic finite state automata if the states of the deterministic model represent subsets of possible states of the nondeterministic case.

Exercise 5.1: Formalize the above discussion into a correct proof.

Regular languages

In Section 5.1.2, the concept of a grammar was introduced to describe the characteristics of certain sets. The purpose of this section is to show that the regular languages are nothing more than an alternative notation for a finite state automata.

Reviewing from the previous section, a regular grammar is a quadruple (N, T, P, S), where:

N is a finite set of nonterminals.
T is a finite set of terminals.
S is the nonterminal start symbol.
P is a set of productions of the form: $X \longrightarrow Ya$ or $X \longrightarrow a$.

Theorem: G is a regular grammar if and only if there is a finite state automata M such that:

$$T(M) = L(G)$$

Outline of proof: Let $G = (N, T, P, S)$ be a regular grammar.
Let $M = (K, I, d, s, F)$ be a finite state automata, such that

$$\begin{aligned} K &= N \cup \{f\} \\ I &= T \\ F &= \{f\} \\ s &= S \\ d(X, a) &= Y \text{ if } X \longrightarrow aY \\ d(X, a) &= f \text{ if } X \longrightarrow a \end{aligned}$$

To see that this construction works, the following must be proven:

1. The states of M are just the nonterminals of G.
2. Each move of M corresponds to one step in the derivation tree for a string in L(G).
3. Terminating the derivation for a string in L(G) corresponds to moving to the final state (f) in M.

In order to complete the proof, the following must also be proven: Let M be a finite state automata. Then there is a regular grammar G such that T(M) = L(G). The proof is similar, and will be left as an exercise.

5.2.3 Postfix

A program is normally written to perform operations on data. Usually these operators are expressed in a notation called *infix* where the operation is between the operands. For example, in $(A*B)+C$, the multiplication operator ($*$) is between the operands A and B while the plus operator ($+$) is between the expression $(A*B)$ and the operand C.

The evaluation of such an expression is not a simple process. For example, the $+$ operation above cannot be performed until the second (C) operand is read. If C itself is a complicated expression, then many tokens have to be read before the expression can be computed.

An alternative notation avoids these problems. It is called *postfix*, and the operator follows the operands. Thus the infix expression $(A+B)$ is $AB+$ in postfix.

Postfix for an expression has two very desirable properties, especially in a compiler:

1. Parentheses are never needed to express any expression. Since the operator immediately follows its operands, it is unambiguous what the operands are. Thus the expression $(A+B)+C$ in infix, will be $AB+C+$ in postfix, and the expression $A+(B+C)$ will be $ABC++$ in postfix.
2. Whenever an operator is scanned, its operands have already been read. Thus there is no case where an operator's evaluation must be delayed until more data is read.

While this discussion has centered on binary operators, the extension to unary operators is the same. Thus unary minus (call it $\sim$) will simply follow its arguments. Thus $\sim A$ in infix will be $A\sim$, and $\sim(A+B)$ in infix will be $AB+\sim$. (Note that the $-$ in infix can stand for both unary or binary minus operations, and its correct definition is known from context. This is much harder to do with postfix.)

Because of these properties for postfix expressions, a simple algorithm exists for evaluating an expression in postfix. This algorithm is:

```
do while(more tokens in expression);
    get (next token);
    if token is operand
        then push token onto stack;
    if token is operator
        then perform operation on top stack
             elements, and replace these elements
             by result of operation;
    end;
```

The result of the expression is now the only element on stack.

This stack-based algorithm is at the heart of almost every compiler. In general the parser converts a program to postfix, and then the code generator generates code to evaluate all the expressions according to the above algorithm.

However, how does one convert an expression to postfix? Since a compiler is based upon grammars, the following technique applies. Assume that a production for the language is the following:

$$A \longrightarrow B\, u\, C$$

where A, B, and C are nonterminals and u is a terminal. Assume that the terminals of the production are operators. Then this production states that the nonterminal A is the "infix" of operands B and C with operator u. Therefore the "postfix" will be A, B followed by operator u. Thus for this production, the postfix is:

Postfix for A
Postfix for B
u

If terminal symbols are output in this order, then the postfix for sentences in the language will be produced.

5.3 PROJECT METHODOLOGY

In implementing any software project, we have identified several distinct steps. The failure of some projects to be completed on time, within budget, or to be reliable can usually be traced to the failure to plan adequately for all the necessary steps. Reviewing Chapter 1, we recall that the six steps of the *software life cycle* are:

1. *Requirements.* The first task is to clearly define the task. What is the program supposed to do? What real-world problems is it to solve? What are the inputs to the program? What are the outputs? What resources (in hardware, personnel, and software) are available?

2. *Specifications.* The requirements must then be translated into a set of explicit specifications for a computer program. What are the desired operating characteristics of the resulting program? That is, is execution speed, portability, modifiability, size, or some other characteristic most important?

3. *Design.* In this phase the overall structure of the program is designed, depending upon the specifications. For example, for a compiler, the basic structure, as described previously, will be determined. In addition, the overall flow of control and interfaces between the various sections must be defined.

4. *Implementation.* In this phase the program is coded. In general the program design language is expanded into the implementation programming language.

5. *Testing*. In this phase the software routines that are coded are integrated into a final system and then tested. All interface problems should be discovered before the system is turned over to the user.

6. *Operation*. In this phase the system is in use; however, no large system is ever static. Additional features are always desired, and some errors that were not detected previously must be fixed.

In describing a translator, there are two primary considerations: the input and the output. The input will be a source program written in some programming language, and the output will be the translation of the program into some other form—usually machine language for some computer.

5.3.1 Source Programming Language

The source programming language may or may not be an option which can be defined by the project. If the task is to "implement ANSI standard FORTRAN" [ANSI, 66], then the source input is fixed; however, if the project is to "implement a language to solve graph algorithmic problems," many options are available. The goals of the language must be described by the users of this language, and a consistent definition formed.

This language definition phase can itself fill a chapter of a book. For further information on this problem, see references such as [SIGPLAN, 76]. We will assume that the language is specified. Figure 5.10 gives the syntax of the language we will implement. It is a simple language, although it has most of the features present in languages like FORTRAN or PL/1.

The language, called NIP,[1] has the following characteristics. A program consists of a set of procedures. Each procedure consists of a sequence of ASSIGNMENT, CALL, IF, WHILE, READ, and WRITE statements. Arguments to procedures in the CALL statement are assumed call-by-reference. All variables are integers, are either local variables or parameters, and must be declared. The START phrase specifies the procedure where execution is to begin. There are no logical variables; so "true" will be defined as any nonzero value, while "false" will be defined as zero for IF and WHILE statements. This language is a simplification of the language SIMPL-T developed at the University of Maryland [Basili and Turner, 75].

5.3.2 Target Machine Language

In describing the output for our translator, we need knowledge of the computer on which the program is to execute. We will assume that we are writing a standard compiler that outputs machine language instructions for

[1]NIP means nothing in particular.

```
<PROGRAM> ::= <PROCEDURE> <PROGRAM> | START <ID>
<PROCEDURE> ::= <ID> PROCEDURE <PARAMLIST><STATEMENTLIST>END
<PARAMLIST> ::= ( <IDLIST> ) | ε
<IDLIST> ::= <IDLIST> , <ID>  | <ID>
<STATEMENTLIST> ::= <STATEMENTLIST>;<STATEMENT>|<STATEMENT>
<STATEMENT> ::= <ID> := <EXPRESSION> | DECLARE <IDLIST> |
                IF <EXPRESSION> THEN <STATEMENTLIST> END |
                IF <EXPRESSION> THEN <STATEMENTLIST>
                                  ELSE <STATEMENTLIST> END |
                WHILE <EXPRESSION> DO <STATEMENTLIST> END |
                CALL <ID> ( <EXPRESSIONLIST>) | CALL <ID> |
                READ( <IDLIST>) | WRITE (<EXPRESSIONLIST>)
<EXPRESSIONLIST> ::= <EXPRESSIONLIST>,<EXPRESSION> | <EXPRESSION>
<EXPRESSION> ::= <EXPRESSION> <ADDOP> <TERM> | <TERM>
<TERM> ::= <TERM> <MULTOP> <PRIMARY> | <PRIMARY>
<PRIMARY> ::= <ID> | <CONSTANT> | (<EXPRESSION>)
<ADDOP> ::= + | -
<MULTOP> ::= * | /
<ID> ::= any string of up to 12 characters starting with a letter and containing only
         letters and digits
<CONSTANT> ::= any string of up to 10 digits

Blanks may appear before or after any non-terminal symbol
Comments may appear wherever a blank may appear, and have the syntax $ any string
   except $ followed by $
```

Figure 5.10 Syntax of the NIP language.

this computer. For now we will hold off the formal description of this machine until we describe the code generation phase in some detail; however, we will assume that it is a "standard" machine with directly addressable main memory and several registers and index registers. This includes most major computers sold today.

5.3.3 Iterative Enhancement

In scanning the NIP language, there are two obvious omissions: arrays and character strings. This is intentional. In describing this compiler, we will use the technique of "iterative enhancement" mentioned in Chapter 1. In using this approach, only the minimal subset of the final product will be implemented. This will simplify the design and greatly shorten the time to implement. By finishing the design earlier, any flaws that may appear during the implementation phase will be discovered earlier. Also, users will have access to the compiler earlier, and any defects in its operation can be corrected with much less effort.

After this initial design, the system will be redesigned with additional features. The redesigned system is recoded, possibly using some of the modules in the previous design. This process is repeated until the final product is finished. In keeping with this philosophy, Section 5.9 will describe enhancements to the language and compiler.

We shall use a program design language, or PDL, to design the compiler. This use of such a design language permits top-down development and better design techniques. As mentioned in Chapter 2, the PDL which will be used will be patterned after PL/1, which will be the language the compiler will ultimately be written in—although that certainly is not necessary. The design can easily be translated into some other programming language.

Note that this "one step at a time" is a recurring theme. Each step in the development of a project should be planned. In designing software, stepwise refinement should be used to control the growth and understanding of the program. Previously, iterative enhancement was described as a technique to control the complexity of the implementation. In both cases, designers avoid the "kitchen-sink" approach, where everything is defined and is implemented without worrying about the structure of the design and its manageability. Our goal here will be to keep the design manageable and understandable.

5.4 COMPILER ORGANIZATION

The time has come to describe the compiler we are to implement. We have already been given the source language to compile, and we have some idea about the target machine that will execute the resulting program. As the previous section explains, we must first analyze the requirements for our project before beginning any design or implementation.

5.4.1 Requirements Analysis

In deciding on a basic structure for our compiler, we have to choose a basic strategy for the compiler as described by Figure 5.1. Because the goal of this project is to give insights into compiler implementation, we will keep the design simple. We will do this by designing the entire compiler to be in memory at one time. Although this will increase the size of the system, the resulting program should not be too large.

Since the use of an operating system's file space is generally an expensive operation, it is desirable to keep file operations to a minimum for student usage. This argues for the design of a one-pass compiler. If we use more than one pass, the entire program must be stored, either in memory or in a file, for pass 2. If it is in memory, we are arbitrarily limiting the size of the program by the available memory space. As we shall see shortly, a one-pass design only needs memory space for a single statement, which is not a significant amount.

This one-pass design should also lead to efficient compiler execution. This is also a desirable trait for a student project.

While on the subject of efficient execution, another aspect of system design should be stressed. The efficiency of a system is measured in "seconds," not "microseconds." A system is efficient by its overall design, not by using every known trick to write efficient but unreadable code. For every language, there are easy (but slightly inefficient) and "sneaky" (but unreadable) ways to write programs. Every experienced programmer knows some of them. The benefits to using them are nil since the resulting program is unreadable to any other programmer (or often to the writer more than three days after being written). In an industrial organization, where programs may be used for years and maintained by many different programmers, inscrutability is a most unwelcome trait.

The seeming sacrifice of efficiency for understandability does not really exist, however. Several examples come to mind. For example, the PL/C PL/1 compiler [Conway and Wilcox, 73] for the IBM 360/370 series is a three-pass compiler which stores all data in main memory. As a result, it is extremely efficient and costs less to use than any of the standard production compilers. While it does not generate as efficient code as the manufacturer-supplied software and is not able to compile very large programs, its overall design goal was to compile small programs quickly. In this respect, it is quite successful.

This author was in charge of a similar compiler development—the PLUM compiler for the Univac 1100 series computer [Zelkowitz, 75]. Since the design goals were similar to the PL/C project, the structure of the PLUM compiler will be described. The compiler was to be used by students in a university environment. That implied several considerations.

1. Execution speed of the compiled programs was not important. A study of student programs demonstrated that most of them executed for under one second, and almost never for more than 10; therefore, the standard compiler and loader which took over 10 seconds for most student runs was most impractical. While it could generate inefficient code, the compiler itself had to be efficient.

2. File operations on the Univac system (or almost any other system) are slow and should be avoided.

3. Student programs are generally short, so that the compiler did not need to handle programs of many thousands of statements.

4. Over 50% of all programs compiled contain errors. Therefore, the compiler had to be written to detect as many of these errors as possible. Diagnostic facilities in the compiler were extremely important.

The result of these decisions was a three-pass compiler that saved the total program, in a parsed form, in memory. Because memory is limited, the compiler can handle only 1500 statements per program—sufficient for most student applications. Even though the compiler uses three passes, it is still the most efficient product on the Univac system. By avoiding all file operations, most of the overhead of other compilers is avoided. Although it is true that the code produced executes two to three times more slowly than an equivalent FORTRAN program, execution time is practically irrelevant for student programs.

5.4.2 Top-level Design

In designing our NIP compiler, we shall try and keep each phase independent of any other phase. This will have the desirable property that changes to one section will not affect changes to any other.

Since we have chosen a compiler of one pass, we have three basic components to write: a scanner to read in tokens, a parser to parse the program, and a code generator. How should these be organized?

One approach would be to assume that the parser uses tokens as primitive symbols in its grammar. This would simplify the grammar that the parser needs since the details of each token need not be specified. This structure is given by the following program:

```
do while (more tokens to read);
        Get next token;
        Parse this token;
        if postfix-produced then
            call CODEGENERATOR;
end;
```

The scanner would read in the program and produce tokens. Its overall structure would then be:

```
do while (more characters in token);
        Get next-input-character;
        IF end-of-next-token then
            return (token);
end;
```

It should immediately become apparent that there must be an interface between the parser and the scanner. In order to define a token, the purpose of a scanner must be explained. Each source language statement contains several components. For example, the statement:

```
ABC := D+6;
```

contains six tokens. There are two variable names (*ABC* and *D*), one constant (6), an assignment operator (:=), an arithmetic operator (+), and a statement delimiter (;). In parsing a program it is generally unimportant what variables or constants appear in an assignment, only that a single variable name appears to the left of the := in such a statement. However, for code generation it is extremely important that code be generated for the correct variable.

Thus tokens need two components. One is a class component to be used by the parser. Classes would consist of variable names, constants and operators, among others. A second component would indicate a member of a particular class. This would be the value of a constant, or some identification of which variable is being specified.

Immediately another problem arises. How are variable names handled? If the same name appears in two different statements, we may want the name to refer to the same variable. This means that we need to keep track of all variable names. This is generally handled by a symbol table.

Whenever the scanner sees a string that refers to a variable name, it must first check to see whether the name appeared previously. In order to keep our system modular, we will assume that all of this is handled by this separate symbol table routine. Thus a section of the scanner logic:

```
if end-of-next-token then
    return token;
```

could be expanded to:

```
if end-of-next-token then do;
    if end-of-variable-name then
        call SYMBOLTABLE with variable-name;
    return (token);
    end;
```

We will assume that the SYMBOLTABLE routine simply returns a code that the scanner uses as a reference to that variable name. Thus the token returned by the scanner will be the pair (token-class, unique-number).

How the symbol table is organized is unimportant to either the scanner or parser. All that is necessary is that both routines have access to the unique number identifying the variable and can return that information to the symbol table routine for further information about the identifier.

We have already given preliminary specifications for the scanner and parser—now for the code generator. Our top-level design for the parser states:

```
if postfix-produced then
    call CODEGENERATOR;
```

The code generator needs to know the structure of tokens so that the appropriate code can be produced. In a one-pass compiler this code generator simply generates code for this token; however, the same parser strategy can be used in a multipass compiler. The parser could pass the tokens to a routine that simply writes the information into a file. A second-pass code generator could reread this file and generate code.

So far our compiler consists of four basic components: a scanner, a parser, a symbol table routine, and a code generator. However, how will we know that the components work correctly? In order to test our design, we will build diagnostic features directly into the compiler. For example, the scanner can be tested by printing out the tokens which are read in some easily readable format. Similarly, the code can be checked by printing out the generated code, again in an easily readable format. Therefore, one of the first decisions will be to design a diagnostic feature for that particular phase. With the PLUM compiler, the most important and first facility added to the compiler was a routine to symbolically print the generated code. Many errors in programming became apparent just by reading this code.

Figure 5.11 shows the overall structure of our compiler. The data that

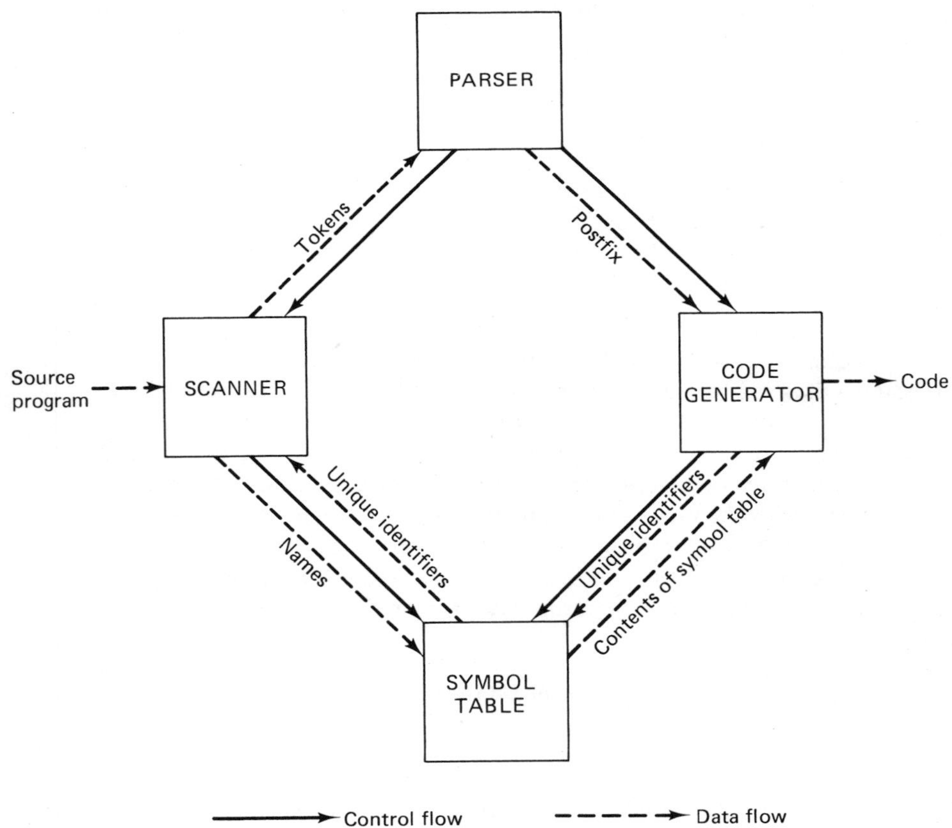

Figure 5.11 Control and data flow through NIP compiler.

passes between each of the various components comprises the interfaces in our system. Having described the gross structure of our proposed NIP compiler, the next four sections will contain descriptions for each of these. Each phase is basically independent of the others, which helps in making the project modular and easy to implement.

5.4.3 Diagnostic Features

Since diagnostic data is important, let us assume that each phase of our compiler will be built with internal diagnostics which can check on the proper development of that phase. We need a way to invoke these, so we will create an array called *DEBUG*. *DEBUG*(1), *DEBUG*(2), *DEBUG*(3), and *DEBUG*(4) will refer to the symbol table, scanner, parser, and code generator phase, respectively. If *DEBUG*(*I*) is true (set to the value '1' B), the corresponding phase will generate diagnostic data. This enables the compiler writer to turn such diagnostic tables dynamically on and off.

We have to provide some mechanism to invoke the diagnostic routines. For our development project we will assume that the first input to the compiler is a list of diagnostic routines to be activated. Thus the input to the compiler would be:

```
diagnostic data
NIP program
```

If we assume that we use a single letter to represent each phase to debug, then the NIP compiler would begin with the following code:

```
declare DEBUG(4) FIXED BINARY INITIAL('0'B, '0'B, '0'B, '0'B),
     T INITIAL(1),
     S INITIAL(2)
     P INITIAL(3),
     C INITIAL(4);
get first card;
if 'T' on card then DEBUG(T) = '1'B;          /*symbol Table */
if 'S' on card then DEBUG(S) = '1'B;          /*Scanner */
if 'P' on card then DEBUG(P) = '1'B;          /*Parser */
if 'C' on card then DEBUG(C) = '1'B;          /*Code gen. */
call COMPILER;                                /*compile */
```

For example, if we want to monitor the symbol table routine and the code generator, the first card could be TC.

Note that once our compiler is operational, we will want to change this structure. Most users do not know, or care, about the internal structure of the compiler; therefore, this first card is quite a nuisance. Compilers (or any piece of software for that matter) should be designed for the users, not for the people writing the compiler. While this seems to me to be obvious, it is truly amazing how many systems are totally incomprehensible to use because they were designed for easy use by systems programmers.

Exercise 5.2: Write down at least five different error messages generated by your own local operating system that are totally incomprehensible unless you know its internal structure.

One way of hiding this debugging information once the NIP compiler is operational is to locate the equivalent of the first card in a place that most users don't know or care about. For example, in IBM systems this could be the PARM field of the EXEC JCL card as in:

```
//    EXEC    PGM=NIP,PARM='DEBUG=TC'
```

With Univac it could be:

```
@NIP ,,,TC
```

On a DEC System 10 a switch could be used:

```
RUN NIP/DEBUG:TC
```

With other systems, similar techniques exist. Thus the debugging code will be hidden from most casual users.

5.5 SYMBOL TABLE ORGANIZATION

In designing the symbol table, we first have to study the information it will contain. Given the statement:

```
NEXTSPACE := NEXTSPACE + 14;
```

we would like both instances of the variable name *NEXTSPACE* to refer to the same variable. If the names occurred in different statements, this may not necessarily be so. If both statements are in the same procedure, then the variables will be the same. However, since NIP has no global data, if the variables occur in different procedures, the names will refer to different variables. Therefore the current procedure and the name of the variable are both parameters to our symbol table routine.

The structure of NIP lends itself to the use of a shortcut. Since NIP has no global data, and there are no nested procedures, variables from only one procedure can ever be accessible at any given time. Thus the current procedure name is not necessary. However, we will keep this as a parameter in case we add block structure at some later date.

A third necessary component is the type of variable accessed. We have several classes even in our simple language. The basic variable is of type INTEGER. We may also have procedure names. We may want to create other types, so let us maintain flexibility by making the type another field in the entry.

When we access the symbol table during code generation, we would like to use an efficient search strategy rather than having to use the character string representation. To do this, the symbol table will initially return a code number that uniquely identifies the variable. This number has significance only to the symbol table routine and is ignored by other routines.

A further consideration, needed at code generation time, is the location of the storage allocated to that variable. This information is necessary to generate code for the variable. Because at this time we have not studied the run-time structure for our language, let us leave it unspecified.

Our symbol table has two major functions: to enter a new name into the table (usually in a DECLARE statement) and to retrieve a name previously entered (as in an assignment statement). Thus the function is another parameter.

Combining all of this, our interface to the symbol table routine is:

```
SYMBOLTABLE: procedure(FUNCTION, NAME, TYPE, LOCATION,
                                  PROC, other);
declare FUNCTION,     /* ENTER NAME, or RETRIEVE NAME */
        NAME,         /* CHARACTER string for name */
        TYPE,         /* INTEGER, FUNCTION or other */
        LOCATION,     /* unique ID for name */
        PROCNAME,     /* procedure declared in */
        other;        /* code generation information */
```

As stated above, this routine has two basic functions: to enter a name or to retrieve a name. Two error conditions are possible. One is retrieving a name that has never been declared. This may mean that the programmer forgot the declaration. In order to handle this, after printing an error message let us assume that a DECLARE statement was omitted, and simply add the declaration. The second error that can occur is the declaration of a new variable with the same name as an entry already in the symbol table. This can occur if two identical DECLARE statements are in the same procedure. We can handle this by simply ignoring the second declaration after printing a warning.

Note that these repairs may not always work or may not be the correct repair. If the new variable is a misspelling of another name, then by adding a new declaration for this new variable, we may not retrieve the variable that was desired. An alternative error correction could be spelling correction. If a variable is searched for in the symbol table and is not found, then it could be a misspelling of some other variable. If so, then that variable should be used. Only if the spelling test fails should a new variable be added. A simple spelling correction algorithm has been coded into the Cornell CORC and PL/C compilers, and has been found to discover about 80% of all spelling errors [Morgan, 70].

Let us now give the basic top-level design for our symbol table routine. Remember it is unimportant to the rest of the system what algorithm is used, only that the interface specifications should hold. Our basic logic is dependent upon two considerations: (1) Is the entry in the table already? and (2) Do we want to enter a new name or retrieve a name already in the table? This can be specified by the following matrix, which gives the operation of the routine:

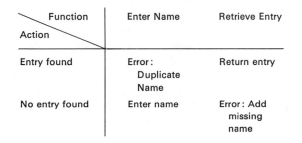

Action \ Function	Enter Name	Retrieve Entry
Entry found	Error: Duplicate Name	Return entry
No entry found	Enter name	Error: Add missing name

Let us base our top-level logic on the function desired. This will allow us to easily add other functions later, should that be required.

```
SYMBOLTABLE: procedure(FUNCTION, NAME, TYPE, LOCATION,
                       PROCNAME, other);
        if DEBUG(T) then output debugging data;
        if FUNCTION=ENTER then do;
             Search table for (NAME,PROCNAME);
             if entry-found then
                Message('Duplicate '||NAME||' ignored');
             else Add new (NAME,PROCNAME,TYPE) to table;
             return (LOCATION);
             end;
        else if FUNCTION=RETRIEVEID then do;
             Search table for (NAME,PROCNAME);
             if entry-found then do;
                  Retrieve it;
                  return(LOCATION); end;
             else do;
                  Message('Missing declaration');
                  Add (NAME,PROCNAME,INTEGER) to table;
                  return (LOCATION);
                  end;
             end;
```

```
        else do;
             Message('Invalid command'||FUNCTION);
             call ABORTRUN; /* compiler error - stop */
             end;
        end SYMBOLTABLE;
```

5.5.1 Keywords and Constants

In the design of our compiler, there are many types of tokens which we have so far ignored: numeric constants and special keywords of the language, such as PROCEDURE, IF, DO and END. We must decide where such constructs are recognized. Since we have already assumed that the parser reads the primitive tokens of the language, these constructs must be recognized before they reach the parser.

Let us consider the case of keywords first. A keyword is just a string of letters, like any other identifier. Therefore the scanner will assume that it is just a variable name at first. This is required since the string may not actually represent a keyword.

Consider the strings C, CA, CAL, CALL, and CALLA. Only the fourth refers to the CALL statement keyword. All the others refer to variable names. Therefore the scanner has to handle them the same way until the end of the string is found.

After finding the end of the string, the scanner could search a list and see if the string represents a special keyword of the language. Unfortunately, this adds complexity to our scanner. An alternate strategy would be to let the symbol table routine find the token. Since we already have two TYPEs (INTEGER and FUNCTION), we can simply add a third type called KEYWORD.

The problem then reduces to how these special keywords are placed in the symbol table in the first place. Two general approaches can be used. One is to define the entries to be already in the symbol table when the compiler is created. The other is to add them before compilation begins; that is, the compiler begins with the following statements:

```
     do I = 1 to NUMBERENTRIES;
          call SYMBOLTABLE(ENTER, KEYWORD(I), keywordtype,
                                   LOC,0,other);
          end;
     call PARSER;
```

This second method has the disadvantage of using extra execution time to add the entries into the table; on the other hand, it is much more flexible since the keywords can be changed by simply changing the array *KEYWORD*. If the first approach is used, then the names will be added into fixed locations in the symbol table based upon the accessing algorithm. The second technique is independent of accessing method used.

The second technique is quite useful when a new language is being designed. The syntax is frequently modified, which allows the changes to be added easily to the developing compiler. After the language is "frozen," the names can be added directly into the table to save compilation time.

This latter technique will be used in our NIP compiler. Note, however, that this description has already restricted our language. If the string CALL always refers to the CALL statement token, then the user cannot create a variable named CALL. Thus, our keywords are actually reserved words. Since we have total control over our language, we are making this restriction for reliability.

Unfortunately, not every language uses reserved words. PL/1 is one such example. As an example of the problems that can arise, the following is a valid PL/1 statement:

```
IF IF=THEN THEN IF = ELSE; ELSE THEN = IF;
```

Consider also the following two statements:

```
DO I = A TO B WHILE(C);
DO I = A TO B, WHILE(C);
```

The first executes a loop with *I* ranging between *A* and *B* as long as *C* remains true. The second, however, has *I* ranging between *A* and *B* and then sets *I* equal to the array element or functional value *WHILE*(*C*) and executes the loop once more. If the comma is in error, it will be almost impossible to find. The use of reserved words makes it easier; in this case the string WHILE could not refer to an array or function.

The use of constants poses a slightly different problem from the case of keywords. Because in NIP all constants are integers, it is easy for the scanner to recognize them. However, this would require that the scanner convert each such constant into its numeric value. While we can convert each constant to its numeric value, we may choose to convert the string to its value once and leave this value in the symbol table. Therefore, we can ignore the differences between constants and variables—both are used in expressions and any address problems can be ignored until code generation. Thus constants will form another type for our symbol table routine.

5.5.2 Detailed Design

Having given the top-level design for our symbol table routine, it is time to specify the detailed design structure for this routine. Given what was said before, our interface can now be specified as:

```
SYMBOLTABLE: procedure(FUNCTION, NAME, TYPE, LOCATION,
                       PROCNAME, other);
    declare FUNCTION FIXED BINARY,                    /* Type */
                ENTERID FIXED BINARY INIT(1),
                RETRIEVEID FIXED BINARY INIT(2),
            NAME CHAR(*) VAR,                         /* ID */
            TYPE FIXED BINARY,                        /* Type */
               INTTYPE FIXED BINARY INIT(1),     /* Int */
               PROCTYPE FIXED BINARY INIT(2),  /* Proc */
               KEYWDTYPE FIXED BINARY INIT(3), /* Reserved */
               CONTYPE FIXED BINARY INIT(4), /* Constant */
            LOCATION FIXED BINARY,               /* Sym Tab */
            PROCNAME FIXED BINARY,               /*Proc ID */
            other;                    /* To be filled in later */
                                      /* for code generator */
```

Note that we have given all parameters symbolic names. When we actually write the compiler, these definitions will be moved to the main procedure to be accessible by other routines calling the symbol table routine. Thus, to enter a new name into the table, the statement

```
call SYMBOLTABLE( ENTERID, . . . .)
```

is used rather than the unclear

```
call SYMBOLTABLE (1, . . . .)
```

No constants should appear in your code. For example, if the number 14 appears somewhere in your program, then it was probably an arbitrary decision on your part. To change it, however, every occurrence must be altered. If this number is specified once and is symbolically referenced, such changes are easy to make. Other than the constants 0 or 1, we will refer symbolically to all other constants in our program.

In designing the symbol table, the following data structures are needed:

```
declare SYMBOLNAME(STSIZE) CHAR(SYMBOLSIZE)
                           INIT(. . . keyword values . . .),
        SYMBOLTYPE(STSIZE) FIXED BINARY INIT( . . . init for
                           keywords . . .),
        SYMBOLVALUE(STSIZE) FIXED BINARY,
                           /* value for constants */
        SYMBOLPROC(STSIZE) FIXED BINARY,
        other; /* for code generator information */
declare NUMBERSTENTRIES FIXED BINARY INIT (. . .);
                        /* set to number of keywords */
```

We will let *STSIZE* be the maximum symbol table size needed, and *SYMBOLSIZE* will be the maximum number of characters allowed in each variable name. Note that this design fixes the maximum number of symbol table entries. For our language we are making that assumption. By constrast, we may want to alter that strategy for other languages. In addition, *NUMBERSTENTRIES* will always contain the number of entries in our symbol table. Since the keywords are already in the table initially, we set this variable to be the number of keywords already present.

Since we are now interested in getting a first working version of our compiler, let us use an extremely simple symbol table searching routine—linear search. Obviously this is inefficient since about half the table must be searched each time, but we can easily change this later since only this routine accesses the table. Also, since our NIP procedures only have local variables, if we search the table backwards, we will shorten the average search time since only local variables need to be searched. Finally, we will let the unique identifier for a given variable be its index in the various arrays.

In our top-level design for this routine, we had the statement

```
Search table for (NAME, PROCNAME);
```

twice. Let us make that a separate routine. It can simply be:

```
LOOKUP: procedure (NAME,PROCNAME,FOUND, LOC);
      declare NAME CHAR(*),               /*name to look up*/
              PROCNAME FIXED BINARY, /* proc dcl'd in */
              FOUND BIT(1),               /* result */
              true BIT(1) INIT('1'B),
              false BIT(1) INIT('0'B),
              LOC FIXED BINARY;           /* sym tab loc */
do LOC = NUMBERSTENTRIES to 1 by -1;
   if SYMBOLNAME(LOC)=NAME & SYMBOLTYPE(LOC)=KEYWDTYPE then
       return (LOC) and FOUND = true;   /* return keyword */
   if SYMBOLNAME(LOC)=NAME & SYMBOLPROC(LOC)=PROCNAME then
       return (LOC) and FOUND = true;
   end;
FOUND = false;                            /* entry not found */
end LOOKUP;
```

We also refer to an error routine. This can be coded as:

```
ERROR: procedure( MESSAGE);
      declare MESSAGE (CHAR(*);
      PUT SKIP LIST('***ERROR***' || MESSAGE);
end ERROR;
```

It will simply print the message and return.

Referring to our original top-level design for the symbol table routine, we can now refine it by incorporating the reserved word code and constant code. Reserved words will always be of type KEYWDTYPE and will have a *PROCNAME* of 0. In addition, multiple constants with the same value are allowed.

```
SYMBOLTABLE: procedure( FUNCTION, NAME, TYPE, LOCATION,
                        PROCNAME, other);
Declarations for parameters;
if DEBUG(T) then output (NAME, PROCNAME, TYPE);
if FUNCTION=ENTERID then do;
    call LOOKUP(NAME, PROC, FOUND, LOCATION);
    if FOUND then do;
        /* constants can be duplicated */
        if TYPE≠CONTYPE then
            call ERROR('DUPLICATE '||NAME||
                 IGNORED');
        end;
    else /* FOUND=false, add name */
        Add new (NAME,PROCNAME,TYPE) to table;
    return LOCATION and TYPE;
    end;
else if FUNCTION=RETRIEVEID then do;
    call LOOKUP(NAME, PROCNAME, FOUND, LOCATION);
    if FOUND then
        return LOCATION and TYPE;
    else do;
        call ERROR('Missing declaration');
        Add (NAME, PROCNAME, TYPE) to table;
        return LOCATION and TYPE;
        end;
    else do;
        call ERROR('INVALID COMMAND'||FUNCTION);
        call ABORTRUN;
        end;
    end SYMBOLTABLE;
```

The statement

```
Add new (NAME,PROC,TYPE) to table;
```

can be expanded as:

```
Add 1 to NUMBERSTENTRIES;
if NUMBERSTENTRIES>STSIZE then
    do;
    call ERROR('Symbol table overflow');
    call ABORTCOMPILE; /* stop compilation */
    end;
```

```
SYMBOLNAME(NUMBERSTENTRIES) = NAME;
SYMBOLTYPE(NUMBERSTENTRIES) = TYPE;
SYMBOLPROCNAME(NUMBERSTENTRIES) = PROCNAME;
if TYPE = CONTYPE then /* numeric constant */
    SYMBOLVALUE(NUMBERSTENTRIES) = value;
```

It should now be an easy matter to fill in the remaining details to finish the routine.

5.6 SCANNER

In Section 5.4 we have already given the interface between the scanner and the parser. The scanner, at the top level of design, is given by the code:

```
SCANNER: procedure( CLASS, IDENTIFIER);
        declare CLASS, /* class of token */
                IDENTIFIER; /* unique member of class */
        do while (more characters in token);
                Get next-input-character;
                if end-of-token then
                    return (token);
        end;
end SCANNER;
```

We also know from Section 5.5 the interface with the symbol table. This symbol table routine will be used to add variables and constants and to retrieve keywords.

Our scanner will return tokens as members of a class. We already have variable name, constant, and keyword as classes. There are others. One is arithmetic operator (+, —, *, and /). There are also several other symbols such as :=, ;, (, and). We will call this fifth class a SPECIAL_CLASS class. Therefore the five classes can be defined as:

```
declare OPERATOR_CLASS FIXED INIT(1),
        SPECIAL_CLASS FIXED INIT(2),
        KEYWORD_CLASS FIXED INIT(3),
        ID_CLASS FIXED INIT(4),
        CONSTANT_CLASS FIXED INIT(5);
```

We also need codes for the unique members of each class. For constants and identifiers they are the location returned by our symbol table routine. However, for the other three classes, we need a unique identifier. Let us use negative numbers in order to distinguish them from symbol table addresses. This will allow the unique member of the class to distinguish operators from operands. This will be useful later when we create postfix for each token. We can simply use this unique identifier as the token symbol.

Therefore, for each of the special symbols, we need symbolic names, as in:

```
declare PLUS_OP FIXED INIT(-1),
        MINUS_OP FIXED INIT(-2),
        MULT_OP FIXED INIT(-3),
        . . . /* other symbols */
        WD_START FIXED INIT(-10), /* START */
        WD_PROC FIXED INIT(-11)   /* PROC */
        WD_END FIXED INIT(-12),   /* END */
        WD_IF FIXED INIT(-13),    /* IF */
        . . .               /* remaining special symbols */
```

The design of our scanner can follow a simple finite state automata. Constants are any string of digits. Therefore, if the first character is a digit, characters are read until the first nondigit is found. Similarly, an identifier is a letter followed by any string of letters or digits. Keywords are just (special) identifiers, and the special symbols are in a class by themselves.

We already know that the symbol table will be used both to add and to retrieve variable names. However, which function is the scanner to assume when an identifier is found? By looking at the language syntax, new names are only added by the DECLARE statement, and retrieved elsewhere. Thus, we will assume that the parser sets a flag for each statement (which we will call *DECLARE_SWITCH*) signifying which is the case. Note that this is another part of the interface between the scanner and parser.

Also, when a name is searched for in the symbol table, we have to know in which procedure the name was declared. Therefore, we will assume that the variable *CURRENT_PROC* contains the unique identifier that identifies the procedure currently being parsed. This identifier will be appended to all variable names in order to separate identical names from separate procedures.

We are now ready to give our top-level design for the scanner. For several tokens, only one symbol is read (e.g., *), for others two are read (e.g., :=), and for others an arbitrary number is read (e.g., constants). In this latter case, an additional character, not part of the token, must be read in order to determine the end of the previous token. This character must be saved (as a PL/1 STATIC or ALGOL **own** variable) for the next token in order not to lose it.

The first line of our scanner is currently coded as:

```
Get next-input-character;
```

Because we have not as yet decided on our source input, i.e., teletypewriter, cards, or disk file, let us simply write that now as a subroutine NEXTCHAR. Later we will fill in the details.

Combining all these details, we can now write our scanner as:

```
SCANNER: PROCEDURE(CLASS, IDENTIFIER);
        DECLARE CLASS, IDENTIFIER;
        IF DEBUG(S) THEN output debugging code;
        NEXT = NEXTCHAR;   /* get next character */
        DO CASE (NEXT); /* transfer to token class */
        \ operator class \
             RETURN (OPERATOR_CLASS,type);

        \ symbols ( ) , \
             RETURN (SPECIAL_CLASS, type);

        \ : \ /* see if := */
             NEXT = NEXTCHAR;
             IF NEXT = '=' THEN
                   RETURN (SPECIAL_CLASS, ASGN_OP);
                    ELSE DO;
                          CALL ERROR(': IS ILLEGAL');
                          CALL BACKUP; /*RESET NEXT AS FIRST */
                                       /* CHAR TO READ LATER */
                          END;

        \ digit \ /* read all digits */
             DO WHILE (NEXT=digit);
                     Save digit;
                     NEXT = NEXTCHAR;
                     END;
             CALL BACKUP; /* RESET NEXT AS NEXT READ */
             CALL SYMBOLTABLE(ENTERID, collected-digits, CONTYPE,
                    LOCATION, 0, 0);
             RETURN (CONSTANT_CLASS, LOCATION);

        \ letter \
             DO WHILE (NEXT= (letter or digit));
                     save character;
                     NEXT = NEXTCHAR;
                     END;
             CALL BACKUP; /* SET NEXT AS NEXT READ */
             IF DECLARE_SWITCH THEN SWITCH=ENTERID;
                   ELSE SWITCH=RETRIEVEID;
             TYPE = ID_TYPE;
             CALL SYMBOLTABLE(SWITCH, collected-characters, TYPE,
                    LOCATION, CURRENT_PROC, other);
             RETURN (TYPE, LOCATION);
```

```
\ blank \ Ignore blanks between tokens;
          Restart at top of SCANNER;

\ $ \    /* comment */
         Read until corresponding $, then restart at top
             of SCANNER;
END CASE;
END SCANNER;
```

Exercise 5.3: Code for blanks and comments seems to indicate a **goto** back to the top of SCANNER. Since **goto**s are unnecessary, and are frowned upon in well-written programs, redesign this routine to avoid them.

The NEXTCHAR routine must also be specified. Our scanner already ignores blanks. Therefore, this NEXTCHAR routine simply returns the next character on the current source image. This can be specified as:

```
NEXTCHAR: procedure;
     Set character_position = character_postion+1;
     if end-of-image then do;
         get next image;
         if end-of-file on read then do;
             Set end of file indicator;
             return (end-file symbol);
             end;
         put image for listing;
         Set character-position = 1;
         end;
     return (character at position character_position);
end NEXTCHAR;
```

For correct programs the compiler should detect the end of the source program (START ⟨ID⟩) at the same time that an end of file is reached on the input stream; however, if there are any errors in the program this may not happen. Let us take the precaution and have NEXTCHAR check for end-of-file conditions before it reads any more images. The easiest way to handle this is to simply let the scanner not know anything about end of files. If NEXTCHAR returned a special end-of-file character, then SCANNER could simply return this to the parser. The parser would simply use this to terminate the program, and the scanner would be unaware of this problem. For this special character, we can use any character that is impossible to be read. For example, if the source images are ASCII characters, a binary 0 character is meaningless to the source program and can be used by NEXTCHAR as the special end-of-file character.

5.7 PARSER

5.7.1 Interface Specifications

As mentioned in Section 5.1, it is the function of the parser to perform the actual transformations on the source program. Tokens are read, and a transformed postfix for the program is produced. From the previous section, we have already designed the "front end," or interface between the scanner and the parser. This interface consists of three components.

1. The scanner subroutine, called via

```
call SCANNER(CLASS, IDENTIFIER);
```

We will use the term *TOKEN* to refer to the (*CLASS*, *IDENTIFIER*) pair.

2. The global variable *DECLARE_SWITCH*, which signifies that a list of declarations is being declared.

3. The global variable *CURRENT_PROC*, which gives the symbol table identifier for the current procedure being parsed.

For the "back end" of the parser, let us produce postfix. This will allow us to postpone the actual code generation process as a separate phase of this compiler. Therefore our top-level design for the parser can be written as:

```
PARSER: procedure;
do while (more tokens);
        call SCANNER(CLASS,IDENTIFIER);
        Parse new token;
        if DEBUG(P) then output parser diagnostics;
        if more postifix to be produced then
              call POSTFIX(postfix-token);
        end;
end PARSER;
```

We already have five classes of tokens: special symbols, operators, keywords, identifiers, and constants. For the latter two classes, the *IDENTIFIER* returned by the scanner will be the unique symbol table address for the variable; and for the first three, *IDENTIFIER* will be a unique negative number. Therefore, this identifier uniquely specifies that a given token is an operator or an operand. This means we can use this value as our postfix value when we parse the program. This simplifies the design since we can now use the same symbols.

As mentioned previously, error detection should be an important part of our design. That means that the following sequence will probably appear frequently in our code:

```
if token-is-not-desired-token then do;
    call ERROR(message);
    Fix up error;
    end;
```

The easiest way to fix the error is to make the current token be the required one. For now, let us use that strategy and modify it accordingly. Currently most error repair is ad hoc, although a few formal studies have been done [Levy, 75]. While we may often give the wrong repair, the use of reserved words enables us to realign ourselves at each statement, and thus we can keep the error localized. Even if our repair is not the appropriate one, we should still be able to parse the remainder of the program correctly and find any additional errors.

Since the above **if** statement will occur frequently, let us make it a separate procedure. It has two arguments: the desired token and the current token. (There are actually four arguments since each token contains two components.) Let us also add the desired error message to be printed as a fifth argument. This then will localize all the error correction to one routine, and we can consequently avoid it in the main parser. Let us call this routine TEST and describe it as follows:

```
TEST: procedure( WANTED_TOKEN, CURRENT_TOKEN, MESSAGE);
        if classes don't match then error;
        if ID class or CONSTANT class
            then ignore which member of class
            else special symbol so check that they
                are same member of class;
        end TEST;
```

This can be expanded into the following routine:

```
TEST: PROCEDURE(WANTED_CLASS, WANTED_ID,
                CURRENT_CLASS, CURRENT_ID,
                ERROR_MESSAGE);
      IF WANTED_CLASS≠CURRENT_CLASS THEN DO;
          /* classes don't match, error */
          CALL ERROR(ERROR_MESSAGE);
          Set Current_token = Wanted_token;
          RETURN;
          END;
```

```
            /* classes match, if ID or constant, */
            /* any value will do */
            IF WANTED_CLASS= ID_CLASS or CONSTANT_CLASS THEN
                 RETURN;
            /* see if correct member of class */
            IF WANTED_ID≠CURRENT_ID THEN DO;
                 CALL ERROR(ERROR_MESSAGE);
                 Set Current_token=Wanted_token;
                 RETURN;
                 END;
            /* have correct token */
            RETURN;
       END TEST;
```

In this design, we represent *WANTED_TOKEN* as the desired character string for understanding (e.g., '+' will be written instead of (OPERATOR _CLASS, ADD_OP).)

We now have all the interface that we need for our parser. This consists of:

1. Procedure SCANNER with global variables *DECLARE_SWITCH* and *CURRENT_PROC*
2. Procedure ERROR for printing messages
3. Procedure POSTFIX for writing of postfix for the program
4. Procedure TEST for making sure that the current token is the one needed at the current point in the parse

At this point we have to make a decision as to which parsing technique to use. Let us use recursive descent, for the simple reason that it is the easiest to program.

5.7.2 Recursive Descent Parsing

For a review of context-free grammars, see Section 5.1.2. The following is a brief summary of recursive descent parsing. See any standard textbook such as Aho and Ullman [72] for more details on parsing techniques.

In recursive descent, each production in the grammar for the source language corresponds to one procedure in the parser. For example, the production:

⟨PROGRAM⟩ ::= ⟨PROCEDURE⟩ ⟨PROGRAM⟩ | START ⟨ID⟩

means that a program is either a procedure followed by a program or the reserved word START followed by an identifier. This can be specified by the following procedure:

```
PROGRAM: procedure;
        if current_token=START then
            Parse START <ID>;
        else do;
            Parse <PROCEDURE>;
            Parse <PROGRAM>;
            end;
        end PROGRAM;
```

The procedure that parses <PROCEDURE> will produce the postfix for a procedure and then return. At this point the current token should be the first token of <PROGRAM>, and hence the procedure PROGRAM can be called recursively. If it always can be unambiguously determined which production to call, recursive descent can be used.

Note that recursive descent will not work on every grammar. Even in our NIP language, there are problems. For example, consider the following production:

<TERM> ::= <TERM> <MULTOP> <PRIMARY> | <PRIMARY>

There are two problems here. First, a <TERM> is either <TERM>... or <PRIMARY>, however, which procedure should our TERM procedure call —TERM or PRIMARY? As in the example of PROGRAM, we have to be able to unambiguously decide.

Assuming we can solve that problem, we also have the problem that the first thing TERM does is call TERM. This leads to an endless recursive chain of calls on TERM. Obviously we have to avoid this.

Therefore, before we make the decision to use recursive descent, we first have to be sure that it will work in our case. As we develop the top-level design of our parser, we will also be modifying the grammar to use this technique.

5.7.3 Parser Design

In generating our parser, let us assume that each of the recursive descent procedures returns after it outputs the postfix for its own section of the source language and leaves the current token as the first token of the next section of the source program. If so, we can design the parser as follows.

Main driver

The starting symbol of our grammar is <PROGRAM>, so we can write our main procedure for our compiler as follows: (Remember we first have to process debugging code.)

```
MAIN_DRIVER: procedure;
        Process first card and set array DEBUG;
        Compiler initialization code;
        call SCANNER(. . .); /* get first token */
        call PROGRAM; /* parse program */
end MAIN_DRIVER;
```

The production for ⟨PROGRAM⟩ was given as:

⟨PROGRAM⟩ ::= ⟨PROCEDURE⟩ ⟨PROGRAM⟩ | START ⟨ID⟩

This says that a program is any number of procedures followed by START ⟨ID⟩. Or in other words, if we use $\{x\}^*$ to mean 0 or more instances of x, we can rewrite the production as:

⟨PROGRAM⟩ ::= {⟨PROCEDURE⟩}* START ⟨ID⟩

This format lends itself nicely to an algorithmic solution.

Since the procedure to parse ⟨PROCEDURE⟩ will output the postfix for it, we can end our parser by outputting the procedure name where execution is to begin. This we can do by outputting the postfix: ⟨ID⟩, START, or as symbolically defined in Section 5.6 the tokens ⟨ID⟩, WD_START. Therefore the top-level design can be given as:

```
PROGRAM: procedure;
        do while (current_token≠'START');
                call PROCEDURE_STMT;
                end;
        call SCANNER; /* pass over START */
        call ID; /* get starting procedure name */
        call POSTFIX(WD_START); /* output postfix */
end PROGRAM;
```

One problem has already appeared. In the line **call** ID, ID refers to the starting procedure name; however, the symbol table routine will look up the name in the current procedure (as defined by *CURRENT_PROC*). Procedure names are actually global names defined across all procedures. We can specify this by reserving procedure number 0 to refer to these global names. Thus, the statement CALL ID should actually be the two:

```
CURRENT_PROC = 0;
call ID;
```

This will cause the procedure ID to look in procedure 0 (global names) for this name.

Note also that procedure names may be used before they are declared (e.g., a CALL statement calling a procedure that has not as yet been parsed). Our symbol table routine will now require a change of specifications to avoid the missing declarations if retrieving a name which is defined in procedure 0.

Procedures

Procedure organization is governed by the production

```
<PROCEDURE> ::= <ID> PROCEDURE <PARAMLIST>
                <STATEMENTLIST> END
```

This syntax poses the same problem as with START. In this case, we want to define a new procedure even though we are not in a DECLARE statement. We can do this by simply setting the global variable *CURRENT_PROC* to 0. Therefore, our top-level design copied directly from the <PROCEDURE> production, is simply:

```
PROCEDURE_STMT: procedure;
        Find and output ID;          /* output ID */
        Find PROCEDURE;              /* PROCEDURE*/
        Find and output PARAMLIST; /* <PARAMLIST> */
        Find and output STATEMENTLIST; /* <STATEMENTLIST>*/
        Find END and output END_PROC; /* END */
end PROCEDURE_STMT;
```

Note that we have used the token END_PROC. The source language allows END to appear in several places: at the end of a procedure and at the end of an IF or WHILE statement. By using separate tokens for these, the postfix becomes unambiguous. This design can be expanded to the following:

```
PROCEDURE_STMT: PROCEDURE;
        DECLARE_SWITCH = true;
        CURRENT_PROC = 0;     /* global procedure name */
        CALL ID; /* parse identifier, add to symbol table */
        DECLARE_SWITCH=false;
        CURRENT_PROC=CURRENT_ID; /* set current proc name */
        CALL TEST('PROCEDURE',current_token,message);
        CALL POSTFIX(WD_PROC); /* output PROCEDURE */
        CALL SCANNER; /* point to parameter list */
        CALL PARAMLIST;
        CALL STATEMENTLIST;
        CALL TEST('END',current_token,message);
        CALL POSTFIX(END_PROC); /* output proper END */
        CALL SCANNER; /* ignore END */
END PROCEDURE_STMT;
```

The procedures for a parameter list and statement list can be handled very simply. These are:

```
PARAMLIST: procedure;
        if current_token≠ '(' then return; /* no list */
        call SCANNER; /* ignore ( */
        do while (current_token ≠ ')');
              call ID;
              Check for comma or right parenthesis;
              end;
        end PARAMLIST;
```

As in the procedure statement, the identifiers in a parameter list will appear before their declaration, so we again have a symbol table problem. In this case by setting *DECLARE_SWITCH* each identifier in the parameter list will be added to the symbol table. However, just making that change will result in duplicate declaration error messages when the parameters are actually declared in the DECLARE statement. We can avoid this by adding a global variable *PARAMETER_SWITCH* such that any variables declared when this switch is set will be of type PARAMETER. Parameters will also turn off the duplicate declaration messages.

Therefore, the **call** ID statement above should be replaced by:

```
DECLARE_SWITCH = true;
PARAMETER_SWITCH = true;
call ID;
PARAMETER_SWITCH = false;
DECLARE_SWITCH = false;
```

Note that each statement type begins with a special reserved word. Also, any list of statements must be terminated by the word END or by the word ELSE (in an IF statement). Because of this, we can code STATEMENTLIST as:

```
STATEMENTLIST: procedure;
      do while current_token≠ 'END' or 'ELSE';
            do case(current_token);
                  \DECLARE\ call DECLARE_STMT;
                  \IF\ call IF_STMT;
                  \READ\ call READ_STMT;
                  \WRITE\ call WRITE_STMT;
                  \WHILE\ call WHILE_STMT;
                  \CALL\ call CALL_STMT;
                  \ID\ call ASSIGNMENT_STMT;
```

```
                        else do; /* ERROR */
                                call ERROR(message);
                                call SCANNER;
                                end;
                        end; /* case */
                if current_token ≠'END' or 'ELSE' then /* not done */
                        call TEST(';',current_token,'missing ;');
                call SCANNER; /* ignore ; */
                end;
        end STATEMENTLIST;
```

Statements

Assignment statement. The syntax of the assignment statement is

```
⟨ASSIGNMENT_STMT⟩ ::= ⟨ID⟩ := ⟨EXPRESSION⟩
```

Postfix for it can be:

```
⟨ID⟩
⟨EXPRESSION⟩
:=
```

This will first evaluate the left-hand side variable, then the expression, and then cause the expression to be assigned. This can be coded directly as:

```
ASSIGNMENT_STMT: PROCEDURE;
        CALL ID /* get left hand side ID */
        CALL SCANNER; /* point to := */
        CALL TEST(':=',CURRENT TOKEN,'missing :=');
                    /* check for := */
        CALL SCANNER; /* start of right hand side expr */
        CALL EXPRESSION; /* get postfix for expression */
        CALL POSTFIX(ASGN_OP); /* output := */
END ASSIGNMENT_STMT;
```

IF statement. The IF statement has the syntax:

```
⟨IF_STMT⟩ ::= IF ⟨EXPRESSION⟩ THEN ⟨STATEMENTLIST⟩
                                 {ELSE ⟨STATEMENTLIST⟩}
                                  END
```

To execute this statement, we would like to evaluate the expression and execute a jump to the ELSE (if present) or to the END if the expression is false (zero). However, we have not seen the ELSE or END yet, so we have no reference point to use for our forward branch.

We can solve this by defining such a reference point. We will call this a system label, and at this time we will simply place it into our postfix after the expression. When we finally process the END (or ELSE), we will set the system label into the postfix at that point also. This means that the system label exists in two places in the parsed program: after the expression at the point of the forward branch and at the point where the forward should resolve to. This allows the code generator phase to fix up the addresses, as we shall shortly see.

This problem is one of the most significant problems in deciding on the format of compiler to build. For our one-pass organization, we are ultimately going to generate code for the IF statement before processing the corresponding END. For example, we can generate a forward branch, but leave the target address empty. By saving the address of this jump instruction, we can go back and insert the address when the forward location becomes known at the ELSE or END statement.

Let us therefore define a new entity called a system label. This will be used by the IF statement routine to keep track of forward branches. It can be coded as:

```
SYSTEM_LABEL:procedure(LABEL);
      declare LABEL; /* identifier for created label */
      Generate new internal name for system label;
      call SYMBOLTABLE(ENTERID,LABEL,TYPE,LOCATION,
          CURRENT_PROC,other);
      return(LOCATION); /* return ID for label*/
end SYSTEM_LABEL;
```

Since we may need other forms of internally generated data, let us keep this option available by making the type of the generated label a parameter. Thus the call to SYSTEM_LABEL would actually be:

```
call SYSTEM_LABEL(LABEL, TYPE);
```

where *TYPE* is an input parameter to the routine.

We are almost ready to code our IF statement routine. We are now able to generate a forward branch around the THEN statement list, but we have one small problem with our END statement. If no ELSE clause was present, the END should be the targeting point of our IF system label. However, if there was an ELSE clause, the ELSE should be the point of the jump and should generate a branch from the THEN clause around the ELSE to the END. This action prevents the THEN code from also executing straight through the ELSE. Notice, however, that in both cases, the END resolves one forward branch. As a result the ELSE code can be made transparent to this END code.

Merging all of this, we can define the postfix for our IF statement as follows:

```
<EXPRESSION>
forward_label for IF
IF
<STATEMENTLIST>
{else_label   /* jump around ELSE  LIST */
forward_label /* resolve jump around THEN  LIST */
ELSE
<STATEMENTLIST>}
system_label for forward_label {or else_label}
END_IF
```

where IF is a binary operator that tests ⟨EXPRESSION⟩ and jumps to *forward_label* if false (zero), and ELSE is a binary operator that generates a forward jump to *else_label* and defines *forward_label*. Similarly for END_IF.

We are now ready to code the IF statement procedure:

```
IF_STATEMENT: PROCEDURE;
      CALL SCANNER; /* already have IF, point to expression */
      CALL EXPRESSION; /* postfix for IF expression */
      CALL SYSTEM_LABEL(forward_label,LABEL_TYPE);
                                  /* around THEN */
      CALL TEST('THEN',CURRENT_TOKEN,'missing THEN');
                    /* see that THEN is next*/
      CALL POSTFIX(forward_label); /* get forward branch */
      CALL POSTFIX(WD_IF); /* setup postfix for IF test */
      CALL SCANNER; /* point to start of statement list */
      CALL STATEMENTLIST; /* process THEN clause */
      IF CURRENT_TOKEN is ELSE THEN DO; /* ELSE CLAUSE */
            CALL SYSTEM_LABEL(else branch,LABEL TYPE);
                                    /* around ELSE */
            CALL POSTFIX(else_branch);
            CALL POSTFIX(forward_label); /* IF branch to here */
            CALL POSTFIX(WD_ELSE); /* ELSE is next */
            CALL SCANNER; /* point to start of ELSE clause */
            CALL STATEMENTLIST; /* ELSE CLAUSE */
            forward_label = else_branch;
                  /* END shouldn't know if ELSE appeared */
            END; /* end of ELSE code */
      CALL TEST('END',CURRENT_TOKEN,'missing END');
      CALL POSTFIX(forward_label); /* IF or ELSE branch */
      CALL POSTFIX(END_IF); /* end IF statement */
      CALL SCANNER; /* point to next statement */
END IF_STATEMENT;
```

By making *forward_label* and *else_branch* local variables to this routine, if the statement list also contains IF statements, the appropriate *forward_label* variables will be automatically stacked by the PL/1 compiler and all addresses will be resolved correctly. This is one of the main benefits of a recursive descent parser. Note also that we were able to give essentially straight PL/1 code for this routine, without the need to expand our pseudo code very much.

WHILE statement. The parsing of the WHILE statement is very similar to the parsing of the IF statement. The major difference is that the WHILE statement always generates a jump back to the expression to test whether the loop is to be reexecuted. Therefore, the postfix can be defined as follows:

```
loop_label /* for return point */
WHILE /* define top of loop */
⟨EXPRESSION⟩ /* WHILE expression */
forward_label /* jump out of loop if expr false */
DO
⟨STATEMENTLIST⟩ /* WHILE statements */
loop_label /* branch back to top of loop */
forward_label /* branch out of loop */
END_WHILE
```

where WHILE is a unary operator defining the head of the loop, DO is a binary operator defining the expression to test and the exit point of the loop, and END_WHILE a binary operator defining the label at the end of the loop. The actual design of the WHILE PROCEDURE will be left as an exercise due to its similarity to the IF statement.

CALL statement. For the CALL statement, we have the straightforward syntax:

```
⟨CALL STMT⟩ ::= CALL ⟨ID⟩ {(⟨EXPRESSIONLIST⟩)}
⟨EXPRESSIONLIST⟩ ::= ⟨EXPRESSIONLIST⟩ , ⟨EXPRESSION⟩ |
                     ⟨EXPRESSION⟩
```

To execute this statement, the compiler will have to pass each expression to the corresponding parameter in the called procedure. We will discuss this in the code generation section; however, we do know that we have to evaluate all the expressions before we can call the procedure. This means that an appropriate postfix for this statement can be as follows:

```
⟨EXPRESSION¹⟩
COMMA_CALL      /* CALL arg. list comma */
⟨EXPRESSION²⟩   /* second argument */
COMMA_CALL      /* CALL ARG. list comma */
. . .
```

```
<EXPRESSIONⁿ>     /* last argument */
RP_CALL           /* right paren for arg. list */
<ID>              /* name of function to call */
CALL
```

Note that we have made COMMA_CALL and RP_CALL unary operators in our postfix. Thus after scanning each expression in the code generator, we immediately get the operator to create the next procedure argument.

The scanning of this statement has the one complication that the ID for the function name is global to the program. Therefore, we will associate a *CURRENT_PROC* of 0 with the procedure name to signify a global name not part of any procedure.

With these considerations, the structure of our CALL statement routine is as follows:

```
CALL_STMT: procedure;
    call SCANNER; /* skip over CALL */
    Save current value of CURRENT_PROC and set it to 0;
    call ID; /* get name of procedure */
    Save ID of procedure name;
    Restore value to CURRENT_PROC;
    if CURRENT_TOKEN='(' then do; /* optional arg list */
        call SCANNER; /* Ignore first left parenthesis */
        do while( CURRENT_TOKEN ≠ ')'); /* until ) */
            call EXPRESSION; /* postfix for argument */
            if CURRENT_TOKEN ≠ ')' then do; /* more */
                call TEST(',', CURRENT_TOKEN,message);
                call POSTFIX (COMMA_CALL);
                call SCANNER;
                end;
            end; /* end arg list code */
        call POSTFIX(RP_CALL); /* Output special ) */
        end; /* end optional arg. list */
    call POSTFIX(saved procedure name);
    call POSTFIX(WD_CALL); /* Output CALL token */
    call SCANNER; /* Go past end of CALL statement */
    end CALL_STMT;
```

READ and WRITE statements. These statements have the syntax:

```
<READ_STMT> ::= READ ( <IDLIST> )
<WRITE_STMT> ::= WRITE( <EXPRESSIONLIST> )
```

These are essentially identical to the previous CALL statement and will be left as exercises.

Expressions

The purpose of the procedure EXPRESSION is to output the postfix for an expression. This is almost always the example which is demonstrated for recursive descent, so that it will be given a cursory treatment here.

The syntax for expressions is given as:

```
⟨EXPRESSION⟩ ::= ⟨EXPRESSION⟩ ⟨ADDOP⟩ ⟨TERM⟩ | ⟨TERM⟩
⟨TERM⟩ ::= ⟨TERM⟩ ⟨MULTOP⟩ ⟨PRIMARY⟩ | ⟨PRIMARY⟩
⟨PRIMARY⟩ ::= ⟨ID⟩ | ⟨CONSTANT⟩ | (⟨EXPRESSION⟩)
⟨ADDOP⟩ ::= + | -
⟨MULTOP⟩ ::= * | /
```

As we mentioned earlier, in order to use recursive descent we must rewrite the productions as:

```
⟨EXPRESSION⟩ ::= ⟨TERM⟩ { ⟨ADDOP⟩ ⟨TERM⟩ }*
⟨TERM⟩ ::= ⟨PRIMARY⟩ { ⟨MULTOP⟩ ⟨PRIMARY⟩}*
⟨PRIMARY⟩ ::= ⟨ID⟩ | ⟨CONSTANT⟩ | (⟨EXPRESSION⟩)
⟨ADDOP⟩ ::= + | -
⟨MULTOP⟩ ::= * | /
```

Thus the structure of the expression recognizer is simply:

```
EXPRESSION :procedure;
        call TERM;
        do while (CURRENT_TOKEN is '+' or '-');
                call SCANNER; /* pass over operator */
                call TERM;
                end;
        end EXPRESSION;
```

Code for TERM and PRIMARY is similar. In order to convert these recognizers to output postfix, we have to output the operators at the correct time. For example, in EXPRESSION, the output for $A+B$ should be $AB+$. Since each procedure outputs the postfix for its own syntax, EXPRESSION can assume that TERM will output the postfix for any term it parses. Thus the expression routine need only output the correct ADDOP used to combine the expressions. This leads to the following structure for EXPRESSION:

```
EXPRESSION: procedure;
        call TERM; /* first operand */
        do while (CURRENT_TOKEN is '+' or '-');
                SAVE type of ADDOP;
                call SCANNER;
                call TERM; /* operand 2 */
                call POSTFIX (Saved ADDOP);
                end;
        end EXPRESSION;
```

5.7.4 Parser Summary

In designing our parser, we have had to make several changes in the specifications of our scanner. These are:

1. For global procedure names, treat the identifier as being in procedure *CURRENT_PROC* = 0 and do not generate the message that a duplicate name has been declared.
2. If *PARAMETER_SWITCH* is true, the IDs declared are parameters, so PARAMETER_TYPE should be appended to the type of the ID.
3. If a variable is of type *PARAMETER_TYPE*, duplicate declaration error messages are ignored.

At this point in our design we have finished what is usually considered to be the "front end" of a compiler. This is graphically demonstrated by Figure 5.12, which shows all sections designed so far.

The routine NEXTCHAR will read in the source input and pass characters to SCANNER. SCANNER will assemble these characters into tokens and pass them back to the parser, after calling the symbol table routine for constants and identifiers. Finally, the parser is a set of recursive descent routines that reads tokens from SCANNER, creates special labels for IF and WHILE statements and outputs a stream of postfix for the program to the routine POSTFIX. In the next section we will describe POSTFIX and the actual code generation process in greater detail.

Exercise 5.4: Program the parser using some other parsing technique, such as operator precedence or SLR(1).

5.8 CODE GENERATION

At this point in our development, the parser for our NIP compiler is generating a stream of tokens that represent the postfix for a given program. The task is now to convert those tokens into a set of instructions that can be interpreted by a given computer.

Before we can even begin to evaluate the various strategies available, we have to have an idea of the type of machine for which we are compiling code. If the machine was stack-oriented and its primitive operations were postfix, then the output of our parser could be the finished product. For example, our parser will output for the statement:

```
Y := Y + Z
```

the postfix:

```
Sy Sy Sz PLUS_OP  ASGN_OP
```

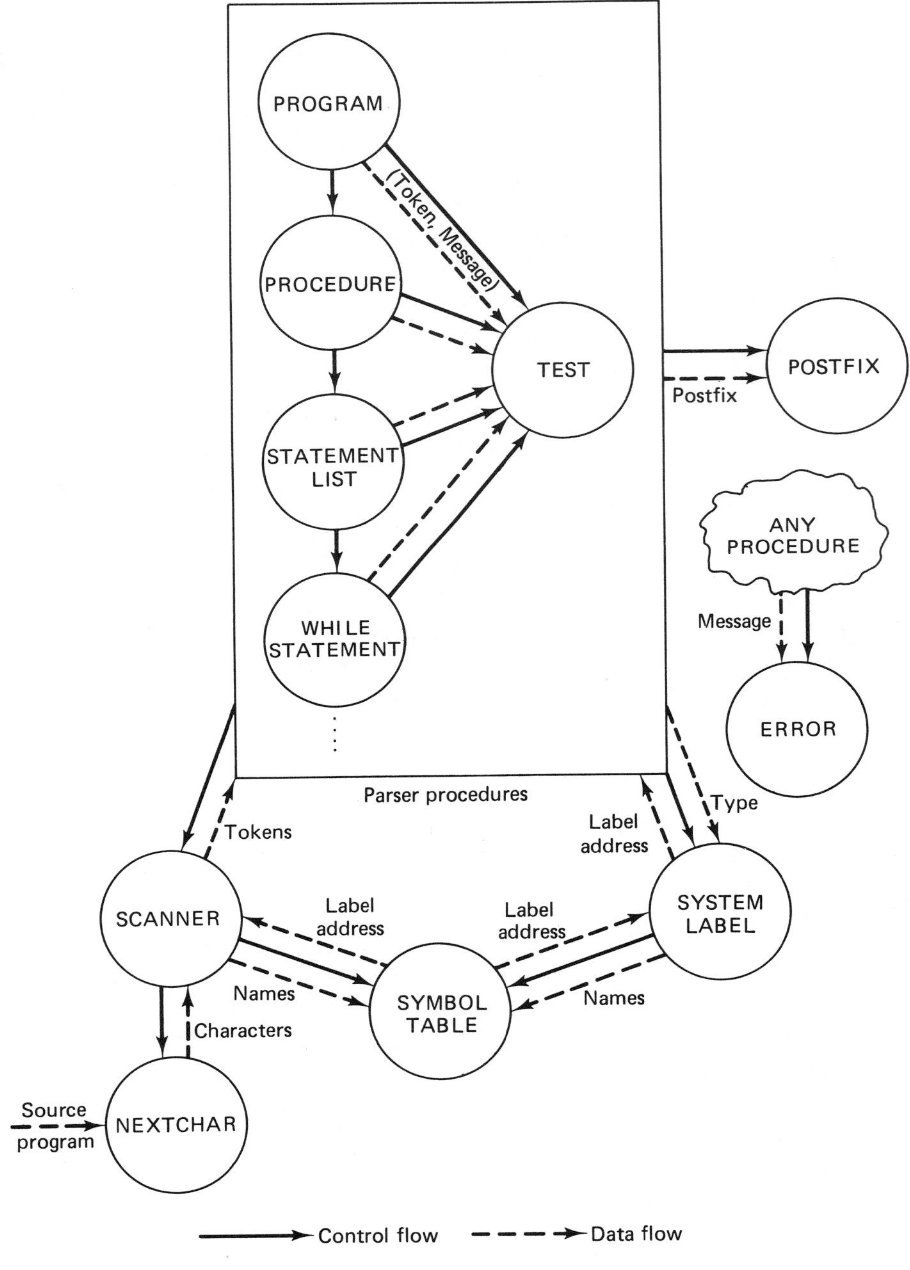

Figure 5.12 Parser organization.

where Sy and Sz are positive unique numbers representing the identifiers or constants Y and Z, and PLUS_OP and ASGN_OP are negative numbers for the operations + and :=, respectively. If our hardware simply stacked all positive tokens (addresses) and used each negative token as an operation, then we would be able to directly execute this postfix.

In most cases, the target computer does not have such a structure, so that we must further translate the postfix into a form that can be executed.

5.8.1 Internal Forms

Straight postfix notation is generally not well suited for code generation. For example, it is difficult for an optimizer to optimize such code. Most compilers use a technique called quadruples for the storage of the intermediate form.

A *quadruple* is simply that—a list of four items: an operation, two operands, and a result. If the result of an operation is the name of a variable, then code can be generated very easily. For example, for the statement:

```
Y := Y + Z
```

the quadruple for this becomes:

```
(PLUS_OP, Sy, Sz, Sy)
```

which says to add (PLUS_OP) the variable defined by symbol table location Sy to the variable defined by Sz and store the result defined by Sy. This is now a self-contained unit that the code generator can use regardless of where the quadruple is located. Thus an optimizer can alter the sequence of operations (or quadruples), yet code can still be generated easily.

For unary operators, we can simply ignore the second operand field of the quadruples; and for operations that seemingly take more that two operations, we can write those as a sequence of successive operations. For example, if we need an operation:

```
X := F(A,B,C,D)
```

we can write it as a set of three quadruples as follows:

```
(F1,A,B,T1)
(F2,T1,C,T2)
(F,T2,D,X)
```

Each of the functions F1 and F2 are intermediate functions, and the purpose of T1 and T2 are as intermediate place holders for the operations F1 and F2. When it actually comes time to generate code, the code generator knows what to do when it sees F1 (i.e., F2 and F must follow) so that correct code can be generated.

The role of T1 and T2 above must be further explained. Consider the following statement:

X := X + Y * Z

with the postfix:

Sx Sx Sy Sz * + :=

This statement consists of a multiplication of Y and Z, an addition of X, and an assignment to X. In generating quadruples (or simply *quads*) after the multiplication, we need a place to store the intermediate result. We will assume that a temporary, or internal, variable is generated for that purpose. Thus quads for the above statement would be:

```
(MULT_OP, Sy, Sz, T1)
(ADD_OP, Sx, T1, Sx)
```

where the first quad says to multiply Y with Z and store the result in T1, and the second quad says to add X to T1 (which is the result of Y*Z) and store the result in X. When we discuss storage allocation, we will discuss the actual location of T1. The symbol table address for T1 can be allocated by the parser by calling the routine *SYSTEM_LABEL* described previously for the IF statement. This will be explained more fully shortly.

5.8.2 Code Generation Techniques

From the above discussion, we already have an inkling of the basic code generation technique. Each operation is in the form of a quad; each quad specifies a set of operations. In general, a given quad will generate the same machine language instructions. For example for the PLUS_OP quad, we can always generate the code:

```
LOAD    register,operand 1
ADD     register,operand 2
STORE   register,result
```

This code is always correct, although it may not be optimal. For example, in the statement X := X+Y*Z, that would result in the following six instructions:

```
LOAD    register,Y      (MULT_OP quad)
MPY     register,Z
STORE   register,T1
LOAD    register,X      (ADD_OP quad)
ADD     register,T1
STORE   register,X
```

where the sequence:

```
LOAD    register,Y
MPY     register,Z
ADD     register,X
STORE   register,X
```

would give the same answer. As we develop our code generator, we will look into developing such optimization techniques. It is important to know that the straightforward techniques generate code that is correct, but not always optimal. We want operations we can perform that alter the code but do not alter the correctness of such operations.

Since each quad generates a generally unique set of machine instructions, our code generator is usually a separate set of subroutines, one for each quad. Thus it is usually of the form:

```
CODEGEN: procedure;
        do case (quad operation);
              \MULT_OP\ ...
              \ADD_OP\ ...
              \ASGN_OP\ ...
              ...        /* separate routine for each quad type */
        end;
end CODEGEN;
```

5.8.3 Machine Organization

For a machine organization we use the structure that exists on most real machines available today. There is a large main memory which ranges from a few thousand to a few million words. The access time to retrieve information from this memory ranges from about .3 to about 1 microsecond. There are also a few, usually less than 100, high-speed memory locations, called registers or accumulators, with an access time frequently under .1 microsecond. The basic machine language instruction retrieves a word in memory and performs some operation, such as ADD or MULTIPLY, between that word and one of the registers. This simple description essentially describes the IBM 360/370 series, Univac 1100, DEC System10, all minicomputers, and most other commonly used computers.

For our own machine, let us use a hypothetical design that has most of the characteristics of many current computers but avoids some of the problems. The machine will have 32-bit words and 8 registers; each instruction word will be broken down into 5 fields, as follows:

1. *Operation code* (6 bits). This permits 64 different instructions. The available operation codes are given in Figure 5.13.

Operation Code	Bit value	Function
LOAD	000001	Move contents of EA to register
STORE	000010	Move contents of register to EA
ADD	000011	Add contents of EA to register
SUB	000100	Subtract contents of EA from register
MPY	000101	Multiply register by contents of EA
DIV	000110	Divide register by contents of EA
LOADIM	000111	Move EA to register
ADDIM	001000	Add EA to register
READ	010000	Read number into register
WRITE	010001	Write numeric value from register
SHIFTLEFT	010010	Shift register left EA bits
SHIFTRT	010011	Shift register right EA bits
SUBCALL	100000	Current address in register and jump to EA.
JUMP	110xyz	Conditional jump. Test register and jump to EA depending upon setting of x, y, and z. x=1 jump if register zero y=1 jump if register negative z=1 jump if register positive

The following 'nonprimitive' operation codes will be of some use:

JUMPZERO	110100	Jump register zero
JUMPPLUS	110001	Jump register positive
JUMPNEG	110010	Jump register negative
JUMPUNC	110111	Unconditional jump

EA stands for effective address and is defined by the mode switch, index register, and address field of the instruction.

Figure 5.13 Machine language instructions.

2. *Operation register* (3 bits). This is the register number (from 0 to 7) of the register that the operation is applied to.

3. *Index register* (3 bits). This permits the address accessed in main memory to be modified by adding the contents of a register. This is useful, for example, when indexing through arrays. The base address of the array is stored in the instruction, and the index, or offset from the beginning of the array, is placed in the index register. Since index registers are not always needed, a value of 0 means no indexing is to be performed. Thus only registers 1 through 7 may be used as index registers. Register 0 can be used only as an operation register.

4. *Mode switch* (1 bit). If 0, the fifth field refers to an address in main memory. If set to 1, the address field refers to one of the 8 available registers, and register-to-register operations may be performed. An alternate way of looking at this bit is to consider it a seventh bit on the operation code (similar to the IBM 360 or DEC System10 approach). Thus a LOAD from memory to a register would be operation 0000010, while a LOAD REGISTER would be 0000011.

5. *Address* (19 bits). If the mode switch is 0, this refers to an address in main memory. With 19 bits, memory size is limited to about a half million words. If the mode switch is set, the high-order 16 bits of this field must be zero, and the low-order three bits represent a register which contains the operand.

We shall refer to (index register, mode switch, address) as the *effective address* since this is the address that is actually accessed by the hardware.

As stated previously, this organization is typical of most machines with the following exception: in our case, two operation codes (READ and WRITE) directly access their respective I/O devices. With modern operating systems, how can we justify that?

In a small, single-user minicomputer system, I/O is generally handled as described. By contrast, the operating system usually performs the I/O operation in a large multiprogramming system. The system will read the program onto a disk storage unit, and then the program will ask the operating system for the information via a special instruction such as a SUPERVISOR CALL or EXECUTIVE REQUEST. The operating system will then retrieve the information from the disk and pass it to the program.

Consequently a supervisor request can be considered to be a single instruction: get next input. From our compiler point of view, in response to a READ statement, we can generate either the direct READ instruction or a pseudo READ by actually generating the supervisor call. In either case, the actions performed by the compiler are similar.

5.8.4 Code Generator Organization

In organizing our code generator, we have already made some top-level design decisions. Our current design is pictured in Figure 5.14. The parser outputs tokens which represent the postfix for the program. The routine POSTFIX converts this stream of tokens into quads and then passes the quads to the routine CODEGEN. CODEGEN will generate machine language instructions for these quads. Let us now give the detailed design for each of these two routines.

The POSTFIX routine receives tokens from the parser and creates quads which are passed to the code generation routines. Since a quad generally has

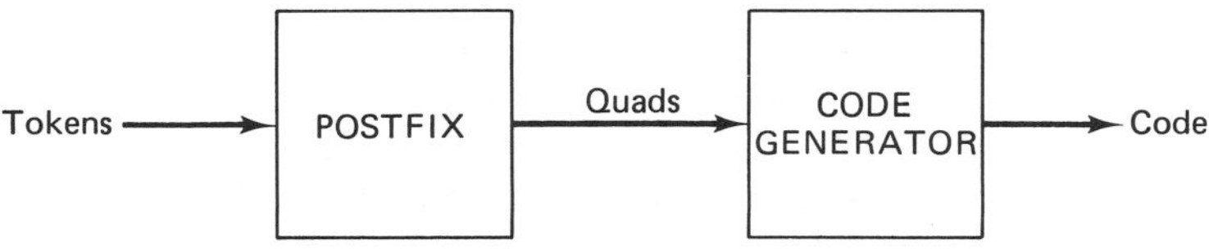

Figure 5.14 Current code generation structure.

four arguments, and POSTFIX receives tokens one at a time, provision must be made for saving intermediate results until an entire quad is formed. If we assume that the routine CODEGEN has four parameters—OPERATOR, OPERAND1, OPERAND2, and RESULT—our basic POSTFIX routine is as follows:

```
POSTFIX: procedure(TOKEN);
    declare TOKEN;
    if TOKEN completes next quad
      then call CODEGEN(OPERATOR,OPERAND1,OPERAND2,RESULT);
      else Save TOKEN;
    end POSTFIX;
```

The basic algorithm on converting from postfix to quads is well known and is the same as the algorithm which evaluates an expression written in postfix. Since the stream of tokens is already in postfix with each operator immediately following its operands, it is only necessary to stack the operands and apply them to the operator, when seen. Thus for the expression X+Y (with postfix XY+), POSTFIX should perform the following operations:

Stack X
Stack Y
Output quad for X+Y

We still have one further consideration. Where is the result of this operation? Consider the more complex example X+Y*Z (or in postfix XYZ*+). If we were evaluating the expression, the sequence of operations would be as follows:

Stack X
Stack Y
Stack Z
Apply * top 2 on stack (Y, Z) and replace by Y*Z
Apply + to top 2 on stack (X, Y*Z) and replace by X+Y*Z

To create quads for this expression, we must employ a similar type of operation. Thus we can perform the following operations:

Stack X
Stack Y
Stack Z
Output quad for Y*Z and replace top 2 on stack (Y, Z) with location of result
Output quad for top 2 on stack (X, loc for Y*Z) and replace top 2 on stack with location of result

For some readers this last operation is hard to grasp in understanding the operation of a code generator. Note that we are not evaluating the expression; we are producing a set of instructions (quads in this case) that will evaluate the expression when the compiled program is later executed. This distinction must be carefully understood. Our compiler is simply a program that is operating on a NIP program as data—not evaluating the operations specified in the NIP program.

One last consideration: In describing the conversion from postfix to quads we used a statement of the form:

```
Output quad for Y*Z and replace top 2 on stack
  (Y, Z) with location of result
```

Where is that result? For an expression like (XYZ*+) we do not have any specified location for the result of first applying the * operation. We can solve this problem by creating new, temporary variables to contain the location. We already have the routine SYSTEM_LABEL from our parser to create forward jumps from IF and WHILE statements; we can simply use this routine and create system labels for arithmetic identifiers by specifying the correct type. Thus for the operation Y*Z we can perform the following actions:

```
Create new system label T1
Output quad (*, Y, Z, T1)
Remove Y and Z from the stack
Stack T1
```

If a similar operation is performed for the + operator, the quad produced will be:

```
(+, X, T1, T2)
```

If the code generator generates code to put the result of Y*Z into T1, the code for the + operation will correctly find that value of Y*Z at T1. Note that as we stated earlier, this will by no means be the most efficient code, although it will necessarily be correct. Later we will look at refining the code to improve it further.

In scanning the list of postfix tokens, we notice that not every token is a binary operator using two operands. For example, the postfix for the WHILE statement is:

```
loop label
WD_WHILE
. . .
```

so WD_WHILE is a unary operator that has only the system label specifying the return point in the loop. Also, WD_WHILE does not need a result location specified. Similarly, in an assignment statement whose postfix is

〈ID〉
〈EXPRESSION〉
:=

ASGN_OP (:=) has an operand1 (〈EXPRESSION〉) and a result (〈ID〉), but no second operand. Therefore, several options are available for each token. In order to allow the most versatility from our postfix to quad routine, let us create two vectors: *POSTFIX_FUNCTION* and *POSTFIX_RESULT*. For each value of *TOKEN*, *POSTFIX_FUNCTION*(*TOKEN*) will hold the number of operands needed for the quad (0, 1, 2, or a value of 3 if the postfix operator is to be totally ignored), which should be popped off the stack. This should be general enough to cover all cases. Similarly, *POSTFIX_RESULT* (*TOKEN*) will contain the value of 0 or 1 depending upon whether a new system label is needed to contain the result of the operation. Some representative values for these vectors are as follows:

TOKEN	POSTFIX_FUNCTION	POSTFIX_RESULT	Operation
+	2	1	System label is result of operand 1 + 2
:=	2	0	Operand 1 gets value of operand 2
COMMA_CALL	1	1	Save function argument in system label
END_IF	1	0	Set forward branch from operand 1 (label at IF)

Exercise 5.5: Complete the vectors *POSTFIX_FUNCTION* and *POSTFIX_RESULT* for all valid tokens. We will describe the operations in greater detail when we describe the code generator routine.

Given the above decisions, we can specify the routine POSTFIX as follows:

```
POSTFIX: procedure(TOKEN);
      if TOKEN is identifier then stack token;
      else do; /* operator */
           do case (POSTFIX_FUNCTION (TOKEN));
                \0\ Set OPERAND1 and OPERAND2 to 0;
                \1\ Set OPERAND1 to top of stack, OPERAND2=0
                    and pop 1 element from stack;
                \2\ Set OPERAND2 to top of stack and pop;
                    Set OPERAND1 to top of stack and pop;
                \3\ return; /* ignore token */
                end; /* case */
```

```
        if POSTFIX_RESULT(TOKEN)=1 then do; /*set result*/
            RESULT = new systemlabel of INTTYPE;
            Stack RESULT;
            end;
        else RESULT=0;
        call CODEGEN(TOKEN, OPERAND1, OPERAND2, RESULT);
        end;
    end POSTFIX;
```

5.8.5 Execution Environment

In deciding on the form of code to generate, we now have to make some decisions about the structure—or environment—of the executing program. We need some organization to generate code for correctly accessing variables and procedures and for calling functions.

In deciding on the form of variable storage, we note there are two basic forms: static storage and dynamic storage. In static storage each variable has a unique location in memory that is constant for the life of the program; this is the storage that is used by languages like FORTRAN. It has the obvious advantage that code to access each variable is efficient since the compiler can generate code to directly access the variable. It is inefficient, however, in that it wastes space. If a procedure is currently not being executed, its storage is still allocated. Static storage also has the disadvantage of not allowing recursive procedures, as there is only one reserved location for each variable.

The alternative strategy is to use dynamic storage. In this case, storage for all variables in a procedure is allocated when the procedure is called. This means that inactive procedures do not use any storage space. Although a great savings in space, it requires additional execution overhead in creating this space, although in many cases the overhead is minimal. Since each activation of a procedure allocates storage for its variables, recursion is no problem for a dynamic allocation strategy.

Although storage may be dynamic, we do not have total chaos in the execution of a recursive procedure. For each procedure, the number of words of storage necessary to contain the variables of that procedure will be fixed. Thus we can talk about the first variable of a procedure, the second, etc. If we simply knew where the first word was located, then we could find any one of the variables easily.

For each procedure we will have an *activation record* or *stack frame* that contains all the local storage for that procedure. Each variable within a procedure will have a unique location within that activation record. Upon calling a procedure, we see that it is necessary only to allocate an area large enough for the entire activation record and make the first address of this activation record known.

This then is the basic two-level accessing necessary in dynamic allocation strategies. If a variable is at location *N* in an activation record, accessing the variable requires the operations:

Find start of activation record for procedure.
Access word *N* after this start address.

In describing the NIP language, every variable must be declared, and each declaration follows the procedure statement of the procedure in which it is declared. Thus if we set a counter to 0 in the procedure name's symbol table entry, and increment it by 1 for each declaration of a variable within that procedure, then at the end of the procedure we have the following two desirable features:

1. The symbol table entry for each procedure contains a field giving the total size of the activation record.
2. Each variable has been assigned a unique location within that activation record.

Remember when we defined our symbol table routine we had additional information which we simply described as "other." This is the information that we need. We can provide the above information by adding the following code to our symbol table routine:

```
if adding new procedure name then
     Set activation record size to MINIMUM_VALUE;
else if new variable then do;
     Increment activation record size by 1;
     Set offset field in variable's symbol table entry
          to be proc's current activation record size;
     end;
```

This requires the addition of the statement

```
DECLARE SYMBOLOFFSET(STSIZE) FIXED BINARY;
```

to the set of symbol table arrays that have been declared previously. Note that we set the initial value to *MINIMUM_VALUE*, rather than to 0 in case we need additional information later.

In the execution of a NIP program, space for the procedure's local variables must be allocated every time a procedure is called. Similarly, whenever a procedure returns, the space can be released. Note that procedure activation is a last-in, first-out strategy. That is, if procedure A calls procedure B, B must return to A before A may return. This last-in, first-out strategy is best implemented as a push-down stack. If all the available memory is considered available for a stack, it is necessary only to set the stack pointer to the next available location. All local variables may be accessed relative to that location. On procedure exit, we have only to reset the stack pointer to the appropriate value for the preceding procedure to again be able to access the variables of that procedure.

However, to reset this stack pointer, we have to be able to save its value in order to be able to restore it on procedure exit. Therefore, the type of code we have to generate to enter a procedure is something of the form:

```
SAVE current location of stack pointer
SET new stack pointer value
```

The best place to save this value would be in the activation record itself. Thus, the return value of the stack pointer is an "overhead" item that must be considered in every activation record. This is therefore one of the items covered by the space needed by *MINIMUM_VALUE.*

Figure 5.15 may help clarify this situation. In this example, a program is executing in procedure A (5.15(a)). Some fixed location (usually a register) points to the activation record of A, and all local variables are addressed relative to this fixed location. If A returns to the procedure that called it, we have to be able to reset our activation record pointer. Let us assume that the first word of the activation record contains this address. (If we consider the activation record to be an array with zero origin indexing, the first element being subscript 0, we can call this location *ACTIVATION_*

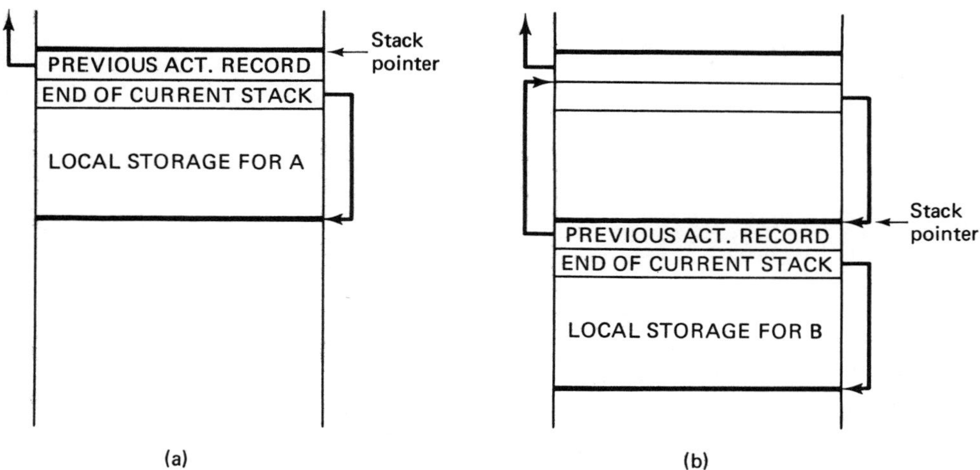

Figure 5.15 Run-time stack organization: (a) Stack while in procedure A; (b) Stack after A calls procedure B.

RECORD(0).) Similarly, we need to be able to know the end of the current activation record. Let this be contained in *ACTIVATION_RECORD*(1). If A now calls procedure B, the sequence of necessary operations is as follows (Figure 5.15(b)):

The current end of stack (*ACTIVATION_RECORD*(1)) becomes the new stack pointer.
The old stack pointer is to be new *ACTIVATION_RECORD*(0) in order to be able to return to A later.
A new *ACTIVATION_RECORD*(1) in the new activation record must be set to include all local variables from the new procedure B. This is just the activation record size in B's symbol table entry.

Given a machine with several registers, then this operation can be performed by the following sequence of instructions (assuming *STACKREG* is the register containing the stack pointer, and *SCRATCH* is some other register).

```
LOAD SCRATCH,STACKREG              /* save stack pointer */
LOAD STACKREG,STACKREG,ACTIVATION_RECORD(1) /* new stack */
STORE SCRATCH,STACKREG,ACTIVATION_RECORD(0)
                 /* back pointer in new ACT. REC. */
LOAD SCRATCH,STACKREG       /* compute end of stack */
ADDIM SCRATCH,0,size /* add size of activation record */
STORE SCRATCH,STACKREG,ACTIVATION RECORD(1) /* new end */
IF SCRATCH is illegal address THEN CALL OUT_OF_SPACE
```

In order to return to the calling procedure, it is only necessary to reset *STACKREG*, i.e., generate the instruction

```
LOAD STACKREG,STACKREG,ACTIVATION_RECORD(0)
```

Thus while procedure activation takes about 10 instructions, we can return in one. (Note, instead of *ACTIVATION_RECORD*(0) and *ACTIVATION_RECORD*(1), symbolic names like *A_R_STACKLINK* and *A_R_END* should be used.)

Returning is actually a bit more complex in that we have to know what is the address of the next instruction to execute. Thus, when B returns to procedure A, not only does A's environment have to be restored, but the address of the next statement in A to execute must be obtained. Therefore we need *ACTIVATION_RECORD*(2) to contain this return address. Our current value for *MINIMUM_VALUE* is now up to 3; that is, the first allocated variable will begin at *ACTIVATION_RECORD*(3). As we develop our code generator, we may need other "housekeeping" words, so the symbolic identification of this value helps.

5.8.6 Machine Dependencies

Up to now we have made minimal decisions based upon the resulting machine to execute the compiled program. About the only decision made so far is that our run-time environment will be stack-oriented, and that we need two registers (which we have called *STACKREG* and *SCRATCH*) for use in procedure activation and termination. Even this decision is not firm since we need only a fixed location (*STACKREG*) for use in local variable addressing. If two registers are not available, then we can develop alternative code sequences for creating new activation records. However, the time has come where we have to start generating code for our target machine, so we must study its structure to develop an optimal design. For our initial implementation, our goal is correct code generation; therefore, we will not be concerned too much with efficiency. Later enhancements will optimize the code further.

For our machine we have eight registers available. Since register 0 cannot be used as an index register (dictated by the hardware) let us use that as our accumulator for results of arithmetic operations. Let 1 be our stack register, and let 2 be a register to contain the return address from a subroutine. Register 3 will be our scratch register. For symbolically referring to all these registers, Figure 5.16 gives the declarations for the named variables which we will use. Each register will be prefixed by the letter *R*, so register 0 will be *R0*, register 1 will be *R1*, etc. Since an index register is not always needed to compute an address, the variable *NO_REG* will be used to represent no index register in the effective address. Note that we have not used registers *R4* through *R7* yet. As we develop the code generator, we will take that into account and try to use them effectively.

```
declare R0 BIT(3) INIT('000'B),
        R1 BIT(3) INIT('001'B),
        R2 BIT(3) INIT('010'B),
        R3 BIT(3) INIT('011'B),
        R4 BIT(3) INIT('100'B),
        R5 BIT(3) INIT('101'B),
        R6 BIT(3) INIT('110'B),
        R7 BIT(3) INIT('111'B),
        NO_REG BIT(3) INIT('000'B);
```

Figure 5.16 Symbolic register assignments.

5.8.7 Symbolic Code Generation

At the base level of our code generator, we want to generate words consisting of 32 bits each. Therefore let us create such a routine with the following description:

```
GENERATE_WORD: procedure(ADDRESS,INSTRUCTION);
   declare ADDRESS FIXED BINARY, /* address of instruction */
           INSTRUCTION BIT(32); /* word to generate */
   Output INSTRUCTION at address ADDRESS;
end GENERATE_WORD;
```

The output statement will be dependent upon the operating system for which the compiler is written. Every system has some type of loader format and provides either a system routine or a clearly defined format which the loader or linkage editor accesses to load the program into memory.

Most operating systems have provided a feature that will be of use in our design. Remember that for IF and WHILE statements we do not know the address of the forward jumps. Therefore, we cannot generate instructions sequentially, one at a time. For the IF (when the END_IF token is seen), we must generate the forward branch from the IF test expression code. Most loaders provide the ability of loading code out of sequence; thus whenever we want to generate the IF or WHILE jump, we can simply write

```
call GENERATE_WORD(if_address, jump_instruction)
```

and have the instruction inserted at the correct location.

If the system does not have such a sophisticated loader and instructions must be generated sequentially, the code generator must be more complex. Briefly, it can be organized as follows.

1. For the vast majority of sequentially generated instructions, place the output from GENERATE_WORD into a file.
2. For the relatively few "patched" jumps, place them into a second file.
3. After the code generation phase is completed, sort this small jump file into ascending addresses.
4. Reread both files, merge the data, and output into loader format.

This last operation takes an extra pass over the program; however, it is a quick pass (which fortunately does not have to be done in most systems).

Since we are only creating code for a hypothetical machine, we will assume for NIP that GENERATE_WORD simply prints each word as it is received.

Most of the time our code generator will generate sequential machine language instructions. Most instructions have a similar format; thus, a single routine to combine all of the fields into a 32-bit word will help the code generation process. Therefore, we can use the routine INSTRUCTION with the structure:

```
INSTRUCTION: procedure( OPCODE, ACC, INDREG, DISPLACE);
      declare OPCODE BIT(6), /* operation code */
              ACC BIT(3),        /* operand register */
             INDREG BIT(3), /* index register */
             DISPLACE FIXED BINARY; /* act rec offset */
      Convert DISPLACE to BIT(20) value
      Compute instruction as concatenation of 4 fields
      call GENERATE_WORD(location,new instruction);
end INSTRUCTION;
```

We need to know the location to pass to GENERATE_WORD. Let us assume that *LOCATION_COUNTER* is a global variable used for this purpose. Thus, we expand that line of INSTRUCTION as follows:

```
call GENERATE_WORD(LOCATION_COUNTER, NEW_INSTRUCTION);
LOCATION_COUNTER = LOCATION_COUNTER +1;
if LOCATION_COUNTER > memory_size then
      call ABORT (overflow_message);
```

Similarly, converting the displacement into bits may be a common operation, so let us make it a subroutine:

```
DISPLACEMENT_TO_BITS : procedure(DISPLACE, OFFSET);
      declare DISPLACE FIXED BINARY, /* displacement */
                 OFFSET BIT(20);           /* returned value */
         OFFSET = bit value of DISPLACE;
end DISPLACEMENT_TO_BITS;
```

If all these fields are coded as symbolic constants, we can write direct assembly-like language statements for our constructs. Consider the following example. Assume we want to generate code for $X + Y$. This is represented by the quad:

(ADD_OP, Sx, Sy, T)

If *Dx* is the displacement of *X* within its activation record (pointed to by *R1*), and *Dy* and *Dt* are similar values for *Y* and *T* respectively, the code to be generated can be written as:

```
call INSTRUCTION(LOAD, ACC, R1, Dx);
call INSTRUCTION(ADD,  ACC, R1, Dy);
call INSTRUCTION(STORE,ACC, R1, Dt);
```

where *ACC* stands for an appropriate register name.

At this point we are removing ourselves from the idiosyncracies of any particular piece of hardware. Nevertheless, we still must use the *R1* stack register for each variable. Also, this assumes that we know how to access any given variable. So far all variables are accessed the same way as offsets past *R1*; however, this may not always be so. What about strings and arrays which we would like to add later? We also have not considered parameters to subroutines or constants. Therefore, let us go one step further. If *Sx* is a symbol table address for program variable *X*, let us create a routine GENERATE which will generate instructions for NIP variables. With this routine, the above ADD can be coded as:

```
call GENERATE(LOAD,  ACC, Sx);
call GENERATE(ADD,   ACC, Sy);
call GENERATE(STORE, ACC, St);
```

GENERATE will be concerned with the actual addressing of each variable. Its structure might be as follows.

```
GENERATE: procedure(OPCODE, ACC, VARIABLE);
    Convert VARIABLE to (INDREG,DISPLACE) pair;
    call INSTRUCTION(OPCODE, ACC, INDREG, DISPLACE);
end GENERATE;
```

So far we only have arithmetic variables, thus the CONVERT statement above expands to the following:

```
if variable type is local ID then do;
    INDREG = R1; /* local activation record */
    DISPLACE = offset in SYMBOLOFFSET(VARIABLE);
    end;
else do;
    . . . /* other variable types still undefined */
    end;
```

One type of variable which we have so far ignored is constants. We have designed our internal form so far in order to hide the fact that they were different from variables. However, they do differ in one important respect: no storage is allocated for constants, and therefore the above code to load the value will not work.

We can solve this in several ways. One way would be to define for each constant a fixed location for its value. Let us use another approach. Note that in NIP all constants are positive since the symbol — will be interpreted as an operator. We also have the instruction LOADIM which loads the effective address into a register. Thus for a constant data type, we can add the section of code to GENERATE:

```
if variable is constant then do;
    call INSTRUCTION(LOADIM, R2, NO_REG, value);
    DISPLACE = R2;
    INDREG = NO_REG;
    end;
```

This will have the effect of loading *R2* with the value of the constant, and then returning *R2* as the register with that value.

Note that this restricts constants to a value which can be represented by 19 bits—the size of the effective address field. This is probably sufficient for our initial implementation. If we want larger constants, other techniques, such as the following, can be used.

We can always use the first technique above and allocate a fixed location for each such constant. However, we can be clever if we wish. We can divide each such constant by 2^{18} (which will fit in a LOADIM instruction), and generate the following sequence:

```
Let X be value of constant/2^18;
Let Y be remainder of (constant - X*2^18)
        (e.g., Y = MOD(constant value, 2^18))
LOADIM call INSTRUCTION(ACC,NO_REG,X);
SHIFTLEFT call INSTRUCTION(ACC,NO_REG,18);
ADDIM call INSTRUCTION(ACC,NO_REG,Y);
```

Thus constants can be loaded with three instructions. While not as efficient as possible, it does simplify the design since no storage is now needed for constants. (Study the code carefully to see that it indeed does work.)

We should now consider the fact that we still have four unused registers (*R4* through *R7*). Using only one accumulator is most inefficient. One way to increase efficiency is to assume that we have many registers. Every time we want to perform an arithmetic operation that needs a register, we can allocate a register, and every time we no longer need the register, we can free it. This dynamic pool of registers usually makes for more efficient execution. For example, given the postfix $XYZ*+$, our straightforward code generator would generate six instructions (three for each operator); however, the following sequence would generate only four:

```
call GENERATE(LOAD, ACC1, Sy); /* load Y */
call GENERATE(MULT, ACC1, Sz); /* Y*Z in ACC1 */
call GENERATE(LOAD, ACC2, Sx); /* get X */
call GENERATE(ADD, ACC2,ACC1); /*compute X+Y*Z in ACC2*/
```

At this point *ACC2* would contain the result. Note that we still do not have optimal code, even in this simple case. Since addition is a commutative operation, the result of computing $X+(Y*Z)$ is the same as $(Y*Z)+X$. Therefore we could have saved an additional instruction by adding X to *ACC1* and leaving the result in *ACC1* instead of computing the value in *ACC2*.

This type of optimization is generally called *peephole* optimization. We are looking at only a small segment of the program, and via this peephole into the program we are attempting to optimize the code. We shall employ this technique whenever it is convenient; after all there is no virtue in generating more inefficient code than is necessary. This technique can improve the code from 30% to 50% from the straightforward approach, and any decent compiler performs several of these optimization "tricks."

However, to what extent should we optimize the code? Each special case that must be checked adds onto our compilation time. Also, there is no coherent theory for all peephole optimization. This points out the difficult nature of code generators. While the scanner and parser phases of a compiler are based upon formal mathematical theories of languages, most code generators produce code in a somewhat ad hoc fashion depending upon the cleverness of the compiler writer. However remember this point: if one gets too clever, then no one else can understand what has been written, and any errors in the compiler can often not be easily corrected. In our design, we shall employ only obvious (almost) optimization techniques.

Back to our design. Since we want the ability of using multiple registers, but want an easy design now, let us assume that a routine ALLOCATE is used to allocate a register to use and always returns register *R0*, while routine FREEREGISTER frees registers. Thus we can code these as follows:

```
ALLOCATE: procedure(ACC);
       declare ACC BIT(3);
       ACC = R0; /* always use R0*/
       end ALLOCATE;
FREEREGISTER: procedure(ACC);
       declare ACC BIT(3);
       end FREEREGISTER; /* do nothing now */
```

Later we can modify these to use registers *R4* through *R7* in addition to *R0*. In Section 5.9, where we discuss enhancements, we will discuss this further.

Our current code generation structure is now pictured in Figure 5.17. We can call ALLOCATE to obtain a register and then call GENERATE or INSTRUCTION to produce the actual machine language instructions. Most of the inner details of our machine language have been hidden from our top-level design.

As we stated earlier, the code generator is actually a large **case** statement where each quad generates a unique sequence of instructions. That is, it has the structure:

```
CODEGEN: procedure( OPERATOR, OPERAND1, OPERAND2, RESULT);
      do case(OPERATOR);
            \ASGN_OP\ GENERATE OPERAND1 := OPERAND2;
            \ADD_OP\ GENERATE RESULT := OPERAND1 + OPERAND2;
            \MULT_OP\ GENERATE RESULT := OPERAND1 * OPERAND2;
                        . . . /* other arithmetic operators */
            \WD_PROC\ /* new procedure */
                        GENERATE creation of new act. record;
```

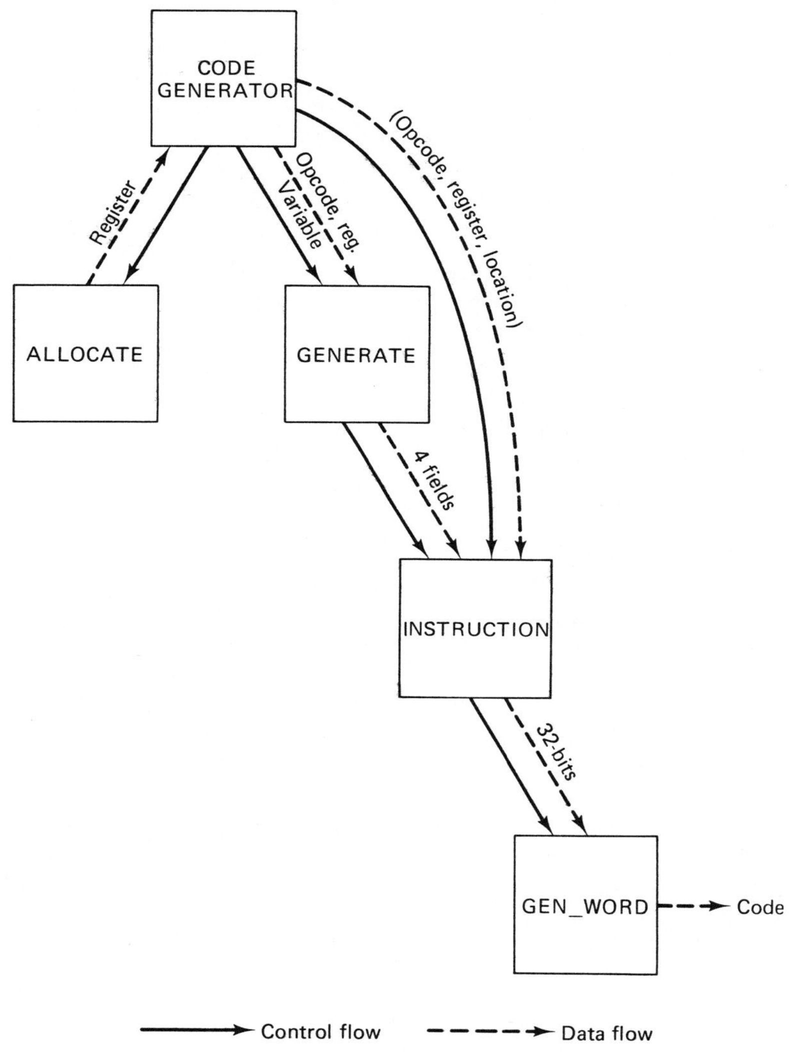

Figure 5.17 Code generator structure.

```
        \END_PROC\  GENERATE return to calling procedure;
                    . . . /* all other operators */
        end; /* end case */
    end CODEGEN;
```

Let us now study selectively several of these code generation routines.

ADD_OP, MULT_OP, DIVIDE_OP, SUBTRACT_OP

In these cases we simply want to set *RESULT* to *OPERAND1* operator *OPERAND2*. Operands 1 and 2 are both either variables or temporaries from previous computations. In either case the quad operands are pointers to symbol table entries for variables in locations in the current activation record. Therefore, the routine is simply:

```
call ALLOCATE(ACC);
call GENERATE(LOAD, ACC, OPERAND1);
call GENERATE(OPERATOR, ACC, OPERAND2);
call GENERATE(STORE, ACC, RESULT);
call FREEREGISTER(ACC);
```

ASGN_OP

This is similar to the above. We set *OPERAND1* to be the current value of *OPERAND2*.

Procedure activation

Several quad operators signify the start and end of a new procedure. For WD_PROC, *OPERAND1* is the symbol table address for the procedure being defined. Since this is the point at which the CALL statement will generate code to call, we want to perform two actions:

1. Generate code to create an activation record for this procedure.
2. Save the current instruction address so that if any other procedures call this one, we will know what address to generate.

This last operation poses a problem. If some earlier routines had calls to this one, the entry point location to call had not as yet been defined. We can solve this in either of two ways. One would be to pick a fixed location to contain the address of the entry point. Then each subroutine call would simply load this address and jump to it via the code:

```
LOAD    R2,0,FIXED_ADDRESS
SUBCALL R2,R2,0
```

(The SUBCALL instruction leaves the current address in *R2* after computing the transfer location.) Since the procedure must be seen sometime during the code generation phase, we simply have to make sure that when WD_PROC is seen, code is generated to initialize FIXED_ADDRESS to the correct value (e.g., **call** GEN_WORD(*FIXED_ADDRESS*, *LOCATION_COUNTER*)). Thus when the program is executed, *FIXED_ADDRESS* will have the correct value. Note that this is another case where it is important to distinguish the difference between compile-time operations and execution-time code. While the address of the procedure must be known at execution time, all that we need to know at compile time is the location that will contain that address (*FIXED_ADDRESS*).

> **Exercise** 5.6: Where is *FIXED_ADDRESS* located? It cannot be within an activation record, since these are dynamically allocated.

This first technique generates two instructions for each subroutine call; however, one will do. Therefore a second approach can be considered. For each CALL statement leave the SUBCALL instruction empty if the location of the procedure is still unknown. Keep a list of these addresses. When the procedure is finally scanned, generate the SUBCALL at the correct location be scanning the list of saved references. This is similar to the "patching" of forward references for the IF and WHILE statements.

We will use this second approach since it will save one instruction per subroutine reference at a cost in compile time to maintain the back references. You must decide whether this is worth it. Since we have a field in the symbol table that contains the starting address of the procedure, let this be used as a pointer to a list of references to this procedure if the procedure has not as yet been defined. Therefore, the sequence of operations to be performed can be modified to be:

```
if previous references to this procedure then do;
    do for each such reference in list;
        GENERATE for each address
            (SUBCALL, R2, NO_REG, LOCATION_COUNTER)
        end;
    end;
Set SYMBOLTABLEVALUE(OPERAND1) :=
        LOCATION_COUNTER;
GENERATE code to create new activation record;
```

For processing all the references in the list, let us assume that we have an array in memory that contains all such references and the symbol table contains a pointer to it. Each such array element contains two fields: the address for generating the subroutine call and the index of the next array element. We can also have two routines GETFORWARDREF(*INDEX*) which allocates an array element and returns its index in *INDEX* and the routine FREEFORWARDREF(*INDEX*) which returns the array element *INDEX* to the free list. These routines are straightforward list processing routines and will not be further defined.

> **Exercise** 5.7: Note that we are sacrificing compile time for increased execution speed. Redesign the CALL sequence to use the *FIXED_ADDRESS* technique mentioned above.

At this point we now have to consider the role of parameters to procedures. We have in NIP call-by-reference parameters, i.e., the address of the argument is passed to the subroutine. When the parameter is accessed, then the passed address is used to point to the actual argument. Thus if the argument is a variable name, any changes to the parameter will affect the value of the argument. However, if the argument is an expression, the address which is passed is simply the address of the temporary value containing the expression. Therefore changes to the parameter representing this argument will not be reflected back to changes in the calling program.

To provide this facility, let us assume that each parameter has one word allocated within the local activation record which contains the address of the actual argument that was passed. How can we provide this? The contents of this word will contain a pointer to the actual argument, and so the code necessary to access that word would be:

```
LOAD SCRATCH,R1,local offset
LOAD ACC,SCRATCH,0
```

That is, the first instruction loads a pointer into a scratch register, while the second instruction accesses the variable using that scratch register as the index register. Remember that we have register *R3* used only as a scratch register during procedure activation. Let us use that register as the scratch register in this case. To add parameter usage to our language, we only have to add to the CONVERT sequence in the routine GENERATE:

```
if variable type is local ID then do;
     INDREG = R1;
     DISPLACE = offset in SYMBOLOFFSET(VARIABLE);
     end;
if variable is constant then do;
     Generate code to load constant in R2;
     end;
if variable is parameter then do;
     call INSTRUCTION(LOAD, R3, R1, act. rec. offset)
          /* pointer to argument */
     INDREG = R3;
     DISPLACE = 0;
     end;
```

We must now make sure that the code at the start of a procedure sets up the environment so that the above sequence of operations is correct.

From the output of POSTFIX for a procedure, we get the following sequence of quads:

```
(WD_PROC, procname,0 0)
{(COMMA_PARAM, parameter,0 0)}*      (for any parameters)
{(RP_PARAM,parameter,0 0)}           (')' for last parameter)
```

For WD_PROC we will create an activation record, and for each parameter we will move its corresponding argument address into the corresponding parameter location. However, how is that parameter list passed from the calling procedure to the called procedure?

The basic way of calling a procedure is to use the SUBCALL instruction. This leaves the next instruction address in the operand register and jumps to the effective address. Let us assume that the *N* parameters are just the next *N* words in memory. Since *R2* will point to the return point upon entry to a procedure, we also have a pointer to the parameter list.

At this point we can generate code for WD_PROC. Similar to what was said in Section 5.8.4, the sequence of instructions to generate is:

```
LOAD    R3,R1,1      get end of current act. rec.
STORE   R1,R3,0      point to old act. rec. for return
LOAD    R1,0,R3      set new act. rec. pointer
ADDIM   R3,0,size    point to new end of stack
STORE   R3,R1,1      (Size from symbol table for proc)
```

At this point *R2* contains either the return point or a pointer to the first parameter, if any. Therefore, we should include the following sequence:

if no parameters **then** GENERATE STORE *R2,R1*,2

How do we know if there are any parameters? We can assume that the procedure's symbol table entry contains this information. If there are any parameters, then RP_PARAM will generate this store.

For each COMMA_PARAM operator we simply want to move the next parameter into its appropriate address. Let us assume that *R2* always contains a pointer to the next entry of the parameter list. This is certainly true for the first parameter since this token is preceded by the WD_PROC token just described. Therefore, we need to generate the following instructions:

```
LOAD SCRATCH,R2,0     address of next parameter
STORE SCRATCH,R1, act. rec. offset of parameter
ADDIM R2,0,1          point to next parameter
```

Since *R3* is again available, we can use that for *SCRATCH*. Calls to INSTRUCTION should generate these directly.

For the RPP_ARAM quad we have two operations to perform:

1. Set the address of the last parameter.
2. Save the return address.

Therefore for this operator, we first generate the same three instructions as for COMMA_PARAM. At this point *R2* points to the first instruction after the parameter list, which is just where execution is to resume. Thus we have only to generate

```
STORE R2,R1,2
```

in order to complete this process.

Given the environment that we have organized, the return code at the end of the procedure is quite simple. We have to reset *R1* to point to the old activation record, and we have to return to the address that followed the parameter list on the CALL. Since these addresses are just the first and third words of the current activation record, the END_PROC quad generates the instructions:

```
LOAD    R2,R1,2         get return address
LOAD    R1,R1,0         reset stack to previous value
JUMPUNC 0,R2,0          return
```

Since the environment for each activation record is described by the housekeeping words within itself, this is all the code that is necessary. The only minor problem is to be careful to load *R2* with the return address before resetting the activation record pointer (*R1*), or else the return address accessed will be the return address from the procedure that you are supposed to return to.

Exercise 5.8: The code for each parameter can be shortened from three to two instructions. Redesign this code sequence to accomplish this.

CALL statement

Perhaps the most complex code will be needed for the CALL statement. From what was written above for procedures, the CALL statement should generate the following code:

```
SUBCALL R2,procedureaddress
parameter list
```

The quads for this statement are as follows:

```
{(COMMA_CALL, parameter,0,0)}* (for each parameter)
{(RP_CALL, parameter,0,0)} (for last parameter)
(WD_CALL, procedurename,0,0)
```

Note that we have to evaluate all the arguments before we generate the SUBCALL code. For example, if we have any argument expressions, we should evaluate them first. Let us use the following sequence for the CALL statement:

```
do for each argument;
      GENERATE code to evaluate each argument;
      STORE each argument value into memory;
      end;
GENERATE code to call procedure
do for each argument;
      GENERATE address of argument in parameter list;
      end;
```

The sequence

```
GENERATE code to evaluate each argument;
STORE each argument value into memory;
```

can be expanded into:

```
if OPERATOR = COMMA_CALL | RP_CALL then do;
      /* RESULT is location of */
      /* value of argument     */
      Save RESULT in list;
      end;
```

For the CALL operator we have to generate the code to call the procedure and to set up the argument list. Remember that we may have the problem of calling a procedure that we have not seen as yet. Thus the sequence of instructions is:

```
if procedure already defined then
     call INSTRUCTION(SUBCALL,R2,0,SYMBOLVALUE(procname));
     else add LOCATION_COUNTER to list of addresses to call
          this procedure when ultimately defined;
do for each argument in argument list;
     Move address to parameter list;
     end;
```

The generation of the subroutine call code is straightforward; however, the argument list code requires some thought.

Since storage is dynamic, we have to create the argument list at execution time and cannot simply use GEN_WORD to place the address of the arguments into the parameter list. For each argument that is in memory we can generate the two instructions:

```
LOADIM    ACC,REG,argument          address of argument
STORE     ACC,parameterlist
```

We have to generate these two instructions for each argument before we generate the code to call the subroutine. At the WD_CALL quad, if there are N arguments, the SUBCALL instruction will be at address $LOCATION\_COUNTER + 2*N$ with the actual parameter list being locations $LOCATION\_COUNTER+2*N+1$ through $LOCATION\_COUNTER+2*N+N$. If we let $SUBCALL\_LOC$ be at $LOCATION\_COUNTER + 2*N$, for argument i we should generate:

```
LOADIM  ACC,address of argument
STORE   ACC,0,SUBCALL_LOC+i
```

We can easily keep count of the number of arguments for each RP_CALL or COMMA_CALL quad processed. When we see the WD_CALL quad we need to know the address of each argument.

We can use the GETFORWARDREF routine described before for procedure activation. For each argument we can save its address. Thus we need only to scan this list and to generate the appropriate load instructions. At the RP_CALL quad:

```
do for all arguments;
    Generate 2 word sequence to move
            address to argument list;
    call FREEFORWARDREF(index);
    end;
```

If the procedure has already been defined, a SUBCALL instruction to it should be generated, otherwise the address should be saved until the procedure is seen. Thus for WD_CALL, the sequence is:

```
call ALLOCATE(ACC);    /* register to use */
do i = 1 to number_parameters;
    if local variable then do;
        call GENERATE(LOADIM,ACC,symboltable address)
        call INSTRUCTION(STORE,ACC,NO_REG,SUBCALL_LOC+i);
        end;
    if parameter then do;
        call GENERATE(LOAD,ACC,symboltable address)
        call INSTRUCTION(STORE,ACC,NO_REG,SUBCALL_LOC+i);
        end;
    if expression then do;
        call GENERATE(LOADIM,ACC,tempvalue);
        call INSTRUCTION(STORE,ACC,NO_REG,SUBCALL_LOC+i);
        end;
    call FREEFORWARDREF; /* free list element */
    end;
call FREEREGISTER(ACC);
```

We should now be at location *SUBCALL_LOC* and must generate code to actually call the procedure and to leave space for the parameter list:

```
if procedure already defined then
        call INSTRUCTION(SUBCALL,R2,0,SYMBOLVALUE(procname));
    else do;
        Add LOCATION_COUNTER to list of unresolved refs.;
        LOCATION_COUNTER = LOCATION_COUNTER + 1;
        end;
do for all parameters;
    call GEN_WORD(LOCATION_COUNTER,0);
    LOCATION_COUNTER = LOCATION_COUNTER + 1;
    end;
```

For example, the statement

```
CALL X(Y,Z)
```

will generate the quads

```
(COMMA_CALL, Y, 0, 0)
(RP_CALL, Z, 0, 0)
(WD_CALL, X, 0, 0)
```

Assuming we are currently at location 600, the code that will be generated will be the following:

```
600    LOADIM    R,Y      COMMA_CALL for Y
601    STORE     R,605    address of Y at loc. 605
602    LOADIM    R,Z      RP_CALL for Z
603    STORE     R,606    address of Z at loc. 606
604    SUBCALL   R2,X     WD_CALL for X
605    +0                 first parameter address (Y)
606    +0                 second parameter address (Z)
```

Note that locations 605 and 606, while not containing any address will contain values during executing time due to the instructions at locations 601 and 603. Also, note that the code is not reentrant. That is, the instructions modify themselves. For programs that are used frequently, this is generally a poor programming practice and is often avoided.

Exercise 5.9: Rather than placing the parameter list immediately following the SUBCALL instruction, another common technique is to place the parameter list in the activation record and simply pass this single address to the subroutine. This avoids writing self-modifying code. Redesign the calling sequence for subroutine arguments so that self-modifying code does not have to be generated.

IF statement

The IF statement is controlled by two quads: the IF quad that appears immediately after the expression to be tested and the END_IF quad after the IF statement. (The case where ELSE appears is similar and will be left as an exercise.)

The IF quad has the structure

(IF, forwardlabel, expression, 0)

The code that we want to generate is

IF expression=0 THEN jump to forwardlabel

The IF expression will be false if the expression evaluates to zero, therefore we want to generate a JUMP on zero to *forwardlabel.* However, we still do not know what address to use for the label. If we simply save the address of the jump instruction, we can fill the value in later when the END_IF is seen. Therefore, the IF statement can be coded as:

```
call ALLOCATE(ACC); /* get accumulator to use */
call GENERATE(LOAD, ACC, OPERAND2); /* IF expression */
Save in symbol table ACC and LOCATION_COUNTER;
ADD 1 to LOCATION_COUNTER; /* space for jump */
```

The END_IF code is therefore:

```
Let ACC be register in label's symbol table location;
Let ADDRESS be saved address of IF test;
Generate at ADDRESS, JUMPZERO, 0, LOCATION_COUNTER
```

Other statements

The WHILE statement is handled in a manner similar to the IF statement and will not be considered further. Similarly the READ and WRITE statements are handled by simply reading or writing from a register. The code is straightforward and is left as an exercise.

START

This quad specifies the procedure name where execution is to begin. Since it is last, all unresolved forward references to procedures should by now be fixed. Thus the design for this quad is:

```
if any allocations left in GETFORWARDREF then
    call ERROR('Undefined procedures remain');
if OPERAND1 is defined then Set initial entry point
    else CALL ERROR('START procedure not defined');
Output initial entry point;
```

5.8.8 Code Generator Summary

At this point we have completed the designs for our NIP compiler. The code, while not optimal, should be correct, and is straightforward to understand and modify. In the next section we will discuss the problems of enhancing the compiler in terms of the language compiled and the features of the compiler itself, such as the efficiency of the resulting code.

5.9 ENHANCEMENTS

By this time we have given the detailed design for our NIP compiler. However, we are not quite finished with the product. Much needs to be done before we have any sort of compiler that can meet the needs of day-to-day operation. For one, there are still features that must be added in order to bring the NIP language up to minimal standards. Therefore, this section will be divided into three parts: improving the characteristics of the compiler, improving the code that is generated, and finally, extending the NIP language.

5.9.1 Compiler Improvements

Perhaps the most important consideration in any compiler is the detection of error conditions. While some of these have been built into the design, we can still add more. This section will outline several changes which can be added in order to help in error determination.

Perhaps the biggest failure right now is the way we coded the TEST subroutine to compare the desired token with the current token. We can use part of the syntax of the NIP language in order to improve on this strategy. For example, users can probably remember the few reserved words in our language. Also, a semicolon appears between statements in a statement list. Let us use this fact to localize errors by enabling the parser to "recover" between statements.

We can implement this by assuming that TEST never modifies a token that is a reserved word. Similarly SCANNER will never read in a new token if the current token is a reserved word. Thus whenever a reserved word is found, the input will never move past that point until explicitly told to do so. This condition should exist whenever a new statement is to be parsed (e.g., semicolon desired).

Therefore, the first line of SCANNER should be modified to include:

```
if CURRENT_TOKEN is RSWD_CLASS then return;
```

Similarly, we can modify the parser procedure STATEMENTLIST from the present:

```
call TEST(';', CURRENT_TOKEN, 'missing ;');
```

to the following:

```
call TEST(';', CURRENT_TOKEN, 'missing ;');
CURRENT_TOKEN = 0; /* force SCANNER past ; */
```

With these changes, the parser "recovers" at each statement boundary.

Exercise 5.10: Complete the remaining changes to add this error detection feature.

A second improvement in the compiler is in the symbol table organization. Note that throughout the rest of the compiler it is assumed that the symbol table routine only returns a pointer to the proper symbol table entry. There is no assumption of how that pointer is obtained. Therefore if we alter the search mechanism of the symbol table routines, this should be transparent to the remainder of the compiler. Since the current design uses a rather slow linear search, we can modify it to use a hash or a binary search.

Exercise 5.11: Modify the symbol table routine LOOKUP to use a different search strategy.

Our compiler should also do as much internal error checking as possible. For example, the current version of NIP has only integer variables; however, we may want to add strings and arrays later. In every expression, are we using variables correctly? We should probably add code for each arithmetic operator and for procedure arguments, in the code generator, to make sure that each such argument is an arithmetic variable. Thus when other typed variables are added, the changes will not affect current programs. Also, whenever a function is called, code should be added to make sure that the number of arguments in the CALL statement is the same as the number of parameters in the procedure.

Exercise 5.12: Modify CODEGEN to test the validity of each variable before it is used.

5.9.2 Code Improvements

Besides improving the error detection within the NIP compiler, we can also improve the code that gets generated. For example, registers *R4* through *R7* are totally ignored by the current compiler. We can often make use of them to improve the code. In addition, not every expression needs to be stored into memory after each operation. We can leave the results in a register and store the results only for an := operator.

To add this feature, we have to be able to test whether a *RESULT* operand (which is a temporary) has actually been stored. However, we do know, when we use the temporary, what the symbol table address is. Therefore, we can store in the symbol table for the temporary a flag signifying that the temporary has not actually been used, and place the name of the register actually containing the value.

Thus to add these changes, modifications to the specifications of some of the routines must be made. For example:

ALLOCATE and FREEREGISTER. In this case, ALLOCATE will have a list of five registers (R0, R4 through R7). Each call to ALLOCATE will take one of these off the list and return its name to the caller. Similarly, FREEREGISTER will return the register to the free list.

CODEGEN. For each use of an operator, instead of generating code to store the result in the temporary *RESULT*, the symbol table entry for *RESULT* should be modified to state that the results are actually in a register.

GENERATE. When a temporary result is used, the symbol table must be checked to see whether the results are actually in the temporary or whether they are actually in a register. If in a register, then a register-to-register effective address should be generated rather than an effective address which points to a word in the local activation record (the address of the temporary).

Just making this change by itself will still cause unnecessary instructions to be generated. For example, the + quad causes *OPERAND1* to be loaded into a register. If it is already in a register, an unnecessary LOAD instruction will be generated. We can avoid this problem by adding a routine LOAD_IF_MEMORY, which will generate a load instruction only if the operand is in a memory location. Thus the statements:

```
call ALLOCATE(ACC);
call GENERATE(LOAD, ACC, OPERAND1)
```

would be replaced by

```
call LOAD_IF_MEMORY(ACC, OPERAND1)
```

This routine would either return the register (as *ACC*) containing *OPERAND1* or would generate code to acquire a new register and load it with the operand.

These changes are actually very easy to make, and should decrease the code produced for expressions by 30% to 40%. For example, the statement $X := X + Y * Z$ which generates the quads:

```
(*, Sy, Sz, St1)
(+, Sx, St1, St2)
(:=, Sx, St2, 0)
```

will now generate the code:

```
LOAD  R0,R1,Dy          Load Y from local ACT. REC.
MPY   R0,R1,Dz          MPY by Z. Set T1 to be register R0
LOAD  R4,R1,Dx          For + get new register to load
ADD   R4,NO_REG,R0      Add T1 which is actually in R0
                        Set T2 to be R4
STORE_R4,R1,Dx          Set result (T2) into X
```

This five-instruction sequence is a great improvement over the eight instructions we would have generated previously.

Note however, that it still is not optimal; rather than loading *R4* with *X*, we could have directly added *X* to *R0* and saved one instruction. The inefficiency is because our code generator assumes that the first operand must be in a register. Since + is a commutative operation, we could have made the improvement by first checking whether either operand was in a register before forcing a load of the first operand.

Unfortunately, these simple changes are insufficient since expressions can be arbitrarily complex. It is possible to write an expression that requires an arbitrary number of registers. We avoided this before since the result of every operation was immediately stored. However, now that we are saving information in registers, we have to be sure that ALLOCATE always has an available register.

Since multiple registers in use occurs in complex expressions, one simple approach to an unavailable request for ALLOCATE would be to print an error message stating that the expression is too complex for the compiler, and quit compiling. If the probability of this occurrence is extremely low, then this is often an effective means to handle the problem. With five available registers to use, this approach might not be a bad idea.

Exercise 5.13: Write an expression that actually requires six registers at one time to contain temporary results. Long, isn't it?

A seemingly similar approach that states that since the probability of occurrence is extremely low, the error condition can be ignored, is unacceptable, since the error *will* occur. If you don't consider the error happening, your compiler will do unpredictable things when the error does occur.

A more effective solution to this problem is not very difficult, so we will use it here. We will simply allocate one of the available registers and store its contents. Note that we have still allocated a memory location in *ACTIVATION_RECORD* for each such temporary. Thus whenever we need a register, and none are available, we can do the following:

Let *X* be a register from the set {*R0*, *R4*, *R5*, *R6*, *R7*}.
Find temporary variable (*T*) currently stored in *X*;

Generate STORE X,T;
Set symbol table for T to state results in memory;

All that we need to complete this is to keep, for each register, a pointer to the symbol table entry of the variable currently in that register. This can be done with a small array in ALLOCATE.

5.9.3 Language Extensions

As mentioned previously, there are several additional features which we would like to add to our NIP compiler. Some of the most important additions are discussed in the following sections.

Arrays

Most programs, if they perform any sort of calculation repeatedly, use arrays. Syntactically, arrays present few problems; we must modify the DECLARE statement production to include array references. Similarly, we have to modify an expression to include an array reference to the ⟨PRIMARY⟩ production.

To the parser, we simply have to add an array reference as a valid operand to an arithmetic operator. This we can simply do by adding the tokens ARRAY_COMMA and ARRAY_PAREN to delineate array references. These then become two new quads for our code generator to handle.

Before discussing code generation for arrays, we should make sure that we understand the run-time structure of arrays. Arrays are usually accessed via *dope vectors*. An array dope vector contains the virtual origin for the array and multipliers for each of the subscripts. If V_0 is the virtual origin, and M_i is the ith multiplier, the address of $A(s_1, s_2, s_3, \ldots s_n)$ is given by $V_0 + M_1{*}s_1 + M_2{*}s_2 + \ldots + M_n{*}s_n$. (See Gries [71] for further information.) Given this formula, we can simply compute a subscript in a register, and modify the GENERATE procedure in CODEGEN to return an effective address of (*REG*, 0) where *REG* is the register containing the computation.

Strings

Strings can be handled in a manner analogous to the techniques for arrays. The syntax poses no problems, and neither does the code generation phase. However, we have one additional problem. So far, all the code has been in-line; that is, no additional routines must be called. Since string operations (such as concatenation) often are long subroutines, in-line code would not be practical. In this case we have to generate code to call a subroutine.

For all the built-in routines we can simply have a table giving the name of the routine and the entry point. We will simply let the operating system loader fix up this address when the program is loaded.

Functions

In NIP, all procedures are called via CALL statements. Often, functions are present in a language. Functions behave very much like a procedure subroutine except that a returned value is generated. Also, a reference to a function may appear within any expression. Therefore, functions pose the following two problems:

1. Where is the returned value to be located?
2. What if several registers contain values when a function must be called?

The first of these problems is usually handled by always returning the value of a function in a specified location, usually one of the registers. Thus we can assume that register *R0* always contains the value of the function. If the syntax for returning a value is:

```
RETURN(⟨EXPRESSION⟩)
```

the code for the RETURN would be:

```
LOAD  R0,expression
Return code from procedure
```

Upon return, the code generator would generate code knowing that *R0* would contain this value.

However, what if *R0* already contained a temporary variable? Before calling the function we would have to make sure that it was empty. Thus the calling sequence would be:

```
if R0 contains a result then
      Generate code to store R0 in memory;
Create parameter list;
call function;
```

(Note that if ALLOCATE always allocated *R0* last, then it would almost always be empty, and no code would have to be generated to clear its contents.) This solves the problem with *R0*, but what if other registers contained values? What if *R4* contained a value and *R4* was also used by the function? We can solve this in either of two ways. One would be to make sure that all registers were stored before calling a function. Thus nothing would be in a register when a function was called. The other approach would be to store all registers upon creating a new activation record.

This latter technique is the approach most production compilers use. Frequently it is called a *save area.* Upon creating a new activation record, space will be allocated for all of the register which can contain values, in this case *R0* and *R4* through *R7*. Thus for our NIP language, the value of MINIMUM_VALUE would be 8 (3 for the linkage information described previously and 5 for the register save area).

Note that the code to call a procedure is now getting long. Frequently this code is a subroutine, and the compiler simply generates code to call this routine for all linkages.

5.10 INTERPRETERS

As we stated early in this chapter, interpreters have a structure very similar to the design of a compiler. Interpreters still have to analyze the syntax of a program much like the front end of a compiler. In the following paragraphs, we will give the outline of an interpreter for NIP.

For efficiency we will assume that our interpreter executes postfix. Thus the entire parser of our NIP compiler can be used; however, instead of the POSTFIX routine outputting quads, it will simply store the postfix into memory, for later execution.

After the entire program has been scanned, the routine INTERPRETER is called. Similar to the POSTFIX routine for the NIP compiler, INTERPRETER will read the postfix and perform the desired actions. However, rather than outputting quads which represent the desired actions, it will perform the action directly. Thus for $XY+$, the interpreter will:

Stack X.
Stack Y.
Access value of X and value of Y and add them.
Replace top two stack locations with X+Y.

All that is necessary is to make sure that storage locations exist for *X* and *Y*. This can be easily done by assuming the existence of a run-time stack for activation records. Whenever a procedure token is seen, the interpreter creates the structure that would be interpretively created by the compiler. Since the designs are so similar to the designs for POSTFIX and CODEGEN, it will be left as an exercise.

Exercise 5.14: Write an interpreter for the NIP language.

5.11 SUMMARY

We have attempted to describe the process of designing a compiler. In addition, many of the techniques used by compiler writers have been identified. It is hoped that this chapter will give you a better understanding of the compilation process.

It should also be apparent by now that there is no one correct way to build this piece of software. Many ways are correct, and each depends upon the design goals for the finished product. We also hope that by now you realize that conceptually a compiler is rather simple; however, there is a vast array of details which must be taken care of. We have only given a brief overview of some of the problems. A most important consideration—how to generate relocatable output that can be linked together—has not even been mentioned. Accessing separately compiled procedures does add some complexity. Also, problems like arrays and strings have only been given the quickest glance.

Bibliography

[Aho et al., 74] AHO, A., J. HOPCROFT, AND J. ULLMAN, *The Design and Analysis of Computer Algorithms*, Addison-Wesley Publishing Company, Inc., Reading, Mass., 1974.

[Aho and Ullman, 72] AHO, A. AND J. ULLMAN, *Theory of Parsing, Translation, and Compiling*, Prentice-Hall, Inc., Englewood Cliffs, N.J., 1972.

[Ambler et al., 77] AMBLER, A. L., D. I. GOOD, J. C. BROWNE, W. F. BURGER, R. M. COHEN, C. G. HOCH, R. E. WELLS, "Gypsy: A Language for Specification and Implementation of Verifiable Programs." (See [LDRS, 77].)

[ANSI, 66] American Standard FORTRAN, *American National Standards Institute*, ×3.9–1966, March 1966.

[ANSI, 76] American Standard PL/1, *American National Standards Institute*, ×3.53–1976, August 1976.

[Baker, 72] BAKER, F. T., "Chief Programmer Team Management of Production Programming," *IBM Systems Journal*, 11, no. 1, 1972, 56–73.

[Basili, 78] BASILI, V., "A Panel Session: User Experience with New Software Methods," National Computer Conference, Anaheim, Calif., June 1978.

[Basili and Zelkowitz, 78] BASILI, V. AND M. ZELKOWITZ, "Analyzing Medium Scale Software Development," Third International Conference on Software Engineering, Atlanta, Ga., May 1978, 116–123.

[Basili and Turner, 75] BASILI, V. AND A. J. TURNER, "Iterative Enhancement: A Practical Technique for Software Development," *IEEE Transactions on Software Engineering*, 1, no. 4, December 1975, 390–396.

[Boehm et al., 75] Boehm, B., R. McClean, and D. Urfrig, "Some Experience with Automated Aids to the Design of Large Scale Reliable Software," International Conference on Reliable Software, Los Angeles, Calif., April 1975, 105–113.

[Boehm, 77] Boehm, B., "Seven Basic Principles of Software Engineering," *Infotech State of the Art Report on Software Engineering*, 1977.

[Brinch Hansen, 77] Brinch Hansen, P., *Architectures of Concurrent Programs*, Prentice-Hall, Inc., Englewood Cliffs, N.J., 1977.

[Brooks, 75] Brooks, F. P., *The Mythical Man Month*, Addison-Wesley Publishing Company, Inc., Reading, Mass., 1975.

[Caine and Gordon, 75] Caine, S. H. and E. K. Gordon, "PDL: A Tool for Software Design," National Computer Conference, 44, 1975, 271–276.

[Constantine and Yourdon, 79] Constantine, L. and E. Yourdon, *Structured Design: Fundamentals of a Discipline of Computer Program and Systems Design*, Prentice-Hall, Inc., Englewood Cliffs, N.J., 1979.

[Conway, 78] Conway, R., *A Primer on Disciplined Programming*, Winthrop Publishers, Cambridge, Mass., 1978.

[Conway and Wilcox, 73] Conway, R. and T. Wilcox, "Design and Implementation of a Diagnostic Compiler for PL/1," *Communications of the ACM*, 16, no. 3, March 1973, 169–179.

[Cooley and Tukey, 65] Cooley, J. W. and J. W. Tukey, "An Algorithm for the Machine Calculation of Complex Fourier Series," *Mathematics of Computation*, 19, no. 90, 1965, 299–301.

[Dahl and Hoare, 72] Dahl, O. J. and C. A. R. Hoare, "Hierarchical Program Structure," in *Structured Programming*, Academic Press, Inc., New York, 1972, 175–220.

[Davis and Vick, 77] Davis, C. G. and C. R. Vick, "The Software Development System," *IEEE Transactions on Software Engineering*, 3, no. 1, January 1977, 69–84.

[Denning, 76] Denning, P. J., "Fault-tolerant Software for Real-time Applications, *Computing Surveys*, 8, no. 4, December 1976, 359–389.

[Dijkstra, 68a] Dijkstra, E., "GOTO Statement Considered Harmful," *Communications of the ACM*, 11, no. 3, March 1968, 147–148.

[Dijkstra, 68b] Dijkstra, E., "The Structure of the THE Multiprogramming System, *Communications of the ACM*, 11, no. 5, May 1968, 341–346.

[Dijkstra, 76] Dijkstra, E., *A Discipline of Programming*, Prentice-Hall, Inc., Englewood Cliffs, N.J., 1976.

[Dolotta and Mashey, 76] Dolotta, T. A. and J. R. Mashey, "An Introduction to the Programmer's Workbench," Second International Conference on Software Engineering, San Francisco, Calif., October 1976, 164–168.

[ENR, 61] "Everything about the Narrows Bridge is Big, Bigger, or Biggest," *Engineering News Record*, 166, June 29, 1961, 24–28.

[ENR, 64] "Narrows Bridge Opens to Traffic," *Engineering News Record*, 173, November 19, 1964, 33.

[ENR, 77] "Alaskan Pipe Cost Probe Hits Snag," *Engineering News Record*, 198, April 7, 1977, 14.

[Fife, 77] FIFE, D., "Computer Software Management: A Primer for Project Management and Quality Control," National Bureau of Standards, Institute for Computer Sciences and Technology, Special Publications, April 1977.

[Gallagher, 65] GALLAGHER, P. F., *Project Estimating by Engineering Methods*, Hayden Book Company, Inc., New York, 1965.

[Gerhart and Yelowitz, 76] GERHART, S. AND L. YELOWITZ, "Observations of Fallibility in Applications of Modern Programming Methodologies," *IEEE Transactions on Software Engineering*, 2, no. 3, September 1976, 195–207.

[Gill, 51] GILL, S., "The Diagnosis of Mistakes in Programming on the EDSAC," *Proceedings of the Royal Society of London*, 206A, 1951, 538.

[Goodenough and Gerhart, 75] GOODENOUGH, J. B. AND S. GERHART, "Toward a Theory of Test Data Selection," *IEEE Transactions on Software Engineering*, 1, no. 2, June 1975, 156–173.

[Gries, 71] GRIES, D., *Compiler Construction*, John Wiley & Sons, Inc., New York, 1971.

[Halstead, 77] HALSTEAD, M., *Elements of Software Science*, Elsevier North-Holland, New York, 1977.

[Hamilton and Zeldin, 76] HAMILTON, M. AND S. ZELDIN, "Higher Order Software: A Methodology for Defining Software," *IEEE Transactions on Software Engineering*, 2, no. 1, March 1976, 9–32.

[Hoare, 69] HOARE, C. A. R., "An Axiomatic Basis for Computer Programming," *Communications of the ACM*, 12, no. 10, 1969, 576–580, 583.

[Huang, 75] HUANG, J. C., An Approach to Program Testing, *Computing Surveys*, 7, no. 3, September 1975, 113–128.

[Jackson, 75] JACKSON, M. A., *Principles of Program Design*, Academic Press, New York, 1975.

[Jeffery and Linden, 77] JEFFERY, S. AND T. LINDEN, "Software Engineering is Engineering," IEEE Computer Science and Engineering Curricula Workshop, Williamsburg, Va., June 1977, 112–115.

[Jones and Liskov, 77] JONES, A. K. AND B. LISKOV, A Language Extension for Controlling Access to Shared Data, *IEEE Transactions on Software Engineering*, 2, no. 4, 1976, 277–285.

[Knuth, 68] KNUTH, D., *The Art of Computer Programming*, vols. 1, 2, and 3, Addison-Wesley Publishing Company, Inc., Reading, Mass., 1968, 1970, 1972.

[Knuth, 71] KNUTH, D., "An Empirical Study of FORTRAN Programs," *Software Practice and Experience*, 1, no. 2, 1971.

[Knuth, 74] KNUTH, D., "Structured Programming with GOTO Statements," *Computing Surveys*, 6, no. 4, 1974, 261–301.

[LDRS, 77] Proceedings of the ACM Symposium on Language Design for Reliable Software, Raleigh, N.C., March 1977 (*SIGPLAN Notices*, 12, no. 3, March 1977).

[Levy, 75] LEVY, J. P., "Automatic Correction of Syntax Errors in Programming Languages, *Acta Informatica*, 4, 1975, 271–292.

[Liskov and Zilles, 75] LISKOV, B. AND S. ZILLES, "Specification Techniques for Data Abstractions," *IEEE Transactions on Software Engineering*, 1 no. 1, 1975, 9–19.

[Liskov et al., 77] LISKOV, B., A. SYNDER, R. ATKINSON, AND C. SCHAFFERT, "Abstraction Mechanisms for CLU," *Communications of the ACM*, 20, No. 8, 1977, 564–576.

[Lowry and Medlock] LOWRY, E. S. AND C. W. MEDLOCK, "Object Code Optimization," *Communications of the ACM*, 12, no. 1, 1969, 13–22.

[Mills, 72] MILLS, H. D., "Mathematical Foundations for Structured Programming," IBM Technical Report FSC-72-6012, 1972.

[Mills, 76] MILLS, H. D., "Software Development," *IEEE Transactions on Software Engineering*, 2, no. 4, 1976, 265–273.

[Morgan, 70] MORGAN, H. L., "Spelling Corrections in Systems Programs," *Communications of the ACM*, 13, no. 2, February 1970, 90–94.

[Norden, 64] NORDEN, P., "Manpower Utilization Patterns in Research and Development Projects," IBM Technical report TR-00.1191, September 1964.

[Parnas, 72] PARNAS, D. L., "On the Criteria for Decomposing Systems into Modules, *Communications of the ACM*, 15, no. 12, 1972, 1053–1058.

[Parnas, 75] PARNAS, D. L., "The Influence of Software Structure on Reliability," International Conference on Reliable Software, Los Angeles, Calif., 1975, 358–362 (*ACM SIGPLAN Notices* 10, no. 6, June 1975).

[Popek et al., 77] POPEK, G. J., J. J. HORNING, B. W. LAMPSON, J. G. MITCHELL, AND R. L. LONDON, "Notes on the Design of Euclid." (See [LDRS, 77].)

[Putnam, 78] PUTNAM, L., "A General Empirical Solution to the Macro Software Sizing and Estimating Problem," *IEEE Transactions on Software Engineering*, 4, no. 4, 1978, 345–361.

[Putnam and Wolverton, 77] PUTNAM, L. AND R. WOLVERTON, *Quantitative Management: Software Cost Estimating* (tutorial), IEEE Computer Society, November 1977.

[Ramamoorthy and Ho, 75] RAMAMOORTHY, C. V. AND S. F. HO, "Testing Large Software with Automated Software Evaluation Systems," *IEEE Transactions on Software Engineering*, 1, no. 1, 1975, 46–58.

[Reifer, 76] REIFER, D. J., "The Structured FORTRAN Dilemma," *SIGPLAN Notices*, 11, no. 2, 1976, 30–32.

[Ritchie and Thompson, 74] RITCHIE, D. M. AND K. THOMPSON, "The UNIX Time-sharing System," *Communications of the ACM*, 17, no. 7, 1974, 365–375.

[Ross and Schoman, 77] ROSS, D. T. AND K. E. SCHOMAN, "Structured Analysis for Requirements Definition," *IEEE Transactions on Software Engineering*, 3, no. 1, January 1977, 6–15.

[Shaw, 74] SHAW, A., *The Logical Design of Operating Systems*, Prentice-Hall, Inc., Englewood Cliffs, N.J., 1974.

[Shaw, 75a] SHAW, A., "Systems Design and Documentation Using Path Descriptions," Proceedings 1975 Sagamore Conference on Parallel Processing, Summary, 180–181.

[Shaw et al., 75b] SHAW, A., N. WEIDERMAN, G. ANDREWS, M. FELCYN, J. RIEBER, AND G. WONG, "A Multiprogramming Nucleus with Dynamic Resource Facilities," *Software Practice and Experience*, 5, 1975, 245–267.

[Shaw and Weiderman, 71] SHAW, A. AND N. WEIDERMAN, "A Multiprogramming System for Education and Research," Proceedings IFIP Congress 71, North-Holland Publishing Company, Amsterdam, 1971, 1505–1509.

[Shaw, 78] SHAW, A., "Software Descriptions with Flow Expressions," *IEEE Transactions on Software Engineering*, 4, no. 3, 1978, 242–254.

[Sibley, 76] SIBLEY, E. (ed.), "Special Issue on Data Base Management Systems," *ACM Computing Surveys*, 8, no. 1, March 1976.

[SIGPLAN, 76] SIGPLAN, "Proceedings of conference on Data: Abstraction, Definition, Structure," *ACM SIGPLAN Notices*, Special Issue, 1976.

[Teichroew and Hershey, 77] TEICHROEW, D. AND E. A. HERSHEY, "PSL/PSA: A Computer Aided Technique for Structured Documentation and Analysis of Information Processing Systems," *IEEE Transactions on Software Engineering*, 3, no. 1, 1977, 41–48.

[Walston and Felix, 77] WALSTON, C. E. AND C. P. FELIX, A Method of Programming Measurements and Estimation, *IBM Systems Journal*, 16, no. 1, 1977, 54–73.

[Weide, 77] WEIDE, B., "A Survey of Analysis Techniques for Discrete Algorithms," *Computing Surveys*, 9, no. 4, 1977, 291–313.

[Weinberg, 71] WEINBERG, G. M., *The Psychology of Computer Programming*, Van Nostrand Reinhold, New York, 1971.

[Wilkinson, 75] WILKINSON, R., "A Nucleus Based Single Language Dedicated Time Sharing System," M.S. Thesis, Department of Computer Science, University of Washington, July 1975.

[Wirth, 71] WIRTH, N., "Program Development by Stepwise Refinement," *Communications of the ACM*, 14, no. 4, 1971, 221–227.

[Wirth, 74] WIRTH, N., "On the Composition of Well-structured Programs," *Computing Surveys*, 6, no. 4, 1974, 247–259.

[Wolverton, 74] WOLVERTON, R. W., "The Cost of Developing Large Scale Software," *IEEE Transactions on Computers*, 23, no. 6, 1974, 615–636.

[Wright, 75] WRIGHT, J. W., "The Change Making Problem," *Journal of the ACM*, 22, no. 1, January 1975, 125–128.

[Wulf et al., 76] WULF, W., R. LONDON, M. SHAW, "An Introduction to the Construction and Verification of ALPHARD Programs," *IEEE Transactions on Software Engineering*, 2, no. 4, 1976, 253–264.

[Younger, 67] YOUNGER, D., "Recognition and Parsing of Context-free Languages in Time n^3," *Information and Control*, 10, no. 2, 1967, 189–208.

[Zelkowitz, 75] ZELKOWITZ, M. V., "Third Generation Compiler Design, ACM National Conference, Minneapolis, Minn., 1975, 253–258.

[Zelkowitz and Larsen, 78] ZELKOWITZ, M. V. AND H. J. LARSEN, "Implementation of a Capability Based Data Abstraction," *IEEE Transactions on Software Engineering*, 4, no. 1, January 1978, 56–64.

Index

A

Abstraction, 60, 128–129, 135, 158–167 (*see also* Data abstraction)
Abstract machines, 51–52 (*see also* Virtual machines)
Access rights (*see* Data abstraction)
Accounting, 188, 199, 201
Activation record, 291–293
Active job, 199
Addressing, 297–298
Administrative manager, 15
Aho, A., 33, 99, 270
ALGOL, 30, 45, 59, 65, 79–80, 235, 265
Allocation, 202
Alphabet, 234
Alphard, 37, 80–81
Ambiguous, 239
Ambler, A., 87, 96
ANSI, 248
ASCII, 267
Assembly languages, 61
Assertions, 28, 96 (*see also* Verification)
Auxiliary storage, 181
Axioms, 81–85 (*see also* Assertions)
  arithmetic, 85
  iteration, 84

Axioms *(cont.)*:
rule of assignment, 83
rules of consequence, 82
selection, 84
sequencing axiom, 84

B

Backtracking, 108–109, 153
Backup programmer, 15
Backus, J., 235
Backus-Naur form, 235
Baker, F. T., 15
Balancing, 100, 122
Baseline diagram, 6, 42, 50
BASIC, 103, 226
Basili, V., 23–24, 38, 40, 54
Bell Telephone Laboratories, 24
Best fit (*see* Storage allocation)
Binary search (*see* Searching, binary)
Binary semaphore, 194 (*see also* Critical section)
Bit map, 194
Blocked state, 189, 191–192, 204
BNF, 235
Boehm, B., 7, 15, 26, 43
Bottom-up design, 50–51, 180
Bottom-up implementation, 52–53
Breadth-first search, 144–147, 152 (*see also* Searching, trees)
Brinch Hansen, P., 51
Brooks, F., 2, 11, 17, 30, 54
Buddy system (*see* Storage allocation)
Buffer, 204–205
disk, 205
ring, 204

C

Caine, C., 31
Call by reference, 49, 304
Capability, 52, 78
Certification, 8, 81–88, 92 (*see also* Verification)
Chief programmer team, 15–16
Clu, 37, 69, 80–81
COBOL, 3, 65, 90
Code, 7, 26, 228, 247, 291
reading, 26
Code generator, 227, 231, 252–254, 281–311
Code improvement, 312–314

Code sequence, 293–294, 297–299, 302–310
  arithmetic operation, 302
  assignment statement, 302
  CALL statement, 306–309
  IF statement, 310
  parameters, 304–306
  procedure activation, 293–294, 302–303
  READ statement, 310
  START, 310
  WHILE statement, 310
  WRITE statement, 310
Collector, 232 (*see also* Linkage editor)
Command language (*see* Job control language)
Compiler, 226–233, 250–253, 276
  cross, 232
  One-pass, 228–229, 250–253, 276
  Three-pass, 228–229, 251–252
  Two-pass, 228–229
Compiler aids, 93
Complete test, 97
Component (*see* Module)
Conceptual integrity, 24–25
Concurrency, 204
Conditional code, 95
Constantine, D., 41
Constants, 259–260, 298
Context free language (*see* Formal languages, context free)
Control oriented, 66–67
Conway, R., 27, 87, 93, 251
Cooley, J., 33
CORC, 258
Coroutines, 112–115
Correctness, 8 (*see also* Verification)
Critical section, 184, 193
Cross compiler, 232

D

Dahl, O. J., 79
Data abstraction, 37, 48, 61, 65–80, 89
  access rights, 77–79
  protected, 73–77
  static, 70–73
Data structures, 60
Data type, 60–70, 145, 147–148, 153, 164, 167, 174, 176–177, 179, 191, 193, 195, 200–203, 216–217, 292–293
  binary tree, 176–177
  directed graphs, 64

Data type *(cont.)*:
FIFO lists, 63, 179, 193, 195, 202–203, 217
LIFO lists, 64, 292
linked lists, 164, 167, 174, 176, 191, 193
lists, 62
messages, 193
queues, 63, 191, 216
sets, 64
stacks, 64, 153, 292–293
trees, 65, 145, 147–148, 174, 200–201
Davis, C., 24, 41
Deadlock, 186, 202–203, 206, 211, 218–219, 223
Debugging compiler, 93
DEC:
PDP-11, 24
System-10, 256, 285–286
Definition (*see* Specification)
Denning, P., 8
Depth-first search, 144, 153 (*see also* Searching, trees)
Derivable, 236
Derivation, 236, 238–240
derivation tree, 238–240
leftmost, 239
Design, 5, 247
Design examples:
airline reservation, 157–178
coin changing, 138–144
compiler design, 226–318
Fibonacci sequence, 117–119
operating system design, 179–225
parking cars, 127–138
path through a maze, 144–157
sort a list, 119–127
Design techniques:
balancing, 100
coroutines, 112–115
divide and conquer, 99–100
dynamic programming, 101
finite state, 109–110
recursion, 100–101
searching, 102–107
simulation, 101–102
sorting, 107–109
storage allocation, 111–112
Deterministic finite state automata (*see* Finite state automata)
Development tools, 24
Diagnostic features, 255–256, 312

Dijkstra, E., 28, 37, 179
Directed graph, 145
Direct execution, 283
Directory, 200, 217–218
Direct search (*see* Searching, direct)
Disk, 181
Divide and conquer, 99–100, 107, 119, 137
DoLotta, T., 24
Dope vectors, 315
Dump, 27
Dynamic programming, 101, 118–119, 141
Dynamic storage, 291–292

E

Effective address, 286–287
Efficiency, 251
Encapsulation, 73 (*see also* Data abstraction)
Enhancements, 311–312
Environment, 291–294
Error day, 30
Errors, 8
Estimation techniques, 17–19, 23
Euclid, 37
Exchange sort (*see* Sorting, exchange)

F

Failures, 8
Faults, 8
Felix, C., 24
Fibonacci number, 117–119
FIFO lists (*see* Data type: FIFO lists)
Files, 186, 199–200, 217–223
  accounting, 199
  directory, 199
  initialization, 218
  measurement of, 200
  termination of, 218
Finite state automata, 110, 233, 240–245, 265
Finite state techniques, 109–110, 154–156
First fit (*see* Storage allocation)
Flows, 182
Forest, 145
Formal languages, 233–237, 245
  context free, 237
  context sensitive, 237
  regular, 237, 245

Formal languages *(cont.)*:
semantics, 233–234
syntax, 233–236
unrestricted, 237
Formal testing (*see* Testing, formal)
FORTRAN, 8, 25, 30, 43, 59, 61, 66, 70, 73, 89, 104, 113, 226, 230, 232–233, 248, 252,
Forward branch, 275–276, 278, 296, 303, 310
Frequency histogram, 33, 96

G

Gallagher, P., 17
Gerhart, S., 8, 29, 97
Gill, S., 1
Goodenough, J., 8, 97
Gordon, E., 31
Gotoless programming (*see* Structured programming)
Grammars, 233, 236, 236–237, 245
nonterminal symbol, 236
productions, 237
start symbols, 236
terminal symbol, 236
Graph, 145, 151
Gries, D., 315
GYPSY, 87, 96

H

Halstead, M., 30
Hamilton, M., 7, 37
Handle, 239
Hash code, 104
Hash search (*see* Searching, hash)
Hershey, E., 24, 37
Hierarchy, 186–187
Higher order software, 37
Ho, S., 27
Hoare, C. A. R., 28, 79, 81
Huang, J., 8
Human engineering, 25

I

IBM, 2, 15, 25–26, 30, 55, 93, 230–232, 251, 256, 285–286
360/370, 231, 251, 285–286
360/370 OS, 2, 25–26, 93, 256
704, 230
709, 230

Index register, 286
Indivisible operation, 192
Infix, 246
Information hiding, 65–66, 68
Inherently ambiguous, 239
Input-Output, 196–198
Interfaces, 11
Interpreter, 182–185, 231, 317
Interrupt, 180, 196
Interval time, 182
Invariant, 84–85, 91 (*see also* Assertions)
ISDOS (*see* PSL/PSA)
Iterative enhancement, 54–55, 249–250

J

Jackson, M., 42
Jeffery, S., 2
Job control language, 187–188, 256
Job descriptor (*see* Job table)
Job file, 190
Job supervisor, 185, 202, 207–209
Job table, 182, 198–199, 211
Jones, A., 78
Junior programmer, 15

K

Kernel, 180 (*see also* Nucleus)
Keywords, 259–260
Knuth, D., 33, 37, 58, 61, 99, 102, 108, 147

L

Language extensions, 315–316
Languages, 234, 237, 242 (*see also* Formal languages)
Larsen, H., 73
Levy, J., 269
Lexical analysis, 227–228
Librarian, 15–16, 23
LIFO lists (*see* Data type: LIFO lists)
Linden, T., 2
Linear search (*see* Searching, linear)
Lines of code (*see* Productivity)
Linkage editor, 232, 296
Liskov, B., 37, 69, 78, 80
Loader, 185, 207, 209–210, 232
Lock, 194, 203
Lowry, E., 33

M

Machine address, 287
Machine language, 248
Machine organization, 285, 295
Maintenance, 9–10, 248
  parts number explosion, 10
  releases, 10
Management, 11–14
Manifest constants, 90
Man-month, 17 (*see also* Productivity)
Mashey, J., 24
Medlock, C., 33
Merge sort (*see* Sorting, merge)
Methodology (*see* individual techniques: Bottom up, Chief programmer team, Iterative enhancement, Jackson Methodology, PSL/PSA, SADT, SREM, Stepwise refinement, Structured design, Structured programming, Top down)
Milestone, 23
Mills, H., 30, 55, 60
Model, 127
Mode switch, 286
Module, 18, 42
Morgan, H., 258
MULTICS, 33
Multiplexor channel, 181, 204
Multiprocessing, 185
Multiprogramming, 179, 182, 190, 224
  batch, 182
  level of, 190, 224

N

NASA, 7
Naur, P., 235
NIP, 248–249, 252, 255–256, 260, 262, 271, 281, 289, 292, 298, 311–312, 315–317
  arrays, 315
  basic syntax, 249
  functions, 316
  strings, 315
NIP compiler:
  code generated (*see* Code sequence)
  run time environment (*see* Environment)
  syntax (*see* Recursive descent)
Nondeterministic finite state automata, 243–245
Nonterminal symbols, 236
Nucleus, 180, 186, 189

Null set, 234
Null string, 234

O

Object code, 228
Object deck, 232
Object oriented, 66
Operating system, 184–187
Operation (*see* Maintenance)
Operation code, 285
Operation register, 286
Operator communication, 203, 214, 216
Operator precedence, 281
Optimization, 230, 285, 299–300, 312–314

P

Parameters, 304–306
Parkinson, C., 19
Parnas, D., 8, 37
Parser, 231, 237–239, 252–254, 268–281 (*see also* Syntax analysis)
PASCAL, 31, 33, 43, 59, 66
PDL (*see* Program design language)
Peephole optimization, 299–300
Performance evaluation, 32–33, 180, 200, 223, 251
Peripheral devices, 185
Personnel, 12–14
Phrase, 236
PL/C, 27, 87, 93–95, 251, 258
PL/CS, 87, 95–96
PL/1, 8, 25, 30, 35, 43, 45–50, 59, 61, 65–66, 70–71, 73, 75, 77, 89–90, 95, 97, 113–115, 226, 248, 250–251, 260, 265, 278
PLUM, 27, 47,. 73, 78–81, 93–97, 251, 254
Popek, G., 37
Portability, 228
Postconditions, 28, 96 (*see also* Assertions)
Postfix, 228, 233, 246–247, 268, 272–273, 275–280, 283, 287, 289–290
Preconditions, 28, 82, 88, 96 (*see also* Assertions)
Predicates, 28
Preemption, 183, 195, 203
Prime program, 57–58
Priority, 195, 203–204
Procedure activation, 302–303
Process, 180, 184–186, 189–190, 195–197, 203–204, 206–207, 210–211, 216
  asynchronous, 197
  elaboration of, 206

Process *(cont.)*:
  management of, 189
  pseudo, 195–197
  root, 186, 203, 216
  structure of, 184–186, 189
  termination of, 207, 211
  user, 210–211
Production, 236–237
Productivity, 11–12, 14, 30
Program design language, 31–32, 45–50, 55, 59, 250
  inner syntax, 31, 46
  outer syntax, 31, 46
Programming languages (*see* Specific language)
Program state word, 182
Project notebook, 16
Proof of correctness (*see* Certification)
Proper program, 56–58
Pseudo code, 50 (*see also* Program design language)
Pseudo comments, 95
PSL/PSA, 24, 27, 32, 37–38, 40
  syntax, 38
PSW, 182
Putnam, L., 20

Q

Quadruple, 283–284, 287–291, 304, 306, 309, 313

R

Ramamoorthy, C. V., 27
Random number, 127–128
Rao, R., 225
Rayleigh curve, 20–23
Ready state, 189, 192, 204
Record, 200, 221–222
  logical, 200, 221
  physical, 200
Recursion, 100–101, 107, 117–118, 122–123, 136–141, 153, 176
Recursive descent, 270–280
  assignment statement, 275
  CALL statement, 278–279
  expressions, 280
  IF statement, 275–277
  main driver, 271
  procedure statement, 273
  program, 272
  READ statement, 279

Recursive descent *(cont.):*
statement list, 274
WHILE statement, 278
WRITE statement, 279
Recursive procedure, 291
Reentrant code, 309
Register allocation, 299–300, 313–314
Regular language (*see* Formal languages, regular)
Reifer, D., 59
Reliability, 8, 24–25, 29–30
human engineering, 25
mean time between failures, 29–30
Reliable test (*see* Testing, formal)
Relocatable element, 232
Representation, 163, 167
Requirements, 3–4, 247, 250
Reserved words, 260, 269
Resource, 180, 189, 191–192
consumable, 191
reusable, 191
Resource management, 191
Resources, 4
Return address, 294
REVS (*see* SREM)
RFQ, 17
Ritchie, D., 32
Ross, D., 39
RSL, 24, 41
Running state, 189

S

SADT, 39–40
Save area, 316
Scaffolding, 52
Scanner, 231, 237, 241, 252–254, 259, 264–267, 281, 311 (*see also* Lexical analysis)
Scheduler, 180, 192, 195–196, 202–203
Searching, 102–109, 202
binary, 102–103
direct, 102–103
hash, 102, 104–105, 202
linear, 102–103, 262
trees, 105–107, 109
Sector, 181, 202
Seed, 128
Sentence, 234
Sentential form, 236

Shaw, A., 179, 182, 192, 194–195, 225
Shooman, K., 39
Side effects, 89
SIGPLAN, 248
Simple phrase, 236
SIMULA67, 79–80
Simulation, 101–102, 126–129, 135–136
SofTech, Inc., 39
Software engineering:
  definition, 1
  goals, 10
Software life cycle, 2, 43, 247
Sorting, 107–108, 119–125
  exchange, 107, 119–122
  merge, 107–108, 122–125
Specification, 4–5, 29, 35, 81–82, 89, 91–92, 247
  database, 4
  functional document, 4
  theory of, 35
Spool, 179–180, 182, 184, 199, 204–205, 211, 214
  input, 182, 184, 199, 204
  output, 184, 199, 205, 214
SREM, (*see* RSL)
Stack frame (*see* Activation record)
Stack pointer, 293–294
Start symbol, 236
Starvation, 202–204
State diagram, 240–244
Static storage, 291
Stepwise refinement, 51, 57, 89, 250
Storage allocation, 111–112, 194–195, 205
  best fit, 111
  buddy system, 111–112
  first fit, 111
String, 234
String generation, 238
String recognition, 238
Structured design, 41–42
Structured programming, 31, 37, 55–58, 89
Stubs, 53, 91, 94
Subroutine call, 294
Successful test (*see* Testing, formal)
Supervisor (*see* Job supervisor)
Symbol table, 253–264, 272–274, 292, 312–313
Syntactic classes, 235
Syntax analysis, 227–228
System label, 276

T

Table driven algorithm (*see* Finite state techniques)
Teichroew, D., 24, 37
Temporary variable, 284, 289–290, 312–314
Terminal symbols, 236
Termination, 87–88, 133–135
Testing, 5, 7–9, 27, 88–97, 248
  acceptance, 7
  benchmark, 7
  conditional code, 95
  criterion for, 97
  data for, 5, 93
  evaluation, 7
  formal, 97–99
  integration, 7
  module, 7, 27
  pseudo comments, 95
  top down, 53, 89
  unit, 7
Thompson, K., 32
Throughput, 202
Time-of-day clock, 182
Tokens, 227, 264–265, 268, 270, 287–288, 311
Top-down design, 31, 50–51, 55–56, 180
Top-down implementation, 52–54, 91
Trace, 27
Translator, 233, 248
Traps, 196–197 (*see also* Interrupt)
Tree chart (*see* Baseline diagram)
TRW, 26
Tukey, J., 33
Turnaround time, 202, 223
Turner, A. J., 54
Type (*see* Data type)

U

Ullman, J., 33, 270
Univac, 25–26, 232, 251–252, 256, 285
  1100, 25–26, 251–252, 285
  1100 O S, 93, 256
UNIX, 32–33
User interface, 187–189
User job flow, 182–184

V

Validation, 8, 27
Valid test (*see* Testing, formal)
Variables, 90
Verification, 8, 27–28, 81 (*see also* Certification)
Vick, C., 24, 41
Virtual hardware, 180
Virtual machines, 51, 179, 186–187
Vocabulary, 234

W

Walkthrough, 26
Walston, C., 24
Weide, B., 33
Weiderman, N., 225
Weinberg, G., 16
WHIZBANG, 232–233
Wilcox, T., 27, 93, 251
Wilkinson, R., 225
Wirth, N., 51
Wolverton, R., 14, 18, 20
Workspace, 184, 190, 210
Wright, J., 141
Wulf, W., 37, 80

Y

Yelowitz, L., 29
Younger, D., 33
Yourdon, E., 41

Z

Zeldin, S., 7, 37
Zelkowitz, M., 23–24, 27, 73, 93, 225, 251